POST-CONFLICT PEACEBUILDIN

This book is a result of a research program funded by the
Geneva International Academic Network (GIAN)

RU|G
G|AN

This book has been developed in co-operation with the

Académie de droit international humanitaire
et de droits humains à Genève
Geneva academy of international humanitarian law
and human rights

Adh
genève

Post-conflict
Peacebuilding: A Lexicon

Edited by
VINCENT CHETAIL

OXFORD
UNIVERSITY PRESS

OXFORD
UNIVERSITY PRESS

Great Clarendon Street, Oxford OX2 6DP

Oxford University Press is a department of the University of Oxford.
It furthers the University's objective of excellence in research, scholarship,
and education by publishing worldwide in

Oxford New York

Auckland Cape Town Dar es Salaam Hong Kong Karachi
Kuala Lumpur Madrid Melbourne Mexico City Nairobi
New Delhi Shanghai Taipei Toronto

With offices in

Argentina Austria Brazil Chile Czech Republic France Greece
Guatemala Hungary Italy Japan Poland Portugal Singapore
South Korea Switzerland Thailand Turkey Ukraine Vietnam

Oxford is a registered trade mark of Oxford University Press
in the UK and in certain other countries

Published in the United States
by Oxford University Press Inc., New York

British Library Cataloguing in Publication Data

Data available

Library of Congress Cataloging in Publication Data

Data available

Typeset by Newgen Imaging Systems (P) Ltd., Chennai, India
Printed in Great Britain
on acid-free paper by
CPI Antony Rowe, Chippenham, Wiltshire

ISBN 978–0–19–956815–4 (Hbk.)   978–0–19–956816–1 (Pbk.)

1 3 5 7 9 10 8 6 4 2

Contents

Foreword

This Lexicon is the result of an international research project undertaken over three years (2006–2008) by thirty-four international experts supported by a team of three researchers and three translators. It was coordinated by the Graduate Institute of International and Development Studies and the European Institute of the University of Geneva, in close cooperation with the Geneva Academy of International Humanitarian Law and Human Rights, the School of Translation and Interpretation of the University of Geneva, the Library of the United Nations Office in Geneva, and the Archive Service of the Office of the United Nations High Commissioner for Refugees.

The publication of this research coincides with a crucial time for post-conflict peacebuilding. With its move towards the top of the international political agenda comes added scrutiny, as the international community seeks to meet the multi-dimensional challenges of building a just and sustainable peace in societies ravaged by war. It requires the cooperation of a plethora of actors, often with varied and even conflicting agendas, who must be induced to create together a state of security, justice, the rule of law, democratic governance, and reconciliation.

Beyond the strictly operational dimension, there is considerable ambiguity in the concepts and terminology used to discuss post-conflict peacebuilding. This ambiguity undermines efforts to agree on common understandings of how peace can be most effectively 'built', thereby impeding swift, coherent action. Accordingly, this Lexicon aims to promote a more cohesive frame of reference for the multiple facets of post-conflict peacebuilding, by presenting its major themes and trends from an analytical perspective. To this end, the Lexicon opens with a general introduction on the concept of post-conflict peacebuilding, followed by twenty-six essays on its key elements.

These essays do not seek to be an exhaustive treatment of the theme, but to illustrate some of the most salient issues that confront post-conflict peacebuilding. The essays were entrusted to international experts from a range of disciplines, including political science and international relations, international law, economics, and sociology. Each study was prepared following the disciplinary perspective and individual specialization of the author. It should be added that the authors have enjoyed academic freedom in preparing their contributions, so their views should not be seen as necessarily reflecting those of their own institutions or of the partner institutions of the project.

In reflecting a diversity of perspectives the Lexicon is able to shed light on many different challenges associated with post-conflict peacebuilding. For each key concept a generic definition is proposed, which is then expanded through discussion of three main areas: the meaning and origin of the concept; its content and essential components; and its means of implementation, including difficulties that commonly arise and relevant lessons learned from past practice. Each entry illuminates a particular aspect of post-conflict peacebuilding, while also acknowledging the profound interaction between them.

The Lexicon is intended for a broad readership, including decision-makers, diplomats, international civil servants, members of non-governmental organizations, journalists, practitioners, researchers and students. A French version is also available under the title: V Chetail (ed), *Lexique de la consolidation de la paix*, Collection de l'Académie de droit international humanitaire et des droits humains à Genève, Bruylant, Brussels.

This project has been a collective endeavour which would not have been possible without the support of many people. I would like to thank especially the Geneva Academic International Network (<http://www.ruig-gian.org/>) for the financial support it provided, and in particular Jean-Marie Dufour and Randall Harbour. My sincere gratitude is accorded to Professors Philippe Burrin, Director, and Michel Carton, Vice-Director, of the Graduate Institute of International and Development Studies, and to Professors Philippe Braillard, former Director, and Nicola Levrat, current Director, of the European Institute at the University of Geneva. I am also grateful to individual members of the different partner institutions for their constant support of the project. Reference is made in particular to Genevieve Bador, Principal Administrator, Private Sector and Public Affairs Service of UNHCR, to Bruno de Bessé, Professor at the Geneva School of Translation and Interpretation, to Andrew Clapham, Director of the Geneva Academy of International Humanitarian Law and Human Rights, to Yvan Droz, Lecturer at the Graduate Institute of International and Development Studies, to Lance Hewson, President, Geneva School of Translation and Interpretation, to Pierre Le Loarer, Chief Librarian, Archives Service, Library of the United Nations Office, Geneva, and to Meredith Peters, Chief, UN Documents Indexing Unit, Library of UNHCR, Geneva.

Thanks is equally due to Marc Roissard de Bellet, Stéphane Pfister and Gilles Giacca for their thorough and professional research work throughout the project; and to Corinne Leuenberger, Alia Rahal and Ashley Riggs who carried out the very substantial work of translation which has enabled the same texts to be published in both French and English. The work of Stuart Maslen, Marian Casey, Anyssa Bellal, Magali Husler Leemann, Mary Picard and Nathalie Tanner in reviewing the text and advising on corrections to the manuscript has also been much appreciated. Finally, I extend my most profound gratitude to the group of experts who agreed to participate in writing this Lexicon, as it is their expertise and insight which has given life to the original concept.

Dr Vincent Chetail
Research Director, Geneva Academy of International
Humanitarian Law and Human Rights
Associate Professor in Public International Law,
Graduate Institute of International and Development Studies

List of Abbreviations

ACT	Alliance for Conflict Transformation
AU	African Union
AXO	Abandoned explosive ordonance
BINUB	UN Integrated Office in Burundi
BONUCA	UN Peacebuilding Office in the Central African Republic
CCA	Common Country Assessment
CCW	Convention on Certain Conventional Weapons
CEP	(1) Corporate Engagement Project
	(2) Community Empowerment Project
CERI	Centre d'études et de recherches internationales (SciPo/CNRS)
CEWARN	Conflict Early Warning and Response Mechanism
CFSP	Common Foreign and Security Policy
CIDA	Canadian International Development Agency
CIMIC	Civil-Military Cooperation
CIS	Commonwealth of Independent States
CMAC	Cambodian Mine Action Centre
CMCO	Civil-Military Coordination
CMCoord	Humanitarian Civil-Military Coordination
CMO	Civil-Military Operations
CMOC	Civil-Military Operations Centre
COE	Council of Europe
COPRET	Conflict Prevention and Transformation (SDC)
CPA	Coalition Provisional Authority (Iraq)
CSCE	Commission on Security and Cooperation in Europe
DAC	Development Assistance Committee (OECD)
DDR	Disarmament, Demobilisation, and Reintegration
DFAIT	Department of Foreign Affairs and International Trade
DFID	Department for International Development (United Kingdom)
DPKO	See 'UNDPKO'
DRP	Demobilisation and Reintegration Programmes
EC	European Community
ECHA	Executive Committee on Humanitarian Affairs (OCHA)
ECHR	European Court of Human Rights
ECOSOC	UN Economic and Social Council
ECOWAS	Economic Community of West African States
ERW	explosive remnants of war
ESDP	European Security and Defence Policy

EU	European Union
EUFOR	European Union Forces
EUPM	European Union Police Mission
FAO	Food and Agriculture Organisation (UN)
FYROM	Former Yugoslav Republic of Macedonia
GICHD	Geneva International Centre for Humanitarian Demining
GTZ	German Technical Cooperation
HALO	Hazardous Area Life Support Organisation
HI	Handicap international
IADB	Inter-American Development Bank
IASC	Inter-Agency Standing Committee
ICC	International Criminal Court
ICISS	International Commission on Intervention and State Sovereignty
ICJ	International Court of Justice
ICBL	International Campaign to Ban Landmines
ICRC	International Committee of the Red Cross
ICTJ	International Centre for Transitional Justice
ICTR	International Criminal Tribunal for Rwanda
ICTY	International Criminal Tribunal for the Former Yugoslavia
IDDRS	Integrated Disarmament, Demobilisation and Reintegration Standards
IDEA	International Institute for Democracy and International Assistance
IDP	Internally Displaced Person
IEOM	International Election Observation Missions
IICP	Institute for Integrative Conflict Transformation and Peacebuilding
ILO	International Labour Organization
IMAS	International Mine Action Standards
IMF	International Monetary Fund
INGO	international non-governmental organization
IO	international organization
IOM	International Organization for Migration
KFOR	Kosovo Force
KOFF	Centre for Peacebuilding
LPI	Life and Peace Institute
MACs	National Mine Action Centres
MAG	Mines Advisory Group
MCDA	Military and Civil Defence Assets
MINURCAT	UN Mission in the Central African Republic and Chad
MINUGUA	UN Verification Mission in Guatemala
MINUSTAH	UN Stabilisation Mission in Haiti
MONUC	UN Mission in the Democratic Republic of Congo

MRRD	Ministry of Rural Rehabilitation and Development (Afghanistan)
NATO	North Atlantic Treaty Organization
NCCR	Swiss National Centre of Competence in Research
NGO	non-governmental organization
NMAA	National Mine Action Authority
NMAS	National Mine Action Standards
NPA	Norwegian People's Aid
OAS	Organization of American States
OAU	Organization of African Unity
OCHA	UN Office for the Coordination of Humanitarian Affairs
ODIHR	Office for Democratic Institutions and Human Rights
OECD	Organization for Economic Cooperation and Development
OHCHR	Office of the UN High Commissioner for Human Rights
OHR	Office of the High Representative and EU Special Representative (in Bosnia and Herzegovina)
ONUMOZ	UN Operation in Mozambique
ONUSAL	UN Observer Mission in El Salvador
OSCE	Organization for Security and Co-operation in Europe
PRSP	Poverty Reduction Strategies Papers
PRT	Provincial Reconstruction Teams
PSO	Peace Support Operations
QIP	Quick-Impact Project
SCSL	Special Court for Sierra Leone
SDC	Swiss Agency for Development and Cooperation
SEEMACC	South East Europe Mine Action Coordination Council
SFOR	Stabilisation Force in Bosnia and Herzegovina (NATO)
SG	UN Secretary-General
SOPs	standing operating procedures
SRSG	Special Representative of the UN Secretary-General
SSR	Security Sector Reform
SWAPO	South West African People's Organisation
TRC	Truth and Reconciliation Commission
UN	United Nations
UNAMA	UN Assistance Mission in Afghanistan
UNAMI	UN Assistance Mission for Iraq
UNAMIC	UN Advance Mission in Cambodia
UNAMID	African Union/UN Hybrid Operation in Darfur
UNBIS	Thesaurus of the United Nations
UNDAF	UN Development Assistance Frameworks
UNDG	UN Development Group
UNDOF	UN Disengagement Force
UNDP	UN Development Programme
UNDPI	UN Department of Public Information

UNDPKO	UN Department of Peacekeeping Operations
UNESCO	UN Educational, Scientific and Cultural Organization
UNFICYP	UN Peacekeeping Force in Cyprus
UNFIL	UN Interim Force in Lebanon
UNFPA	UN Population Fund
UNHCR	Office of the UN High Commissioner for Refugees
UNICEF	UN Children's Fund
UNIOSIL	UN Integrated Office in Sierra Leone
UNITAR	UN Institute for Training and Research
UNMAS	UN Mine Action Service
UNMEE	UN Mission in Ethiopia and Eritrea
UNMIBH	UN Mission in Bosnia and Herzegovina
UNMIK	UN Interim Administration Mission in Kosovo
UNMIL	Un Mission in Liberia
UNMIN	UN Mission in Nepal
UNMIS	UN Mission in Sudan
UNMIT	UN Integrated Mission in Timor-Leste
UNMOGIP	UN Military Observer Group in India and Pakistan
UNOC	UN Operation in the Congo
UNOCI	UN Operation in Côte d'Ivoire
UNOGBIS	UN Peacebuilding Support Office in Guinea-Bissau
UNOMIG	UN Observer Mission in Georgia
UNOSOM	UN Operation in Somalia
UNOWA	UN Office for West Africa
UNPOS	UN Political Office for Somalia
UNPROFOR	UN Protection Force
UNSC	UN Security Council
UNSCO	Office of the UN Special Coordinator for the Middle East
UNSG	UN Secretary-General
UNTAC	UN Transitional Authority in Cambodia
UNTAES	UN Transitional Administration for Eastern Slavonia, Baranja and Western Sirmium
UNTAET	UN Transitional Administration in East Timor
UNTAG	UN Transitional Assistance Group
UNTEA	UN Temporary Executive Authority in West New Guinea (West Irian)
UNTOP	UN Tajikistan Office of Peacebuilding
UNTSO	UN Truce Supervision Organization
US	United States of America
USAID	US Agency for International Development
UXO	unexploded ordnance
WFP	World Food Programme
WHO	World Health Organization

List of Authors

Riccardo Bocco

Professor at the Graduate Institute of International and Development Studies of Geneva, he received his PhD from the Institut d'Etudes Politiques in Paris. He has been working for the CNRS-Maison de l'Orient (University of Lyon II), has been the Director of the CERMOC in Amman (the French research centre in social sciences based in Jordan) and Research Director of the Graduate Institute of Development Studies in Geneva. During the past 15 years, he has focused his research on Palestinian refugees and humanitarian policies in the Middle East, as well as on the role of the international aid in conflict and post-conflict contexts. A list of his publications is available at: <http://graduateinstitute.ch/corporate/teaching/professeurs.html>.

Richard Caplan

Richard Caplan is Professor of International Relations at the University of Oxford. He has written widely on international organizations and conflict management. He is the author of *International Governance of War-Torn Territories: Rule and Reconstruction* (Oxford University Press, 2005) and *Europe and the Recognition of New States in Yugoslavia* (Cambridge University Press, 2005).

Gilles Carbonnier

Gilles Carbonnier is Professor at the Graduate Institute of International and Development Studies in Geneva, where he heads the development studies unit. He holds a PhD in economics, and specializes on the political economy of war, corporate responsibility, public-private partnerships, and humanitarian action. Gilles Carbonnier has eighteen years of professional experience in the fields of international trade negotiations, development cooperation, and humanitarian action.

Vincent Chetail

Dr Vincent Chetail is Associate Professor in International Law at the Graduate Institute of International and Development Studies and Research Director of the Geneva Academy of International Humanitarian Law and Human Rights. He was the coordinator of the present research project on post-conflict peacebuilding, and has been supervising other research projects related to peacekeeping, armed conflicts, and migration. Vincent Chetail is Editor-in-Chief of *Refugee Survey Quarterly* (Oxford University Press) and co-director of the collections

'Organisation internationale et relations internationales' and 'Axes' at Bruylant (Brussels). He also regularly serves as a consultant to UNHCR. His recent publications include *Globalization, Migration and Human Rights: International Law under Review* (Bruylant, Brussels, 2007).

Andrew Clapham

Andrew Clapham is Professor of Public International Law at the Graduate Institute of International and Development Studies in Geneva and the Director of the Geneva Academy of International Humanitarian Law and Human Rights. Prior to coming to the Institute in 1997 he was the Representative of Amnesty International at the UN in New York. His publications include *Human Rights Obligations of Non-State Actors* (Oxford University Press, 2006), and *International Human Rights Lexicon,* with Susan Marks (Oxford University Press, 2005).

Suzanne Damman

Suzanne Damman is currently working for the Centre for Humanitarian Dialogue (HD Centre) in Geneva, Switzerland. She is part of the HD Centre's mediation programme and works on several projects in Africa and Asia. Before joining the HD Centre in October 2007, she worked at the Geneva International Centre for Humanitarian Demining, the Global Fund to Fight Aids, Tuberculosis and Malaria in Geneva, and at the permanent Mission of the United Kingdom of the Netherlands to the UN in New York. She has a Masters' degree in International Relations and International Organizations from the University of Groningen in the Netherlands.

Marwa Daoudy

A Doctor in Political Science, Marwa Daoudy is visiting Lecturer at the Graduate Institute of International and Development Studies, Geneva. She also works as a consultant for international organizations and the private sector. Her publications and courses cover non-traditional security studies, water conflict, and negotiation analysis, with a special focus on the Middle East conflict and peace negotiations. She is the author of *The Water Divide between Syria, Iraq, and Turkey, Negotiation, Security and Power Asymmetry* (CNRS, Paris), which received the 2005 Lémonon Prize of the Institut de France, and *The Long Road to Damascus, Syria and the Peace Negotiations with Israel* (Les Etudes du CERI, 2005). She has recently published in *The Economics of Peace and Security Journal*, *Négociations* and *Alternatives Internationales* (2007), and her papers are forthcoming in *The Journal of International Affairs, Middle East Institute's Viewpoints, Natural Resources Journal,* and *Water Policy* (2008).

Louise Doswald-Beck

Louise Doswald-Beck is Professor of International Law at the Graduate Institute of International and Development Studies and at the Geneva Academy of

International Humanitarian Law and Human Rights. She was formerly the Director of the University Centre for International Humanitarian Law (CUDIH) from 2003 to 2007. She has been a consultant for the Federal Department of Foreign Affairs of the Swiss Confederation. She was Lecturer at Exeter University, and later at University College London. Professor Doswald-Beck previously headed the Legal Division of the ICRC. She participated in the negotiations on the Rome Statute and headed the ICRC delegation to the diplomatic conference that drafted the Elements of Crimes for the International Criminal Court. She is the former Secretary General of the International Commission of Jurists (2001–2003) as is presently a member of the Commission.

Victor-Yves Ghebali†

Victor-Yves Ghebali was Honorary Professor at the Graduate Institute of International and Development Studies (Geneva). His fields of specialization covered European security, with particular focus on the OSCE, and the United Nations system. He published in English and French some fifteen books and over 200 academic articles on both topics. His latest works are *The OSCE Code of Conduct on Politico-Military Aspects of Security. Anatomy and Implementation*, 2005), *The OSCE Between Crisis and Reform: Towards a New Lease of Life* (2005) and *Democratic Governance of the Security Sector Beyond the OSCE Area: Regional Approaches in Africa and the Americas* (2007).

Gilles Giacca

Gilles Giacca is research assistant at the Geneva Academy of International Humanitarian Law and Human Rights and PhD candidate in international law at the Graduate Institute of International and Development Studies in Geneva. His fields of interest focus on collective security, human rights law and international migration law.

Vera Gowlland-Debbas

Vera Gowlland-Debbas is Professor of Public International Law at the Graduate Institute of International and Development Studies in Geneva. She has been an Honorary Professor at University College London, a Visiting Fellow at All Souls College, Oxford, and a Visiting Professor at Université Panthéon-Assas Paris II and the University of California at Berkeley. Her fields of interest and publications focus on UN law, particularly Security Council sanctions, refugee and human rights law, treaty-making, state responsibility, and international courts. As a practioner, she has counselled governments, international organizations, and law firms.

Laurent Goetschel

Laurent Goetschel is Professor of Political Science at the Europe Institute of the University of Basel and Director of the Swiss Peace Foundation (swisspeace) in

Berne. He has worked as a journalist with the Associated Press (AP) and conducted research with the Graduate Institute of International and Development Studies in Geneva and the Centre for European Studies at Harvard University. From 2003 to 2004, he served as political advisor to the Swiss Minister for Foreign Affairs. His main research interests lie in the fields of foreign policy analysis, and peace and conflict issues. He received his PhD from the University of Geneva in 1993.

Heiner Hänggi

Heiner Hänggi is Assistant Director and Head of Research at the Geneva Centre for the Democratic Control of Armed Forces (DCAF). He is also a Titular Professor of Political Science at the University of St. Gallen, Switzerland. His recent research and publications concentrate on the concepts of security sector reform and security governance in post-conflict peacebuilding. Most recently, he has been working with the UN and member states on the development of a UN policy for security sector reform.

Pierre Harrisson

Pierre Harrisson is a former Lecturer at the Graduate Institute of International and Development Studies in Geneva. He holds a PhD in Sociology (Rural and Development Studies) and works as a freelance expert in international cooperation. He has more than 20 years of experience in Africa, Europe, and Central, North, and South America, in evaluation and institutional support, decentralization and public administration, conflict situations and peacekeeping, policy analysis and strategic planning, agrarian policy and peasant organization, water resources management, EU integration, and human rights. He has worked with non-governmental organizations, farmworkers' federations, bilateral and multilateral agencies, and academic institutions.

Pierre Hazan

Pierre Hazan is Visiting Lecturer at the Graduate Institute of International and Development Studies in Geneva. Previously, he was the political advisor on the Durban Review Conference for Louise Arbour, the UN High-Commissioner on Human Rights. In 2005–2006, he was a Senior Fellow at the US Institute of Peace (USIP) in Washington DC and in 2004–2005 he was a fellow at Harvard Law School. Pierre Hazan holds a PhD in Political Science from the University of Geneva. Prior to that, as a UN correspondent in Geneva for the French newspaper *Libération* and with the Swiss newspaper *Le Temps*, Pierre Hazan has covered a number of conflicts, focusing on humanitarian action and peace-keeping operations. He has written a number of books on Transitional Justice. He is the laureate of the 2008 Georges Dreyfuss Prize for his book, *Juger la guerre, juger l'Histoire* (PUF, September 2007).

Jana Krause

Jana Krause is a research assistant at the Centre on Conflict, Development and Peacebuilding at the Graduate Institute of International and Development Studies, and previously worked for the Geneva Centre for the Democratic Control of Armed Forces (DCAF). She is a PhD candidate at the Graduate Institute of International and Development Studies. Her research focuses on armed conflict and post-conflict peacebuilding in Southeast Asia and West Africa.

Keith Krause

Keith Krause is Professor of International Politics at the Graduate Institute of International and Development Studies in Geneva, and Director of its Centre on Conflict, Development and Peacebuilding. He is also the founder and Programme Director of the Small Arms Survey project, and has jointly edited its annual yearbook since 2001. His current research interests are concentrated in three areas: the nature of contemporary political violence; the emergence of transnational state and non-state action to combat small arms and light weapons proliferation; and state formation and insecurity in the post-colonial world.

Anne-Marie La Rosa

Anne-Marie La Rosa is a Legal Adviser in charge of questions related to international justice in the Legal Department of the ICRC since 2005. Before this date, she worked for more than ten years as a lawyer in Canada before joining in 1994 a UN specialized agency and being actively involved in the implementation of fundamental human rights. She is the author of a number of books, papers, and contributions in this field, and teaches international criminal law and international humanitarian law. She also holds a doctorate in international relations, with specialization in international public law, from the Graduate Institute of International and Development Studies.

Rama Mani

Dr Rama Mani served as Executive Director of the International Centre for Ethnic Studies, Colombo Sri Lanka from 2007 to mid-2008. From 2004 to 2006, she was the Director of the New Issues in Security Course at the Geneva Centre for Security Policy. In the past she also served as the Africa Strategy Manager and Policy Coordinator to Oxfam GB, based in Ethiopia and Uganda, Senior Strategy Advisor to the Centre for Humanitarian Dialogue and Senior External Relations Officer to the Commission on Global Governance. She is a Founding Councillor of the World Future Council. She serves on the International Advisory Board of the Global Centre for the Responsibility to Protect and of the International Journal on Transitional Justice, and also on the Board of the Institute for Peace Studies in Alexandria, Egypt. She holds a PhD in Political Science from the University of Cambridge, UK, and a Master's in International

Affairs from Johns Hopkins University. She is the author of *Beyond Retribution: Seeking Justice in the Shadows of War* (Polity Blackwell, 2002) and numerous articles on peacebuilding.

Robert Muggah

Dr Robert Muggah is the Research Director of the Geneva-based Small Arms Survey and a Social Science Research Council Fellow. He earned a DPhil at Oxford University and an MPhil at the Institute of Development Studies, University of Sussex, in the UK. Dr Muggah has worked in more than twenty post-conflict countries for multilateral and bilateral donors and serves as a consultant to several governments and UN expert panels. His latest books include *Security and Post Conflict Recovery: Dealing with Fighters in the Aftermath of War* (New York: Routledge, 2009) and *Relocation Failures in SriLanka: A Short History of Internal Displacement and Resettlement* (London: Zed, 2008).

Lucas Oesch

Lucas Oesch is a teaching assistant and PhD student at the Graduate Institute of International and Development Studies in Geneva. He holds a Master's in Geography and Development Studies. He is working on issues related to governmentality and security, urban territories, and refugee camps.

Davide Orifici

Davide Orifici worked from 2002 to 2008 as Head of Policy and External Relations at the Geneva International Centre for Humanitarian Demining (GICHD). He dealt with policy issues, international humanitarian law, disarmament, and external relations. Before joining the GICHD, he was a diplomat with the Swiss Federal Department of Foreign Affairs from 1998 to 2001, and served in Bern and at the Swiss Mission to NATO in Brussels. After completing studies in Political Science at the University of Pavia, Italy, he received a Master of Arts in International Relations and wrote a PhD thesis on Co-operative Security Relations in the Western Mediterranean at the Graduate Institute of International and Development Studies in Geneva. He holds an Executive MBA from HEC University of Geneva.

Thania Paffenholz

Thania Paffenholz is a Lecturer at the Graduate Institue of International and Development Studies, Geneva, as well as a Senior Researcher at the Centre for Conflict, Peacebuilding and Development at the Graduate Institue of International and Development Studies. Her main fields of research are peacemaking and peacebuilding strategies, the role of civil society in peacebuilding, evaluation in peacebuilding, and the conflict/peace-development nexus. Thania Paffenholz has also many years of experience as a policy advisor for national and international organizations.

Vassilis Pergantis

Vassilis Pergantis is a teaching assistant and PhD candidate in international law at the Graduate Institute of International and Development Studies, Geneva. His fields of interest focus on general international law, specifically theory of international law and sources doctrine. He is writing a doctoral thesis on the element of state consent in the law of treaties.

Xavier Philippe

Xavier Philippe is Professor of Public Law at the University Paul Cézanne – Aix-Marseille III (France). He teaches international humanitarian law, international criminal law, and transitional justice. From 1995 to 2001, he was seconded to the French Embassy in South Africa as legal advisor and worked closely with the South African Ministry of Justice. He was at the same time Professor at the University of the Western Cape, in Cape Town. From 2004 to 2006, he was Regional Legal Advisor for the ICRC for Eastern European Countries, based at the ICRC Delegation in Moscow. Today, he is a member of the Research Institute Louis Favoreu and is also extraordinary Professor at the University of the Western Cape in South Africa.

Béatrice Pouligny

Béatrice Pouligny is a Senior Researcher at the Centre for International Studies and Research (CERI/Sciences-Po/CNRS) in France, currently based in Washington, DC. She is a Visiting Scholar at the Edmund A. Walsh School of Foreign Service at Georgetown University and also works as a senior consultant for the Peacebuilding Initiative, a project led by the International Association for Humanitarian Policy and Conflict Research (HPCR International), in partnership with the Humanitarian Policy and Conflict Research Program, at Harvard University, and the UN Peacebuilding Support Office, in New York. She has worked for the UN and international and local NGOs in different parts of the world. In 2002–2003 and in 2004, she received two awards from the Fulbright Commission (New Century Scholar and Alumni Initiative Award).

Bertrand Ramcharan

Bertrand G. Ramcharan is Professor of International Human Rights Law at the Graduate Institute of International and Development Studies in Geneva, Chancellor of the University of Guyana, and Senior Fellow at the Ralph Bunche Institute for International Studies at the CUNY Graduate Center. He has a doctorate from the London School of Economics and is a Barrister of Lincoln's Inn. He was a member of the UN Secretariat for thirty-two years. He served in the position of Deputy and then UN High Commissioner for Human Rights a.i. (2003–2004). Previously he had been Director in the Office of the Secretary-General's Special Representative for the Former Yugoslavia and Director of the

Secretariat of the International Conference on the Former Yugoslavia, then Director of the Africa I Division of the Department of Political Affairs, and head of the speech-writing service of the UN Secretary-General. He has taught as an Adjunct Professor at Columbia University and as Visiting Professor of International Law in Lund University, Sweden. He is the author or editor of some twenty-five books on international law, human rights, and the UN, including a book on *Preventive Diplomacy at the UN: The Journey of an Idea* for the UN Intellectual History Project.

Marco Sassòli

Marco Sassòli is Professor of International Law at the University of Geneva and chairs the Boards of the Geneva Academy of International Humanitarian Law and Human Rights and of Geneva Call. From 2001 to 2003, he taught at the University of Quebec in Montreal, Canada, where he remains Associate Professor. He is also Associate Professor at the University of Laval. Marco Sassòli obtained an LLD at the University of Basel (Switzerland) and is member of the Swiss bar. From 1985 to 1997, he worked for the International Committee of the Red Cross at its headquarters, *inter alia* as Deputy Head of its Legal Division, and in the Middle East and the Balkans. He has published on international humanitarian law, human rights law, international criminal law, international law and private actors, the sources of international law, and on state responsibility.

Thierry Tardy

A doctor in Political Science, Thierry Tardy is a Faculty Member and Director of the European Training Course at the Geneva Centre for Security Policy. His areas of research and teaching include crisis management, UN peacekeeping, the role of the UN in security governance, and European security. His latest work addresses the relations between the UN and the European Union in crisis management.

Vicky Tennant

Vicky Tennant is a Senior Policy Officer in the Policy Development and Evaluation Service at UNHCR. She is a barrister, and holds a Master's degree in Human Rights Law from Queen's University, Belfast. She has undertaken a number of field assignments with UNHCR, including in Pakistan, Afghanistan, Sudan, and Somalia, and is now based in Geneva. From 1994 to 2000 she worked as a refugee law specialist at the Refugee Legal Centre in London, and at the Northern Ireland Law Centre in Belfast.

Volker Türk

Volker Türk is currently Director for Organizational Development and Management at the headquarters of UNHCR in Geneva. He has had a number of UNHCR assignments in various parts of the world, including in Bosnia and Herzegovina, the Democratic Republic of Congo, Malaysia, Kosovo, and Kuwait. From 2000 to 2004, he was Chief of the Protection Policy and Legal Advice Section at UNHCR. Before his time with UNHCR, he worked as university assistant at the Institute of International Law at the University of Vienna, where he finished his doctoral thesis on *UNHCR and its mandate* (published in German by Duncker & Humblot, Berlin, 1992). From 1985 to 1988, he was research assistant at the Institute of Criminal Law at the University of Linz, Austria. He has published widely on international refugee and human rights law.

Daniel Warner

Daniel Warner is Deputy to the Director of the Graduate Institute of International and Development Studies in Geneva and Executive Director of its Program for the Study of International Organization(s). He holds a doctorate in political science from the Institute. In addition to his academic work, he has organized more than twenty courses for young government officials in twenty-seven countries.

Achim Wennmann

Achim Wennmann is Researcher at the Centre on Conflict, Development and Peacebuilding (CCDP) of the Graduate Institute of International and Development Studies in Geneva. He works on the dynamics of contemporary armed conflict and violence, and was a co-editor (with Keith Krause and Robert Muggah) of the 'Global Burden of Armed Violence Report' of the Geneva Declaration on Armed Violence and Development. He has a specific interest in the economic dimensions of armed conflict including its financing and mobilization cost. Current work includes research on the economic issues and tools in peace processes and, more broadly, how their content and design could facilitate post-conflict peacebuilding.

Nigel White

Dr Nigel D White is Professor of International Law at the University of Sheffield and Director of the Centre for the Study of Law in Its International Context. He was formerly Professor of International Organisations at the University of Nottingham. He is co-editor of the *Journal of Conflict and Security Law* and author of numerous articles and books including *Keeping the Peace* (1997) and *The Law of International Organisations* (2005).

Introduction: Post-conflict Peacebuilding—Ambiguity and Identity

Vincent Chetail[*]

I. The Meanings and Dilemmas of Post-conflict Peacebuilding

Origin and context

Although the term 'peacebuilding' appeared as early as the 16th century, the theme of peacebuilding did not become a subject of study in its own right until the 1960s and 1970s within the framework of peace research. Its conceptual origins lie in the distinction between 'positive peace' and 'negative peace' developed by the Norwegian sociologist and researcher Johan Galtung. Whereas negative peace is defined as the 'absence of direct and organised violence between human groups or nations', the notion of positive peace is part of a longer term conception according to which establishing a sustainable peace is made possible through cooperation between these groups or nations and the eradication of the root causes of the conflict (Galtung, 1975: 29). To this end, Galtung's 'triangle of violence' identifies three types of violence: direct violence, cultural violence, and structural violence. From this tripartite model three complementary approaches to peace are derived:

- *peacekeeping*, the aim of which is to end the immediate violence and hostilities;
- *peacemaking*, in order to resolve the conflict peacefully through negotiation, mediation, or arbitration; and;
- *peacebuilding*, which focuses on the root causes of the conflict with a view to establishing a sustainable peace.

The pioneering work of Johan Galtung has inspired—and continues to inspire—numerous studies on the dynamics of conflicts and methods of peaceful settlement of disputes (Senghaas, 2001; Lund, 1996 & 2004; Azar, 1990; Burton, 1990). Among the other key scholars in the field of peace research, John Paul Lederach has made a major contribution to the understanding of peacebuilding,

* The drafting of this introduction was made possible thanks to the comments and assistance of Gilles Giacca, Stuart Maslen, Stéphane Pfister, and Marc Roissard de Bellet.

arguing that the concept means much more than just reconstruction after a peace agreement, and should be understood as:

> a comprehensive concept that encompasses, generates, and sustains the full array of processes, approaches, and stages needed to transform conflict toward more sustainable, peaceful relationships. The term thus involves a wide range of activities that both precede and follow formal peace accords. Metaphorically, peace is seen not merely as a stage in time or a condition. It is a dynamic social construct (Lederach, 1997: 20).

Notwithstanding reflections in earlier publications on peace studies, the term 'peacebuilding' only officially entered the diplomatic lexicon in 1992. Its endorsement as a sector in its own right is largely due to Boutros Boutros-Ghali's *Agenda for Peace* published that year. Amid the widespread enthusiasm which characterized the immediate aftermath of the Cold War, the former UN Secretary-General categorized conflict management into four key activities: preventive diplomacy, peacemaking, peacekeeping, and peacebuilding. Despite its new exalted position at the heart of the UN's *raison d'être* (the promotion of peace), peacebuilding was defined in only very general terms as an 'action to identify and support structures which will tend to strengthen and solidify peace in order to avoid a relapse into conflict' (UN, 1992: para 21). Assisting in post-conflict peacebuilding in its differing contexts thus means 'rebuilding the institutions and infrastructures of nations torn by civil war and strife; and building bonds of peaceful mutual benefit among nations formerly at war' (*ibid*: para 15). Such an ambitious objective requires a considerable number of enabling measures if the implementation of a ceasefire agreement is to be sustained:

> [T]hese may include disarming the previously warring parties and the restoration of order, the custody and possible destruction of weapons, repatriating refugees, advisory and training support for security personnel, monitoring elections, advancing efforts to protect human rights, reforming or strengthening governmental institutions and promoting formal and informal processes of political participation (*ibid*: para 55).

In this way, peacebuilding is seen as linear, a natural extension of the three other types of activity identified in *An Agenda for Peace*. From this perspective:

> Preventive diplomacy seeks to resolve disputes before violence breaks out; peacemaking and peacekeeping are required to halt conflicts and preserve peace once it is attained. If successful, they strengthen the opportunity for post-conflict peace-building, which can prevent the recurrence of violence among nations and peoples (*ibid*: para 21).

Although peacebuilding has its own specific content, it is sometimes difficult to disassociate it from the other approaches promoted by the UN. This is especially true for preventive diplomacy with which peacebuilding has long been confused. Highlighting the interaction of these two corollary concepts, *An Agenda for Peace* explains that:

> In surveying the range of efforts for peace, the concept of peace-building as the construction of a new environment should be viewed as the counterpart of preventive diplomacy,

which seeks to avoid the breakdown of peaceful conditions. When conflict breaks out, mutually reinforcing efforts at peacemaking and peace-keeping come into play. Once these have achieved their objectives, only sustained, cooperative work to deal with underlying economic, social, cultural and humanitarian problems can place an achieved peace on a durable foundation. Preventive diplomacy is to avoid a crisis; post-conflict peacebuilding is to prevent a recurrence (*ibid*: para 57).

The concept of peacebuilding has been taken up again and clarified in the *Supplement to An Agenda for Peace*, published in 1995. While restating the 'validity of the concept of post-conflict peacebuilding', the Supplement emphasizes the need for 'integrated action' (UN, 1995: paras 47–8), observing that:

Most of the activities that together constitute peace-building fall within the mandates of the various programmes, funds, offices and agencies of the United Nations system with responsibilities in the economic, social, humanitarian and human rights fields. In a country ruined by war, resumption of such activities may initially have to be entrusted to, or at least coordinated by, a multifunctional peace-keeping operation, but as that operation succeeds in restoring normal conditions, the programmes, funds, offices and agencies can re-establish themselves and gradually take over responsibility from the peace-keepers (*ibid*: para 53).

The same year as the publication of the Supplement, the Secretary-General created an inter-departmental Task Force to identify post-conflict peacebuilding activities that could be undertaken by UN agencies; these are described in *An Inventory of Post-Conflict Peace-Building Activities*, published in 1996. Along with this, the publication of *An Agenda for Development* (1994), *An Agenda for Democratization* (1996), as well as the *UNDP Report on Human Security* (1994) have helped to explain the UN's perspective on the interaction between four central concerns: security, development, democratization, and human rights.

The many peace operations undertaken during the 1990s were thus intended to be part of a broader strategy on post-conflict peacebuilding. In reaction to the often-mixed results of such operations, the Brahimi Report, published in 2000, stresses the need to promote more coherent strategies 'to reassemble the foundations of peace and provide the tools for building on those foundations something that is more than just the absence of war' (UN, 2000: 3). This in turn demanded better coordination of the various stakeholders and recognition of the intersectoral nature of the many areas of peacebuilding activities inherent to such a process.

Since 1992, the UN conception of post-conflict peacebuilding has thus evolved from an essentially linear approach into one which is meant to be more integrated (Tschirgi, 2004). This evolution culminated in the 2005 World Summit, which emphasized 'the need for a coordinated, coherent and integrated approach to post-conflict peacebuilding and reconciliation with a view to achieving sustainable peace' (UN, 2005b: 25). The decision to establish a Peacebuilding Commission was adopted at the Summit with a view to resolving the institutional deficit that had long prevailed in efforts to ensure effective coordination. This quest has generated a new impetus for shaping the UN's strategy and conception of peacebuilding. In May 2007, the UN Secretary-General's Policy Committee agreed on the following conceptual basis to inform the UN practice in the field of post-conflict peacebuilding:

Peacebuilding involves a range of measures targeted to reduce the risk of lapsing or relapsing into conflict by strengthening national capacities at all levels for conflict management, and to lay the foundations for sustainable peace and development. Peacebuilding strategies must be coherent and tailored to the specific needs of the country concerned, based on national ownership, and should comprise a carefully prioritized, sequenced, and therefore relatively narrow set of activities aimed at achieving the above objectives. (UN Peacebuilding Commission, 2007: 2).

Identifying this 'relatively narrow set of activities' may, however, prove particularly perilous given the wide range of activities and actors involved in post-conflict peacebuilding. In parallel with the reflections initiated within the UN, post-conflict peacebuilding has been developed and strengthened well beyond the confines of that world body, being rapidly incorporated into the mandates of numerous other governmental and intergovernmental agencies. For example, in 1996, Canada launched the 'Canadian Peacebuilding Initiative' in the form of a joint programme led by the then-Department of Foreign Affairs and International Trade (DFAIT) and the Canadian International Development Agency (CIDA), thereby highlighting the interaction between peace and development. Among multilateral institutions, the World Bank established a 'Post-Conflict Unit' in 1997, the same year that the Organisation for Economic Co-operation and Development (OECD) created the 'Conflict Prevention and Post-Conflict Reconstruction Network', the aim being to bring together bilateral and multilateral aid agencies to better coordinate their actions. From then on, interest in peacebuilding continued to grow, but without an accompanying clarification of the meaning of this now essential concept.

Definitions and meanings of post-conflict peacebuilding

Indeed, far from becoming more sharply defined, as peacebuilding was institutionalized, its scope and ambit actually became increasingly ambiguous. Although the expression 'post-conflict peacebuilding' has become an integral part of diplomatic vocabulary, states and international organizations often—deliberately—avoid giving it a precise definition. The waters have been further muddied by the proliferation of terminological substitutes and other hybrid expressions. A study of the terminology used by twenty-four governmental and non-governmental agencies has highlighted the vast diversity of expressions used to describe post-conflict peacebuilding (Barnett *et al*, 2007).

Aside from the difficulties in comprehension this may cause, the profusion of terms reflects more fundamentally the differences in the mandates and political and/or institutional interests of the various actors involved in the process of post-conflict reconstruction. For instance, the North Atlantic Treaty Organization (NATO) privileges the terms 'stabilization' and 'peace support' in line with its military mandate, while the European Union employs the expression 'civilian crisis management' within the framework of its European Security and Defence Policy (ESDP). Among the many other regional organizations involved in this sphere, the African Union (AU) speaks of 'post conflict reconstruction and development (PCRD)', defined as:

a comprehensive set of measures that seek to: address the needs of countries emerging from conflict, including the needs of affected populations; prevent escalation of disputes; avoid relapse into violence; address the root causes of conflict; and consolidate sustainable peace. PCRD is conceived within the African vision of renewal and sustainable development and while its activities are integrated, and many must be pursued simultaneously, they are envisaged in the emergency (short-term), transition (medium-term) and development (long-term) phases. The scope of these activities encompasses six indicative elements, namely: security; humanitarian/emergency assistance; political governance and transition; socio-economic reconstruction and development; human rights, justice and reconciliation; and women and gender (AU, 2006: para 14).

With respect to UN agencies and international financial institutions, such as the UN Development Programme (UNDP) or the International Monetary Fund (IMF), the expression 'post-conflict peacebuilding' is generally associated with the concepts of reconstruction and recovery. In UNDP's view:

crisis and post-conflict situations present a major challenge to development assistance but also constitute a unique opportunity for UNDP to demonstrate the importance of its own core mandate – that of building national capacity for long-term growth and sustainable development (UNDP, 2000: 8).

Among the rare official definitions, that of the UN Thesaurus (UNBIS) merely repeats verbatim the definition proposed by Boutros Boutros-Ghali in his *An Agenda for Peace*. The on-line glossary of the UN Department of Peacekeeping Operations (DPKO) proposes a slightly more substantive definition:

[I]n the aftermath of conflict; it means identifying and supporting measures and structures which will solidify peace and build trust and interaction among former enemies, in order to avoid a relapse into conflict; often involves elections organized, supervised or conducted by the United Nations, the rebuilding of civil physical infrastructures and institutions such as schools and hospitals, and economic reconstruction (<http://www.un.org/Depts/dpko/glossary/p.htm>).

More recently, DPKO's 2008 *United Nations Peacekeeping Operations: Principles and Guidelines* outlines its own definition of peacebuilding:

Peacebuilding involves a range of measures targeted to reduce the risk of lapsing or relapsing into conflict by strengthening national capacities at all levels for conflict management, and to lay the foundation for sustainable peace and development. Peacebuilding is a complex, long-term process of creating the necessary conditions for sustainable peace.

It works by addressing the deep-rooted, structural causes of violent conflict in a comprehensive manner. Peacebuilding measures address core issues that effect the functioning of society and the State, and seek to enhance the capacity of the State to effectively and legitimately carry out its core functions (UN, 2008: 18).

Definitions used by governmental agencies are even more diverse. For instance, DFAIT defines peacebuilding as designating a set of measures that create a sustainable infrastructure for human security (DFAIT, 1996). This dense and concise formula attests to Canada's desire to promote the concept of human security which it has placed at the heart of its foreign policy. Thus, the way peacebuilding is defined remains highly dependent upon the political motivations of its promoters. In some cases, for example in Japan or the United Kingdom, meaning can even vary internally within the government, depending on whether the department involved is responsible for defence or development. The banner of post-conflict peacebuilding is indeed large enough and vague enough to encapsulate different interpretations of its exact meaning. Its volatility represents both its main strength and weakness. Barnett *et al* observe that:

[T]he willingness of so many diverse constituencies with divergent and sometimes conflicting interests to rally around peacebuilding also suggests that one of the concept's talents is to camouflage divisions over how to handle the post conflict challenge. In this respect, it functions much like a favored political symbol. Symbols are often highly ambiguous. Ambiguity can facilitate collective action because different constituencies can support the symbol without necessarily achieving consensus on the substance (Barnett *et al*, 2007: 43–4).

The recurrent ambiguity of post-conflict peacebuilding perpetuates the ongoing debates among policy-makers, practitioners, and analysts as to its exact scope and meaning. Although there is a general agreement that post-conflict peacebuilding is more than the elimination of armed conflict, three different approaches to peacebuilding may be identified:

- *Maximalist:* addressing roots causes of armed conflict;
- *Minimalist:* no renewed armed conflict;
- *Middle Ground:* no renewed armed conflict plus decent governance (Call & Cousens, 2007: 4–6).

These different approaches echo the long-standing discussions on the interaction between peacebuilding and development. While development is essential for lasting and sustainable peace (Collier *et al*, 2003), the muddling of the difference between peacebuilding and development could result in practical problems, because 'the most important factors driving potential conflict may not be addressed' (Lund, 2003: 27). Accordingly, it has been argued that:

A line needs to be drawn between peacebuilding and maximizing the various levels of social, economic and political development possible in a given society. Otherwise, if the term peacebuilding becomes a synonym for all the positive things we would want to include in development in order to reduce any and all of a society's ills, it becomes useless for guiding knowledge gathering and practical purposes (*ibid*, 28).

Dilemmas and controversies surrounding post-conflict peacebuilding

In short, post-conflict peacebuilding is a polymorphous concept that never fails to provoke lively debate. While in-depth analysis is not possible here, it is important to point out early on that the political essence of such a concept easily explains why it has become the battleground for ideological confrontations that go well beyond the individual issue of post-conflict reconstruction. The many controversies provoked by peacebuilding are part of the larger and constant confrontation between different schools of thought in international relations: the realist and neo-realist schools; the theory of dependence; constructivism; functionalism; and neo-functionalism, or critical theories.

Many have called into question the ideological underpinnings of post-conflict peacebuilding, which they say is being exploited by Western states to justify a new form of interventionism or to promote the post-9/11 agenda of stabilization (Richmond, 2004; Pugh, 2004; Bellamy, 2004). On another level, the strategies applied by the international community are often criticized for not giving adequate consideration to local realities and the actual needs of the concerned populations (Chopra & Hohe, 2004). The importing of a neo-liberal model combining democracy with a market economy may be indeed particularly counterproductive in societies weakened by years of war (Kumar, 1997). Roland Paris has shown on the basis of different case studies that accelerated economic liberalization and strong efforts to democratize can cause a recurrence of violence (Paris, 1997). The impossibility of standing up to extreme economic competition may cause new social inequalities, whereas premature democratization is thought to lead to the polarization of political antagonisms within already destabilized societies. It raises in turn the validity of the 'liberal peace', as embedded in the particular Western paradigm of the state, by opposition to 'real peace' in non-Western post-conflict societies.

Over and above underlying ideological issues, what is most worrying is that the multiple actions undertaken by the international community have brought so few positive results. Post-conflict peacebuilding remains an eminently precarious process. Various estimates suggest that the risk of conflict recurrence is between 20 to 50 per cent in the first five years after a conflict ended (Suhrke and Samset, 2007: 195–7; Call & Cousens, 2007: 3–4; Collier and Hoeffler, 2004; Doyle & Sambanis, 2000). Thus, numerous conflicts labelled 'recidivist' (Woodward, 2007: 3) require repeated peace operations. In other cases, countries coming out of an armed conflict get stuck in a grey area of 'neither war nor peace'. As the hope inspired by the end of the fighting gives way to disillusionment, the involvement of the international community decreases or even disappears, at the very moment when the populations are most in need of assistance.

Such a feeling of failure is obviously not independent of the particularly high—even disproportionate for some—expectations that the ambitious concept of peacebuilding encourages. The ever-present gap between theory and practice is a reminder of the extent to which post-conflict peacebuilding is a complex, multifaceted, and long-term process. It is 'not only *multi-dimensional* but also *multi-sectoral* in terms of *what* the international community should be doing on the ground, *multi-leveled* in terms of *how much* should be done, and *multi-staged* in terms of *when* the international community should be involved' (Lund, 2003: 13). Although each post-conflict context is unique, peacebuilding typically involves a triple transition: a *security* transition, from a situation of open violence to the progressive establishment of sustainable peace; a *socio-economic* transition, from conflict economies to a peace economy which is more open to the private sector and to international trade; and a *democratic* transition, from an authoritarian system to one of representative government (David, 1998). While the concept of transition is controversial in itself, there is consensus that post-conflict peacebuilding is composed of three core components: security, socio-economic recovery, and democracy.

The establishment of sustainable peace requires simultaneous action in each of these areas, which are so interdependent that they are difficult to dissociate. The first challenge of post-conflict peacebuilding is clearly that of taking security measures, in order to avoid a recurrence of hostilities and thus to support the peace process. The implementation of this security aspect involves many tasks: maintaining law and order through civil and military means, undertaking mine action, effecting the disarmament, demobilization, and reintegration of former combatants, ensuring security sector reform, facilitating the return and reintegration of refugees, and so on. Peacebuilding strategies rapidly become split between the contradictory objectives of negative peace and positive peace. All at the same time, it becomes necessary to stabilize the situation in the field for the short- and medium-term while addressing the root causes of the conflict through long-term action. In short, this dilemma illustrates the traditional opposition between the logic of security and the logic of development (Krause & Jütersonke, 2005; Junne & Verkoren, 2004; Keating & Knight, 2004; Duffield, 2001).

Faced with these contradictions, the concept of human security tries to reconcile the traditional understanding of security with development by focusing on the protection of individuals. Its objective is to free individuals not only from 'fear', but also from 'need'. The second challenge highlighted by UNDP, recovery, has to make it possible to optimize the passage from emergency assistance to development. Capacity-building, especially through local ownership, is then a crucial factor for minimizing the perverse phenomenon of assistance. Aside from getting infrastructure back in working order, boosting the economy requires structural reform to facilitate the passage from conflict economies to peace-time economies. It notably includes the stimulus of the private sector, combating corruption and shadow economies, as well as encouraging investment by diasporas and multinational companies.

The third challenge of post-conflict peacebuilding, democratization, often supposes state-building reforms through a whole battery of legislative or even constitutional measures aimed at restoring the authority and representativeness of institutions damaged during a civil war (Daudet, 1995). The essential, if not vital, issue is to foster—to the extent possible—an impartial state that respects the rights of all, including those of minorities. In practice, however, the principle of democratic governance and its corollary concept—free and fair elections—frequently come up against the persistence of clan and/or party loyalties inherited from the war. Indeed, 'the lines of division that led to conflict escalation normally survive the peace process: if war is continuation of politics by other means, peace is generally the resumption of the same politics, often by the same pre-war means' (Smith, 2004: 27). Implementing a policy of reconciliation that closely involves civil society is therefore essential for encouraging a culture of peace. Ball observes that:

Successfully ending the divisions that lead to war, healing the social wounds created by war, and creating a society where the differences among social groups are resolved through compromise rather than violent conflict requires that conflict resolution and consensus building shape all interactions among citizens and between citizens and the state (Ball, 2005: 619).

No reform of institutions which are seen as the guarantors of the rule of law can succeed in a lasting way if such reform is imposed from outside. Over and above institutional engineering, it is the citizens' confidence in the primacy of law which must be restored.

II. The Actors of Post-conflict Peacebuilding

The diversity of actors

Taking stock of the many actors involved in post-conflict reconstruction is another way of understanding the complexity and multi-dimensional nature of the peacebuilding process (Cutillo, 2006). Here again, the issue can be examined from various perspectives: external or exogenous actors versus local or endogenous actors; state actors versus non-state actors; decision-makers versus civil society; civilians and the military; political leaders and economic agents. Attempting to make a complete and systematic list quickly becomes a perilous exercise, as one could add categories indefinitely. Moreover, all of these actors are involved—and interconnected—to different degrees.

Beyond the operational difficulties inherent in coordinating a plethora of stakeholders, one of the major challenges centres on the collaboration between the state concerned and the international community. Indeed, the viability of this collaboration conditions the effectiveness of peacebuilding efforts (hence the eternal tension between national sovereignty and international intervention). The terms of this contradiction are even enshrined in the UN Charter: on the one hand, the principle of non-intervention in domestic affairs, reflected in Article 2(7) of the Charter, is a natural extension of the concept of sovereignty; while on the other, apart from the explicit reservation mentioned in Chapter VII, specifically created to address threats to peace, the principle of non-intervention in domestic affairs must be squared with the 'universal respect for, and observance of, human rights and fundamental freedoms for all' proclaimed in Articles 1(3) and 55 of the Charter. How can the world body's founding principles be reconciled, when they endorse sovereignty while at the same time suggesting infringing upon it in order to protect collective interests such as peace and human rights?

The concept of responsibility to protect suggests shifting the terms of the debate by moving 'from sovereignty as control to sovereignty as responsibility' (ICISS, 2001: para 2.14). From this perspective, 'sovereignty implies a dual responsibility: externally—to respect the sovereignty of other states, and internally, to respect the dignity and basic rights of all the people within the state' (*ibid*: para 1.35). Although the exact content of the responsibility to protect remains uncertain (which explains its success), one of its core components derives from the principle of subsidiarity: the international community is supposed to act as a substitute to a failed state which must be rebuilt. In practice, however, such endeavours have proven to be extremely hazardous, in cases where the international community intervenes without the consent of the state and, more generally, without the consent of all of the former belligerent factions (Kreilkamp, 2003; Han, 1994).

While the intervention of the international community can become necessary, it is important to recognize that local actors, and in particular civil society, are best equipped to take their fate in hand and bring a sustained end to conflict. External intervention can never be an end in itself. Its *raison d'être* is to support the indigenous forces of a country coming out of conflict. The primary actor of peacebuilding remains the population affected by war. Capacity-building and local ownership are thus crucial to the success of any post-conflict peacebuilding process.

Too often, however, external actors have privileged formal institutions over informal or traditional structures for the purpose of restoring the authority of the state. Support to the formal institutions of the state is certainly critical, for peacebuilding is by essence 'a highly political project involving the creation of a legitimate political authority that can avoid the resurgence of violence' (Tschirgi, 2004: 9). It should not, however, be carried out to the detriment of the informal sector at the societal or micro level (Tschirgi, 2006). Initiatives towards civil society and the population at large prove crucial for fostering reconciliation and ensuring that peacebuilding programs are locally owned, people-centred, and rights-based.

The important work of John Paul Lederach showed how important it is to reconcile and combine a 'top-down' with a 'bottom-up' approach to peacebuilding. Both approaches are closely interconnected and complementary in the establishment of a sustainable peace. Constructing a peace process in deeply divided societies therefore requires consideration of 'the *legitimacy, uniqueness,* and *interdependency* of the needs and resources of the grassroots, middle range and top level' (Lederach, 1997: 60). His analytical framework is succinctly summarized in the pyramid shown in Figure 1, which identifies three categories of actors and three correlative approaches to peacebuilding, whose impact on the population varies from one to another.

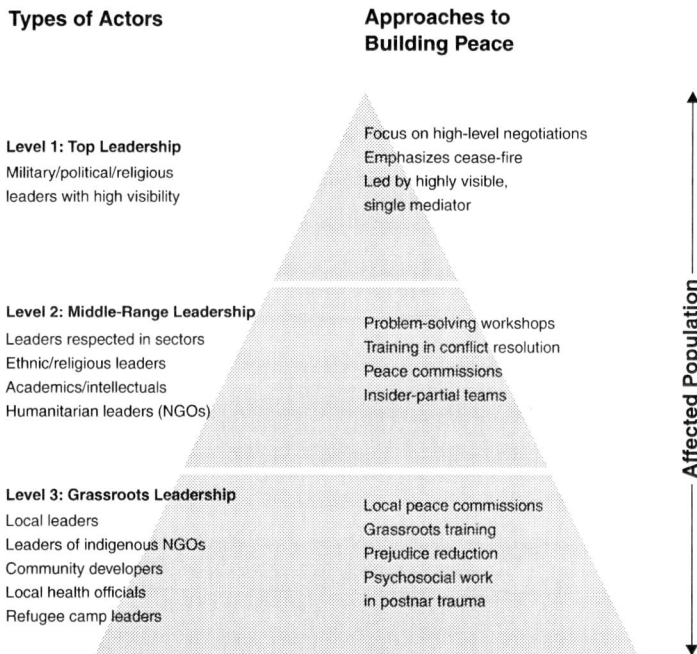

Types of Actors

Approaches to Building Peace

Level 1: Top Leadership
Military/political/religious leaders with high visibility

Focus on high-level negotiations
Emphasizes cease-fire
Led by highly visible,
single mediator

Level 2: Middle-Range Leadership
Leaders respected in sectors
Ethnic/religious leaders
Academics/intellectuals
Humanitarian leaders (NGOs)

Problem-solving workshops
Training in conflict resolution
Peace commissions
Insider-partial teams

Level 3: Grassroots Leadership
Local leaders
Leaders of indigenous NGOs
Community developers
Local health officials
Refugee camp leaders

Local peace commissions
Grassroots training
Prejudice reduction
Psychosocial work
in postnar trauma

Affected Population

Figure 1 Peacebuilding Pyramid

Derived from John Paul Lederach, *Building Peace: Sustainable Reconciliation in Divided Societies* (Washington, DC: United States Institute of Peace Press, 1997), 39.

Peacebuilding operations and missions

Regardless of the limitations inherent in any external intervention, the deployment of an impartial international presence is as much an element of stability—the prerequisite for reconstruction—as it is a means of keeping the international community's attention focused on countries devastated by war. Furthermore, as most peacebuilding activities involve many different actors, supporting and coordinating these activities can require the setting up of comprehensive and multifaceted peace operations.

The very concept of peace operations has thus evolved considerably as its missions have developed. Given the difficulty of constructing a global and coherent typology, such operations are often described by generic—and revealing—terms such as 'complex' or 'multidimensional'. Their hybrid character becomes even more accentuated with the involvement of two or more international organizations responsible for different—and sometimes identical—activities in one country. This evolution is mainly due to the increasing role played by regional organizations in peace operations, including the AU, the EU, the Economic Community of West African States (ECOWAS), NATO, and the Organization for Security and Co-operation in Europe (OSCE). While regional organizations offer the advantage of being more familiar with local conditions and enjoy a special legitimacy among local actors, they may also be dominated by regional hegemons that may be counter-productive to efforts to foster capacity-building and local ownership. Against this backdrop, complex peace operations carried out by the UN may appear more impartial and benefit from a relatively longer experience in the field of post-conflict peacebuilding.

Within the UN, the first peace operation specifically tasked with peacebuilding was the UN Transition Assistance Group (UNTAG), which accompanied Namibia's passage to independence between April 1989 and March 1990. Its primary mandate was to supervize the organization of free and fair elections. It also required a multitude of related activities: restoring public order, confining of troops to base, and, in the case of South Africa's troops, ensuring their withdrawal from Namibia; as well as ensuring that discriminatory laws were repealed, political prisoners were released, and Namibian refugees were permitted to return.

Since then, many operations have been deployed to help implement peace agreements. This was the case, for example, in El Salvador (UN Observer Mission in El Salvador, ONUSAL, 1991–1995); in Cambodia (UN Advance Mission in Cambodia, UNAMIC, 1991–1992, UN Transitional Authority in Cambodia, UNTAC, 1992–1993); in Mozambique (UN Operation in Mozambique, ONUMOZ, 1992–1994); in Guatemala (UN Verification Mission in Guatemala, MINUGUA, 1997); in Bosnia and Herzegovina (UN Mission in Bosnia and Herzegovina, UNMIBH, 1995–2002); and in Burundi (UN Operation in Burundi, ONUB, 2004–2006).

Today, such peacebuilding operations are the rule rather than the exception. Indeed, almost all of the peace operations in progress, listed in Table 1, fulfil reconstruction and peacebuilding functions.

Table 1 United Nations Peace Operations

Peace operations in progress		*Date for initiation*
UNTSO	United Nations Truce Supervision Organization	May 1948
UNMOGIP	United Nations Military Observer Group in India and Pakistan	January 1949
UNFICYP	United Nations Peacekeeping Force in Cyprus	March 1964
UNDOF	United Nations Disengagement Observer Force	June 1974
UNIFIL	United Nations Interim Force in Lebanon	March 1978
MINURSO	United Nations Mission for the Referendum in Western Sahara	April 1991
UNOMIG	United Nations Observer Mission in Georgia	August 1993
UNMIK	UN Interim Administration Mission in Kosovo	June 1999
MONUC	UN Organization Mission in the Democratic Republic of the Congo	November 1999
UNMIL	United Nations Mission in Liberia	September 2003
UNOCI	United Nations Operation in Côte d'Ivoire	April 2004
MINUSTAH	United Nations Stabilization Mission in Haiti	June 2004
UNMIS	United Nations Mission in the Sudan	March 2005
UNMIT	United Nations Integrated Mission in Timor-Leste	August 2006
UNAMID	African Union/United Nations Hybrid Operation in Darfur	July 2007
MINURCAT	United Nations Mission in the Central African Republic and Chad	September 2007

Source: United Nations Peacekeeping operations. Peace and Security Section of the United Nations Department of Public Information, in consultation with the Department of Peacekeeping Operations, Peacekeeping Financing Division of the Office of Programme Planning, Budget and Accounts, and the Department of Political Affairs—DPI/1634/Rev.79—February 2008: <www.un.org/Depts/dpko/dpko/bnote010101.pdf>

In addition to these peace operations managed by DPKO, peacebuilding missions and support offices are directed by the Department of Political Affairs (DPA). As of 31 July 2008, 12 missions of this type involving 3,944 civilian and military staff were being conducted in Africa, Asia, and the Middle East. The peacebuilding missions underway in 2008 are summarized in Table 2.

The overall results of the various peacebuilding operations and missions are mixed, as they vary significantly from one situation to another, depending on the local context and the degree of involvement of the international community. The major operational difficulty lies in coordinating a multitude of civilian and military actors whose areas of expertise are extremely diverse. One of the solutions put forward to this implementation challenge has been the notion of 'integrated mission', whose goal is to enable all participants to cooperate closely and in a coordinated manner in order to ensure the implementation of a comprehensive peacebuilding strategy (Eide *et al*, 2005). However, the tangible results of such integrated missions proved themselves so mixed that a new step toward institutionalizing coordination efforts was necessary through the creation of a Peacebuilding Commission.

Table 2 United Nations Peacebuilding Missions

Missions in progress	
UNPOS	Since 15 April 1995
UN Political Office for Somalia	
UNOGBIS	Since 3 March 1999
UN Peacebuilding Support Office in Guinea-Bissau	
UNSCO	Since 1 October 1999
Office of the United Nations Special Coordinator for the Middle East	
Special Coordinator for the Middle East Peace Process and Personal Representative of the Secretary-General to the Palestine Liberation Organisation and the Palestinian Authority	
BONUCA	Since 15 February 2000
UN Peacebuilding Office in the Central African Republic	
UNSCOL	Since 16 February 2007
Office of the United Nations Special Coordinator of the Secretary-General for Lebanon (formally known as Office of the Personal Representative of the Secretary-General for Southern Lebanon established in August 2000)	
UNOWA	Since 29 November 2001
Office of the Special Representative of the Secretary-General for West Africa	
UNAMA*	
UN Assistance Mission in Afghanistan	Since 28 March 2002
UNAMI	
UN Assistance Mission for Iraq	Since 14 August 2003
UNIOSIL*	
UN Integrated Office in Sierra Leone	Since 1 January 2006
BINUB*	
UN Integrated Office in Burundi	Since 1 January 2007
UNMIN	
UN Mission in Nepal	Since 23 January 2007
UNRCCA	Since 10 December 2007
United Nations Regional Center for Preventive Diplomacy for Central Asia	

* Mission directed and supported by the Department of Peacekeeping

Source: Peace and Security Section, United Nations Department of Public Information, in consultation with the Department of Political Affairs and the Department of Peacekeeping Operations—DPI/2166/Rev.53—December 2007: <http://www.un.org/Depts/dpko/dpko/ppbm.pdf>

The Peacebuilding Commission

The Peacebuilding Commission was established on 20 December 2005 by the Security Council and the General Assembly (UN Security Council, 2005; UN, 2005b; Ponzio, 2005; Schneckener & Weinlich, 2005; Stahn, 2005a). This 'double paternity' is an important novelty: in UN history the Commission is the first subsidiary organ to belong to both the General Assembly and the Security Council. This specificity anchors it solidly at the centre of the UN system. In return, however, the effectiveness of its action is dependent upon the often equivocal relations between the Security Council and the General Assembly in the area of international peacekeeping and collective security.

The key mission of this new institution is to better coordinate post-conflict strategies in order to ensure that they can be sustainable in the long-term and be more coherent. The three main functions assigned to it by the aforementioned resolutions are:

(a) To bring together all relevant actors to marshal resources and to advise on and propose integrated strategies for post-conflict peacebuilding and recovery;
(b) To focus attention on the reconstruction and institution-building efforts necessary for recovery from conflict and to support the development of integrated strategies in order to lay the foundation for sustainable development;
(c) To provide recommendations and information to improve the coordination of all relevant actors within and outside the United Nations, to develop best practices, to help to ensure predictable financing for early recovery activities and to extend the period of attention given by the international community to post-conflict recovery (resolution 1645 (2005), para 2).

The institutional void the Commission is supposed to fill is nevertheless a relative one. The Commission is not intended to take the place of other UN bodies. It is an instrument of support for the many existing institutions, all of which can call on it for help or advice. As a consequence, the Commission is nothing but an advisory body: it does not have the authority to make binding decisions opposable to any of the numerous actors involved in post-conflict peacebuilding efforts. As a way of attenuating this significant limitation, the Security Council and the General Assembly invite 'all relevant United Nations bodies and other bodies and actors, including the international financial institutions, to take action on the advice of the Commission, as appropriate and in accordance with their respective mandates' (*ibid*: para 14).

The Peacebuilding Commission thus resembles in many ways a forum for discussion, exchange, and reflection as a support to the various actors involved in the complex post-conflict process. It is thereby constrained to favour an integrated approach to the management of post-conflict situations by acting as the key interface between all UN agencies involved in reconstruction (such as DPA, DPKO, UNHCR, OHCHR, UNDP, and UNICEF), but also between the other bodies that are becoming more and more involved in this process (even though it is not at the core of their respective mandates), such as the World Health Organization (WHO) or the International Labour Organization (ILO).

All the other relevant actors are also closely associated to the work of the Peacebuilding Commission. According to the resolutions establishing this new body, 'representatives from the World Bank, the International Monetary Fund and other institutional donors shall be invited to participate in all meetings of the Commission' (para 9). Moreover, in addition to its collaboration with the authorities of the state concerned, the Commission shall work in consultation with 'regional and subregional organizations' (para 11) and with 'civil society, non-governmental organizations, including women's organizations, and the private sector engaged in peacebuilding activities' (para 21).

Development of the working methods of the new Commission is entrusted to a permanent Organizational Committee (para 4), whose composition was decided with the utmost care. The Committee comprises thirty-one members elected for renewable terms of two years, including: seven members chosen by the Security Council (and including permanent members); seven members elected by the Economic and Social Council; five of the ten top providers of financial contributions to UN budgets; five countries from among the ten top providers of military personnel and civilian police to UN missions; and, lastly, seven members elected by the General Assembly. The diversity of these members and their experience in post-conflict activities gives the Commission undeniable legitimacy, although its reactivity may be hindered by the number of its members and the use of consensus for decision-making. In parallel to country-specific meetings, a Working Group on Lessons Learned was also established to accumulate best practices and lessons on critical peacebuilding issues with a view to develop recommendations for future post-conflict strategies and implementation.

In order to carry out the difficult mandate entrusted to it, the Peacebuilding Commission is supported by two other key components: the Peacebuilding Support Office and the Peacebuilding Fund. Together, these three new bodies form what is labelled the 'UN peacebuilding architecture'. The Peacebuilding Support Office enables the Commission to benefit from the different services of the Secretary-General and to help the latter integrate peacebuilding strategies on a UN-wide scale. It thus serves as interlocutor between the UN system and the Commission.

The Peacebuilding Fund is by far the most crucial pillar of this new peacebuilding architecture, with a funding target of US$250 million. The Fund, managed by UNDP, must mobilize the resources necessary to undertake activities 'of direct and immediate relevance to the peacebuilding process' (UN, 2006: para 5; Annex, para 2.1). Its priority is to foster activities that support the implementation of peace agreements, reinforce the beneficiary country's capacities for the peaceful resolution of conflict, and help combat the sources of a recurrence of conflict, such as disarmament, demobilization, and reintegration programmes. The Peacebuilding Fund thus serves as a catalyst for more sustainable investments by development agencies and bilateral donors. However, the Fund is not part of the UN's regular budget, as its financing depends entirely on states' voluntary contributions.

The main challenge facing the Peacebuilding Commission is to maximize its impact on the ground to make the UN peacebuilding architecture an effective instrument of international collaboration in support of countries emerging from conflict. A key political instrument for the Commission is the potential to negotiate an Integrated Peacebuilding Strategy (IPBS) with the focus-country government. Once jointly endorsed by the government and the Commission, the IPBS provides an agreed framework for the government's commitments and the international community's overarching support to peacebuilding activities. IPBS is thus conceived as 'a flexible and practical instrument for facilitating political dialogue, analysing the sources of conflict, enhancing coordination among key national and international actors, marshalling resources and monitoring progress' (UN Peacebuilding Commission, 2008a: para 63). It should therefore cover all aspects that are critical to sustain a country's transition from conflict to sustainable peace, notably the following:

(a) a consultative process based on the principle of national ownership;
(b) an integrated approach to ensure that political, security and development dimensions reinforce rather than undermine each other;
(c) succinct identification and analysis of key peacebuilding priorities and commitments on the part of all stakeholders;
(d) a nationally led monitoring and review mechanism on the basis of concrete, measurable and time-bound indicators to assess progress as well as setbacks towards agreed commitments;
(e) coherence with existing national strategic frameworks, such as the Poverty Reduction Strategy Papers; and
(f) ways to support national capacity for peacebuilding and enhance aid effectiveness (*ibid*).

Although it is too early to make a full assessment of the Commission's activities, it is clear that this young child of the UN family is still in search of an identity. This is a predictable consequence of its double paternity. One thing is sure: the success of the UN in this area now goes hand-in-hand with that of the Peacebuilding Commission. As one of the participants in the Security Council's 31 January 2007 session stated:

in order to benefit from [the Commission], the Security Council, the General Assembly and the Economic and Social Council should all continue to adapt to ensure that they too achieve a level of effectiveness that meets both their Charter objectives and general expectations. In other words, to use the metaphor of parent and child, the existence of the Peacebuilding Commission should ease the conscience of those who established it, just as parents pass on to their children the dreams and ambitions that they themselves could not realise. The Commission would otherwise be just another body in an insufficiently reformed international institutional framework (UN Security Council, 2007: 19).

III. A Legal Framework for Post-conflict Peacebuilding

Jus post bellum: an emerging field

Just as there are multiple actors involved in post-conflict reconstruction, the law applicable to peacebuilding is made up of various components. Far from being based upon a coherent and uniform set of standards, the delicate transition from war to peace is located at the intersection of various branches of law, as much international as domestic law. From the perspective of public international law, the law which applies to post-conflict peacebuilding is scattered throughout a multitude of domains including—to mention only the most recurrent—international humanitarian law; international human rights law; international criminal law; international refugee law; international development law; international economic law; the law of international organizations; the law of international responsibility; the law relating to the peaceful settlement of disputes; treaty law which governs, in particular, ceasefire agreements; and the law relating to the succession of states in the case of territorial dismemberment due to conflict.

The fragmenting of the legal system applicable to post-conflict peacebuilding is due, in part, to the compartmentalizing of branches so common in contemporary international law. But it is also, and above all, a reflection of the contradictions and ambiguities inherent in the very concept of peacebuilding. The result is a heterogeneous mixture of standards which are not at all, or only loosely, linked to each other. The fragmentation of the norms applicable to post-conflict peacebuilding makes them difficult to understand, and difficult to apply effectively in war-torn societies.

The generic expression *jus post bellum* nevertheless captures in a single term the extreme diversity of the branches of law which can be applied at the close of armed conflicts. Beyond the traditional couplet *jus in bello* (law governing the conduct of hostilities) and *jus ad bellum* (law regulating the resort to force), it is more important than ever to recognize post-war law as a concept in its own right, as has been demonstrated by recent international practice (Stahn, 2007). Following this perspective, *jus post bellum* can be generally defined as the set of norms applicable at the end of an armed conflict—whether internal or international—with a view to establishing a sustainable peace. Far from a stylistic device of the sort dear to academics, the grouping of disparate standards within the same frame of reference underscores the need for a comprehensive and coordinated approach to the numerous rules governing post-conflict situations. From a systemic perspective, it paves the way for a contextualized interpretation—and, by extension, a contextualized application—of existing norms in order to better take into account the specificities which characterize the difficult transition from war to peace.

Although the expression *jus post bellum* is not widely used in contemporary international law, it is part of a long tradition of the doctrine of the law of nations introduced by Francisco de Vittoria in the 16th century. His disciple, Francisco Suarez, put particular emphasis on the tripartite concept of *jus ad bellum, jus in bello*, and *jus post bellum* (*Disputationes* XIII, 1621). But it is thanks to the works of Emmanuel Kant that this tripartite notion was systematized. In *The Metaphysics of Morals*, he distinguishes between '(1) the right of "going to" war; (2) right "during" war; and (3) right "after" war, the object of which is to constrain the nations mutually to pass from this state of war and to found a common constitution establishing perpetual peace' (Kant, 1796: 226–7).

The components of *jus post bellum*

The various norms governing the end of hostilities are now receiving renewed attention which is not yet systematic or in-depth. Although an exhaustive analysis of all of its components is beyond the scope of this introduction, one could highlight some of them to assess the multifaceted legal challenges of post-conflict peacebuilding.

International humanitarian law

International humanitarian law is a key component of *jus post bellum* at least with respect to the rules governing military occupation. Bearing this in mind, the other rules of international humanitarian law are not applicable, as the threshold of their applicability depends on the existence of an armed conflict and they therefore cease to be applicable 'on the general close of military operations' (Geneva Convention IV, Article 6; Additional Protocol I, Article 3).

There are, however, various exceptions which led the International Criminal Tribunal for the former Yugoslavia to state that 'the temporal scope of the applicable rules clearly reaches beyond the actual hostilities' (ICTY, 1995: para 69). This is particularly true for the rules applicable to prisoners of war and civilian internees, as they remain under the protection of the Geneva Conventions and their Additional Protocols until their final release and repatriation (Convention III, Article 5; Convention IV, Article 6; Protocol I, Article 3; Protocol II, Article 2(2)). The rules relating to the control of weapons are also applicable at the end of the armed conflict. For example, the 1996 Protocol on Prohibitions or Restrictions on the use of Mines, Booby-Traps and other Devices requires states parties to take measures to remove and destroy mines 'without delay after the cessation of active hostilities' (Article 9). The parties are also encouraged to reach agreements, if necessary, with other states or with international organizations, in order to receive technical and material assistance in fulfilling their responsibilities.

Aside from the various rules of international humanitarian law likely to be applied upon cessation of hostilities, the law of occupation has seen renewed interest in light of recent international practices in Iraq and elsewhere. Although military occupation is traditionally defined by reference to a 'territory [. . .] actually placed under the authority of the hostile army' (Hague Regulations, Article 42), its meaning has been progressively enlarged by subsequent practice to encapsulate other kinds of occupation without armed resistance or state of belligerency (Adams, 1984). The threshold for military occupation is thus factual in essence. It is satisfied by effective control by a foreign military force over a territory of a state. Against this background, it has been argued that the law of occupation may apply to complex peace operations (Benvenisti, 1993: 3–5; Kolb *et al*, 2005: 204–32). Although this last issue remains controversial, this was clearly the case for the multinational forces present in Iraq and Afghanistan after armed intervention, which had been carried out outside of UN auspices.

While it is not possible to analyse here the complex and detailed legal regime governing military occupation, its content is organized around two essential axes: the protection of individuals and maintenance of territorial and legislative *status quo*. The first normative axis prohibits, in particular, forcible transfer and deportation (Geneva Convention IV, Article 49), forced labour (*ibid*: Article 51) and the destruction of real or personal, individual or collective property located in an occupied territory (*ibid*: Article 53). Furthermore, the Occupying Power 'has the duty of ensuring food and medical supplies of the population' (*ibid*: Article 55). The second normative axis aims to maintain the *status quo ante*, just prior to the occupation, the latter being considered a transitional phase by definition. Occupation cannot thus generate any transfer of sovereignty of the territory in question, as annexation by threat or through the use of force is prohibited by the UN Charter. The legislative *status quo* has, though, proven highly problematic, especially in light of the prevailing situation in Iraq (Sassòli, 2005; Boon, 2005; Dinstein, 2004). The principle of maintaining in force the legislation of the occupied territory blocks all legislative and constitutional reform, which is often necessary for establishing the rule of law.

It has to be observed, however, that a simple appeal to the norms of international humanitarian law does not resolve the issue of which law to apply during any given occupation. In each case, the issue must also be examined in light of relevant Security Council resolutions and with regard to peremptory norms of general international law (*jus cogens*). From that perspective, respect for fundamental norms of international human rights law has been interpreted as involving, for the Occupying Power, 'an obligation to abolish legislation and institutions which contravene international human rights standards' (Sassòli, 2005: 676).

International human rights law

International human rights law plays a crucial role in restoring the rule of law and the citizen's confidence in their own state. It offers a normative framework which is mainly based upon the two UN Covenants of 1966, whose universality is well established. But the issue is not so much the opposability of human rights law as its effectiveness in a less-than-favourable environment, where the state and its legislative, judiciary, and even executive bodies often need to be rebuilt. That is the fundamental question, as genuine respect of fundamental rights is both a precondition and a component of peacebuilding (Quast, 2004; Ahlund, 2004). It requires not only the incorporation of international norms into domestic law, but also, and above all, that they inform the practices of national and local authorities.

From that angle, the right to an effective remedy, and the right to a fair trial, play key roles in incorporating international standards into the domestic legal order. They presuppose, however, the establishment of a transparent and effective judicial system. The effectiveness of human rights is therefore closely dependent on the operational and structural measures adopted after the cessation of the hostilities (OHCHR, 2006; Strohmeyer, 2001). Such an endeavour is nevertheless bound to fail if it is limited to the passing on of a sort of Western ready-made model, totally detached from the local context, and incompatible with the legal traditions of the country (Danne, 2004).

Following the same logic, the relevant applicable human rights cannot be limited to civil and political rights. The prohibition of arbitrary deprivation of life, torture, inhuman or degrading treatment, and arbitrary detention is surely the most visible indication that an armed conflict, during which these fundamental human rights are so often flouted, has ended. Nevertheless establishing a sustainable peace requires an integrated—and therefore ambitious—approach that gives appropriate consideration to economic and social rights, which are just as fundamental. Notably they include the right to a decent standard of living, the right to adequate housing, the right to health, and the right to education. While the state retains its primary responsibility for implementing human rights, realizing economic and social rights in post-conflict contexts largely depends upon international assistance for fostering the capacity-building and recovery of the state and its population. It echoes in turn the long-standing debate on a putative right to development regularly asserted by the General Assembly.

At the state level, the adoption of legislation protecting individual freedoms is also closely linked to free and fair elections, which concretize the right to vote and to be elected, as enshrined in Article 25 of the 1966 Covenant on Civil and Political Rights (Goodwin-Gill, 2006; Samuels, 2005–2006; Fox, 2003). Such elections guarantee the legitimacy of the Parliament in its efforts to repeal exceptional legislation, which is commonly passed in times of armed conflict. In practice, however, recourse to elections has often proven premature in the socio-political context prevailing at the end of an armed conflict, as the former belligerents often attempt to obtain by means of the ballot box what they gained or lost through the use of arms. In this context, free and fair elections presuppose the prior safeguarding—in fact as in law—of other related freedoms. Promoting freedom of opinion, of association, and of assembly is essential if an active and open civil society is to be fostered.

In post-conflict situations, the prohibition of 'any propaganda for war' and 'any advocacy of national, racial or religious hatred', set out in Article 20 of the 1966 Covenant, takes on a largely symbolic dimension unless it is accompanied by a policy of national reconciliation. Particular emphasis needs to be placed on freedom of the press, especially when some media have been used during the conflict to propagate hatred of others. Moreover, one of the frequent underlying causes of conflict is an unresolved minority issue. Ensuring equal access to essential public services and protecting cultural rights (including the right to enjoy one's culture, the right to profess and practise religion, and the right to use one's own language) is central for promoting reconciliation and building confidence among the entire population. While a paternalistic approach towards minority groups should be avoided (and may be counter-productive), harmonious relations between minorities and majorities and between different minority groups within a state contribute greatly to its stability.

International criminal law

In the heated context that follows an armed conflict, judging war criminals is an essential—albeit highly sensitive—step in restoring peace and breaking with the past. The concept of transitional justice has thus become a full-fledged component of post-conflict peacebuilding, so much so, that legal writings focus on this aspect to the detriment of the other relevant domains of public international law. Aside from the definition of international crimes, a central concern relates to the different forms that transitional justice can take. It is possible to identify five different scenarios and to classify them according to their degree of internationality as shown in Table 3.

Table 3 Models of Transitional Justice

Typology of transitional justice	Mechanisms implemented
Permanent international criminal justice	International Criminal Court. Cases in progress concerning: the Central African Republic, the Democratic Republic of the Congo, Uganda, and Sudan.
Ad hoc international criminal justice	International Criminal Tribunal for the former Yugoslavia
	International Criminal Tribunal for Rwanda
Hybrid criminal justice	Special Court for Sierra Leone
	Extraordinary Chambers in the Courts of Cambodia
	Serious Crimes Unit and Special Panels created by UNTAET in East Timor
	Internationalized Courts in Kosovo: International Judges and Prosecutors programme established by UNMIK
	Special Chamber within the State Court of Bosnia and Herzegovina
	Special Tribunal for Lebanon
Ad hoc internal criminal justice	Iraqi Special Tribunal
	Gacacas courts in Rwanda
	Truth and Reconciliation Commissions in South Africa, Argentina, Burundi, Chile, East Timor, El Salvador, Ghana, Guatemala, Morocco, Peru, and Sierra Leone.
Internal criminal justice under domestic law	Territorial jurisdiction of states after conflict: ordinary Timorese courts, ordinary Congolese courts
	Universal jurisdiction of third-party states: Germany, Belgium, Spain in particular

Choosing among the different forms of transitional justice does not depend on any specific legal rule. Stahn rightly recalls that:

[T]here is no blueprint for transitional justice. The choice and design of each formula must be adjusted to the particular needs of each individual case, taking into account factors such as the nature of the underlying conflict, the commitment of parties to the peace process, the need and degree of protection for particular groups (minorities, displaced persons, abducted children), the potential for public and victim consultation, and the condition of the country's legal and political system, in general (Stahn, 2005b: 426–7).

Furthermore, the different possible forms of transitional justice are not mutually exclusive (Mobekk, 2006; Chesterman, 2005; Seibert-Fohr, 2005; Bassiouni, 2002). On the contrary, experience has shown that the reconciliation and reparation of victims benefits from an approach which combines domestic and international aspects of justice, whose ultimate goal goes well beyond the simple criminal repression of past crimes.

However, the design and formula of transitional justice depends more fundamentally on the political will of the state involved as well as of the international community (which raises the possibility of their doing nothing to prosecute past crimes). Although it is increasingly acknowledged that peace and justice are not contradictory but complementary, states are frequently tempted to enact amnesty laws on the assumption that prosecution would be politically charged and could destabilize the fragile new government or even hinder the reconciliation process. Conversely, abstaining from prosecution of international crimes encourages a culture of impunity, which not only undermines the very notion of rule of law but represents a major cause of the perpetuation of violence and human rights abuses.

From the perspective of international law, human rights treaty bodies have asserted an obligation to prosecute serious human rights violations, such as torture, extrajudicial, summary, or arbitrary execution, and forced disappearance (Olson, 2006; Ratner, 1999). But while amnesty is also prohibited in the case of genocide and war crimes committed in international armed conflicts, international law is more ambiguous with regard to other violations of humanitarian law committed in the wake of a civil war (Dugard, 1999). Article 6(5) of 1977 Additional Protocol II to the Geneva Conventions provides that:

At the end of hostilities, the authorities in power shall endeavour to grant the broadest possible amnesty to persons who have participated in the armed conflict, or those deprived of their liberty for reasons related to the armed conflict, whether they are interned or detained.

This provision, originally intended to facilitate reconciliation at the end of a civil war, has subsequently been construed as excluding war crimes from its scope. The same conclusion may be argued for crimes against humanity under customary law. In line with other UN bodies, the Security Council has recalled that amnesty 'shall not apply to international crimes of genocide, crimes against humanity, war crimes and other serious violations of international humanitarian law' (UN Security Council, 2000).

International refugee law

Among the various other relevant branches of public international law, international refugee law deserves special attention, as it is well-known that armed conflicts are one of the main causes of forced displacement. When hostilities end, withdrawal of the refugee status, granted by a host country on the basis of the 1951 Geneva Convention, is inevitably posed (Chetail & Flauss, 2001). While the principle of non-refoulement prohibits a State from returning to a territory a person who fears for his/her life or freedom, Article 1C of the convention states that refugee status will cease to apply to such a person if circumstances in that person's country of origin have fundamentally changed. This represents a crucial dilemma, inherent to the very process of post-conflict peacebuilding: can one consider that the end of a conflict constitutes in and of itself a fundamental change of circumstances, when a sustained peace has not been established and the massive return of refugees may serve as an additional source of destabilization? On the other hand, it has been argued that the return and reintegration of refugees can be a decisive factor in the reconstruction of the country (Black & Koser, 1999).

An empirical solution to this normative and political dilemma has been found through the promotion of programmes of voluntary repatriation which are generally organized in close cooperation with the country of asylum, the country of origin, and UNHCR (Chetail, 2005). From a normative point of view, while it is not explicitly addressed by the 1951 Geneva Convention, voluntary repatriation is provided for in Article 5 of the 1969 OAU Convention governing the Specific Aspects of Refugee Problems in Africa. At the universal level, international human rights law gives it a broader and more solidly anchored legal foundation via the right to return to his own country, notably as enshrined in Article 12(4) of the 1966 Covenant on Civil and Political Rights (Chetail, 2003).

The situation of internally displaced persons (IDPs) raises an additional legal difficulty linked to the absence of a distinct legal regime specifically devoted to those who are forced to flee their homes but who, unlike refugees, have not crossed an international border. In recognition of their specific needs, the Guiding Principles on Internal Displacement, adopted in 1998, restate and refine, in the particular context of internal displacement, the key provisions of international human rights law, humanitarian law and—by analogy—refugee law. Although the Guiding Principles are not formally binding, they have been endorsed by the General Assembly and incorporated into the domestic law of an increasing number of states. In particular, they require competent authorities to create conditions and provide the means to enable IDPs 'to return voluntarily, in safety and with dignity, to their homes or places of habitual residence, or to resettle voluntarily in another part of the country'.

The voluntary nature of return does not, though, make it a panacea. Successful returns of refugees and IDPs require a wide range of other conditions, including first of all the safety of returnees. Reintegration also presupposes that they will have access without discrimination to basic public services and employment opportunities. The restitution of housing, land, and property, as well as other forms of reparation is also needed not only to facilitate their reintegration but also to restore a sense of normalcy, thereby fostering the reconciliation process. More generally, if the return is to be viable in the medium- and long-term, it must be coupled with economic cooperation agreements between donor countries and the home country so as to stimulate recovery and the sustainable development of the country. Implementing durable solutions for refugees and IDPs is therefore an integral component of post-conflict peacebuilding. It 'can simultaneously address the root causes of a conflict and help prevent further displacement' (Koser, 2007: 12). The concept of return and reintegration thus condenses the great diversity of the challenges typically associated with post-conflict processes.

As we can see, the multi-faceted issues surrounding post-conflict peacebuilding cannot be addressed through a narrow disciplinary approach in which each of the relevant branches of public international law develops in isolation, in a sterile and outmoded environment. On the contrary, the specificities of post-conflict peacebuilding call for a global and integrated approach within a more general and comprehensive legal framework, which can truly be labelled a *jus post bellum*.

IV. Concluding Remarks: Post-Conflict Peacebuilding—Crossing the Bridge from Rhetoric to Reality

The existence of legal norms should not hide the fundamentally political essence of peacebuilding processes. The means of achieving a sustainable peace are well known. They demand an unfailing determination from the international community, the mobilization of resources over the long term, and a better understanding of the true needs of the populations involved. One cannot, however, help but notice that the concept of post-conflict peacebuilding is still struggling to move from rhetoric to reality. Its popularity in diplomatic circles certainly owes much to the broad and equivocal nature of this concept.

In the absence of a definition accepted by all of the actors involved, post-conflict peacebuilding remains an easy target for all sorts of manipulation and ideological machination. Owing to the prevailing terminological and operational confusion surrounding the term, it may become a convenient smoke-screen, used to justify the institutional mandate of international agencies or to defend a security agenda. Since 9/11, post-conflict peacebuilding has been conflated with the discourse of 'nation-building' and 'stabilization'. Such a reformulation driven by external actors is likely to undermine 'the basic agreement that peace, security and stability cannot be imposed from outside but need to be nurtured internally through patient, flexible, responsive strategies that are in tune with domestic realities' (Tschirgi, 2004: 9).

The chronic ambiguity of post-conflict peacebuilding stems from the fact that it designates both the *process* of establishing a sustainable peace, and the political and institutional *strategies* used to do so. Nevertheless, these different—albeit overlapping—meanings share two essential attributes and one common purpose: post-conflict peacebuilding is a long-term process; and it is multidimensional in nature; the ultimate objective being to reconcile security, development, and justice. The rhetorical interest in post-conflict peacebuilding has yet to translate into effective coordination and a broader strategy for the countries ravaged by war. Policy coherence and coordination remain one of the key challenges at all levels between international and domestic actors, among departments and ministries of states, within the UN as well as between the UN and regional organizations. Different actors are likely to make different choices in line with their own mandates and priorities, which frequently counteract each other's actions. The strategic deficit has been notably exemplified by the Utstein Study which evaluated 366 peacebuilding projects financed by Germany, Norway the Netherlands, and the UK. It concluded that:

More than 55 per cent of the projects do not show any link to a broader strategy for the country in which they are implemented. Some projects are not linked to a broader strategy because there is no strategy for them to be linked to. In other cases, the broader strategy exists but projects show no connection to it (Smith, 2004: 10–11).

Nonetheless, despite its strategic limitations, during the last decade, post-conflict peacebuilding has evolved significantly as a field of practice in its own right. External actors have become more conscious of their own limitations, and of the correlative need for a context-specific approach determined by, and tailored to, local needs and realities. Analysts have observed that:

On the one hand, the international architecture for peacebuilding has improved considerably over the past fifteen years, as noted at the outset. There is a much greater understanding of the complexities of peacebuilding, more self-critique about the limits of international assistance, and increasing appreciation of the unique demands of specific situations, particularly over questions of state society relations and governance. As peacebuilding has become a comparative growth industry, there have also been waves of effort to reform, streamline, specialize, or coordinate among international actors, both multilaterally and bilaterally. Within the UN system and within donor governments, agencies are much more aware of functional priorities for post-war societies, which has spurred specialization of specific international offices dedicated to tasks including transitional justice; police development; disarmament, demobilization, and reintegration of combatants; refugee return; and economic recovery. On the other hand, these advances have not yet sufficiently diminished persistent and serious shortcomings in international responses to war-torn societies, which the Peacebuilding Commission and related bodies have just been created to fill. Whether they are able to do so will be an important determinant of the effectiveness and appropriateness of international architecture on these issues for some time to come (Call & Cousens, 2007: 10).

The Peacebuilding Commission represents a unique opportunity to mainstream and prioritize peacebuilding efforts worldwide. However, institutional engineering cannot be a substitute, but rather it represents a complement to a more coherent and comprehensive strategy. The establishment of the Commission intervenes at a crucial moment as consensus coalesces around the core components of an effective and holistic strategic framework. While acknowledging that there is no 'one-size-fits-all' model (nor will there ever be), its Working Group on Lessons Learned identified a set of twelve key principles. They are summarized in the following terms:

Specificity of peacebuilding: in order to address drivers of conflict that are context-specific, peacebuilding strategies have to be informed by accurate analysis of country realities.

National ownership: the primary responsibility and ownership for peace consolidation rests with the Government and the people of the host country.

Strengthening national capacities: the international partners' focus to get things done quickly and effectively should not undermine efforts over the medium- and long-term to strengthen national capacities for conflict management.

Holistic approach: Since peacebuilding encompasses security, development and human rights, the linkages between them need to be adequately recognized and prioritized.

Ongoing support for political consolidation: constructive political processes are essential to peace consolidation.

Mutual accountability: sustainable peacebuilding requires a strong partnership based on mutual respect and accountability between the Government and the people of the host country and their international partners.

Sustained engagement: peacebuilding is a long-term process requiring sustained and predictable engagement from all stakeholders. Despite the necessity to implement projects that provide tangible peace dividends, sufficient attention should be given to the sustainability of efforts.

Effective coordination: to avoid duplication as well as gaps in peacebuilding, international, national and local stakeholders need to act in a coherent and mutually reinforcing manner. Existing mechanisms, such as post-conflict needs assessments, integrated peacebuilding strategies, poverty reduction strategies and monitoring and tracking mechanisms, are important instruments for effective coordination.

Tangible peace dividends and quick wins: while peacebuilding requires time, early provision of tangible peace dividends for the population and quick win projects are necessary to build confidence and generate support.

Integrating a gender perspective: men and women are affected differently by conflict. Any peacebuilding strategy should address these differences, especially to ensure the end of impunity for gender-based violence, while contributing to gender equality and supporting women's full participation in and ownership of peacebuilding and recovery.

Encouraging a regional approach: an effective peacebuilding strategy takes into account the regional dimensions of a conflict and provides a regional and/or international solution, in consultation with relevant governments and non-state actors.

Prioritization, sequencing and timing: when building peace in societies ravaged by violent conflict, everything is considered a priority. However, to use the limited resources most effectively, host governments and international actors need to agree on key priorities and to sequence their implementation (UN Peacebuilding Commission, 2008b: 13).

The Working Group on Lessons Learned adds that 'the challenge, therefore, lies in calibrating general principles with country-specific realities based on an accurate analysis of commonalities and differences among countries' (*ibid*: 4). Too often, knowledge about local context has been lacking, thereby impeding the development of strategies tailored to specific environments. External actors need to understand thoroughly the history, politics, and cultures of the countries in which they are attempting to build peace. More fundamentally, they must learn to appreciate that they are not the main actors of the peacebuilding process, but are only facilitators in a leverage process. This supposes a cultural sea-change to an approach based on modesty, flexibility, and patience. This in turn obliges—as the rule rather than the exception—that a comprehensive assessment of the local and regional environment, conflict dynamics, and indigenous capacities pre-dates the design of peacebuilding programs, and that it is undertaken in close collaboration with internal actors. External actors need to seek to fulfil more of a catalytic role—understanding post-conflict peacebuilding as a long-term, home-grown, and political process.

Winning the peace has typically proved far harder than winning the war. If this is to change, we need to speak the same language when we talk about peacebuilding. Otherwise, in the absence of a common identity, peacebuilding will continue to be plagued by ambiguities and misunderstandings. The search for the true meaning of peacebuilding remains one the greatest challenges of our times.

Selected Bibliography

Abi-Saab, G (1995), 'United Nations Peacekeeping Old and News: An Overview of the Issues', in D Warner (ed), *New Dimensions of Peacekeeping*, Dordrecht/Boston/London: Martinus Nijhoff Publishers, 1–9.
Adams, R (1984), 'What is Military Occupation?', *British Yearbook of International Law* 55: 249–305.

African Union (2006), *Report on the Elaboration of a Framework Document on Post Conflict Reconstruction and Development (PCRD)*, EX.CL/274 (IX).

Ahlund, C (2004–2005), 'Major Obstacles to Building the Rule of Law in a Post-Conflict Environment', *New England Law Review*, 39: 39–44.

Azar, E (1990), *The Management of Protracted Social Conflict: Theory and Cases*, Hampshire/Aldershot: Dartmouth.

Ball, N (2005), 'The Challenge of Rebuilding War-Torn Societies', in Chester A Crocker, Fen Osler Hampson, and Pamela Aall (eds), *Turbulent Peace: The Challenge of Managing International Conflict*, Washington, DC: United States Institute of Peace, 719–36.

Barnett, M, Kim, H, O'Donnell, M, & Sitea, L (2007), 'Peacebuilding: What Is in a Name?', *Global Governance*, 13: 35–58.

Bassiouni, C (ed) (2002), *Post-Conflict Justice*, New York: Transnational Publishers.

Bellamy, A (2004), 'The Next Stage in Peace Operations Theory?', *International Peacekeeping*, 11/1: 17–38.

Bellamy, A, & Williams, P (2004), 'What Future for Peace Operations? Brahimi and Beyond', *International Peacekeeping*, 11/1: 183–212.

Benvenisti, E (1993), *The International Law of Occupation*, Princeton: Princeton University Press.

Bertram, E (1995), 'Reinventing Governments: The Promise and Perils of United Nations Peace Building', *Journal of Conflict Resolutions*, 39/3: 387–418.

Black, R, & Koser, K (eds) (1999), *Refugee Repatriation and Reconstruction*, New York: Berghan Books.

Boon, K (2005), 'Legislative Reform in Post-Conflict Zones: *Jus Post Bellum* and the Contemporary Occupant's Law-Making Powers', *MacGil Law Journal*, 285–326.

Burton, J (1990), *Conflict: Human Needs Theory*, London: Macmillan.

Call, CT, & Cousens, EM (2007), *Ending Wars and Building Peace*, Coping with Crisis Working Paper Series, International Peace Academy.

Chesterman, S (2005), 'Rough Justice: Establishing the Rule of Law in Post-Conflict Territories', *Ohio State Journal on Dispute Resolution*, 20/1: 69–98.

Chetail, V (2003), 'Freedom of Movement and Transnational Migrations: A Human Rights Perspective', in Aleinikoff, A, & Chetail, V (eds), *Migration and International Legal Norms*, The Hague/London/New York: TMC Asser, 47–60.

—— (ed) (2004), 'Voluntary Repatriation: Achievements & Prospects', *Refugee Survey Quarterly*, 23(3).

—— (ed) (2005), *Internally Displaced Persons: The Challenges of International Protection*, *Refugee Survey Quarterly*, Oxford: Oxford University Press.

—— (2006), 'La réforme de l'ONU depuis le Sommet mondial de 2005: bilan et perspectives', *Relations Internationales*, 128/2: 79–92.

—— (ed) (2007), *Conflits, sécurité et coopération/Conflicts, Security and Cooperation. Liber Amicorum Victor-Yves Ghebali*, Bruxelles: Bruylant, 125–67.

—— & Flauss, J -F (eds) (2001), *La Convention de Genève relative au statut des réfugiés du 28 juillet 1951—50 ans après: bilan et perspectives*, Bruxelles: Bruylant, collection de l'Institut international pour les droits de l'homme.

Chopra, J, & Hohe, T (2004), 'Participatory Peacebuilding', in T Keating & A Knight *Building Sustainable Peace*, Tokyo: United Nations, 241–62.

Collier, P, & Hoeffler, A (2004), 'Conflicts', in B Lomborg (ed), *Global Crises, Global Solutions*, Cambridge: Cambridge University Press, 129–56.

—— Elliott, L, Hegre, H, Hoeffler, A, Reynal-Querol, M, & Sambanis, N (2003), *Breaking the Conflict Trap. Civil War and Development Policy*, Oxford: Oxford University Press & World Bank.

Cutillo, A (2006), *International Assistance to Countries Emerging from Conflict: A Review of Fifteen Years of Interventions and the Future of Peacebuilding*, Policy paper, Security-Development Nexus Programme, New York: International Peace Academy.

Danne, AP (2004), 'Customary and Indigenous Law in Transitional Post-Conflict States: A South Sudanese Case Study', *Monash University Law Review*, 30/2: 199–228.

Daudet, Y (ed) (1995), *Les Nations Unies et la restauration de l'Etat*, Paris: Pedone.

David, C-P (1998), *La guerre et la paix. Approches contemporaines de la sécurité et de la stratégie*, Paris: Presses de Science Po.

—— (1998), 'Les limites du concept de consolidation de la paix', *La Revue internationale et stratégique*, 31: 57–78.

DFAIT (1996), *Canada to Establish New Peacebuilding Fund* (Press Release, October 30).

Dinstein, Y (2004), *Legislation under Article 43 of the Hague Regulations: Belligerent Occupation and Peacebuilding*, Occasional paper series, Humanitarian Policy and Conflict Research, Harvard University.

Doyle, M, & Sambanis, N (2000), 'International Peacebuilding: A Theoretical and Quantitative Analysis', *The American Political Science Review*, 94/4: 779–801.

Duffield, M (2001), *Global Governance and the New Wars: The Merging of Development and Security*, London: Zed Books.

Dugard, J (1999), 'Dealing With Crimes of a Past Regime. Is Amnesty Still an Option?', *Leiden Journal of International Law*, 12: 1001–15.

Dupuy, P-M (1998), 'Le maintien de la paix', in R -J Dupuy (ed), *A Handbook on International Organisations*, 2nd edn, Dordrecht/Boston/London: Martinus Nijhoff Publishers, 563–604.

Eide, EB, Kaspersen, AT, Kent, R, & von Hippel, K (2005), *Report on Integrated Missions: Practical Perspectives and Recommendations*, Independent Study for the Expanded UN ECHA Core Group.

Fox, GH (2003), 'International Law and the Entitlement to Democracy after War', *Global Governance*, 9: 179–97.

Galtung, J (1975), *War and Defence: Essays in Peace Research*, Vol. 1, Copenhagen: Christian Ejlers, 76–108.

Goodwin-Gill, G (2006), *Free and Fair Elections*, Geneva: Inter-Parliamentary Union.

Han, SK (1994), 'Building a Peace that Lasts: The United Nations and Post-Civil War Peace-Building', *New York University Journal of International Law and Politics*, 26: 837–92.

ICISS (International Commission on Intervention and State Sovereignty) (2001), *The Responsibility to Protect*, Report of the International Commission on Intervention and State Sovereignty, Ottawa: International Development Research Centre.

ICTY (International Criminal Tribunal for the Former Yugoslavia) (1995), *Prosecutor v Tadic, Decision on the Defence Motion for Interlocutory Appeal on Jurisdiction*, available at: <www.un.org/icty/tadic/appeal/decision-e/51002.htm>

Junne, G, & Verkoren, W (eds) (2004), *Post-conflict Development: Meeting New Challenges*, Boulder: Lynne Rienner Publishers.

Keating, T, & Knight, A (2004), *Building Sustainable Peace*, Tokyo: United Nations University Press.

Kolb, R, Poretto, G, & Vité, S (2005), *L'application du droit international humanitaire et des droits de l'homme aux organisations internationales*, Bruxelles: Bruylant.

Koser, K (2007), *Addressing Internal Displacement in Peace Processes, Peace Agreements and Peace-Building*, The Brookings Institution/University of Bern Project on Internal Displacement.

Krause, K, & Jütersonke, O (2005), 'Peace, Security and Development in Post-Conflict Environments', *Security Dialogue*, 36(4): 447–62.

Kreilkamp, JS (2003), 'UN Postconflict Reconstruction', *New York University Journal of International Law and Politics*, 35: 619–70.

Kumar, K (ed) (1997), *Societies after Civil War, Critical Roles for International assistance*, Boulder: Lynne Rienner Publishers.

Lederach, J-P (1997), *Building Peace—Sustainable Reconciliation in Divided Societies*, Washington DC: USIP.

—— & Jenner, J (eds) (2002), *A Handbook of International Peacebuilding: Into the Eye of the Storm*, San Francisco: Jossey-Bass.

Lund, M (1996), *Preventing Violent Conflicts—A Strategy for Preventive Diplomacy*, Washington DC: USIP.

—— (2003), *What Kind of Peace is Being Built? Taking Stock of Post-Conflit Peacebuilding and Charting Future Directions*, Discussion paper prepared for the International Development Research Centre, Ottawa.

—— (2004), 'A Toolbox for Responding to Conflicts and Building Peace', in L Reychler & D Lynch (eds), *Engaging Eurasia's Separatist States—Unresolved Conflicts and De Facto States*, Washington DC: USIP.

Mobekk, E (2006), *Transitional Justice and Security Sector Reform: Enabling Sustainable Peace*, Occasional paper No 13, Geneva: Geneva Centre for the Democratic Control of Armed Forces.

Office of the UN High Commissioner for Human Rights (OHCHR) (2006), *Rule-of-Law Tools for Post-Conflict States. Vetting: An Operational Framework*, United Nations: Geneva and New York, HR/PUB/06/5.

Olson, LM (2006), 'Provoking the dragon on the patio. Matters of international justice: penal repression vs. amnesties', *International Review of the Red Cross*, 88/862: 275–94.

Paris, R (1997), 'Peacebuilding and the Limits of Liberal Internationalism, *International Security*, 22/2: 54–89.

—— (2004), *At War's End: Building Peace after Civil Conflict*, Cambridge: Cambridge University Press.

Ponzio, R (2005), *The Creation and functioning of the UN Peacebuilding Commission*, London: Saferworld, London.

Pugh, M (2004), 'Peacekeeping and Critical Theory', *International Peacekeeping*, 11/1, 39–58.

Quast, SR (2004–2005), 'Rule of Law in Post-Conflict Societies: What is the Role of the International Community?', *New England Law Review*, 39: 45–51.

Ratner, SR (1999), 'New Democracies, Old Atrocities: An Inquiry in International Law', *Georgetown Law Journal*, 87: 707–48.

Reychler, L, & Paffenholz, T (eds) (2001), *Peacebuilding: A Field Guide*, Boulder, Lynne Rienner Publishers.

Richmond, O (2004), 'UN Peace Operations and the Dilemmas of the Peacebuilding Consensus', *International Peacekeeping*, 11/1: 83–101.

Samuels, K (2005–2006), 'Post-Conflict Peacebuilding and Constitution-Making', *Chicago Journal of International Law*, 6: 663–82.

Sassòli, M (2005), 'Legislation and Maintenance of Public Order and Civil Life by Occupying Powers', *European Journal of International Law*, 16/4: 661–94.

Schneckener, U, & Weinlich, S (2005), *The United Nations Peacebuilding Commission. Tasks, Mandate and Design for a New Institution*, Stiftung Wissenschaft und Politik, SWP Comments 38, Berlin: German Institute for International and Security Affairs.

Seibert-Fohr, A (2005), 'Human Rights as Guiding Principles in the Context of Post-Conflict Justice', *Michigan State Journal of International Law*, 113: 179–96.

Senghaas, D (2001), 'The Civilisation of Conflict: Constructive Pacifism as a Guiding Notion for Conflict Transformation', in Ropers, N, & Fischer, M (eds), *Berghof Handbook for Conflict Transformation*, Berlin, Berghof Research Centre.

Smith, D (2004), *Towards a Strategic Framework for Peacebuilding: Getting Their Act Together. Overview Report of the Joint Utstein Study of Peacebuilding*, Royal Norwegian Ministry of Foreign Affairs.

Stahn, C (2005a), 'Institutionalising Brahimi's "Light Footprint". A Comment on the Role and Mandate of the Peacebuilding Commission', *International Organisations Law Review*, 2: 403–15.

—— (2005b), 'The Geometry of Transitional Justice: Choices of Institutional Design', *Leiden Journal of International Law*, 18: 425–66.

—— (2007), '"*Jus ad bellum*", "*jus in bello*" ... "*jus post bellum*"?—Rethinking the Conception of the Law of Armed Force', *European Journal of International Law*, 17/5: 921–43.

Stedman, SJ, Rothschild, D, & Cousens, E (eds) (2002), *Ending Civil Wars: The Implementation of Peace Agreements*, Boulder: Lynne Rienner Publishers.

Strohmeyer, H (2001), 'Collapse and Reconstruction of a Judicial System: The United Nations Missions in Kosovo and East Timor', *American Journal of International Law*, 95: 46–63.

Suhrke, A & Samset, I (2007), 'What's in a Figure? Estimating Recurrence of Civil War', *International Peacekeeping*, 14/2: 95–203.

Tschirgi, N (2004), *Post-conflict Peacebuilding Revisited*, International Peace Academy, WSP, Peacebuilding Forum.

—— (2006), 'L'articulation développement-sécurité. De la rhétorique à la compréhension d'une dynamique complexe', *Annuaire suisse de politique de développement*, 47–68.

UN (1992), *An Agenda for Peace, Preventive Diplomacy, Peacemaking and Peacekeeping*, Report of the Secretary-General Pursuant to the Statement Adopted by the Summit Meeting of the Security Council on 31 January 1992, A/47/277–S/24111, 17 June.

—— (1995), *Supplement to an Agenda for Peace*, Position Paper of the Secretary-General on the Occasion of the 50th anniversary of the United Nations, A/50/60–S/1995/1, 25 January.

—— (2000), *Report of the Panel on United Nations Peace Operations* (Brahimi Report), General Assembly and Security Council, New York A/55/305–S/2000/809.

—— (2005a), Report of the Secretary-General (Kofi Annan), *In Larger Freedom: Towards Development, Security and Human Rights for All*, A/59/2005.

—— (2005b), *The Peacebuilding Commission*, A/RES/60/180, General Assembly, 30 December.

—— (2006), Report of the Secretary-General, *Arrangements for establishing the Peacebuilding Fund*, A/60/984, General Assembly, 22 August.

—— (2008), Department of Peacekeeping Operations & Department of Field Support, *United Nations Peacekeeping Operations: Principles and Guidelines,* available at: <http://pbpu.unlb.org/pbps/Library/Capstone_Doctrine_ENG.pdf>.

UN Development Programme (UNDP) (2000), Executive Board of the United Nations Development Programme and of the United Nations Population Fund, *Role of UNDP in crisis and post-conflict situations*, New York, DP/2001/4, available at: <http://www.undp.org/execbrd/pdf/dp01–4.PDF>.

UN Peacebuilding Commission (2007), Statement by the Assistant Security-General for Peacebuilding Support to the Hiroshima Peacebuilding Center, *the United Nations Peacebuilding Architecture*, Hiroshima, Japan, 15 September, available at: <http://www.un.org/peace/peacebuilding/Statements/ASG%20Carolyn%20McAskie/Japan%20HPC%20Speech%20as%20delivered%2015%20Sept%202007.pdf>.

—— (2008a), *Draft Report of the Peacebuilding Commission on its second session*, PBC/2/OC/L.2.

—— (2008b), Working Group on Lessons Learned, *Synthesis Report and Summary of Discussions. Key Insights, Principles, Good Practices and Emerging Lessons in Peacebuilding.*

UN Security Council (2000), *Security Council resolution 1315 (2000), The situation in Sierra Leone,* S/RES/1315.

—— (2005), *Post-conflict Peacebuilding*, S/RES/1645, 20 December.

—— (2007), 62nd Year: 5627th Meeting, New York, S/PV.5627, 31 January.

White, ND (2001), 'Commentary on the Report of the Panel on United Nations Peace Operations (The Brahimi Report)', *Journal of Conflict and Security Law*, 6: 127–38.

Woodward, S (2007), 'Do the Root Causes of the Civil War Matter? On Using Knowledge to Improve Peacebuilding Interventions', *Journal of Intervention and Statebuilding*, 1/2: 143–70.

Capacity-building

Volker Türk

Definition

Capacity-building—as an integral part of peacebuilding—is understood as a process that reinforces individual, institutional, or community skills and knowledge, develops national structures, and promotes reconciliation on a sustainable basis. In peacebuilding it must respond to the particular challenges of the complex post-conflict setting. It is premised primarily on local ownership and responsibility, requires coordination among a variety of stakeholders at different levels, needs to be participatory, and involves technical, financial, material, and infrastructural assistance, as well as the transfer of knowledge and skills.

I. Term

Origin and context

In ideal circumstances, the state, in the exercise of its sovereignty, provides a safe, secure and stable environment, guarantees the functioning of basic services, and protects human rights. The effective exercise of state power and corresponding state responsibilities are, along with people and territory, core defining features of statehood. However, this ideal is not met in situations of underdevelopment, poor governance, weak or fragile state structures, or violent conflict—all situations in which the state is either unwilling or unable to exercise effectively power and responsibilities through national structures.

Violent conflicts are often generated by such situations, and manifest themselves in sharply deteriorating national protection systems. In turn, conflicts often inflict the most visibly damaging impact on key elements of social systems and national structures. In a post-conflict environment, the provision of key services, a safe and secure environment, and effective human rights protection are therefore among the most immediate needs. Capacity-building is a tool to reconstruct previously existing national structures, or to establish and develop those that have either, not existed before, or that have been so fragile as to require external support.

Following the decolonization process, notably in Africa in the 1950s and 1960s, capacity-building emerged as a central principle for development action. It has been described as a method to ensure self-sustaining local structures with regard to a wide array of development-related issues, including the building of public institutions (Somé, 2004: 5). It has taken on a somewhat new meaning in response to the collapse of the Soviet Union and the transition of former Warsaw Pact countries into free-market democracies, with the consequent need to create representative institutions and democratic governance models. Its emergence in post-conflict environments has been more recent, as a result of the various crises in the former Yugoslavia and the Great Lakes, and the so-called 'nation-building' in Afghanistan and Iraq. This last concept is dealt with in the chapter on state-building.

Linguistic and semantic difficulties

There is no single definition of capacity-building. The term 'capacity-building' could be a misnomer in that it may imply a value judgment about the non-existence of capacities where they actually do exist, at least in a rudimentary form, and simply need to be unfolded, developed, or enhanced. In most situations, capacities, however nascent or fledgling, are indeed present prior to any capacity-building efforts, and work is therefore geared towards updating existing capacities and building on them. In development discourse the word has therefore acquired some less than positive connotations and has gradually been replaced with 'capacity-development'. Linguistically, however, 'building' refers to 'the process of creating or developing something, typically a system or situation, over a period of time' (New Oxford Dictionary of English, 1998). Since conflict often results in serious damage to, or even wholesale destruction of, national capacities in certain areas, the term 'building' therefore encapsulates appropriately what is meant in the post-conflict context.

The French translation of capacity-building as *renforcement des capacités*, as adopted by most international organizations, covers less ambiguously what is commonly understood in English as 'capacity-building'. It also does more justice to the true nature of the process by placing the emphasis on the 'reinforcing' or 'strengthening' aspect of the building process.

The main difficulty in translating capacity-building into a conflict transformation process lies in the common use of the terminology as it has emanated from a development discourse. In the development understanding of the term, capacities can only be built or strengthened in an environment of basic stability and with a measure of political will, both of which may be lacking immediately following an armed conflict. It is therefore essential to explore the concept as it has developed and as it applies to the particular challenges of the post-conflict setting.

Possible understandings

In earlier understandings of capacity-building, the emphasis was primarily on training activities to strengthen national institutions. This was slowly expanded to include strengthening the capacity of communities and civil society actors, and more generally to cover broader institution-building activities, often in the form of administrative reform. Today, capacity-building notions stress the continuing and long-term process of strengthening abilities, ranging across all aspects of human activity, from the development of specific institutions to infrastructure projects. Capacity-building in the broad sense is therefore interpreted by the UN Development Programme (UNDP) to encompass human resource development, organizational development, and institutional and legal framework development. The targets can range from communities and institutions to entire sectors, such as health, or to a societal sub-set.

Given the fundamentally disruptive nature of conflict and its specific impact on society, the nature, content, implementation, and outlook of capacity-building activities are different in countries not marked by conflict than in post-conflict settings. The defining factor is the post-conflict environment, which demands that capacity-building be 'disentangled' from its broader development base and applied to the specific issues that typically arise in peacebuilding settings. The fundamental questions are, therefore, who is in need of capacity-building in a post-conflict situation, as well as when and how should self-sustaining local structures be created, used, or developed?

Official definitions currently used by the main actors

Capacity-building actors are governmental, inter-governmental, and non-governmental. Given the evolution of capacity-building in the development realm, it is not surprising that none of the large development institutions offers a definition of capacity-building specific to the realities of a post-conflict environment.

The UN Terminology Database defines capacity-building as follows:

Process by which individuals, groups, organizations, institutions and countries develop, enhance and organize their systems, resources and knowledge, all reflected in their abilities, individually and collectively, to perform functions, solve problems and achieve objectives (<http://unterm.un.org>).

In a similar vein, the Development Co-operation Directorate (DCD) of the Organisation for Economic Co-operation and Development (OECD) has defined 'capacity' as the ability of people, organizations and society as a whole to manage their affairs successfully, and 'capacity-development' is understood as the process whereby people, organizations, and society as a whole unleash, strengthen, create, adapt, and maintain capacity over time. UNDP defines the concept in terms of capacity development as follows: 'UNDP defines capacity development as the process through which individuals, organisations and societies obtain, strengthen and maintain the capabilities to set and achieve their own development objectives over time' (UNDP, 2008: 1).

The Office of the UN High Commissioner for Refugees (UNHCR) has used the term broadly to describe the wide variety of measures that enable countries to deal with issues relating to populations of concern to UNHCR. The agency defines capacity-building as follows:

Capacity-building is both an approach and a set of activities. In its broadest sense it is directed at the reinforcement of human, institutional or community performance, the strengthening of skills and knowledge, as well as the promotion of positive attitudes, on a sustainable basis. It is based on networking with partners at various levels, is highly participatory by nature and intimately linked to a nationally driven reform process. It involves the provision of technical support, including training, of advisory services, of specialised expertise, and of financial and material assistance (UNHCR, 2002: 2).

The Organization for Security and Co-operation in Europe (OSCE), with its vast experience in post-conflict situations in Europe, defines capacity-building as involving many elements: human, technological, organizational, financial, cultural and institutional. According to the OSCE, the ultimate goal is to enhance the capability of people, institutions, and society in general, to develop their potential, make better use of existing resources, and foster new potential. It is further described as follows:

The most obvious form of capacity-building is developing the skills and performance of both individuals and institutions through training. That's the 'micro' level. But at the 'macro' level—that of a specific sector or society as a whole—there are several other elements. Capacity-building is about improving cooperation; supporting changes in the institutional, administrative and policy environment. It is about taking a multidisciplinary approach to planning and implementation. Emphasising organisational and technological change; new ideas and innovation. Finding ways to sustain progress. Fundamentally, it is about problem solving, involving people in the process and encouraging them to take responsibility for their actions (OSCE, 2002: 1).

Comments on the general definition

What all these definitions have in common are the following notions: (1) process; (2) multiple actors; (3) diverse sets of activities; and (4) emphasis on local sustainability. The general definition offered above takes these notions as the starting point and applies them specifically to the post-conflict setting, while basing itself on the experience and definitions of those actors who have been most exposed to post-conflict work.

II. Content

The nature of conflict has changed in the post-Cold War era and is now often characterized by inter-ethnic or sectarian strife within a country, with a massive impact on the civilian population. At the same time international engagement and involvement throughout the spectrum of conflict has increased, as has the presence of widely diverse actors. These actors range from national and international institutions, whether civilian or military, governmental or non-governmental, through various segments of civil society, such as the media or religious leaders, to the communities at the grass-roots level (see also the chapters on non-state actors; peace operations; civil-military interface).

Countries in post-conflict environments face enormous challenges in re-establishing peace and stability, in achieving stable democracies, in restoring national protection through the rule of law, in ensuring respect for human rights and the protection of minorities, as well as in embarking on economic and social reform. While a given post-conflict environment may be relatively stable, this does not mean that the underlying causes of the conflict have disappeared, especially when they relate to ethnic or religious strife. In rising to these challenges it is important to view capacity-building realistically, not as the be-all and end-all, but rather as a practical tool to re-craft the fabric of war-torn societies. Since the various challenges are interlinked, often interdependent, and provide possibilities for interaction between different communities, a capacity-building methodology helps cut across the various key components of any peacebuilding process. At the same time, it is a vehicle to ensure that all external interventions contain an inherent sustainability factor.

The following paragraphs, grouped around the key components to be addressed in a typical post-conflict setting, set out briefly the core capacity-building elements in such a context, discuss their challenges, needs, objectives, and impact, and give a number of examples.

Safe and secure environment

A safe and secure environment often remains the most serious concern, especially in the immediate post-conflict stage, but also more generally throughout the peacebuilding process. The security of the population, including the return and reintegration of refugees and displaced persons, must be assured by the responsible authorities and, if necessary and appropriate, monitored by the international community. Experience has shown that prompt and decisive action is essential in response to fresh spates of violence or the recurrence of public disorder. The need for prompt action may not necessarily be conducive to capacity-building efforts oriented towards the longer-term, especially in the early phase of the peace process. Moreover, mines and unexploded ordnance remain a direct threat in many post-conflict situations.

To provide the appropriate security framework, capacity-building activities in this area have primarily focused on armed forces reform and disarmament, demobilization, and reintegration of former combatants, as well as police reform, including non-discriminatory community policing, or, if necessary, the creation of well-trained multi-ethnic police forces (see also the chapter on security sector reform). In most situations, such activities require significant external support and supervision, typically provided by the UN or regional organizations, such as the OSCE. In 1999, for instance, the OSCE assisted the UN Mission in Kosovo (UNMIK) with the task of creating a police service in Kosovo. It is important that mine clearance programmes, while often conducted by international actors, use and build local capacity wherever available (for a similar assessment see the chapter on mine action).

In the aftermath of conflict it is not unusual for human rights violations to continue. An effective human rights regime, including independent institutions which sustain it, is essential to redress such violations. Capacity-building activities in this area must therefore be geared towards systematic human rights monitoring and reporting systems, coupled with effective intervention and response mechanisms. Examples in this area include the setting up of national human rights commissions, ombudspersons, or a quasi-judicial mechanism, such as a Human Rights Chamber. At least initially, such efforts require the support of international institutions with expertise in this area, such as the Council of Europe, the OSCE, or the Office of the UN High Commissioner for Human Rights (OHCHR). Given its specific protection mandate for returning refugees and displaced persons, UNHCR also often sets up, in cooperation with other agencies as appropriate, a framework for the systematic monitoring of returnees, with standardized reporting and assessment formats, data collection, and corrective responses through interventions with local authorities. Such monitoring programmes help ensure that returnees enjoy human rights on an equal footing with their fellow citizens. At the same time, they help build local capacity in the human rights protection area by, for example, involving local NGOs in the process.

Rule of law reform

Most post-conflict societies are faced with the need to revive and reform their legal and administrative systems. As a result, continued support for national legal, judicial, and administrative capacity-building is indispensable to ensure the durable restoration of national protection structures. In order to promote and sustain the peacebuilding process, and to ensure that rights of the population, in particular the rights of women, are respected, it is crucial to build confidence in the legal and administrative system. People must be enabled to bring claims before the courts or, perhaps, other more traditional conflict-resolution mechanisms.

Capacity-building activities in this area therefore require continued support for programmes that assist in building an independent judiciary, rebuilding the civil administration, and strengthening lawyers' associations. Such programmes have been carried out by the Council of Europe, the OSCE, various UN agencies, and other actors such as the International Centre for Transitional Justice. There is also a great need for advisory services and training for countries emerging from conflict in preparing legislation, such as that concerning the protection of minorities, property restitution, documentation, equal access to social services, citizenship issues (to avoid statelessness), the civil service, the independence of the judiciary, NGOs, and ombudspersons.

Apart from promoting accession to international human rights treaties and other relevant instruments, capacity-building activities in this area essentially include the promotion of technical expert assistance in the drafting or revision of national legislation, including implementation of administrative instructions, to readjust the country's legal, administrative, or judicial structures to the post-conflict environment. This needs to be accompanied by the provision of material and technical legal support in the implementation phase, including the provision of specialized training and advisory services or other technical assistance (for further discussion on the multifaceted measures for implementing rule of law reform as part of post-conflict peacebuilding, see the chapter on rule of law).

Confidence-building, reconciliation, and civil society

In societies emerging from violent conflict, confidence-building measures and community-based reconciliation initiatives are central to peacebuilding. Capacity-building activities in this area need therefore to foster openness, tolerance, transparency, awareness, and a sense of ownership and responsibility, while ensuring inclusiveness and the participation of all sectors of society, in particular women, community and religious leaders (see also in this sense the chapter on civil society). Activities need to start at the community level, often simply by promoting freedom of movement across former frontlines or the 'enemy's territory, or by bringing communities, women's groups, religious groups, and different ethnic groups together around neutral themes. Capacity-building efforts need to reform the educational system, often with the help of relevant international organizations. Particular emphasis needs to be placed on media work, not least because some media, in particular television and local radio, have often been used during the conflict, such as in Rwanda, to create a climate of fear between different groups and to propagate hatred of others, thus separating communities (for a similar conclusion, see the chapter on peace process). Capacities for the promotion of free, balanced and informed reporting, for media monitoring by independent institutions, and the active countering of hostile messages therefore need to be developed, not least because public expectations of the benefits from peace are usually high.

Examples in this area are numerous, particularly in the former Yugoslavia. There they ranged from UNHCR's Bosnian Women's Initiative, to Ms Sadako Ogata's Project Co-existence, to the Open City Concept. In other situations, reconciliation commissions composed of eminent persons dedicated to reconciliation and human rights have made an important contribution (such as the South African Truth and Reconciliation Commission or Truth Commissions in a number of Latin American countries) (see the chapter on transitional justice). Building local capacity in accounting for missing persons and responding to the consequences is another important contribution, often led by the International Committee of the Red Cross (ICRC).

Often, one of the underlying causes of conflict is an unresolved minority issue, involving at times orchestrated inter-ethnic tensions. Capacity-building activities in this area therefore need to promote policies and measures to preserve and develop the ethnic, linguistic, cultural, and religious identity of persons belonging to minority groups, in accordance with international law and standards. All forms of extremism and racism need to be subjected to political, social and, as appropriate, legal sanctions, while positive attitudes and activities should be rewarded through political, social, and economic incentives.

Of equal importance are measures fostering an active and open civil society committed to human rights, not least to ensure the sustainability of national protection structures, and to develop a sense of local ownership. Capacity-building activities in this area can range from assistance for the conduct of free and fair elections, to rights awareness programmes, to training on a wide range of both substantive and organizational issues, through to helping civil society actors develop diversified funding strategies and broader-based community support. This means support for networking and coordination among civil society actors, including through the involvement of international actors to work collaboratively with national ones to enhance capacity in their respective areas. Capacity-building activities may also involve the provision of material assistance, such as office space and equipment, and financial assistance to civil society actors for the purposes of development, training and general support. The setting up of Legal Aid and Information Centres, as part of NGO capacity-building, is an example of this. Another is the World Health Organization (WHO)'s 'Health as a Bridge for Peace' programme, which is designed to integrate the health-oriented activities of medical agencies and personnel with community-building, thereby contributing to peacebuilding (Macduff, 2001: 1, who describes the programme in more detail, including its origins).

Socio-economic environment

The socio-economic effects of conflict have a major negative impact on the prospect of the peacebuilding process. Destruction of housing, infrastructure, and the environment is often compounded by the fact that most pre-conflict economies no longer function in the same way as before, leading to a lack of employment opportunities and associated social problems. Conflict may also exacerbate extreme poverty and produce large numbers of people who are vulnerable and lack the necessary coping mechanisms. Priorities in the immediate post-conflict environment are: reconstructing, through a capacity-building approach, at least rudimentary housing and infrastructure, and providing access to essential public services, such as water, sanitation, energy (in particular power supply), communications, transport, health, and education. These are central to restoring some sense of normalcy and order, as well as building confidence among the population. As new market forces come into play and economic activity resumes, employment opportunities are crucial for communities to rebuild their lives and promote reconciliation.

It is recognized that addressing such needs goes well beyond the initial humanitarian assistance and capacity-building phase, and often requires massive investment by the international community to help reconstruction and economic recovery, and eliminate economic and social disparities (see also the chapter on private sector). It means enhancing national capacities to absorb external funds (before donor interest wanes), to mobilize internal resources to overcome poverty and vulnerability, and to improve economic security. While this clearly moves into longer-term development, capacity-building activities in this area need to support initiatives that expand local employment in the overall reconstruction phase, especially for former combatants, as well as to improve vital social and economic structures by adding to existing local skills and qualifications, and by providing technical skills development, rights awareness, and community-development activities.

III. Implementation

Challenges and dilemmas

Generally the post-conflict period goes through different phases, starting with the immediate and often volatile post-conflict phase, which is by nature transitory, continuing with the actual peace consolidation phase, and ending with the effective functioning of national structures and the resumption of a full development strategy for the country. Often, a challenge early in the process is that, even after the cessation of hostilities and the conclusion of formal peace agreements, reconstruction and rehabilitation efforts in a post-conflict environment are marked by simmering tensions and ongoing animosities or grievances (see on this issue the chapter on conflict transformation). Although a capacity-building approach needs to be incorporated into the peacebuilding process from the outset, its actual implementation may vary depending on the character of the post-conflict phase and the continuing obstacles it may present to the peace process.

Another dilemma is that most agents of capacity-building are foreign, or at least external to the local context, even while the aim is to empower or strengthen existing local capacities through local participation. In emergency or post-crisis situations, especially, many large international agencies focus on setting up and implementing their programmes with speed, without necessarily investing sufficiently in local institutions. Accordingly, there is often a tension between international initiatives to provide relief assistance and reconstruct war-torn countries, and the sometimes competing, professed international commitment to 'capacitation' (Minear in Smillie, 2001: foreword). It is, however, important not to bypass national structures but to involve them from the start (see in the same perspective the chapters on state-building and local ownership).

While the transition from relief to development is a complex issue in a general sense, it is even more so in relation to the content and implementation of capacity-building and its evolution from the immediate post-conflict relief phase to longer-term reconstruction and rehabilitation issues (see the chapter on recovery). In such an environment the success of a capacity-building approach will not only hinge on the political will of the local authorities and other actors, but also on the real commitment and expertise of external actors to ensure they take a capacity-building approach in whatever they do, by promoting self-help, and reducing the need for continued external support.

In effect, capacity-building in a post-conflict environment needs to pursue a two-pronged approach: (1) to build and enhance the 'capacities' of institutions, civil society actors, and social fabrics, thus enabling them to function effectively on their own, to provide essential services and to guarantee national protection for individuals and groups with special needs; and (2) to contribute to peace-building by instilling confidence and fostering reconciliation and community development. In a post-conflict context, it is therefore necessary to link reconstruction, community development, human rights, and conflict management (Macduff, 2001: 2).

Operational aspects on the basis of lessons learned

There is no 'one-size-fits-all' paradigm for capacity-building. It is, however, possible to discern a number of principles for the implementation of a capacity-building approach in a post-conflict context, based on lessons learnt.

Gaps and needs assessment, including conflict analysis

Successful capacity-building initiatives require: an analysis of the causes, dynamics, evolution, and ending of the conflict; an assessment of the ensuing destruction and of the current capacities, needs, gaps, vulnerabilities, and ongoing obstacles to the peacebuilding process; an identification of the target group, institution or sector; a deep understanding of systemic or endemic structural issues of underdevelopment, inequality, and social and economic disparities; and knowledge of whether key institutions even existed prior to a conflict (for a similar assessment, see the chapter on state-building). In Rwanda, for instance, there had not been a functioning judiciary prior to the 1994 genocide. Such an analysis helps to prevent choosing the wrong actors, such as the Hutu militia in the eastern Democratic Republic of Congo (Smillie, 2001: chapter 1). To give another example, in a country such as Bosnia and Herzegovina which is emerging from conflict of a sectarian nature, reconstruction of public services like health care or education can only succeed if capacity-building is mindful of the underlying attitudes which gave rise to the conflict in the first place, and which produced discrimination and deep-rooted prejudice.

Local ownership and international action

The achievement of peace is, first and foremost, the responsibility of local authorities and of the people themselves. Peace needs to be built from the bottom up, often starting at the village level, and by offering incentives to ensure the support of the local population and national civil service. It is important to recognize that local actors have important capacities and leadership qualities on which to build. Where this capacity is limited, capacity-building activities need to empower them ultimately to become self-reliant. At the same time, in most post-conflict situations, capacity-building will require coherent, resolute, and sustained action by the international community. Capacity-building will not be successful without both. Capacity-building cannot be imposed but must be locally owned. It needs to involve and be attentive to those who will ultimately benefit from it. Planning for it therefore needs to take place at the local level and to be mindful that results are usually influenced by local circumstances and events. Equally, it is essential to develop local resources, to elicit local experience on which skills can be built, and to develop local expertise through, for example, 'training of trainers'. Overall it is important to recognize the point at which external actors need to step back and allow the initiative to develop its local 'voice' (Macduff, 2001: 4). To the extent possible, capacity-building activities should also build upon the positive aspects of the history, traditions, cultures, and values of the societies involved (for further discussion on the role and importance of local ownership, a key component of post-conflict peacebuilding processes, see the chapter on local ownership).

Implementation arrangements

Following a comprehensive assessment of gaps and needs, it is necessary to define clear objectives, priorities and target groups, institutions or sectors as well as verifiable results. Actual implementation arrangements need to include timetables and to be realistic, practical, incremental, transparent, participatory, and nondiscriminatory. They must be designed flexibly, to adapt to the particular needs identified through the assessment process, and to facilitate the peacebuilding process in its respective stages. Throughout implementation the activities need to be designed and delivered within a gender-aware and age-sensitive framework, not least because of the prevalence of violence against women in many post-conflict settings, as well as the often-disproportionate onus on them to take care of their families. Capacity-building initiatives will therefore need to integrate special assistance and protection measures for women and children in particular, but also for people with disabilities, returning refugees and displaced persons, and ex-combatants.

Depending on the type of activity in relation to the area to be addressed, different actors will be required, either to build up and support local expertise or to provide external expertise with a gradual handover to relevant local actors. As experience shows, self-reliant local actors are better equipped to build a durable peace. At the same time, most capacity-building initiatives need to be linked to a long-term development strategy to ensure sustainable change.

In terms of substance, capacity-building in post-conflict settings normally includes the following sets of activities: (1) material, infrastructural, and technical support measures for key institutions involved in post-conflict reconstruction and rehabilitation (see recovery); (2) transfer of skills and knowledge to a variety of governmental, non-governmental, and civil society actors; (3) training, including, for example, through exchange programmes or study visits aimed at strengthening implementation of specific functions; (4) facilitation of planning processes with local actors, including through needs assessments, design of prevention, and adequate response mechanisms and formulation of strategies and budgets; (5) community-based approaches and community development activities. The role and level of involvement of external actors will depend on how disruptive the impact of the conflict has been on the national system and the society.

Integrated, coherent, and consistent approach

Since the key components of peacebuilding and post-conflict reconstruction are intrinsically linked and interdependent, integrated responses are necessary for the implementation of capacity-building activities. Those who work towards building up capacities, be it in the judicial, health, education, or any other sector, should also be aware of the evolution of the conflict and of the political, social, and economic realities in the country. On the basis of such understanding they should be encouraged to help foster a climate of dialogue, confidence-building and reconciliation in their respective technical areas. The 'create opportunity for peace' maxim requires a collaborative approach between technical specialists and those engaged in post-conflict political management. In an interesting example, WHO developed practical guidance on peacebuilding skills for health professionals (Macduff, 2001: 3).

Moreover, success in attaining capacity-building objectives requires integrated action by many different parties, organizations, and bodies, but primarily by the local actors. For instance, in an effort to rebuild the capacities of the education or health system, it is useful to expedite in particular the return and reintegration of refugees who were teachers or doctors before the outbreak of the conflict. If local action is less forthcoming, obstacles can be overcome only by a high level of determined, well-coordinated, and coherent engagement by the international community. A sustained international involvement is generally needed in most capacity-building endeavours in post-conflict settings.

Coordination and partnership

National and international actors, both at the governmental and non-governmental level, civil society and the communities themselves are key partners in the achievement of successful capacity-building strategies. As Macduff puts it: '... the emergence of multiple agencies adds not only flexibility and diversity in terms of responses, it also adds to the possibility of designing interventions specific to the needs of the dispute or for the larger task of peacebuilding' (Macduff, 2001: 6). Given the wide diversity of actors, it is important to avoid duplication and waste and to ensure consistency by building a culture of multi-faceted partnerships among the stakeholders, through coordination arrangements, information exchange, and agreed frameworks for a division of labour.

Monitoring and evaluation

In order to both learn lessons and identify good practices, it should be the norm to conduct regular consultations with the different stakeholders, to monitor activities constantly throughout implementation, against the original objectives and based on measurable results, and to evaluate at the end of a capacity-building project.

Selected Bibliography

Harris, F (2005), *The Role of Capacity-Building in Police Reform*, Pristina: OSCE.

International Rescue Committee (2003), *Capacity-Building of Local Partners: A Core Principle, Post-Conflict Development Initiative*.

Macdonald, M (2005), *Provision of Infrastructure in Post-Conflict Situations*, London: UK Department for International Development.

Macduff, I (2001), 'Capacity-Building in Conflict Transformation: Integrating Responses to Internal Conflicts', *Journal of Humanitarian Assistance*, available at: <http://www.jha.ac/articles/a073.htm>

Mckechnie, AJ (2003), 'Building Capacity in Post-Conflict Countries', World Bank Social Development Notes, No 14, available at: <http://www.worldbank.org/conflict>.

OSCE Mission in Kosovo (2002), *OSCE and Capacity Building*, available at: <http://www.osce.org>.

Rugumamu, S, & Gbla, O (2003), *Studies in Reconstruction and Capacity-Building in Post-Conflict Countries in Africa: Some Lessons of Experience from Mozambique, Rwanda, Sierra Leone and Uganda*, ACBF Occasional Paper No 3, The African Capacity-Building Foundation.

Smillie, I (ed) (2001), *Patronage or Partnership: Local Capacity-Building in Humanitarian Crises*, Bloomfield, CT: Kumarian Press.

Somé, SA (2004), *Méthodologie de renforcement des capacités*, DT-CAPES, no 2004–13, Ouagadougou, 1–15 and 34–35, available at: <http://www.capes.bf>.

The Global Development Research Centre, *Defining Capacity-Building*, Kobe (Japan), available at: <http://www.gdrc.org/uem/capacity-define.html>.

UN Department for Economic and Social Information and Policy Analysis (1996), *An Inventory of Post-Conflict Peacebuilding Activities*, ST/ESA/246, New York: UN.

UNDP (1997), 'Capacity Development', Technical Advisory Paper II, in *Capacity Development Resource Book, Management Development and Governance Division*.

—— (1998), 'Capacity Assessment and Development', Technical Advisory Paper no 3, available at: <http://mirror.undp.org/magnet/docs/cap/CAPTECH3.htm>.

—— (2008), 'Supporting Capacity Development: The UNDP Approach', Capacity Development Group Bureau for Development Policy, available at: <http://www.capacity.undp.org/indexAction.cfm?module=Library&action=GetFile&DocumentAttachmentID=2410>.

UNHCR (1999), *A Practical Guide to Capacity-Building as a Feature of UNHCR's Humanitarian Programmes*, available at: <http://www.unhcr.org>.

—— (2002), *Strengthening Protection Capacities in Host Countries*, EC/GC/01/19, available at: <http://www.unhcr.org>.

UN Terminology Database (UNTERM), <http://unterm.un.org>.

• **Online resources**

For the mission of the International Centre for Transitional Justice, see <http://www.ictj.org>.

Civil-military Interface

Thierry Tardy

Definition

'Civil-military interface' describes the different levels of interaction between military and civilian actors involved in post-conflict peacebuilding activities. Military actors usually comprise units of peacekeeping forces and may also include the local military. Civilian actors make up a broader category comprising the civilian component of a peace operation, government agencies, non-governmental humanitarian and development organizations, as well as other civilian actors involved in the peacebuilding process, including local actors.

I. Term

Origin and context

In the context of post-conflict crisis management, the 'civil-military interface' describes the relationship between military and civilian actors who are involved in peace operations. Such relations are not new: the military has always interacted, in one way or another, with civilians. At the beginning of the 20th century, European armed forces fulfilled humanitarian or social functions in their colonies and were already confronted with certain issues related to the civil-military interface. In different contexts, the counter-insurgency strategies implemented in Indochina or in Vietnam were aimed at winning over the local populations to the cause of the occupying military forces.

Nonetheless, the term 'civil-military interface' (or relations) was first conceptualized and used at the end of the Cold War with the deployment of armed operations with a humanitarian remit. This was the case in 1991 in Iraqi Kurdistan, with Operation Provide Comfort, and later with the UN peace operations in Bosnia and Herzegovina in 1992, and the UN and United States (US) peace operations in Somalia in 1992–1993. In these three cases, the strong presence of numerous humanitarian agencies alongside military troops raised *de facto* the issue of their relationship. This was when the expressions 'civil-military relations' and 'civil-military cooperation' first appeared, the acronym for which is CIMIC.

The US army first opened a Civil-Military Operations Centre (CMOC) in Iraqi Kurdistan in 1991, then in Somalia in 1993, first and foremost with a view to sharing information with the community of humanitarian agencies and, possibly, to provide them with logistical support. In 1993, the UN Protection Force (UNPROFOR) and the Office of the UN High Commissioner for Refugees (UNHCR) set up a similar structure in Bosnia and Herzegovina. At that point, the scope of the civil-military interface was defined fairly narrowly and was mainly used by the military to characterize its relationship with humanitarian agencies. From then on and throughout the remainder of the 1990s, the increasing number of peacebuilding operations and their evolution gave civilian actors an even more important role. This trend raised even more acutely the issue of the relationship between, and coordination of, civilian and military stakeholders. Civilians, particularly in the field of humanitarian activities, took up the debate and suggested another approach, which reflected more accurately their own identity and concerns.

Nevertheless, the growing complexity of peace operations makes the civil-military interface inherently difficult, for three main reasons: differences in terminology and approaches of the different actors; the discrepancy between a state-oriented conception of crisis management and the nature of the conflicts which have to be managed; and the challenging implementation of dialogue and coordination between the different stakeholders in a relationship still dominated by the military-humanitarian dynamic, to the detriment of the many other civilian actors.

Official definitions

First, civil-military relations are confronted with the problem of definition. Thus, the term 'civil-military interface' takes on a different meaning depending on whether it is used by a state's armed forces, an international organization, a humanitarian non-governmental organization (NGO), or a development NGO. Different definitions can even coexist within a single institution. The differences in definitions are reflected by differences in terminology: in addition to CIMIC—which stands for 'civil-military cooperation'—'civil affairs', civil-military action or operations, 'civil-military coordination', or 'humanitarian-military relations' are also in use. These concepts refer not only to different types of stakeholders, but also to differences in the intensity of the relationship. Thus, the terms relations, cooperation, coordination, or integration indicate different levels of interaction, desired or existing.

Furthermore, none of the suggested definitions applies specifically to peacebuilding. Some organizations, such as the International Committee of the Red Cross (ICRC), draw a distinction between armed conflicts and other contexts. Others, such as the European Union, embed civil-military cooperation in the context of post-conflict crisis management. However, peacebuilding is never dealt with specifically.

The notion of the civil-military interface was first developed by the armed forces of a few Western states, at either the national level or within the North Atlantic Treaty Organization (NATO). Initially, it was defined narrowly and placed the military at the heart of the relationship. The aim was to handle the relationship with humanitarian agencies in the best possible way, to the benefit of the armed forces. Thanks to humanitarian-like activities, the military wished to create an environment favourable to its own action. The initial approach of the military then evolved to encompass a wider range of actors, not only humanitarian, but remained influenced by its own interests and constraints.

Most Western countries, NATO, and the European Union (EU) use the acronym CIMIC to refer to civil-military cooperation. The US usually uses the terms 'Civil Affairs' and 'Civil-Military Operations'. NATO doctrine defines CIMIC as follows: 'The coordination and cooperation, in support of the mission, between the NATO Commander and civil actors, including national population and local authorities, as well as international, national and non-governmental organisations and agencies' (NATO, 2003). It also states that 'the immediate purpose of CIMIC is to establish and maintain the full cooperation of the NATO commander and the civilian authorities . . . in order to allow him to fulfill his mission.'

The American terms 'Civil-Military Operations (CMO)' and 'Civil Affairs' are used in a very broad sense that does not specifically apply to post-conflict reconstruction operations. 'Civil-Military Operations' are defined as:

The activities of a commander that establish, maintain, influence, or exploit relations between military forces, governmental and non-governmental civilian organisations and authorities, and the civilian populace in a friendly, neutral, or hostile operational area in order to facilitate military operations, to consolidate and achieve operational US objectives (US Joint Chiefs of Staff, 2001).

Within Civil-Military Operations, it falls to Civil Affairs staff to establish an interface between the military and civilians.

More recently, the EU—whose European Security and Defence Policy (ESDP) promotes an integrated and global approach to crisis management—has also developed its own notion of Civil-Military Cooperation (CIMIC). The EU defines CIMIC as:

the coordination and cooperation, in support of the mission, between military components of EU-led Crisis Management Operations and civil actors (external to the EU), including national population and local authorities, as well as international, national and non-governmental organisations and agencies (Council of the European Union, 2002).

The EU has also developed the notion of Civil-Military Coordination (CMCO) which differs from CIMIC in that it deals with the relationship between the military and civilians within the EU itself (European Council and Commission, 2003).

The civilian approach is essentially presented by humanitarian agencies. Instead of the term 'civil-military cooperation', they prefer 'civil-military coordination' (Office for the Coordination of Humanitarian Affairs—OCHA, 2003) or 'humanitarian-military relations' (Steering Committee for Humanitarian Response, 2004). From a general point of view, humanitarian organizations stress the need to preserve the humanitarian space and to ensure that any relationship with the military is not to the detriment of the fundamental humanitarian principles of independence, impartiality and humanity. The ICRC is prudent by nature in the way it approaches relations with military actors (Studer, 2001; Rana, 2004), but it also acknowledges the fact that, in fulfilling their mission, 'the components of the [International Red Cross and Red Crescent] Movement frequently interact with military bodies' and that their 'respective roles and areas of expertise are widely recognised' (ICRC, 2005).

For the ICRC, such an interaction is part of 'civil-military relations' rather than coordination (ICRC, 2001) and the nature of the relationship means that the participants—and especially the military—must abide by certain key rules. These include respect for the fundamental principles governing ICRC action, ensuring that such relations improve the effectiveness of its assistance, maintenance of a clear distinction between the roles ascribed to military and humanitarian actors, and careful consideration of local perceptions of the relationship and the various actors. Permitted activities related to military forces—whether they are deployed on the national territory or not—such as dialogue and information sharing, participation in training sessions and exercises, the use of military logistics and resources, and the use of military escorts and protection, are intentionally minimized (ICRC, 2005).

Within the UN system, it is OCHA and the Inter-Agency Standing Committee (IASC) which have defined the relationship between the military and humanitarians. They have coined the term 'CMCoord' (Humanitarian Civil-Military Coordination) to describe the civil-military interface, which is based on the need to preserve the integrity of humanitarian action. Documents relating to the concept include the 'Guidelines on the Use of Military and Civil Defense Assets (MCDA) in Disaster Relief', also known as 'the Oslo Guidelines' (May 1994); the 'Guidelines on the Use of Armed and Military Escorts for Humanitarian Convoys' (September 2001); and the 'Guidelines on the Use of MCDA to Support UN Humanitarian Activities in Complex Emergencies' (March 2003). The IASC has also published 'Civil-Military Relations in Complex Emergencies' (June 2004), which uses the definition of civil-military coordination developed by OCHA:

The essential dialogue and interaction between civilian and military actors in humanitarian emergencies that is necessary to protect and promote humanitarian principles.

In addition, the UN Department of Peacekeeping Operations (DPKO) has drafted the 'DPKO Civil-Military Coordination Policy', which deals with civil-military aspects in the specific case of peace operations and goes well beyond humanitarian action:

UN Civil-Military Coordination is the system of interaction, involving exchange of information, negotiation, de-confliction, mutual support, and planning at all levels between military elements and humanitarian organizations, development organizations, or the local civilian population, to achieve respective objectives (DPKO, 2002).

Coordination is envisaged at three different levels: coordination within the UN operation; between the operation and the UN Country Team when the latter is distinct from the operation; and between the operation and other actors present. Yet, despite this effort at clarification, UN documents do not deal specifically with peacebuilding, nor, in any detail, with the relationship to all civilian actors. The conceptualization of civil-military relations remains dominated by the links between the military and humanitarian agencies.

These various approaches reflect the diversity of actors, their identity and the way they understand their roles in the post-conflict setting and, consequently their conception of civil-military relations. However, beyond mere differences in terminology, they foreshadow how difficult it is to implement a suitable relationship, which is a vital factor for success in any peacebuilding initiative.

II. Content

In addition to practical and human problems which stem from the difficulty the two types of actors have in coordinating their activities, the civil-military interface is complex because it pertains to political issues. Among the issues at stake are the respective areas of accountability of the military and humanitarian agencies, the link between state and non-state actors, and the typology of peacebuilding actors.

The difficult coexistence of the military and humanitarian agencies

The difficult coexistence of the military and humanitarian agencies is a well-known feature of peacebuilding. For the military, a critical issue is the evolution of its roles after the end of the Cold War and its ability to take on an ever-growing scope of activities that are not strictly military, while preserving its primary role of soldiering. This is at stake in its participation in peace operations and its direct involvement in humanitarian, development-related, or policing missions. In this context, the military's understanding of civil-military relations—under-conceptualized at the national level in troop-contributing countries to UN operations—is often determined by the need to ensure its own security or to implement the military aspects of peace operations.

For humanitarian agencies, the central issue is that of the impact of military 'interference' in the humanitarian sphere on the integrity of their action. In essence, the principles on which humanitarian action is based cannot apply to the military. In fact, regardless of their own personal motivations, military actors remain instruments of the states that send them. In the field, the independence and credibility of humanitarian agencies are therefore difficult to reconcile with close cooperation with the military. Paradoxically, while humanitarian workers may need protection from the military as they fulfil their missions, their association with the military may jeopardize their own security.

The interaction between state and non-state actors

The second type of problem has to do with the way the state and non-state actors interact. One of the main challenges in contemporary crisis management is the discrepancy between, on the one hand, the nature of the policies implemented and, on the other hand, their principal actors and the nature of conflicts. Peacebuilding and state-building policies are defined and implemented by states and institutions which embody and express a conservative attitude to crisis management, based on state centrality and the imposition of a politically and economically liberal system. In the field of security, this approach is conveyed by the military (as well as police forces) whose mandate is to restore the monopoly on legitimate violence by the host state (see the chapter on security sector reform).

Such an approach faces the following problems: the nature of conflicts and their actors; their intra- or sub-state dimension; and the challenge to the Westphalian model they imply (see also on this issue the chapter on state-building). In post-conflict reconstruction, civilian actors are often much more sensitized to these characteristics when they do not embody them themselves (eg local actors who represent communities, non-state actors). Thus, the military, which is an emanation of the state, and civilian actors, which do not necessarily emanate from the state (see the chapter on civil society) are theoretically opposed. Subsequently, the civil-military interface pits two approaches to the notion of security against each other: a narrow approach focusing on the state, and a broader approach focusing on the individual and which hinges on the notion of human security.

The heterogeneity of the actors

The third kind of problem has to do with the increase and heterogeneity of the actors in the civil-military interface. While military actors make up a relatively homogeneous category, the way the civil-military interface is conceived at the national level varies from one country to the next depending on its military culture and, more generally, on its defence policy. In UN peace operations, few troop-contributing countries have a civil-military relations doctrine and the implementation of the different UN concepts seems problematic (de Coning, 2005).

In addition, since the civil-military interface also involves armed forces in the countries hosting post-conflict reconstruction operations, this poses the question of their identification, culture, will, and capacity to cooperate with external or internal civilian actors. This is the case in the framework of security sector reform and demobilization, disarmament, and reintegration programmes, which, by definition, imply a wide range of military actors (regular armed forces, militias, presidential guard, etc), whose identification and cooperation often remain problematic. Finally, the increasingly important role of private security companies tends to blur even more the line drawn between what falls to the state and what escapes its control (see on this issue the chapters on non-state actors, peace operations, and private sector).

Yet, heterogeneity is even more obvious with civilian actors. In fact, it is extremely difficult to write about civilian actors *per se*. Be they humanitarian agencies, development organizations, or local actors, the notion of civilian actors covers a wide range of entities which may differ greatly from each other and whose only shared characteristic is the fact that they are not military actors. In addition, some civilian actors, such as civil servants in international organizations, are *de facto* emanations of states. In such cases, they have more in common with the military than with representatives of independent civil society organizations. At the local level, civilian actors, such as populations or their representatives, are also difficult to apprehend as a whole, and hence as one element of the civil-military interface.

In all peacebuilding policies, stabilization and reconstruction require ownership of civil society and the private sector—two entities of a different nature from the political authorities, also a civilian entity. Consequently, the mere existence of civilian actors as a category is a challenge to any understanding of the civil-military interface. Finally, civil-military relations suffer from a lack of reflection on the part of civilian actors as to what they cover. Beyond international organizations and humanitarian agencies, a majority of civilian actors involved in peacebuilding activities have not determined the terms of their interaction with the military.

III. Implementation

At the beginning of the 1990s, the emergence of the concept of civil-military relations coincided with the multiplication of peace operations in post-conflict environments, even if the first civil-military units were not set up in the context of post-conflict transitions (Iraqi Kurdistan, Somalia, and Bosnia and Herzegovina). Since then, both military and civilian actors have worked to develop a better understanding of their respective roles, cultures, and expectations. On the ground, they have designed cooperation/coordination mechanisms which have shaped their interface. As a consequence, their interaction has received broader support on both sides and, to a certain extent, has become institutionalized. Fifteen years after the emergence of the term civil-military relations, the debate deals less with the need for this relationship than with the nature and the degree of coordination/cooperation it implies.

Nature and degree of civil-military interaction

Therefore, most UN operations in post-conflict environments include a unit in charge of civil-military cooperation. There are three main types of possible interaction: information-sharing between military and civilian actors (whether they are part of the UN operation or not); support of civilian actors by the military, particularly in terms of logistics and means of communication; and military activities that directly benefit the local populations, eg medical assistance or restoration of public facilities (schools, hospitals, etc). This last type of interaction is quite different from the others in that it covers activities which could equally be carried out by civilian actors. In such cases, the risk of overlapping is the greatest and the civil-military interface is not as well defined. Thus, if a battalion taking part in a UN operation were to help rebuild a school, such an initiative would not necessarily comply with CIMIC provisions as defined by DPKO (de Coning, 2005). In the context of humanitarian operations, such initiatives are common. Beyond UN operations, the fact that the military activity of peace operations in post-conflict environments integrates a humanitarian dimension tends more and more to distort the relationship between the military and civilians, in that they are not systematically distinguishable by the nature of the activities they conduct.

All peace operations that involve the deployment of the military in post-conflict settings, whether led by the UN, NATO, the EU in the Balkans or Afghanistan, or the African Union, include humanitarian activities in which the military participates either directly or indirectly. Nowadays, the extension of its remit is widely accepted by the military and the notion of civil affairs is part and parcel of post-conflict stabilization missions. However, the way things have evolved has often confirmed the fears of humanitarians that different kinds of missions may be confused and give rise to tension. Afghanistan, with the setting up of Provincial Reconstruction Teams (PRTs), is a case in point. In order to win the population over, these teams, which emanate from the states whose militaries are part of the peacekeeping forces, combine security and humanitarian missions. This has, however, undermined the distinction between humanitarian and military actors/activities (Rana, 2004: 565–6), and has resulted in the local population confusing military and external civilian actors. Not only does such a situation blur the identities of the different actors, it may also put their security at risk (Save the Children, 2004: 29–36; Donini *et al*, 2005).

Second, two characteristics of international interventions in post-conflict environments are that, on the one hand, they carry out civilian rather than military tasks, and, on the other, the military is increasingly involved in these civilian activities. This 'civilianization' is evidenced by the growing use of the armed forces for tasks which traditionally fall to the police. For instance, in Kosovo, NATO forces (KFOR) and UN police forces (UN Mission in Kosovo, UNMIK) participated simultaneously in law-enforcement operations, notably in the town of Mitrovica. In a similar way, the remit of the EU military operation in Bosnia and Herzegovina (Operation Althea) was mainly to fulfil police tasks.

Generally, missions assigned to UN peace forces are only marginally of a strictly military nature. Similarly, the participation of the military in demobilization, disarmament, and reintegration; mine action and security sector reform programmes are but a few examples of this trend toward increasing interaction, and again they also point to the potential overlapping of civilian and military efforts.

All of these cases raise the issue of the function of the military in post-conflict settings, as well as that of its interaction with civilian components in the stabilization effort. What is at stake is the extension of the concept of security and of the role taken on by the military in restoring security in post-conflict settings. If security is a necessary condition to economic recovery and peace, the extension of its definition to include non-military aspects bears a direct impact on the civil-military interface, in that it dilutes the differences between those two categories of actors. To a certain extent, this debate has been reflected at UN level by the concept of integrated missions and the 'security-development-human rights' triptych; at EU level, by the notion of 'global planning' of crisis management operations; and, at the national level, by the integration of civilian aspects in the planning of stabilization operations (Gordon, 2006) (for further discussion on integrated missions and other associated concepts see also peace operations).

The challenge of coordination

The coordination of the different actors in the politics of peacebuilding is essential for success. Coordination must take place at different levels: between the different entities of a single organization; between different organizations; between governmental (or intergovernmental) and non-governmental organizations; and between external and internal actors. At each of these levels, civil actors interact with the military. From a general point of view, coordination between the actors in post-conflict transition has improved since the beginning of the 1990s. This is particularly true at the UN where the notion of integrated mission has contributed to better coordination. In addition, the civil-military interface has been made easier by the fact that, in the framework of UN peace operations, civilian actors and the military come from the same organization. The fact that the Force Commander reports to the Special Representative of the Secretary-General *de facto* raises the issue of the civil-military interface.

The situation is different when civilian and military actors do not belong to the same operation or institution. In Afghanistan and Kosovo, for instance, the military and civilian components pertain to different organizations which have their own culture and conception of the civil-military interface. NATO remains an organization with a military culture and its operations are fundamentally different from parallel civilian activities. Within the EU, the distinction that is made between the European Commission, the activities undertaken by the EU intergovernmental entity (in the context of the Common Foreign and Security Policy—CFSP) and, to a certain extent, the military and civilian aspects of crisis management reflect different civil and military identities. These identities are manifested in crisis management policies in post-conflict settings. Thus, EU action in Bosnia and Herzegovina entails three different operations: a military operation (Althea); a civil police operation (EUPM); and the European Commission's support for economic recovery.

The need for a truly inclusive approach

Finally, though civil-military relations are one of the determining factors for the success of any peacebuilding policy, they describe a narrow concept which reflects neither the evolution of each actor in the interface, nor the need for a truly inclusive approach to peacebuilding. First of all, civil-military relations were mainly defined in the context of the interaction between intervening military forces and humanitarians. Thus, many civilian actors, such as human rights officers, election observers, and representatives of development agencies, have been excluded from the concept, although they constantly interact with the military on the ground (de Coning, 2005). Second, the concept of civil-military interface reflects the recurring difficulties of peacebuilding policies to include local actors—the notion of local ownership—in the planning and implementation stages of post-conflict transitional programmes (Khouri-Padova, 2004: 8–9; Harland, 2005: 9; Barth Eide *et al*, 2005: 35–6). In fact, civil-military relations continue to focus on the interaction between external actors, instead of the interaction between external and internal actors, despite the fact that only the participation of the latter can guarantee the sustainability of the peace process. Yet, internal actors are often marginalized in the peacebuilding process. The problem here is that the definition is too narrow to account for the evolution of conflicts and their actors. This narrow definition is reflected by the identification of actors, such as the external or local private sector or private security companies, which play an increasingly important role in the stabilization and reconstruction process, but which are often neglected in the civil-military interface. In this context, analysis of the links between civilian and military actors by Western armed forces, international organizations, and important humanitarian and development agencies, offers only a partial account of peacebuilding activities.

Selected Bibliography

Barth Eide, E, Kaspersen, A, Kent, R, & Von Hippel, K (2005), *Report on Integrated Missions: Practical Perspectives and Recommendations*, Independent Study for the Expanded UN ECHA Core Group.

Council of the European Union (2002), *Civil-Military Co-operation (CIMIC) Concept for EU-led crisis Management Operations*, cl 7106/02, 18 March.

—— (2006), *Civil-military Coordination: Framework Paper of Possible Solutions for the Management of EU Crisis Management Operations*, Bruxelles, 2 May.

Dahrendorf, N (ed) (2003), *A Review of Peace Operations: A Case for Change*, London: Kings College.

de Coning, C (2005), 'Civil-Military Coordination and UN Peacebuilding Operations', *African Journal on Conflict Resolution*, 5/2: 89–118.

DPKO (UN Department of Peacekeeping Operations) (2002), *Department of Peacekeeping Operations (DPKO) Civil-Military Coordination Policy*, 9 September.

Donini, A, Minear, L, Smillie I, van Baarda, T, & Welch, A (2005), 'Mapping the Security Environment. Understanding the Perceptions of Local Communities, Peace Support Operations, and Assistance Agencies', Feinstein International Famine Centre, Tufts University.

Gordon, S (2006), 'The Changing Role of the Military in Assistance Strategies', in Wheeler, V, & Harmer, A (eds), *Resetting the rules of engagement. Trends and Issues in Military-Humanitarian Relations*, Humanitarian Policy Group Research Report 21, Overseas Development Institute, March.

Harland, D (2005), 'UN Peacekeeping Operations in Post-Conflict Timor-Leste: Accomplishments and Lessons Learned', New York: UN Peacekeeping Best Practices Section.

ICRC (2001), *Guidelines for Civil-Military Relations (CMR)*.

—— (2005), *Document d'orientation sur les relations entre les composantes du Mouvement et les organismes militaires*, résolution no 7 et annexe *Relations entre les composantes du Mouvement et les organismes militaires*, Conseil des délégués, Séoul.

Khouri-Padova, L (2004), *Haiti. Lessons Learned*, New York: UN Peacekeeping Best Practices Unit.

NATO (2003), *Doctrine de coopération civilo-militaire (CIMIC) de l'OTAN*, AJP-9, June.

OCHA (UN's Office for the Coordination of Humanitarian Affairs) (1994), *Guidelines on the Use of Military and Civil Defense Assets (MCDA) in Disaster Relief*, known as 'the Oslo Guidelines', May.

—— (2001), *Guidelines on the Use of Armed and Military Escorts for Humanitarian Convoys*, September.

—— (2003) *Guidelines on the Use of MCDA to Support UN Humanitarian Activities in Complex Emergencies*.

Rana, R (2004), 'Contemporary Challenges in the Civil-Military Relationship: Complementarity or Incompatibility?', *International Review of the Red Cross*, 86/855.

Rehse, P (2004), *CIMIC: Concepts, Definitions and Practice*, IESH, Heft 136, Hamburg.

Save the Children (2004), *Provincial Reconstruction Teams and Humanitarian-Military Relations in Afghanistan*, London.

Secrétariat du Conseil et Commission européenne (2003), *Coordination civilo-militaire (CMCO)*, Brussels, 7 November.

Steering Committee for Humanitarian Response, (2004) *SCHR Position Paper on Humanitarian-Military Relations in the Provision of Humanitarian Assistance* (revision of the 2001 version).

Studer, M (2001), 'The ICRC and Civil-Military Relations in Armed Conflict', *International Review of the Red Cross*, 83/842: 367–91.

US Joint Chiefs of Staff (2001), *Joint Doctrine for Civil-Military Operations*, Joint Publication No 3–57, 8 February.

Civil Society

*Thania Paffenholz**

Definition

'Civil society' is generally understood as the arena of voluntary, collective actions of an institutional nature around shared interests, purposes, and values that are distinct from those of the state, family, and market. Civil society consists of a large and diverse set of voluntary organizations and comprises non-state actors and associations which are not purely driven by private or economic interests, are autonomously organized, show civil virtue, and interact in the public sphere. In the context of post-conflict peacebuilding, civil society is understood as an important pillar for stabilizing peace and contributing to the transition from peacebuilding to democratization.

I. Term

Origin and context

Historically the concept of 'civil society' has been an almost purely western concept, tied to the political emancipation of European citizens from former 'feudalistic' ties, monarchy, and the state during the 18th and 19th centuries.

The origins of the concept of civil society go back to a number of political philosophers whose understanding of civil society shapes the way the concept is understood today (Merkel & Lauth, 1998: 5–7). The work of the following authors is therefore worth summarizing. John Locke was the first in modern times to stress that civil society is a body in its own right, separate from the state. People form a community, in which their social life develops and in which the state has no say. The first task of this civil society is to protect the individual— his/her rights and property—against the state and its arbitrary interventions.

Charles de Montesquieu elaborated his model of separation of powers (*De l'esprit des lois*), where he distinguished, as Locke did, between political society (regulating the relations between citizens and government) and civil society (regulating the relations between citizens), but presented a far less sharp contrast

---

* The following article is based on previous works of the author. See Paffenholz & Spurk, 2006.

between the two spheres. Instead, he stressed a balance between central authority and societal networks (*corps intermediaries*), where the central authority (monarchy) must be controlled by the rule of law and limited by the countervailing power of independent organizations (networks) that operate inside and outside the political structure.

Alexis de Tocqueville stressed even more the role of these independent associations as civil society (*De la démocratie en Amérique*). He saw these associations as schools of democracy in which democratic thinking, attitudes and behaviour are learned, also with the aim to protect and defend individual rights against potentially authoritarian regimes and tyrannical majorities in society. According to Tocqueville these associations should be built voluntarily and at all levels (local, regional, national). Thus, civic virtues like tolerance, acceptance, honesty, and trust are integrated into the character of civic individuals. They contribute to trust and confidence, or, as Putnam later described it, to the building of 'social capital' (Putnam, 2000: 19–26).

Antonio Gramsci focused on civil society from a Marxist theoretical viewpoint. He stressed the potentially oppositional role of civil society as a 'public room', upholding the existing order. Gramsci's ideas influenced the resistance to totalitarian regimes in Eastern Europe and Latin America. Jürgen Habermas focused his concept of civil society on its role within the public sphere. He said the political system needs interests to be articulated in the public sphere so that societal concerns can be put on the political agenda, and this function cannot be left purely to establishment institutions such as political parties. Marginalized groups in particular need to organize and find a way to articulate their interests. This is necessary because political parties and parliaments need to '…get informed public opinion beyond the established power structures' (Habermas, 1992: 374).

Other 'civil societies' that might have existed in other countries or continents (Africa, Asia, Latin America, or the Middle East) or different times (pre-colonial, middle ages) are barely reflected in the international debate about civil society (Pouligny, 2005: 498). It continues to be disputed whether the concept is transferable to non-western or other historical contexts with different conditions for democracy, peacebuilding, and economy.

During the last century, the concept of 'civil society' has gained increasing importance in development cooperation, starting in the mid-1980s with the increased involvement of voluntary agencies or non-governmental organizations (NGOs) (both in the North and in the South) in development cooperation. This can be attributed primarily to the 'neo-liberal' policy of the 1980s that encouraged a highly sceptical attitude towards the state and favoured the privatization of state welfare and infrastructure services (see the chapter on private sector). As a result of such policies, NGOs were assigned new service functions, especially in the social and health sectors, that had previously been the responsibility of the state. This trend toward supporting civil society was enforced by a series of UN world conferences in the 1990s that gave substantial incentives to the founding of new NGOs or the enlargement of existing ones. The average amount of funds channelled by OECD countries via NGOs was US$3.1 billion in 1985–86 and increased to $7.2 billion in 2001 (Debiel & Sticht, 2005: 10). Other sources mention even higher figures (Schmidt, 2000: 302).

Civil society gained even more momentum at the beginning of the 1990s as a means of improving governance, democratization, and post-conflict peacebuilding. With the end of the cold war, democratic governance, respect for human rights, and the rule of law became priority objectives in development cooperation, and post-conflict peacebuilding and reconstruction. A vibrant civil society was considered an important pillar for democratization and the medium to long-term support of peace processes (see also the chapters on conflict transformation and local ownership).

Meaning of the concept

Although the term is widely used, there is no commonly agreed definition. The notion that civil society is the arena of voluntary collective actions around shared interests, purposes and values is non-controversial. To define civil society further many authors (see Paffenholz & Spurk, 2006: 2–3) describe its position in relation to other sectors of society, and then to group actors within these sectors. We find two main understandings here as shown in the figure below: first, civil society is seen as a sector on its own *vis-à-vis* the three other main sectors—state, business, and family. Although there is general agreement in the literature on this basic approach, the attribution of actors is contested. For example, some authors argue that family is not a separate sector but belongs to civil society, while others consider business as part of civil society rather than being a sector on its own. Some researchers use a different and more sophisticated segmentation, distinguishing, for example, between the political (state apparatus, political parties, and parliamentarians), economic (companies and markets), and private spheres, and define a space where these spheres overlap. Thus, some actors do not belong just to one sector but operate in various spheres.

Second, civil society is seen as the space between societal sectors (Merkel & Lauth, 1998: 7). Thus, actors are attributed to specific sectors but can also act in civil society. For example, entrepreneurs, usually part of the business sector, are acting in civil society when demanding tax exemptions. This understanding also helps to uncover other actors who have a role in civil society, such as traditional groups in Africa.

And while civil society is independent from the state, it is oriented toward and interacts closely with it, especially in the political sphere (see Figure 2).

Linguistic and semantic distinctions

Civil society as a concept is not much contested in its linguist or semantic understanding. However, two possible distinctions are worth mentioning:

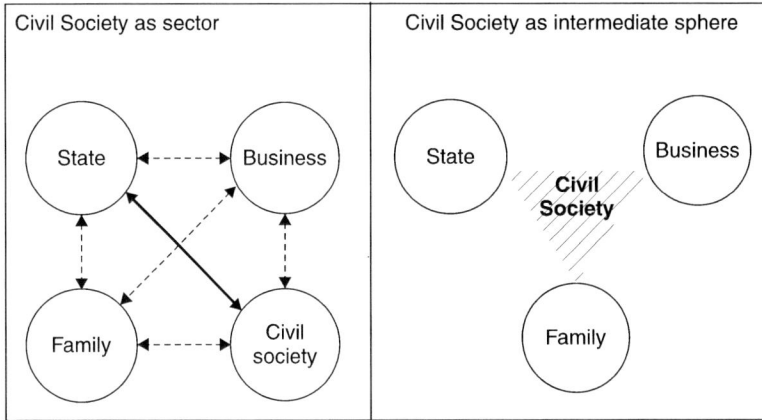

Figure 2 Civil society as sector and as intermediate sphere
Source: Paffenholz & Spurk, 2006: 3.

First, the term 'civic engagement' is widely used by social capital theorists like Robert Putnam and refers mainly to the participation of individuals in civil life and groupings (Putnam, 2000: 31–180). In its civil society discourse the World Bank uses the term 'civic engagement', which is broader than the activities and roles of organized civil society and also includes actions of individuals and loose groupings or associations.

Second, the term 'civil' as part of the term 'civil society' indicates a requirement for civil society actors to be 'civil', ie to respect the values of non-violence and mutual tolerance (Merkel & Lauth, 1998: 7). This distinction—though not entirely agreed upon in the literature—is a core distinction from the concept of 'non-state' actors, which can also include those actors that show 'uncivil' virtues or use violence in their interactions with other groups, for example warlords, militia, and armed liberation movements.

II. Content

Civil society actors and roles

The literature offers two main approaches for analysing the diverse forms of civil society (Paffenholz & Spurk, 2006: 7–9). One of these approaches focuses on actors and their identity, the other structures civil society according to its functions.

Actor-oriented approaches focus the debate on which actors belong to civil society, what their characteristics are, and how they act in the specific historical and political context. Development cooperation actors are inclined to identify 'civil society' only with NGOs. In this NGO category, a very wide array of actors are considered part of civil society, including women, the media, youth, faith-based organizations, educational institutions, the arts, local business, diaspora, and sometimes even soldiers. This broad definition subsumes almost everybody who is not a government actor under the civil society umbrella. Not only does this blur sectoral boundaries (state, market, family), it also fails to identify the different actors' purposes and roles and to clarify their objectives, as well as omitting the distinction between 'civil' and 'uncivil' virtues.

There are two major schools of thought that use a role/functions approach to civil society. One school was formed by Edwards (2004), who has distilled three different 'models' of civil society. The other main school of thought comes from political scientists who have presented the concept of five functions of civil society. These functions were extracted primarily through research into system transformation in Eastern Europe and clarified through a wide array of case studies investigating civil society in different contexts (Merkel & Lauth, 1998). Their concept sees civil society not as a specific historic form, but as an analytical category. This analytical focus not only helps distil the functions of civil society *vis-à-vis* democracy, it also allows one to analyse the role of civil society in different regional, cultural, or societal contexts. In the practice of development cooperation we find another understanding of functions: here the service delivery function is strongest. In merging these different schools/discourses on civil society functions, Paffenholz and Spurk (2006: 13) propose to combine Merkel and Lauth's five functions with two new functions contributed by development cooperation practice. From this integration they get the following list of seven basic civil society functions that further clarify the role of civil society in democratization:

- protection of citizens;
- monitoring of relevant issues for accountability;
- advocacy/public communication;
- socialization within society (bonding ties);
- building community (bridging ties);
- intermediation/facilitation between citizens and state; and
- service delivery.

Relevance and understanding of the concept in post-conflict peacebuilding

Since ancient times, a variety of actors have made contributions to peacebuilding, but since the end of the 19th century international institutions and international law have increasingly developed mechanisms and instruments to make war between states less likely. The main protagonists involved in the development of peacebuilding institutions have been nation states and the UN. Civil society involvement, especially in international conflicts, was considered to complicate the peacebuilding efforts of professional diplomats. Non-governmental actors on the scene such as the Quakers were exceptions (Paffenholz, 2001).

In the 1990s, the main research debate within peacebuilding was which external actors would achieve the best results in efforts to end armed conflicts and sustain peace after war, and with what approach. The practice of peacebuilding during that decade was characterized by the testing of many different approaches. Research has since led to the conclusion that only the involvement of *multiple* actors—including grass-roots organizations or other civil society actors—and a range of approaches can lead to sustainable peace (for overviews, see Reychler & Paffenholz, 2001; Crocker *et al*, 2001).

The main debates within peacebuilding research until the mid-1990s focused on the role of external actors. The important work of John Paul Lederach shifted the focus of attention from external actors to the role of local actors within the conflict country (Lederach, 1997). This research led to a paradigm shift within the international research and practitioner community: from the mid-1990s onwards, the question for external actors was mainly how to support national actors within countries experiencing armed conflict so as to best enhance their capacity-building (see the chapter on local ownership). The interpretation of this conceptual framework gave rise to, and justification for, the mushrooming of international, national, and local peacebuilding initiatives, mainly by civil society actors. Support to civil society became routine in post-conflict peacebuilding and reconstruction.

Many different peacebuilding approaches and initiatives, such as peace funds, dialogue projects, peacebuilding training, and capacity-building programmes for local actors, have been tested during the last decade. Today, a wide array of civil society actors such as NGOs, associations, religious entities, business and grass-roots organizations, communities, or individuals, are increasingly involved in different peacebuilding activities (Paffenholz & Spurk, 2006: 18–19; Richmond & Carey, 2006).

Core components: civil society roles in post-conflict peacebuilding

The seven civil society functions identified from democracy and development research and practice (see above) have been adapted by Paffenholz and Spurk (2006: 27–33) to the context of peacebuilding. Their function-oriented model of civil society helps to better understand the role of civil society in post-conflict peacebuilding.

Protection

In civil society discourse within democracy theory, protection of citizens and communities against the despotism of the state is a core civil society function.

During and after armed conflicts, protection becomes almost a precondition for fulfilling other roles and functions, as civil society actors are substantially hindered from taking up peacebuilding roles when threatened by armed groups. This is particularly true where states weakened by armed conflict cannot properly fulfil their own protection function. In peacebuilding, protection needs to be secured not solely *vis-à-vis* a despotic state, but from any armed actor, be it the national army, militia, or a non-state armed group. The main activities for civil society within this protective function are: international accompaniment, watchdog activities, creation of 'zones of peace', or civil society human security initiatives.

Monitoring/accountability

Monitoring is both a precondition for the 'protection' function and the 'advocacy/public communication' function (see below) as well as a key function in democratization as a means of holding governments accountable (see also on this issue the chapters on democratic governance and rule of law). Within peacebuilding, monitoring remains closely related to (1) protection and (2) advocacy, but also to (3) early warning as a means for early action. International and local groups monitor the conflict situation and give recommendations to decision makers or information to human rights and advocacy groups.

Advocacy/public communication

Advocacy is a core function within the civil society discourse within democracy theory often referred to as 'communication' since it entails civil society bringing relevant social and political themes to the public agenda. In the same vein, advocacy is considered one of the core functions in peacebuilding. The main activities within this function are: agenda setting by local civil society actors, such as bringing themes to the national agenda in conflict countries (road map projects, awareness workshops, public campaigns), lobbying for civil society involvement in peace negotiations, or public pressure (mass mobilization for peace negotiations or against the recurrence of war, for the proper implementation of peace agreements, of reconciliation or of proper disarmament, demobilization, and reintegration processes). Also important is international advocacy for specific conflict issues (banning of landmines or cluster munitions; war diamonds; child soldiers) or for specific countries at conflict.

In-group socialization

Socialization is a key civil society function that supports the practice of democratic attitudes and values within society, realized through the active participation in associations, networks or democratic movements. Naturally this is also a crucial civil society function in peacebuilding which aims at promoting attitudinal change within society towards peaceful conflict transformation and reconciliation. The difference between socialization and social cohesion (see 'inter-group social cohesion' below) is that socialization takes place only within groups and not between former adversary groups (which would be called bridging ties = social cohesion), that is, in a post-conflict setting in-group bonding ties are strengthened. For example, the Geneva-based international NGO 'Interpeace' supports groups on the different sides of the Israel/Palestine conflict separately and works to strengthen each group in their peace efforts and understanding.

Every national or local association that practises peaceful coexistence contributes to this function. From outside, this function is often supported through peace education through different media (radio or TV soap operas, street theatre, peace campaigns, school books, poetry festivals, etc.), conflict resolution, or negotiation training (see the chapter on peace process).

Inter-group social cohesion

In democracy theory 'social cohesion' is seen as an important civil society function that ensures building of community. In fact, this is also an essential civil society function in peacebuilding as 'good' social capital is destroyed during war and needs to be rebuilt, mainly in order to prevent 'uncivil virtues' as well as to revitalize active civic engagement. Therefore, it is crucial that 'bridging ties' across adversarial groups and not only 'bonding ties' within specific groups are built (Putnam, 2000). The objective of this civil society function is to help these groups learn to live together in peaceful coexistence.

Intermediation/facilitation

The facilitation function of civil society within the democracy discourse highlights civil society as an intermediator/facilitator between citizens and the state. In a peacebuilding context intermediation/facilitation can also be an important function that takes place between different groups (not only between state and citizens) and on different levels of society. The main activities within this function are facilitation initiatives (formal or informal): between armed groups; between armed groups and communities; or between armed groups, communities and development agencies.

The contribution of civil society to diplomatic conflict management activities is, however, a limited one and is only taken up in exceptional cases because conflict management is more of a government function for states or the UN (see the chapter on peace process). In the rare cases when this function is taken up by civil society actors, we see the involvement of external civil society actors, such as international NGOs, international networks, or research institutions. For example, the Catholic lay organization San Egidio mediated during the Mozambique peace negotiations in Rome from 1990 to 1992 and the Geneva-based international NGO Centre for Humanitarian Dialogue facilitated the first negotiations between the parties in Indonesia's Aceh province.

Local civil society can often facilitate the relationship between:

- civil society and warring parties at the village or district level. In conflict zones in Nepal civil society representatives have successfully negotiated the release of citizens from custody by armed groups;
- the warring parties in order to negotiate peace zones (see 'protection' above), or violence-free days such as those negotiated by churches during the war in El Salvador;
- international or national aid agencies and the warring parties as a means to ensure the delivery of aid to their communities;
- international or national aid agencies and civil society groups, because NGOs often become the main providers of services in war zones and unstable post-conflict settings. As these NGOs are usually not acquainted with the local context, they are in need of facilitators between themselves and the local communities as well as the armed groups in the area (Paffenholz & Spurk, 2006: 31).

Service delivery

During armed conflict the provision of aid services through civil society actors (mainly NGOs but sometimes also associations) increases tremendously as state structures are either destroyed or weak. There is no doubt that this kind of service is extremely important to help the war-affected population and support reconstruction of the state and society at large (see more generally the chapter on recovery). Nevertheless, the question remains whether and under which circumstances service delivery is also a civil society function in peacebuilding (Paffenholz & Spurk, 2006: 31–3). Some authors see aid service delivery as a separate function of civil society because it saves lives and thus creates the preconditions for civil society to exist. Another line of thinking follows the same argumentation as in democracy theory: usually service delivery is done with an economic, social or humanitarian objective, and therefore it should not be labelled as 'civil society' support. A third argument states that aid service delivery can only be important for civil society peacebuilding when aid donors and agencies explicitly aim also at contributing to local capacities for peace and try to find entry points for peacebuilding through their respective aid interventions (see in this sense the chapter on capacity-building).

Challenges and dilemmas

Civil society is a mirror of society at large. The listing of these constructive civil society functions should thus not blur our views regarding the overall role and function of civil society. Many civil society actors might not fulfil one or more of the above-mentioned constructive functions, and others might develop uncivil virtues, preach hatred against others or even commit violence. We must keep in mind that associations and organizations can be completely destructive in their behaviour to others or at least have both integrative and disintegrative potential.

It must be also clearly stated that these constructive civil society functions are not the exclusive domain of civil society actors; such functions can and are also provided by others. 'Protection', for example, should be provided mainly by the state, the judiciary, and law enforcing authorities. Furthermore, democratic attitudes are not only learned in voluntary associations, but also in the classroom or within the family.

The constructive civil society functions listed above do not describe the enabling environment necessary for their implementation. Theory reminds us that civil society is not to be replaced by the state but should exist separately to improve the interplay between citizens and the state. Thus, it needs to be kept in mind that, especially where the state is extremely fragile or extremely authoritarian, any external support to civil society should be matched by support to the state as well. This support might encompass capacity-building for state structures or enforcement of the rule of law, contingent upon the needs on the ground.

III. Implementation

Challenges of implementation

A core challenge is supporting an enabling environment in which civil society can flourish. This is a context where the state is an adequate counterpart for civil society, where fundamental democratic values such as the rule of law are put into practice, and where associational freedom as well as free media are accepted (for further discussion see also the chapter on democratic governance).

The rise of civil society peacebuilding initiatives also shows the dilemmas of donor-driven NGO civil society support. The mushrooming of peace initiatives and the increased involvement of NGOs in conflict countries has gone hand-in-hand with the professionalization and commercialization of peace work. This 'NGOisation' of social protest (Orjuela, 2004: 255) has led to a 'taming of social movements' (Kaldor, 2003) and has thus shifted the focus of peacebuilding away from peace movements and grass-roots civic engagement for peace.

Following the logic of development aid delivery, most external support from donors goes directly to international NGOs (INGOs) or through them to national, mainly urban, elite-based NGOs. Empirical evidence from different countries (see Paffenholz & Spurk, 2006: 25–26) shows that donors tend to support mainly moderate, middle-class groups that often act as 'gatekeepers' *vis-à-vis* other strata of society. This has resulted in a 'colonization of space' by international and national NGOs. International NGOs have been criticized for 'parachuting in' to conflicts and introducing Western conflict resolution techniques to local people, who are consequently familiarized with the language and expectations of international donors. This argument is countered by others who point to the fact that many INGOs work with national NGOs that are linked to the local context.

Another criticism is that many of these new national urban NGOs have a weak membership base, lack countrywide and/or balanced political or ethnic representation, and are often linked to the political establishment through kin relationships. The reasons for these characteristics are to be found mainly in the 'monetization of peace work'. The fact that these NGOs are only accountable towards their international counterparts and not *vis-à-vis* 'their' constituencies has resulted in the disempowerment of local communities and civic engagement for peace. Donor-driven NGO civil society initiatives have limited the capacity to create domestic social capital and ownership of peace processes. As a result, domestic groups are disempowered and left in a weak and subordinate position (Belloni, 2001). Moreover, resources and opportunities gained in civil society detain talented and motivated citizens from joining political parties, government institutions and contributing to political peace processes (Belloni, 2001). Obviously, the same negative effects of donor-driven support occur in peacebuilding as those already analysed decades earlier in development research.

Studies on the effectiveness of peace work show that many initiatives by national NGOs do not automatically reach the macro peace process level unless certain conditions are met. For example, the Reflecting on Peace Project found that for peacebuilding to be successful either key people must be supported or else a critical mass of people must participate (Anderson & Olson, 2003). Despite this finding, single urban-based or INGOs receive the majority of funds on this level of engagement, because it is easier for international NGOs to work with urban-based elite NGOs as they speak the language of Western INGOs and donors and also understand the culture of project proposals. It is much harder for INGOs and donors to engage with actors in communities: while they possess great knowledge, their ability to cope with Western agency demands is weak (for further discussion see also the chapter on local ownership).

Lessons learned, good practice, and operational aspects

On the positive side, we have seen a general acceptance that national actors from within conflict countries should be the main actors in peacebuilding and that the role of outsiders is limited to supporting them (Lederach, 1997). We have also seen an understanding that civil society peace initiatives are as needed as official or unofficial diplomatic efforts to build peace.

On the international level we have often seen successful lobbying and advocacy for specific peace-related themes (for example 'small arms' or 'conflict economies') but also for specific peacebuilding processes in conflict countries. This is linked to the debate about global civil society (Kaldor, 2003). For example different church-based development and peace organizations have joined hands to create awareness building about the (previously) forgotten war in Sudan. They opened an advocacy liaison office in Europe (Sudan Focal Point Europe) to lobby on the case for Sudan in European Parliaments and other decision-making forums long before Sudan came back to the international agenda.

Cooperation between governmental actors and mainly international NGOs for peacebuilding has become more and more a routine in many countries, accepting each other's comparative advantages. In Switzerland for example, the Centre for Peacebuilding (KOFF; see <http://www.swisspeace.org>) provides an exchange platform between the Swiss government and Swiss civil society groups active in peacebuilding in different countries.

To illustrate lessons learned and operational aspects in the practice of civil society functions in post-conflict peacebuilding, a number of examples have been given here, along with the functions discussed in section II above (see more in Paffenholz & Spurk, 2006: 27–35).

The civil society function of protection is often implemented through external NGOs that support national or local civil society actors either indirectly, as a watchdog through their presence on the ground due to humanitarian or development service delivery, or directly through international accompaniment. A good example of the latter is the work of the international NGO 'Peace Brigades International' that sends outsiders into conflict zones to protect national peace or human rights activists, thus enabling them to fulfil their work. We find, however, that local civil societies also take up protective functions for their communities. For example, communities in the Philippines and Colombia have negotiated 'zones of peace' where no arms are allowed.

The monitoring function of civil society is often implemented through the creation of political early warning systems and human rights monitoring. In both fields we see increasing cooperation between local groups and not only national and international NGOs, but also regional organizations. In Nepal, national human rights organizations, which have close links to Amnesty International, cooperate closely with local groups. These ties between the groups create safe space for the local groups to fulfil their monitoring tasks. Several examples of local–national–regional cooperation in early warning can be seen in Africa, where we find early warning systems of regional organizations (CEWARN in the Horn of Africa) that cooperate with local civil society groups for the actual monitoring. In West Africa, the UN's Office for the Coordination of Humanitarian Affairs (OCHA), the regional organization the Economic Community of West African States (ECOWAS), and a regional NGO peace network have signed a memorandum of understanding for joint early warning.

Advocacy is a core civil society peacebuilding function that is first of all implemented by national and local groups. The strongest form of advocacy is certainly mass mobilization. An interesting example is the mass mobilization against the Nepali King in spring 2006 that started as a political movement of the parties and the armed faction (Maoists) and developed into a countrywide civil society peace and democracy mass movement that brought ten years of armed conflict to an end.

International civil society can also take up important advocacy functions. For example, the Swedish Life and Peace Institute (LPI) has been practicing advocacy for Somalia with the objective of making international actors aware of the need for a people-based peace process, of the special role of women in peacebuilding, and of providing funding for people's involvement. LPI's main advocacy instrument was to provide information. It constantly advocated a bottom-up solution of the Somali crisis in various international forums, such as UN bodies (the UN Operation in Somalia—UNOSOM—in the beginning), the Somali Aid Coordination Body, and international conferences (Paffenholz, 2006).

Advocacy is also a function that is relevant in all phases of armed conflict even though different issues might be more or less relevant in different phases. During armed conflict civil society can advocate for reaching a peace agreement, against violence and human rights violations, for a broad-based participation in the peace process, as well as for relevant themes and issues. The population can be linked to the official negotiation process through broad-based information campaigns, public opinion polls or more direct involvement. For example, during the official peace negotiations in Guatemala from 1994 to 1996, and those for Afghanistan that occurred in Germany in 2001, there were official parallel civil society forums established which gave recommendations to the official peace negotiations. During the peace process in Northern Ireland civil society groups organized 'Yes' campaigns for public support to the peace agreement.

Inter-group social cohesion is seen by many international donors and NGOs as a main role of civil society: to foster joint activities between former or present adversarial groups, such as the formation of joint associations (mixed groups of parents, journalists, teachers, multi-ethnic chambers of commerce, etc), joint cultural events (music, poetry, film festivals), or joint work initiatives. Though many funds are going into these initiatives, research evidence of their impact is mixed. For example, a qualitative and quantitative research evaluation of the impact of peace education on attitude change through peace camps with different groups from both sides of the Georgian/Abkhazian conflict, shows evidence that little attitude change was achieved through various peace education initiatives over a period of four years. However, initiatives promoting and implementing joint work initiatives were possible and were also perceived as fruitful by the adversarial groups, even without any attitude change (Ohanyan with Lewis, 2005, in Paffenholz & Spurk, 2006: 30). Moreover, a research project from India shows that ethnically integrated organizations, including business, trade or other associations, have been an effective means to build bridging ties across ethnically divided groups, even leading to an 'institutionalised peace system' that facilitated the control of violence (Varshney, 2002: 46).

Selected Bibliography

Anderson, MB, Olson, L, & Doughty, K (2003), *Confronting War: Critical Lessons for Peace Practitioners*, Cambridge, MA: The Collaborative for Development Action.

Belloni, R (2001), 'Civil Society and Peacebuilding in Bosnia and Herzegovina', *Journal of Peace Research*, 38/2: 163–80.

Crocker, CA, Hampson, FO, & Aall, P (2001), *Turbulent Peace: The Challenges of Managing International Conflict*, Washington, DC: United States Institute of Peace Press.

Debiel, T, & Sticht, M (2005), *Towards a New Profile? Development, Humanitarian and Conflict-Resolution NGOs in the Age of Globalisation*, INEF Report, no 79, Duisburg: Institute for Development and Peace (INEF).

Edwards, M (2004), *Civil Society*, Cambridge, UK: Polity Press.

Habermas, J (1992), 'Zur Rolle von Zivilgesellschaft und politischer Öffentlichkeit', in Habermas, J, *Faktizität und Geltung*, Frankfurt a.M.: Suhrkamp, 399–467.

Kaldor, M (2003), *Global Civil Society: An Answer to War*, Cambridge, UK: Polity Press.

Lederach, JP (1997), *Building Peace: Sustainable Reconciliation in Divided Societies*, Washington, DC: United States Institute of Peace Press.

Merkel, W, & Lauth, H (1998), 'Systemwechsel und Zivilgesellschaft. Welche Zivilgesellschaft braucht die Demokratie?', *Aus Politik und Zeitgeschichte*, 6–7: 3–12.

Orjuela, C (2004), *Civil Society in Civil War, Peace Work and Identity Politics in Sri Lanka*, PhD Thesis, Department of Peace and Development Research, University Göteborg.

Paffenholz, T (2001), 'Western Approaches to Mediation', in Reychler, L, & Paffenholz, T (eds), *Peacebuilding: A Field Guide*, Boulder, CO: Lynne Rienner Publishers, 75–81.

——(2006), 'Community Peacebuilding in Somalia—Comparative Advantage of NGO Peacebuilding – The example of the Life and Peace Institute's Approach in Somalia (1990–2003)', in Richmond, O, & Carey, H (eds), *Subcontracting Peace: NGOs and Peacebuilding in a Dangerous World*, Aldershot: Ashgate Publishers, 173–182.

—— & Spurk, C (2006), *Civil Society, Civic Engagement, and Peacebuilding*, Social Development Paper, no 100, and Conflict Prevention and Reconstruction Paper, no 36, Washington, DC: The World Bank.

Pouligny, B (2005), 'Civil Society and Post-Conflict Peacebuilding: Ambiguities of International Programmes Aimed at Building "New" Societies', *Security Dialogue*, London: Sage Publications, 36/4, 495–510.

Putnam, RD (2000), *Bowling Alone: The Collapse and Revival of American Community*, New York: Simon and Schuster.

Reychler, L, & Paffenholz, T (eds) (2001), *Peacebuilding: A Field Guide*, Boulder, CO: Lynne Rienner Publishers.

Richmond, O, & Carey, H (2006), *Subcontracting Peace: NGOs and Peacebuilding in a Dangerous World*, Aldershot: Ashgate.

Schmidt, S (2000), 'Die Rolle von Zivilgesellschaften in afrikanischen Systemwechseln', in Merkel, W (ed), *Systemwechsel 5. Zivilgesellschaft und Transformation*, Opladen: Leske + Budrich, 295–334.

Varshney, A (2002), *Ethnic Conflict and Civic Life: Hindus and Moslems in India*, New Haven: Yale University Press.

Conflict Economies

Achim Wennmann

Definition

Conflict economies include all economic activities taking place during armed conflicts. In a narrow sense, these are defined in relation to the mobilization of resources to organize and maintain armed conflict (combat economies). However, in a broader sense, conflict economies also include the activities—often illicit in nature—that emerge as a consequence of armed conflict (shadow economies), as well as the livelihood activities of populations living in conflict zones (survival economies). Combat, shadow, and survival economies are often interwoven and their consequences tend to outlive the end of an armed conflict.

I. Term

Context

Conflict economies are an established concept in the history of warfare and the emergence of the state in Europe. Historically, mobilizing resources for war became one of the major preoccupations of rulers and they consequently devoted the largest share of national revenue to war-making. However, changes in weapons technology increased the cost of warfare and encouraged innovations in fundraising strategies—including the development of state taxation systems, central banking, and the formation of state institutions—that ultimately fostered state-building in Europe between the 16th and 19th centuries (Tilly, 1992). In terms of guerrilla warfare, conflict economies defined the relationship between guerrillas and local populations. As guerrillas were difficult to distinguish from civilian populations, they provided cover from the relatively stronger state armed forces. However, a tension arose once the economic requirements of the guerrillas went above what local populations were willing to provide, thus jeopardizing the provision of protection (Rufin, 1996: 23).

More recently, there has been a growing interest in conflict economies particularly due to the role of natural resources in a number of armed conflicts in Africa. The issue gained prominence in reports to the UN Security Council that detailed the role of so-called 'conflict diamonds' in the wars in Angola, the Democratic Republic of Congo, (DRC) and Sierra Leone. Growing awareness of these linkages fostered multi-stakeholder initiatives, such as the Kimberley Process against conflict diamonds, and voluntary sector-specific codes of conduct such as the Extractive Industry Transparency Initiative or the Forest Stewardship Council Certification. In addition, the World Bank identified armed conflict as an obstacle to development. Contemporary armed conflicts were not a useful force for social change in line with the European history of state-building, but rather 'development in reverse' (Collier *et al*, 2003: 32).

At the same time, scholars sought to find alternative explanations of armed conflict that had previously rested on 'irrational and essentially inexplicably primordial qualities' of ethnic and cultural identities (Pugh and Cooper, 2004: 97). An entire debate focused on whether armed conflict was caused by greed or grievance, and more recently shifted to emphasize 'the primacy of feasibility over motivation' (Collier *et al*, 2007: 21). While popular among policy-makers, a wave of responses exposed methodological problems and situated economic factors of armed conflicts in specific contexts (Ballentine and Sherman, 2003; Arnson and Zartman, 2005; Cramer, 2006). While academia remains divided on statistical methods in the analysis of armed conflict, a consensus seems to suggests that 'the origin of armed conflict cannot be exclusively related to greed or loot seekers' but rather interacts 'with socioeconomic and political grievances, interethnic disputes, and security dilemmas in triggering the outbreak of warfare' (Ballentine, 2003: 259–260).

Another perspective on conflict economies captures the changing international economic and political context after the end of the Cold War. It highlighted the role of new actors in conflict zones—private military companies (PMCs), transnational crime networks, or extractive industries—in shaping the characteristics of so-called 'new wars' (Kaldor, 1999) (see the chapters on non-state actors; private sector). These were described as 'a myriad of transnational connections so that the distinction between internal and external, between aggression (attacks from abroad) and repression (attacks from inside the country), or even between local and global, becomes difficult to sustain' (Kaldor, 1999: 2). The globalization of both formal and informal economies facilitated the commercialization of local resources and the supply of know-how, manpower, and matériel necessary for armed conflict.

Conflict economies were also discussed in the context of 'regional conflict complexes' characterized by 'the cross-border spill over of violence, the empowerment of borderlands as sanctuaries for combatants and nurseries for recruits and also as centres of shadow economic activities, and the interregional commercial or other connections that make for prolonged and intractable conflicts' (Pugh and Cooper, 2004: 2). In these circumstances, armed violence had an economic function and represented 'not simply a breakdown of a particular system, but a way of creating an alternative system of profit, power and even protection' (Keen, 1998: 11).

Possible understandings

Conflict economies have both a broad and narrow dimension, which reflects the efforts of different disciplines to study this phenomenon. In the broadest sense, conflict economies include all economic activities taking place in a specific territory during armed conflict. Macro-economists, for example, capture these conflict economies by looking at the economic performance of states in times of armed conflict (Collier *et al*, 2003: 13–17).

A narrow perspective focuses on the mobilization of resources to organize armed conflict in a combat economy. Such a perspective looks at the various methods of conflict financing or 'conflict goods' that are 'non-military materials, knowledge, animals or humans whose trade, taxation or protection is exploited to finance or otherwise maintain the war economies of contemporary conflicts' (Cooper, 2001: 27). The organization of an armed conflict represents such an enormous transformation of resources and labour that it affects economic and social relations in the long term. The effect of conflict economies therefore outlasts the end of an armed conflict and conditions the post-conflict economy.

Combat economies are frequently interwoven with shadow and survival economies. The shadow economy captures the economic opportunities that emerge as a consequence of armed conflict. These are often illicit in nature as legal systems and property rights break down during armed conflict. These conditions can be exploited for the purposes of weapons or human trafficking, smuggling, natural resources pillage, or drugs production. In most conflict situations, these activities contribute to the reduction of formal economic activities and the growth of the informal sector that often remains the main sector of employment in the post-conflict economy. The informal sector is particularly important for livelihood activities of populations living in conflict zones. Survival economies recognize that people adapt their behaviour in order to survive and maximize the economic opportunities that became available through the economic transformation brought about by armed conflict (Pugh and Cooper, 2004: 8–9). This resilience capacity is an essential attribute of conflict-affected populations and an asset for post-conflict economies.

These different types of conflict economies justify the appropriateness of the concept of conflict economies (plural) and not on any particular conflict economy (singular). Combat, shadow, and survival economies are sub-sets of the concept of conflict economies and all occur during armed conflict. Their effects tend, however, to outlast a conflict and thereby become a concern for peacebuilding.

Linguistic and semantic difficulties

'Conflict economies' are often described as 'war economies'. The label 'war' refers to warfare between states and 'war economies' therefore tend to capture the economies of states during war. This is why in historical work the reference to 'war economies' is common. However, in recent decades the occurrence of inter-state armed conflict has become much less frequent while different forms of armed conflict have gained prominence. The emphasis on 'conflict' is therefore broader to capture the multiple types of armed conflict. French language contributions do not make such a separation (Jean and Rufin, 1996; Daguzan and Lorot, 2003). Conflict economies are usually referred to as *économies de guerres* (war economies) or as *économies de guerres civiles* (economies of civil wars). The direct translation from conflict economies—*économies des conflits armés*—is not common.

Official definitions

Most of the attention on conflict economies at the political level has been devoted to individual commodities such as conflict diamonds, timber, and other natural resources. Even though non-governmental organizations and academia have put forward definitions on 'conflict goods', 'conflict commodities', and 'conflict trade', these have not been officially endorsed by governments in international organizations. One exception is the case of conflict diamonds. The UN Security Council defines conflict diamonds as 'diamonds that originate in areas controlled by forces fighting the legitimate and internationally recognized government of the relevant country' (UN Security Council, 2000: para 145).

This definition highlights the political sensitivities of defining conflict economies. While the in-built state bias of the definition of conflict diamonds is an outcome of a bargaining process between states, it also shows the difficulty to link the financing of armed conflict with the legitimacy to use force. States have a monopoly on the use of force and therefore claim to have the legitimate right to use state resources to pay for coercive means. However, the financing for all those challenging the state is considered illegitimate. Hence, as in the context of Angola in the 1990s, conflict diamonds were an illegitimate source of financing for the *União Nacional Para a Independência Total de Angola* (UNITA) because it was a non-state armed group, while the government could legitimately use oil revenues for conflict financing. Official definitions may therefore be less a reflection of dealing with 'the link between [conflict] goods and violence per se than the role these goods play in supporting actors deemed pariah by the West' (Cooper, 2001: 30).

Comments on the proposed definition

The proposed concept of conflict economies provides the foundation for a broad understanding of the economic aspects of armed conflict relevant for peacebuilding. It considers all economic activities taking place during conflict and captures macro-economic perspectives on conflict economies and their impact on recovery, as well as the transformative effects of armed conflict that have consequences for peacebuilding and post-conflict economies (see more generally the chapter on conflict transformation). In order to mobilize the full potential of post-conflict economies in support of peacebuilding, economic continuities in the transition from war to peace should not be overlooked. Armed conflict has such profound effects on economic relations that reconnecting 'post-conflict' to 'pre-conflict' economies is an illusion. Instead, engagement on post-conflict economies should build on immediate post-conflict economic contexts.

II. Content

Conflict economies have implications for post-conflict peacebuilding in terms of the economic legacies and the cost of conflict, its financing, and the evolution of conflict economies. This content of the concept of conflict economies also illustrates the interlinkages between combat, shadow, and survival economies and their implication for post-conflict economies.

The economic legacies and cost of conflict

Economists often describe armed conflict as an anomaly of 'normal' economic development and look at the direct and long-term economic effects of armed conflict. The direct effects are, of course, the destruction of infrastructure, capital flight, and reduced investment, which together affect the economic performance of a conflict country. In addition, armed conflict reduces human security as violence shortens planning horizons, increases opportunistic behaviour, fosters impunity, and erodes property rights (Collier *et al*, 2003: 16–19).

State finances are also affected by armed conflict. Warfare represents a diversion of productive activity towards destruction and leads to increased military spending while state revenues decline due to lower tax revenues and foreign direct investment (FDI). In addition, economies become less productive due to rising levels of insecurity, a decrease in formal economic transaction, and the undermining of the rule of law. State revenues can also decline if a government loses control over resource-rich areas of the country. To bridge the gaps in public finances, many government resort to printing money and aggressive taxation (Collier *et al*, 2008: 41). As a consequence, post-conflict economies inherit high levels of public expenditure, inflation, and debt that in turn stifle recovery and business confidence in the post-conflict period.

In recent years, a number of attempts have been made to estimate the cost of armed conflict. One estimate suggests that the costs of a civil war are between US$60 and $250 billion, or an average of $123 billion (Collier *et al*, 2008: 22). In Africa, the annual economic costs of armed conflict have been estimated at around $18 billion (IANSA, 2007). Recent endeavours to estimate the cost of interpersonal violence have contributed to a better understanding of the cost drivers of armed violence (Butchart *et al*, 2008; see Table 4). The estimates and cost factors not only exemplify the opportunity costs of armed conflict and violence, they also highlight the challenges of long-term recovery.

Table 4 Cost factors of armed conflict and inter-personal violence

Direct costs	Medical and rehabilitation cost due to casualties, injuries, and increased disabilities
	Policing, criminal justice system, private security
	Military expenditure
	Care for refugees and internally displaced persons
	Physical destruction, including infrastructure and livelihood assets
Indirect costs	Macroeconomic consequences of inflation, reduced savings, losses in investment and exports
	Capital flight
	Loss of development aid
	Wealth transfers from formal to informal economies
Intangible costs	Quality of life (pain, suffering, trauma)
	Reduced job opportunities and access to schools and public services
	Limited participation in community life
	Inter-generational impacts
Economic multiplier effects	Reduced productive activity and productivity losses due to insecurity, limited mobility, a smaller workforce, work hours lost, and lower incomes
	Lower accumulation of human capital
Social multiplier effects	Loss of social capital
	Inter-generational transmission of violence
	The privatization of policing
	Lower political participation

(Butchart *et al*, 2008; IANSA *et al*, 2007)

A review of these cost factors clearly illustrates the fact that armed conflict has long-lasting effects on human security. These effects include, for example, higher levels of military spending, missed investment, capital flight, and the loss of social capital. At societal level, legacies include the psychological scars of war as well as increased illness and disease, such as higher levels of HIV/AIDS. As a result, it is often argued that armed conflict has no positive transformative effects but serves only as an obstacle to development: 'If poor economic conditions cause civil wars, then we may be able to design economic policy interventions that reduce their occurrence, mitigating the human suffering that they cause' (Collier and Sambanis, 2005: xiii). Such a rationale justifies an interventionist agenda and the need for post-conflict aid, peace operations, security guarantees, and caps on military spending (Collier *et al*, 2008).

The financing of conflict

Much of the recent attention on combat economies has focused on natural resources and their relationship to armed conflict. However, natural resources are just one way of financing conflict. Other methods include centralized war economies, external assistance from governments or diasporas, asset transfers from civilians, the printing and forging of banknotes, protection rackets, landing fees, kidnapping, portfolio investments, and legitimate business ventures (Wennmann, 2007a). In order to understand combat economies, it is necessary to differentiate these strategies. Weinstein, for example, affirms that 'patterns of violence are a direct consequence of endowments leaders have at their disposal as they organise' (Weinstein, 2007: 20). Resource-rich groups recruit opportunistic soldiers with coercive strategies; resource-poor groups recruit activist-minded soldiers with participatory strategies. Resource-rich groups can mobilize more quickly than resource-poor groups. This indicates that non-state actors have different organizational and financial requirements at different stages of their formation, which in turn can affect their resilience.

Recent advances in small arms research have made it possible to compare the availability of revenues to the cost of mobilization. Using estimates for the cost of weapons and ammunition, start-up costs have been estimated between US$67,500 and $450,000 per 1,000 soldiers. While these figures are still moderate, the maintenance of armed conflict is much higher: between $2.1 million and $34.8 million per 1,000 soldiers per year depending on the level of intensity (Wennmann, 2007c: 138). These figures suggest that the critical element in conflict financing is the availability of revenue to meet the financial requirements for the type of armed conflict needed to reach a particular objective. Armed conflicts in Angola, Georgia, and Kosovo show that belligerents do not always 'cover their costs during the conflict' (Collier and Hoeffler, 2004: 654) and that this is why these conflicts could not escalate (Wennmann, 2007c).

Potentially, a better understanding of the feasibility of armed conflict could have significant benefits for the sustainability of peacebuilding, especially in terms of reducing the risk of conflict recurrence. There is evidence that the ability of peace spoilers to undermine peacebuilding depends on the means they control for this purpose (Greenhill and Major, 2007: 36).

The evolution of conflict economies

Conflict economies have dynamic characteristics, changing over time and according to the context. One attempt to conceptualize this change is based on the interaction of the type of conflict economy (predation, parasite, or extraction) and the military strategy of armed groups (contention, expansion, or control) (Naylor, 2002: 45–7; 53–4). The different stages in this evolution include:

• *Predation-Contention:* The conflict economy is predatory and the military strategy is based on contention with government forces. Armed groups operate in areas formally under state control and in order to destabilize the state and raise funds, they conduct hit-and-run attacks, such as killings, kidnappings, burglaries, or bank robberies. At this stage, expenditure requirements are small as the armed group itself is small and operations are relatively small scale.

- *Parasite-Expansion:* As armed groups grow in size and territorial reach, the conflict economy becomes increasingly parasitical. Operations take place in a particular geographic area in which the group expands control. The military strategy shifts from hit-and-run attacks to low-intensity warfare and economic strategies to weaken the government. As the formal economy declines and the government loses fiscal revenues, an armed group captures a bigger share of the shadow economy and is strengthened through additional revenues.

- *Extraction-Territorial Control:* Insurgents establish control over an area from which the state is excluded. In this area, an armed group becomes the *de facto* government and runs social services, arbitration and a taxation system. The latter generates funding to continue military activities. These areas can ultimately evolve into a '*de facto* state' in which an armed group establishes control over a territory and its population and then creates institutions.

Armed groups to which this dynamism have applied include the Shining Path in Peru, the National People's Army in the Philippines, the Bougainville rebels in Papua New Guinea, the Khmer Rouge in Cambodia, the Tamil Tigers in Sri Lanka, UNITA in Angola, the Maoist rebels in Nepal, and the *Fuerzas Armadas Revolucionarias Colombianas* (FARC) in Colombia (Naylor, 2002: 45–7, 53–4) (see more generally the chapter on non-state actors).

The importance for peacebuilding of the evolution of conflict economies lies in how it shapes relations between armed groups and local populations. In Colombia, for example, the labour-intensive nature of coca harvesting became the main survival economy in the remote rain forest area under the control of the FARC. By providing the conditions that made a livelihood possible, the FARC could legitimize itself in the eyes of the local population as the authority of a *de-facto* state (Guáqueta, 2003: 79–80). This example illustrates the difficulty faced by peacebuilding in seeking to overcome resistance by local populations and provide livelihoods in areas with few alternative economic opportunities.

These accounts stand in contrast to a more macro-economic understanding of conflict economies as a 'black box' that represents an interruption of a liner process of economic development. This is found, for instance, in the emphasis in peacebuilding terminology on the 're', as in *re*-integration, *re*-habilitation, or *re*-construction. However, the notion of *re*-connecting to the period prior to the onset of fighting may not account for the social and economic transformations taking place during armed conflict (Cramer, 2006: 197). Identifying and maximizing the positive unintended consequences of economic transformations during armed conflict can be used to strengthen peacebuilding.

Actors in conflict economies

Conflict economies are embedded in the globalized economy and transnational networks. These networks link conflict zones to international arms, and commodity and financial markets, and facilitate the conversion of illicit and criminal profits into legitimate sources of revenue. Actors can include transnational organized crime networks (TOCNs), PMCs, and resource-extraction companies (see the chapter on private sector). TOCNs are involved in conflict zones for profit-making and do not tend to be directly involved in the political dimensions of an armed conflict or combat operations. They are profiting from supplying weapons and providing logistical services, or run business operations that are internationally outlawed (Naylor 2002, 31–2).

PMCs are for-profit organizations that offer professional services linked to armed conflict, including implementation and command structures, advice, and training. PMC can give non-state armed groups or governments a military advantage by facilitating their access to international arms markets. Their services can be paid by futures contracts, concessions, or royalties for resource exploitation. In these circumstances, some PMCs have developed vertically integrated business structures that include a resource extraction and logistics component (Singer, 2003: 88–100).

Natural-resource-extracting companies are linked to conflict areas because this is where many natural resource deposits are located. Companies can be trapped if a country slips into conflict and the magnitude of investments makes a retreat commercially ruinous (Wennmann, 2007b: 86). However, most companies shy away from the risks of working in conflict zones even though some smaller 'rough' companies are attracted by the risk premiums of doing business during conflict. Natural-resource companies can also foster grievances among the local population due to unsustainable production processes, environmental impacts, and human rights abuses.

Other actors in conflict economies include relief or development agencies. Even though aid workers provide life-saving support, in a context of scarcity, development assistance and relief are precious commodities. If distributed wrongly, they can reinforce social antagonisms and insecurity, rather than alleviate them (Anderson, 1999: 37–53). More recently, military actors have also become involved in development assistance, reconstruction, and stabilization during conflict as part of a strategy to win the 'hearts and minds' of the people. Examples are Provincial Reconstruction Teams in Afghanistan and Iraq. However, critics highlight that the entry of military actors into the humanitarian space has undermined the neutrality of humanitarian assistance, subordinating it to military objectives (see the chapter on civil-military interface). The way that relief and development aid is delivered during the conflict can shape the attitudes of people towards post-conflict assistance. As distinctions between military stabilization, humanitarian relief, and development assistance become increasingly blurred, local actors can perceive post-conflict economic recovery as a continuation of an externally driven agenda rather than a locally owned peacebuilding process (see the chapter on local ownership).

Identifying which actors have been involved in conflict economies is important for the recovery of post-conflict economies. While many of the profit-oriented intermediaries move elsewhere at the end of the combat economy, others may stay and provide formidable challenges for peacebuilding efforts. These actors may have little interest in peacebuilding if this means state building and the provision of security, representation, and welfare. By controlling the shadow economy in the post-conflict phase, these actors can impede peacebuilding, using armed violence to perpetuate insecurity.

III. Implementation

A better understanding of conflict economies opens new opportunities for peacebuilding and efforts to assist the recovery of post-conflict economies. These opportunities are related to disarmament, demobilization, and reintegration, economic recovery, the private sector, and the inclusion of economic issues in peace processes. However, addressing the remnants of conflict economies in the post-conflict phase also generates dilemmas, especially when seeking to target conflict financing and shadow economies.

Economic policy for post-conflict recovery

Policy engagement on the post-conflict economy lies at the fault line of institutional mandates to address political, security, or economic issues. While the first two usually concern the UN, economic issues fall within the mandate of the International Financial Institutions. The UN Peacebuilding Commission provides a forum to go beyond these divisions and foster a coherent, coordinated and integrated economic approach to peacebuilding and economic recovery.

One contentious area of economic policy is the role of the state in economic affairs. While much of liberal economics seeks to reduce that role, experience from conflict and post-conflict settings highlights the importance of the state as guarantor of security, welfare, justice, and representation. The Organisation for Economic Co-operation and Development (OECD) Principles for Good International Engagement in Fragile States and Situations, for example, recognize the centrality of 'supporting the legitimacy and accountability of states' and 'strengthening the capability of states to fulfil their core functions'. Another complication for economic policy is that the distinction between the political and economic sphere does not always exist in post-conflict settings. Rather, as the 2005 World Summit 'Outcome Document' observes, 'development, peace and security, and human rights are interlinked and mutually reinforcing'. Thus, there is a mutual interdependence between economic policies and peacebuilding strategies, as exemplified by need for peace dividends, employment, and state building.

The signature of a peace agreement is often followed by a transition period in which belligerents are expected to disarm and demobilize in return for the promise of a better future. In this period, belligerents and populations develop expectations of peace dividends that result from the channelling of resources away from war-making to productive uses. In order to avoid public disappointment with the immediate-post-conflict peace process, a priority for post-conflict economic policy is to support the creation of peace dividends (Wennmann, 2007b: 79). As part of the UN Peacebuilding Commission, the Peacebuilding Fund has been created to support this critical time when other funding and assistance mechanisms may not yet be available.

Another economic policy priority is the creation of labour and education opportunities. Many post-conflict contexts face large groups of soldiers who need to be demobilized, and provided with a meaningful alternative occupation (Collier, 2005: 54–5). In the context of depressed post-conflict economies this is a herculean task, particularly if conflict economies made the use of force a function of appropriation and predation. Labour creation can occur through public employment programmes, market based-economic activities, or the toleration of parallel employment opportunities. Public employment programmes are a preferred tool by governments as they support a new state-society relationship and assist in reconstructing infrastructure (see the chapter on recovery). However, they also introduce market inefficiencies though the inflation of the public sector and budget deficits, and can undermine an emerging private sector. Informal markets are important to labour creation because they tend to persist during armed conflict as survival economies (Landow, 2006).

Another priority area for economic policy is in efforts to strengthen the capacity of the state to mobilize, allocate, and spend resources. Such capacity-building is important to consolidate state finances, foster an independent resource base, and prevent aid dependence in the long term. Such a policy often includes the gradual co-option of the informal into the formal economy, increasing the capture of tax revenue, and the promotion of market-based activities. In addition, this promotes the legitimacy of the state in the eyes of the population as it delivers essential services, thereby emphasizing the two-way relationship of fiscal policy in which 'governments need revenue in order to provide services, but they must provide services in order for people to be willing to pay taxes' (Boyce and O'Donnell, 2007: 6).

The development of a unified fiscal system in post-conflict environments also entails security risks, particularly if profitable shadow economies outlive the end of an armed conflict, and its stakeholders use force to protect their spoils (Wennmann, 2005: 487). Fiscal policy in post-conflict context also has to deal with different perspectives on fiscal centralization and decentralization. Governments and International Financial Institutions tend to favour fiscal centralization—the former because of the political functions of redistributing state resources, the latter to prevent budget deficits accrued by sub-national authorities. Many development agencies, however, prefer fiscal decentralization because public investment decision can be more closely determined by local needs and thereby foster democratic governance by increasing local ownership and transparency.

In the long term, state-building certainly also has to address macro-economic, legal, or military issues that in turn foster recovery. Economic policy should occur with due consideration to inflation as increasing prices undermine post-conflict economic growth and peace dividends. Moreover, the re-establishment and enforcement of property rights and the rule of law is essential to foster economic activities of both local and international companies (Collier, 2005: 54–5). In addition, private sector development initiatives can be supported by reforming business regulations and trade policy, promoting geographical and sectoral market linkages and value chains, and supporting local economies through microfinance (Bagwitz *et al*, 2008).

Ultimately, economic policy in post-conflict settings should be placed within broader political contexts. The experience of large-scale privatization schemes or reducing public sector expenditures in the 1990s illustrate, for example, how these were used to transform the governance of fragile states. Privatization and public sector reform were used by some rulers to cut off political opponents from economic opportunities—thereby limiting their power—while fortifying their own patronage network and power base. In this way, governments reduced the political significance of the state and its institutions while increasingly relying on markets and informal networks (Reno, 1998: 21–2).

Private sector investment

Private sector investment is often held to decrease in conflict countries as a reaction to increasing transaction and transport costs, the disruption of labour and goods markets, and attacks on physical assets and staff of companies. Nevertheless, investors are far from homogenous in their sensitivity to political risk, as the consequences of armed violence largely depend on the characteristics of investments. These include, for example, the magnitude of physical assets, the level of exit costs, whether outputs are for foreign or domestic markets, or part of an integrated production cycle. Investments in energy and natural resources are more vulnerable to armed violence while investments in financial, education, other professional services, telecommunication, or construction face a lower exposure to armed violence. These factors may explain why some conflict countries did not experience a downward shift in FDI. Colombia and Algeria, for example, increased its level of FDI during the years of armed conflict and the DRC and Eritrea even had high peaks (Mihalache, 2008: 2–5, 49–50). The risk perception of companies also depends on the distribution of armed violence. If a company has its main activities in the capital but most of the fighting takes place in remote areas of the country, violence has little effect on business.

Such a nuanced analysis of FDI in conflict countries underlines the constructive role that the private sector and FDI could play in fostering economic recovery. Both local and international companies sensitive to violence should be unified as a lobby for violence reduction. Even those companies less affected by violence can play important roles as advocates for the rule of law and property rights. Strategies such as joint ventures, project financing, risk insurance, or export credit guarantees can be used to reduce and spread risk for investors.

Diasporas have a particularly high potential to invest in their home country after an armed conflict. Due to existing family and cultural ties they are less risk-averse and investments—or small scale remittances to family members—can be an immediate relief to a post-conflict economy, representing an important social safety net. However, investment attitudes of diasporas depend on the circumstances and time period of emigration as well as the assimilation policies of host states (Bercovitch, 2007: 34–7).

Targeting the revenue sources of armed groups in post-conflict economies

Targeting conflict financing is a policy that can be used against states and non-state actors. It can involve the use of sanctions but also the tracking of financial transactions of particular companies or black-listing individuals. Most recently, such approaches have been applied against the financing of terrorism. Targeting the revenue sources of armed groups in post-conflict economies is particularly important to prevent the recurrence of conflict.

A widely known initiative against conflict financing is the international diamond certification scheme, the Kimberley Process. A civil society campaign effectively publicized the linkages between diamonds and armed conflict, and changed industry reaction from denial to engagement. However, once the link was exposed, the multi-stakeholder coalition behind the Kimberley Process was mainly motivated by commercial concerns. Diamond companies wanted to address the parallel market in diamonds—of which conflict diamonds were just a small part—and improve competitiveness through vertical integration from the mine to the market. Governments of diamond-producing states saw the Kimberley Process as an opportunity to centralize and expand state revenue (Smillie, 2005: 53–60). Others also point out that the focus on conflict diamonds was part of partisan intervention in the Angola, DRC, Liberia, and Sierra Leone. Policies targeting conflict financing are therefore rarely about peace, but rather part of broader political, economic, or military agendas. This is illustrated by the absence of sanctions against Liberian timber. Chinese and French interests blocked a sanctions regime in the UN Security Council even though timber is easier to target than some other resources (Cooper, 2002: 949–50).

Policies against conflict financing tend to outlast the end of an armed conflict and represent a challenge for peacebuilding. Sanctions, for example, do not end automatically with the end of a conflict. In a post-conflict context, sanctions have been used to compel parties to enact credible reforms and implement peacebuilding provisions. In Liberia, restrictions to participate in the Kimberley Process were not lifted as long as the national diamond industry failed to deliver comprehensive reforms (UN Security Council, 2006: para 52). However, using the withdrawal of sanctions as an incentive for change only works as long as there is a willingness to withdraw them at one point. If not, they may feed public disillusionment and provide political entrepreneurs with a rallying platform against peacebuilding (Wennmann, 2007b: 78).

The management of revenue sources of armed groups is also important in the context of the promotion of democratic governance and a multi-party system. Continued access to revenue sources is essential for an armed group's transformation to political party and the development of an autonomous policy platform. Such continuity, however, often involves difficult judgements on the genuineness of a transformation process and the abuse of party financing as a smoke-screen for the financing of conflict recurrence.

The dilemmas of dealing with shadow economies

Shadow economies often outlive the end of an armed conflict and confront policy-makers with three dilemmas. The first is finding the right balance between the promotion of order and a legitimate economy, and the short-term provision of economic satisfaction of the population. Shadow economies prevent the creation of an independent revenue base and thereby undermine the consolidation of state finances in the long term. They do, however, include livelihood opportunities and contribute to economic satisfaction in the short term. A middle path may be to adopt a sector-specific perspective. Like every regular economy, a shadow economy is composed of different sectors and not a monolithic block. Such an approach separates the shadow economy into separate flows of goods and services, and assesses social impacts and possible areas resistance (Wennmann, 2005: 489–91).

The second dilemma is identifying a short-term balance between confrontation and cooptation in the management of shadow economies. A confrontational approach may provoke violent counter-reactions by those who feel that their profits or livelihoods are being threatened. In Kosovo, for example, a confrontational approach was deemed counter-productive in terms of maintaining security (Yannis 2004: 184). In sensitive post-conflict contexts, the choice is between confronting stakeholders and risking higher levels of post-conflict violence, or coopting them, but with the risk of their entrenchment in the post-conflict economy.

The third dilemma is the management of stakeholders that are more powerful than the state or the donor community. In Afghanistan, the revenues from drugs are far greater then the national budget or international donor assistance. If shadow economy stakeholders are able to hold entire countries hostage to socio-economic destitution or violence, government and donor agencies should find ways to engage with these groups. This involves difficult decisions concerning whether to tolerate the shadow economy in return for the toleration of peace-building activities by the other side. There is, however, also the risk that instead of the state co-opting the shadow economy, the shadow economy co-opts the state in order to to control law-making and security institutions to protect its business.

Economic issues in peace processes and peacebuilding

About one-third of the 58 negotiated settlements that ended armed conflicts between 1990 and 2005 relapsed back into armed conflict in the first five years (HSRP, 2008: 35). This figure underlines the question of whether and how the type, content, and quality of a peace agreement can support peacebuilding. In this perspective, peacebuilding is part of the continuum of conflict management and therefore preceded by mediation processes, a peace agreement, and humanitarian relief or peace operations. As peacebuilding comes at a later stage, it inherits flaws from previous phases. This is why there may be some policy opportunities that derive from moving peacebuilding 'upstream' into the peace process.

An overview of the economic dimension in peace mediation highlights some opportunities for peacebuilding (Wennmann, 2007b). These include, for example, that negotiations on economic issues can help create economic futures and a vision of society by jointly designing institutions for democratic governance. In addition, discussions on economic issues can manage expectations in the economy by making available to the parties knowledge about future production and revenue possibilities. This was the case in Sudan, where representatives from Southern Sudan initially overestimated the revenue potential of oil. Economic provisions in peace agreements could address the spoiler problem by establishing how and by whom the economy will be controlled. However, this is often complicated, as seen in the DRC,—because those implicated in the combat and shadow economy had little interest to be exposed on their business affairs. Ultimately, agreement on economic provisions in the peace agreement assists conflict transformation by shortening the transition period between demobilization and the materialization of peace dividends. Agreement on economic provisions may accelerate the receipt of benefits to ex-combatants and post-conflict populations through employment or education opportunities that in turn support return and reintegration and disarmament, demobilization, and reintegration processes.

Despite these opportunities, their impact on peacebuilding must be considered in relation to the functions that the main parties attach to a peace process. If it is part of a strategic decision to relocate confrontations from the battlefield to the negotiation table, few positive long-term effects can be expected. However, if parties are engaging in peace talks to end an armed conflict, much may be gained for peacebuilding by including economic issues in a peace process.

Selected Bibliography

Anderson, MB (1999), *Do No Harm: How Aid Can Support Peace—or War*, Boulder: Lynne Rienner Publishers.

Arnson, C, & Zartman, IW (eds) (2005), *Rethinking the Economics of War: The Intersection of Need, Creed and Greed*, Washington DC: Hopkins University Press.

Bagwitz, D, Elges, R, Grossmann, H, & Kruk, H (2008), *Private Sector Development in (Post-) Conflict Situations*, Eschborn: Deutsche Gesellschaft für Technische Zusammenarbeit.

Ballentine, K (2003), 'Beyond Greed and Grievance: Reconsidering the Economic Dynamics of Armed Conflict', in Ballentine, K, & Sherman, J (eds), *The Political Economy of Armed Conflict: Beyond Greed and Grievance*, Boulder: Lynne Rienner Publishers, 259–83.

—— & Sherman, J (eds) (2003), *The Political Economy of Armed Conflict: Beyond Greed and Grievance*, Boulder: Lynne Rienner Publishers.

Bercovitch, J (2007), 'The Neglected Relationship: Diasporas and Conflict Resolution' in Smith, H, & Stares, P (eds), *Diasporas in Conflict: Peace-makers or Peace-wreckers?*, Tokyo: UN University Press, 17–38.

Boyce, JK, & O'Donnell, M (eds) (2007), *Peace and the Public Purse: Economic Policies for Postwar Statebuilding*, Boulder: Lynne Rienner Publishers.

Butchart, A, Brown, D, Khanh-Huynh, A, Corso, P, Florquin, N, & Muggah, R (2008), *Manual for Estimating the Economic Costs of Injuries due to Interpersonal and Self-directed Violence*, Geneva: World Health Organization.

Collier, P (2005), 'Economic Policy in Post-conflict Societies', in Kwasi Fosu, A & Collier, P (eds), *Post-conflict Economies in Africa*, Houndmills: Palgrave Macmillan.

—— Elliott, L, Hegre, H, Hoeffler, A, Reynal-Querol, M, & Sambanis, N (2003), *Breaking the Conflict Trap: Civil War and Development Policy*, Washington, DC: World Bank.

—— & Hoeffler, A (2004), 'Greed and Grievance in Civil War', in *Oxford Economic Papers*, 56/4: 563–95.

—— & Sambanis, N (eds) (2005), *Understanding Civil War: Evidence and Analysis*, Washington DC: World Bank.

—— Hoeffler, A & Rohner, D (2007), *Beyond Greed and Grievance: Feasibility and Civil War*, Centre for the Study of African Economies Working Paper Series 2006/10, Oxford: University of Oxford.

—— Chauvet, L, & Hegre, H (2008), *The Security Challenge in Conflict-prone Countries*, Copenhagen: Copenhagen Consensus Centre.

Cooper, N (2001), 'Conflict Goods: The Challenges for Peacekeeping and Conflict Prevention', in *International Peacekeeping*, 8/3: 21–38.

—— (2002), 'State Collapse as Business: The Role of Conflict Trade and Their Emerging Control Agenda', in *Development and Change*, 33/5: 935–55.

Cramer, C (2006): *Civil War is not a Stupid Thing: Accounting for Violence in Developing Countries*, London: Hurst and Company Publishers.

Daguzan, J -F & Lorot, P (eds) (2003), *Guerre et Economie*, Paris: Ellipses.

Greenhill, KM, & Major, S (2007), 'The Perils of Profiling: Spoilers and the Collapse of Intrastate Peace Accords', in *International Security*, 31/3: 1–40.

Guáqueta, A (2003), 'The Colombian Conflict: Political and Economic Dimensions', in Ballentine, K and Sherman, J (eds), *The Political Economy of Armed Conflict: Beyond Greed and Grievance*, Boulder: Lynne Rienner Publishers, 73–106.

HSRP (Human Security Report Project) (2007), *Human Security Brief 2007*, Vancouver: Simon Frazer University.

IANSA (International Action Network on Small Arms), Oxfam International, & Saferworld (2007), *Africa's Missing Billions*, London: IANSA.

Jean, F, & Rufin, J -C (eds) (1996), *Economie des guerres civiles*, Paris: Hachette.

Kaldor, M (1999), *New and Old Wars: Organised Violence in a Global Era*, Cambridge: Polity Press.

Keen, D (1998), *The Economic Functions of Civil War*, Adelphi Papers No 320, London: International Institute for Strategic Studies.

King, C (1997), *Ending Civil Wars*, Adelphi Papers No 308, London: International Institute for Strategic Studies.

Landow, C (ed) (2006), *Guidelines for Employment in Crises*, Geneva: International Labour Organization and the Graduate Institute of International Studies.

Mihalache, AS (2008), 'Gambling on Conflict: Profiling Investments in Conflict Countries', paper dated 20 March for the Midwest Political Science Association 66th Annual Convention, Chicago, April 2008.

Naylor, RT (2002), *Wages of Crime: Black Markets, Illegal Finance, and the Underworld Economy*, Ithaca: Cornell University Press.

OECD – DAC (2007), *Principles for Good International Engagement in Fragile States Situations*, OECD, 4 April.

Pugh, M, & Cooper, N (2004), *War Economies in a Regional Context: Challenges and Transformations*, Boulder: Lynne Rienner Publishers.

Reno, W (1998), *Warlord Politics and African States*, Boulder, Lynne Rienner Publishers.

Rufin, J -C (1996), 'Les économies des guerres dans les conflits internes', in Jean, F & Rufin, J -C (eds), *Economie des guerres civiles*, Paris: Hachette, 19–59.

Singer, PW (2003), *Corporate Warriors: The Rise of the Privatized Military Industry*, Ithaca: Cornell University Press.

Smillie, I (2005), 'What Lessons from the Kimberley Process Certification Scheme?' in Ballentine, K & Nitzschke, H (eds), *Profiting from Peace: Managing the Resource Dimension of Civil War*, Boulder: Lynne Rienner, 47–67.

Suhrke, A, & Samset, I (2007), 'What's in a Figure? Estimating Recurrence of Civil War', in *International Peacekeeping*, 14/2: 195–203.

Tilly, C (1992), *Coercion, Capital and European States, AD 990–1992*, Oxford: Blackwell.

UN General Assembly (2005), *(2005) World Summit Outcome*, A/RES/60/1, New York: UN.

UN Security Council (2000), *Report of the United Nations Sierra Leone Sanctions Committee Expert Panel—December 2000*, New York: UN.

—— (2006), *Report of the Panel of Experts Concerning Liberia*, S/2006/076, New York: UN.

Weinstein, J (2007), *Inside Rebellion: The Politics of Insurgent Violence*, Cambridge: Cambridge University Press.

Wennmann, A (2005), 'Resourcing the Recurrence of Intra-state Conflict: Parallel Economies and Their Implications for Peace Building', in *Security Dialogue*, 36/4: 479–94.

—— (2007a), 'The Political Economy of Conflict Financing: A Comprehensive Approach Beyond Natural Resources', in *Global Governance*, 13/3: 427–44.

—— (2007b), *Money Matters: The Economic Dimensions of Peace Mediation*, PSIS Occasional Paper 4, Geneva: Graduate Institute of International Studies.

—— (2007c), *Conflict Financing and the Recurrence of Intra-state Armed Conflict: What Can Be Done from the Perspective of Conflict Financing to Prevent the Recurrence of Intra-state Armed Conflict?*, Doctoral Dissertation, Geneva: Graduate Institute of International Studies.

Yannis, A (2004), 'The UN as Government in Kosovo', in *Global Governance*, 10/1: 67–81.

Conflict Transformation

*Laurent Goetschel**

Definition

Conflict transformation in the field of post-conflict peacebuilding refers to a process in which parties to a conflict consciously work towards a modification of the structural dimensions of a conflict with the short-term objective of prevention of renewed violence (or a reduction in its intensity) and with the long-term objective of sustainable peace.

I. Term

Origin and context

The concept of 'conflict transformation' emerged in the late 1960s and early 1970s in the context of both early conflict research and, in the field of development research, 'dependency-thinking'. The idea that conflicts are linked to deeper structures in society, at national and international level, was already present in the early work of peace researchers like Senghaas (1973) or Krippendorf (1973). They emphasized the relationship between smaller, national conflicts and larger conflicts embedded in the structure of world society and international economy. For Galtung (1996: 70–126) conflicts are due to contradictions in the structure of society. The incompatibility which arises between parties might be eliminated by transcending these contradictions, by compromise, by deepening or widening the conflict structure, or by associating or dissociating the actors.

Galtung's notion of transcendency builds on the assumption that conflicts have both positive and negative—or life-affirming and life-destroying—aspects. Curle (1971) traces how asymmetric relationships can be transformed through a

---

* This paper is partially based on work supported by the Swiss National Centre of Competence in Research (NCCR) North-South: Research Partnerships for Mitigating Syndromes of Global Change (<http://www.north-south.unibe.ch>).

shift from unbalanced to balanced relationships. Development, a key to Curle's positive peace concept, involves the 'restructuring of a relationship so that the conflict or alienation that had previously rendered it unpeaceful is eliminated and replaced by a collaboration that prevents it from recurring' (Curle, 1971: 259).

The end of the Cold War and the UN Secretary General's 'An Agenda for Peace' in 1992 provided new opportunities to develop the concept of conflict transformation within the framework of peacebuilding. However, the focus on positive aspects of conflicts and on the primordial role of conflict parties themselves fundamentally differentiates a conflict transformation approach from conflict settlement, management, or resolution approaches, as follows:

- The *conflict settlement* approach—mediation, conciliation, negotiation—starts from an acceptance of a given political and socio-economic *status quo*. The transformational approach, however, begins by assuming that there is nothing sacred about the *status quo*; indeed, it is probably the source of the conflict (Mitchell, 2002: 15);

- *Conflict management* sees violent conflicts as a consequence of differences of values and interests within and between communities. The propensity to violence stems from institutions, historical relationships, and the distribution of power. Management is about the art of appropriate intervention to achieve political settlements, particularly by those actors having the power and resources to bring pressure on the conflict parties in order to induce them to settle (Miall, 2004: 69);

- *Conflict resolution* is about how parties can move from zero-sum destructive patterns of conflict to positive-sum constructive outcomes. The aim is to develop processes of conflict resolution that appear to be acceptable to parties and effective in resolving conflict (Azar & Burton, 1986: 1).

Obstacles of linguistic or semantic nature

From a linguistic perspective, the term 'transformation' provides no major problems. It refers to 'a thorough or dramatic change in the form, or appearance' (New Oxford Dictionary of English). In French, its meaning is somewhat broader, as it means 'to transfer from one shape to another, to give a different aspect, other formal features' (Petit Robert). In German, the expression '*Konfliktbearbeitung*' is less well-known to non-specialists. It remains very open, as any work on conflict may be covered. Thus, the English term seems best suited, because it is deeper in nature and more precise. Concerning the term 'conflict', the latter may be defined as a social relation between two or more actors, out of which at least one is being consciously harmed over a longer period of time by one or several of the other parties.

Possible acceptance and meanings

The transformational approach to conflicts builds on a specific understanding of conflicts which combines structural and constructivist elements. Its basic assumption is that conflicts often have causes or reasons more fundamental than the ones directly expressed on the level of disputes. Conflict transformation refers to efforts employed to work on these structural conditions of conflicts, whereby the objective is not to prevent or eradicate conflicts. Conflicts are not seen as deviance from regular social behaviour; on the contrary, they are seen as catalysts of social change and might therefore even be promoted (Kriesberg, 2003). However, for certain reasons, conflicts may be ill-guided and prone to violence. The latter is the real problem, not the conflict itself (Francis, 2002: 54). In line with the assumed understanding of conflicts, the reasons for such violence are of a structural nature.

What should be transformed? The structural conditions of conflict have two dimensions: what may be called a substantive dimension referring to actual political, economic, social, etc, discrimination against conflict parties, and a relational dimension consisting of perceptions and impressions resulting from parties' current and past interactions. The relational dimension is based on a constructivist analytical approach to conflict parties' interests, meaning that these interests should be treated as endogenous to—ie originating from within—any conflict analysis framework. They may be changed using adequate methods and tools (Wendt, 1999). This differentiates the conflict transformation approach from the bulk of conflict theories that regard the issues, actors, and interests as given and on that basis makes efforts to find a solution to mitigate or eliminate contradictions between them. This specificity of conflict transformation sheds light upon the framing and understanding of the contested issues, the acknowledgement of the legitimacy of the other party, the sense of responsibility for the origins of the conflict, consciousness of the other parties' perspectives and objectives, and the acknowledgement of the existence of past grievances (Mitchell, 2002: 9).

The two structural dimensions of conflict are reflected in the contingency approach to conflict intervention developed by Fisher and Keashly (1991: 34) and for whom objective and subjective conflict elements permanently interact. A balanced relevance of both conflict dimensions may also be found in the systemic approach to conflict transformation developed by the Berghof Foundation, which stresses the non-linear features and multiple escalation and de-escalation paths of conflict dynamics (Dudouet, 2006). Most transformational conflict approaches, however, stress the second, relational, dimension of conflicts. In the transformational view, conflict is primarily about human interaction rather than violations of rights or conflicts of interest. Conflict is part of the basic dynamic of human interaction in which people struggle to balance their own concerns with connections to others. When this balance is upset, human interaction becomes alienated and destructive. There is a crisis in human interaction.

The 'transformative framework' (or transformative model of mediation) developed by Bush and Folger (1994) posits that people have the capacity to regain their footing and shift back to a restored sense of strength or confidence in themselves (empowerment shift) and openness or responsiveness to others (recognition shift). The model assumes that this transformation of the interaction itself is what matters most to parties in conflict—even more than resolution on favourable terms. It is based on a relational view of the world. Conflict transformation must actively envision, include, respect, and promote the human and cultural resources from within a given setting. This involves a new set of lenses, through which one does not primarily view the setting and the people in it as the problem and the outsider as the answer. Rather, the long-term goal of transformation is understood as validating and building on people and resources within the setting (Lederach, 1995).

Cross-cutting the categorization between substantive and relational structural conflict causes, several authors have established categories of transformation objects. Vayrynen (1991: 4–7) sees four possible ways of transformation: *actor transformation* (major international changes within the parties or inclusion or exclusion of conflict parties); *issue transformation* (alteration of political agenda, modification of what the conflict is about); *rule transformation* (affecting parties' relationship); and *structural transformation* (applying to inter-party relations). Miall (2004: 78) adds to this *context transformation* (change in the international or regional context) and *personal* or *elite transformation* (change of perspectives and will).

Conflict transformation frameworks usually refer to the importance not only of elites and political leaders, but also of social intermediaries, such as business people, teachers, religious or traditional authorities, as well as grass-roots movements (see non-state actors; civil society; private sector). Lederach (1997) has coined the 'pyramid' perspective of societies (elites, mid-level, grass-roots), in which transformation occurs. Changes are brought about over different time-periods (short-, mid- and long-term), affecting different levels of society at different times. Some authors, such as Rupesinghe (1995), explicitly focus on the grass-roots level. Lederach (1997), however, explicitly stresses the importance of interaction between the different levels.

A further important criterion concerns the role of third parties (see the chapter on responsibility to protect). Conflict transformation does not necessarily include the intervention of a third party. Ideally, it would be implemented by the conflict parties themselves. However, due to the protracted nature of the respective conflicts, this hardly ever happens. External actors participate in the transformation effort, either directly as facilitators, or indirectly by empowering the conflict parties. Fisher and Keashley (1991: 34) differentiate the role of third parties according to the structural dimension (substantive or relational) concerned. Authoritative (and powerful) intervention is appropriate in case of disputes over objective, tangible elements (such as territorial dispute); softer means of intervention are more appropriate in case of disputes over subjective elements (such as misperception and/or lack of communication). Categories of different roles for external interveners have been established by Mitchell (2005: 20). They include fifteen activities such as facilitators, envisioners, enhancers, guarantors, legitimizers, and reconcilers.

Official definitions

Conflict transformation has its main roots in the sphere of academic conflict research and in that of conflict mediation and facilitation. It is thus both a rather complex and a rather technical term. As a consequence, it is rarely used in a meaningful way outside these spheres.

One may find thematically focused bodies, such as the Alliance for Conflict Transformation (ACT), which according to its own saying:

> is dedicated to building peace through innovative education, training, research and practice worldwide. ACT works with educators, youth, community and religious leaders, non-governmental organisations and governmental agencies to transform social conflicts into opportunities for peaceful and positive change (<http://www.conflicttransformation.org>).

Another example is the Institute for Integrative Conflict Transformation and Peacebuilding (IICP), which offers training based on the Transcend methodology developed by Johan Galtung. Its process aims at inspiring analytical empathy of one conflict party for the others and releasing sufficient creativity within a conflict party, so that it can develop possible solutions that would take into consideration the symmetric fulfilment of human basic needs of all conflict parties. The process especially addresses the reciprocal relations of 'deep cultures', 'deep structures', and 'human basic needs', which define and subconsciously guide conflict-handling styles.

The concept of conflict transformation appears in documents of development agencies and peacebuilding divisions of ministries and international organizations. The Swiss Agency for Development and Cooperation (SDC) even called one of its divisions 'Conflict Prevention and Transformation' (COPRET). However, especially with regard to development agencies, individual activities of the respective units are mainly focused on mainstreaming conflict-sensitive thinking and programming within the overall organization.

II. Content

Core components

At the empirical analytical level of conflict research, the concept of conflict transformation was elaborated particularly in response to one prototype of intra-state conflict: the protracted social conflict. This term was first coined by Azar (1990) in the late 1970s. He used the term to describe and explain the difficulty of certain conflicts by pointing out their protracted (or structural) nature. His units of analysis are: discriminated identity groups that have suffered a denial of separate identity; an absence of security of culture; and an absence of effective political participation. Azar's model may explain both the formation and the transformation of such conflicts. It is now widely used to describe long-enduring conflicts that are:

- conflicts between identity groups, of which at least one feels that their basic needs for equality, security, and political participation are not respected;
- essentially about access to state-related power, often in the form of an asymmetric conflict between government and an insurgent party; and
- often based on deeply rooted antagonistic group histories (Fischer & Ropers 2004: 13).

Since the end of the Cold War, these types of conflicts have considerably risen in number. They are seen as a major challenge for peace and development. Their prominence has even increased since the 11 September 2001 attacks, with conflicts and the so-called fragile states in which they often take place seen by some as breeding grounds for terrorism (Schneckener, 2004). From a peacebuilding perspective, conflict transformation has come to be seen as the only sustainable way of dealing with international conflicts in general and protracted social conflicts in particular.

International conflicts are no longer limited to sovereign states, but in most cases include non-state actors who also pursue political objectives by means of organized violence (Daase, 2003: 167–8). This change in actors is joined by modifications in the underlying structures and dynamics of such conflicts, which often include social and economic dimensions in addition to political ones (Ballentine & Nitzschke, 2003). So-called 'environmental conflicts' have emerged as a typical field of application of conflict transformation research. Whereas at the beginning of these studies scarcity of natural resources was seen as a potential cause of direct conflict (Baechler, 1999; Homer-Dixon, 1999), more recent work has underlined the importance of political, social, and cultural factors in determining the use of resources (Goetschel & Péclard, 2006).

Traditional means of intervention in international conflicts have focused on the framework of collective security (see in particular the chapters on peace operations and transitional administration). They have consisted of legally based and reactive types of instruments, and have conceived of the conflict parties as states. Among the approaches discussed in this chapter, conflict management comes closest to collective security which still provides the political and legal core of the UN Charter. Conflict transformation, however, is far more inclusive in nature. It includes all levels of societies, and aims towards long-term reorientation of conflicts. Thus, conflict transformation may be seen as an alternative concept for conflict intervention, which is better adapted to the most frequent types of international conflicts encountered today. It supplements traditional means of collective security without replacing them. It provides a conceptual basis for mitigation measures applied to protracted social conflicts.

Underlying ideological, normative, and institutional issues

Conflict transformation is essentially about the understanding of conflicts, dimensions of interventions, and specific objectives: conflicts are seen as catalysts of change. Interventions should focus on structural dimensions of conflicts with the objective of promoting the constructive impact of conflicts on social change. Thus, conflict transformation is a process of engaging with and transforming relationships, interests, discourses and, if necessary, the very constitution of society that supports the continuation of violent conflicts (Miall, 2004: 70). Transformation should reorient the specific interaction in order to minimize violence and promote the positive outcomes of these human exchanges. It should aim at removing the frequently observed helplessness of conflict parties (Mitchell, 2002: 9).

The clarification of a conflict's constructive impact as such remains an open issue, though ideologically most conflict researchers see this impact ultimately as 'peace'. Lederach (1997) describes the activity of third parties in conflict transformation as peacebuilding, which has the long-term objective of transforming a war system into a peace system inspired by a quest for the values of justice, truth, and mercy. In his view, a comprehensive peace process should address complementary changes at all these levels.

Fischer and Ropers (2004: 13) see conflict transformation as referring to both the structure of conflicts and the process of moving towards 'just peace'. This opens a whole range of issues on the notion and definition of peace and the priorities to be set within conflict transformation. The ways in which structures should be transformed may be normatively preconceived: Francis (2004), for example, conceives of conflict transformation as necessarily linked to power asymmetries, gender inequalities and cultural differences. The normatively tainted long-term objectives of conflict transformation and its rather abstract content definition make it prone to an inflationary inflow of all kinds of problem issues seen by the respective authors as structural dimensions of conflicts. But these dimensions are not all necessarily constitutive elements of conflict transformation. In a short- to mid-term perspective, conflict transformation should allow for an absence, or at least for a reduction, of violence. The envisaged transformation of parties' perspectives and interests occurs with the long-term perspective of fundamental change. But in reality this change may be of a far more limited nature than an all-encompassing notion of peace would suggest. The latter should be seen as a long-term objective, maybe even as a regulative idea, whose components need not all be concretized in real-life conflict transformation.

Institutionally, the structural and long-term nature of conflict transformation brings it close to policies of development cooperation. Conflict transformation is frequently seen as a central political objective and increasingly also as a justification of development programmes in conflict-prone environments (see also the chapter on conflict economies). In a conflict transformation approach, the longer-term perspective of development programmes makes them more attractive as implementation vehicles than other peacebuilding activities looking for political windows of opportunity and which therefore frequently occur on a short-term or even ad hoc basis.

The introduction of a transformation perspective in development and peacebuilding activities has had several positive implications. First, it has strengthened the focus of the concepts and the implementation of such programmes on civil society actors: NGOs, grassroots organizations, and individuals have been implicated. Second, it has offered to such programmes paths of action other than conflict intervention tools directly linked to collective security. Working with non-state actors and using non-coercive means, a conflict transformation approach is far less subject to political stalemates in high political spheres such as typically occur in the UN Security Council. The reason is that the types of action undertaken by conflict transformation are far less sovereignty-sensitive.

When looking at the concrete development and peacebuilding activities associated with conflict transformation, however, there seems to exist some discrepancy between the complex objectives of conflict transformation and the *de facto* implemented programme activities (see notably the chapter on recovery). While the substantive structural dimensions of conflicts may be touched by them, the relational dimension often lies outside the scope of the programme administration logic applied. The biggest danger lies in the tendency to equate 'good' development cooperation with conflict transformation. This might both unnecessarily politicize development activities and reduce the specificity of the transformation approach to an addition of well-intended programme activities which, however, lack an explicit focus. The transformational approach is not just 'wider' and 'longer' than a conflict management or settlement approach. It fundamentally differs from them in its perception of conflicts and their contribution to social development. In a transformation approach conflicts are not primarily something to be solved or eradicated, but something which has to be guided to perform change and ultimately to produce positive outcomes.

In order to perform such change, development and peacebuilding programmes have to be geared specifically towards such outcomes. The constructivist approach underlying conflict transformation should be reflected in concrete programme objectives, which should aim at modifying conflict parties' interests. For example, constructing a bridge over a river may or may not be directed at such an objective. Or, gender mainstreaming activities may or may not comply with conflict transformation objectives. The same applies the other way around: not all conflict transformation activities are necessarily mainstreamed in a gender perspective (Reimann, 2004).

To summarize, conflict transformation has enjoyed unprecedented attention since the end of the Cold War within both the research and policy communities. However, this success has revealed different dangers: conflict transformation has suffered conceptually by its frequently unquestioned attribution to specific visions of peace. It has also suffered operationally by its almost essentialist attribution to specific political aspects of development programmes, being used as an explanatory frame for the latter's political correctness.

III. Implementation

Best practice

The instruments that most directly aim at conflict transformation and which have also been applied in several cases are the so-called interactive or problem-solving workshops. Their objective is to transform the conflict parties' perspectives on specific conflict issues and through this to achieve a transformation of the mutual perspectives of the conflict parties themselves. Famous is the implementation of such workshops with Palestinian and Israeli participants in the 1970s and 1980s by Herbert Kelman, who also claims that his workshops had a positive influence on the later Oslo Peace Talks (Kelman, 2005). A similar framework has been used within applied research on the riparian countries of the Nile River (Mason, 2004). The Berghof Foundation has developed a rather complex systemic approach to conflict transformation (Dudouet, 2006), which integrates many concepts and ideas developed by systemic scholars and by mediation practitioners. This approach was applied by the foundation in a few cases, such as Sri Lanka and the Southern Caucasus, but no published results are yet available.

These examples show that conflict transformation is mostly implemented by practice-oriented researchers and their institutions. Apart from these specific applications, it is hard to judge the extent to which conflict transformation has indeed been thoroughly implemented. This is not due to a lack of advice and concepts (Paffenholz, 2004), but there seems to be a lack of explicitly conflict-transformation-oriented methods and approaches for official agencies at the programme level. This starts with conflict analysis, for which rapid appraisal tools will not do. The same counts for concrete actions which affect selected aspects potentially relevant to conflict transformation, such as the empowerment of civil society, but which are not embedded in an overall long-term strategy, and which are not working towards changing conflict parties' perspectives either. Such actions do not qualify as conflict transformation.

Though notable progress has been made in sensitizing various actors to the needs and pitfalls of working in conflict-prone areas (Anderson, 2004), this is not to be confounded with the needs of conflict-oriented work, which differs again from conflict-transformation-oriented programming and implementation.

Proposal for more efficient implementation

Conflict transformation is not just another concept to be mainstreamed by the development and peacebuilding community. It is based on a philosophy of conflicts and how they should be handled in order to minimize violence and to promote positive social effects. Thus, development and peacebuilding agencies should not integrate conflict transformation just as a wording or as part of a preconceived process; they should adapt their whole strategies (see also the chapter on recovery). This process is rather cumbersome and success is far from sure because the task of transforming conflicts, especially protracted ones, is not an easy one. It is much handier for agencies to design limited and measurable objectives at the programme or even at the project level. However, the following recommendations should contribute to improving the implementation of conflict transformation:

- What is most lacking is adequate conflict analysis and a working interface between it and policy implementation. Appropriate conflict transformation needs conflict analysis which emphasizes the structural causes of a conflict. This requires profound context knowledge and in-depth studies. The challenge is not only to find adequate tools, but also to find adequate analysts. The interface problem touches upon the often-discussed, but rarely resolved, problematique of how to integrate analytical results (from conflict analysis) into strategy building of respective actors (see also on this issue the chapter on state-building).

- The objectives of conflict transformation should not be too ambitious: 'World peace' need not be the declared objective. Depending on the conflict context, a simple lasting reduction of violence might already represent a very noble achievement (<http://www.conflicttransformation.org>).

- This is all the more significant if we take the local ownership criteria of conflict transformation seriously. Thinking rigorously, the 'beneficial effects' expected from conflicts as social catalysts should be defined by the people and conflict parties themselves. The same applies to the content of human security. Conflict transformation is not about implementing northern visions in conflict-prone regions, but about getting the parties concerned to optimize the social outcomes of their strife. External assistance can merely provide a supportive framework (Dudouet, 2006: 72) (see the chapter on capacity-building).

- Furthermore, it should be borne in mind that structural transformation is not equal to development. We may promote development by, for example, knowledge capacity-building or health improvement, without directly affecting conflict structures. Even in a conflict-prone country, not everything outside the short-term political conjunctures is automatically promoting conflict transformation. Long-term structure-affecting measures may be seen as conflict prevention, but this does not mean that they *ipso facto* contribute to conflict transformation.

- Conflict transformation efforts need a medium-to-long-term horizon. This is linked to the necessity of including local stakeholders (ie conflict parties) and the need to transform effectively the substantive and relational dimensions of the conflict's structures.

Finally, it seems almost superfluous to emphasize the all-encompassing nature of a conflict transformation approach to peacebuilding. While specific tasks, such as civil society empowerment, security sector reform, or the issue of non-state actors, may be described and handled separately, they should be embedded in the overall conflict transformation framework. Only with strategies and programmes that obey such a framework will agencies and their partners be able to work effectively towards the transformation of conflicts.

Selected Bibliography

Anderson, MB (2004), 'Experiences with Impact Assessment: Can We Know What Good We Do?', in Austin, A, Fischer, M, & Ropers, N (eds), *Transforming Ethnopolitical Conflict*, The Berghof Handbook, Berlin: Berghof Research Centre for Constructive Conflict Management; Wiesbaden: VS Verlag für Sozialwissenschaften, 193–206.

Austin, A, Fischer, M, & Ropers, N (eds) (2004), *Transforming Ethnopolitical Conflict*, The Berghof Handbook, Berlin: Berghof Research Centre for Constructive Conflict Management; Wiesbaden: VS Verlag für Sozialwissenschaften.

Azar, EE (1990), *The Management of Protracted Social Conflicts: Theory and Case*, Aldershot: Dartmouth.

—— & Burton, JW (1986), *International Conflict Resolution: Theory and Practice*, Boulder: Lynne Rienner Publishers.

Baechler, G (1999), *Violence through Environmental Discrimination*, Dordrecht: Kluwer Law International.

Ballentine, K, & Nitzschke, H (2003), 'The Political Economy of Civil War and Conflict Transformation', in Bloomfield, D, Fischer, M, & Schmelzle, B (eds), *Berghof Handbook for Constructive Conflict Transformation*, Berlin: Berghof Research Centre for Constructive Conflict Management, http://www.berghof-handbook.net.

Bush, BA, & Folger, JP (1994), *The Promise of Mediation: Responding to Conflict through Empowerment and Recognition*, San Francisco, CA: Jossey-Bass.

Curle, A (1971), *Making Peace*, London: Tavistock Publications.

Daase, C (2003), 'Krieg und politische Gewalt: Konzeptionelle Innovation und theoretischer Fortschritt', in Hellmann, G, Wolf, KD, & Zürn, M (Hrsg), *Die neuen internationalen Beziehungen. Forschungsstand und Perspektiven in Deutschland*, Baden-Baden: Nomos, 161–208.

Dudouet, V (2006), *Transitions from Violence to Peace: Revisiting Analysis and Intervention in Conflict Transformation*, Berghof Report No 15, Berlin: Berghof Research Centre for Constructive Conflict Management.

Fischer, M, & Ropers, N (2004), 'Introduction', in Austin, A, Fischer, M, & Ropers, N (eds), *Transforming Ethnopolitical Conflict*, The Berghof Handbook, Berlin: Berghof Research Centre for Constructive Conflict Management, Wiesbaden: VS Verlag für Sozialwissenschaften, 11–22.

Fisher, RJ, & Keashly, L (1991), 'The Potential Complementarity of Mediation and Consultation within a Contingency Model of Third Party Intervention', *Journal of Peace Research*, 28/1: 29–42.

Francis, D (2002), *People, Peace and Power: Conflict Transformation in Action*, London: Pluto Press.

—— (2004), 'Culture, Power Asymmetries and Gender in Conflict Transformation', in Austin, A, Fischer, M, & Ropers, N (eds), *Transforming Ethnopolitical Conflict*, The Berghof Handbook, Berlin: Berghof Research Centre for Constructive Conflict Management; Wiesbaden: VS Verlag für Sozialwissenschaften, 91–107.

Galtung, J (1996), *Peace by Peaceful Means*, London: Sage Publications.

Goetschel, L, & Péclard, D (2006), 'Les conflits liés aux ressources naturelles: résultats de recherches et perspectives', in Schümperli Younossian, C (dir), & Tschumi Canosa, X (resp. du dossier), *Annuaire suisse de politique de développement. Paix et sécurité: les défis lancés à la coopération internationale*, Genève: Institut universitaire d'études du développement, 25/2: 95–106.

Homer-Dixon, TF (1999), *Environment, Scarcity, and Violence*, Princeton: Princeton University Press.

Kelman, HC (2005), 'Interactive Problem Solving in the Israeli-Palestinian case: Past Contributions and Present Challenges', in Fischer, RJ (ed), *Paving the Way: Contributions of Interactive Conflict Resolution to Peacemaking*, Lanham, LD: Lexington Books, 41–64.

Kriesberg, L (2003), *Constructive Conflicts: From Escalation to Resolution*, Oxford: Rowman and Littlefield.

Krippendorf, E (1973), 'Peace Research and the Industrial Revolution', *Journal of Peace Research*, 10/3: 185–201.

Lederach, JP (1995), *Preparing for Peace: Conflict Transformation across Cultures*, New York: Syracuse University Press.

—— (1997), *Building Peace: Sustainable Reconciliation in Divided Societies*, Washington, DC: US Institute of Peace Press.

Mason, SA (2004), *From Conflict to Cooperation in the Nile Basin: Interaction between Water Availability, Water Management in Egypt and Sudan, and International Relations in the Eastern Nile Basin*, Zürich: Forschungsstelle für Sicherheitspolitik, ETH Zürich.

Miall, H (2004), 'Conflict Transformation: A Multi-Dimensional Task', in Austin, A, Fischer, M, & Ropers, N (eds), *Transforming Ethnopolitical Conflict*, The Berghof

Handbook, Berlin: Berghof Research Centre for Constructive Conflict Management; Wiesbaden: VS Verlag für Sozialwissenschaften, 67–89.

Mitchell, CR (2002), 'Beyond Resolution: What Does Conflict Transformation Actually Transform?', *Peace and Conflict Studies*, 9/1, available at: <http://www.gmu.edu/academic/pcs/CM83PCS.htm>.

—— (2005), 'Conflict, Social Change and Conflict Resolution: An Enquiry', in *Social Change and Conflict Transformation*, Berghof Handbook Dialogue Series, No 5, Berlin: Berghof Research Centre for Constructive Conflict Management.

Paffenholz, T (2004), 'Designing Transformation and Intervention Processes', in Austin, A, Fischer, M, & Ropers, N (eds), *Transforming Ethnopolitical Conflict*, The Berghof Handbook, Berlin: Berghof Research Centre for Constructive Conflict Management; Wiesbaden: VS Verlag für Sozialwissenschaften, 152–69.

Reimann, C (2004), *Gender in Problem-solving Workshops: A Wolf in Sheep's Clothing?*, Swisspeace Working Paper No 3, Bern: Swiss Peace Foundation.

Rupesinghe, K (1995), *Conflict Transformation*, New York, NY: St Martin's Press.

Schneckener, U (2004), *Transnationale Terroristen als Profiteure fragiler Staatlichkeit*, Berlin: Stiftung Wissenschaft und Politik.

Senghaas, D (1973), 'Conflict Formation in Contemporary International Society', *Journal of Peace Research*, Vol. 10, No. 3, 163–84.

Vayrynen, R (1991), 'To Settle or to Transform? Perspectives on the Resolution of National and International Conflict', in Vayrynen, R (ed), *New Direction in Conflict Theory*, Thousand Oaks: Sage Publications, 1–25.

Wendt, A (1999), *Social Theory of International Politics*, Cambridge: Cambridge University Press.

Democratic Governance

Rama Mani* and Jana Krause

Definition

Democratic governance refers to the regulation of social matters within a state according to the principles of democracy, including respect for human rights and the rule of law, justice and equity, equality and political participation, and legitimacy and accountability. It derives from the merging of two prominent concepts in the international security and development discourse: democracy promotion as a security strategy, and the promotion of 'good governance' as a developmental concern.

I. Term

The concept of democratic governance appears ubiquitous today but it first appeared in peacebuilding terminology only as far back as the 1990s. It represents the melding of one of the oldest concepts in politics—democracy—with the more recent concept of governance, which, although coined in the 16th century, entered international discourse only in the 1980s. Today, this combined concept of 'democratic governance' has become central to the practice of post-conflict peacebuilding, due to the particular context and exigencies of societies emerging from violent conflict, usually accompanied by dysfunctional or unrepresentative government and a history of political repression.

The emergence of the concept of democratic governance

Democracy

The concept of democracy dates back to ancient Greek political organization and literally means 'rule by the people'. Democracy is often reduced to its most visible lowest common denominator—elections. However, this pragmatic view or

* I would like to express my deep gratitude to Cristina Lopez, Programme Manager/Researcher of the Peace and Justice Programme at the International Centre for Ethnic Studies, Sri Lanka, for her highly professional research assistance.

'formal democracy' as government by, for, and of the people, for which periodic elections are a proxy, is only a basic conception (Mani, 2006: 15). 'Substantive democracy' needs to be more than majority rule disciplined by checks and balances. A consolidated democratic system combines behavioural, attitudinal, and constitutional dimensions. Democracy as a complex system of institutions, rules, and patterned incentives and disincentives has to become 'the only game in town' (Linz and Stepan, 1996: 15).

Democratization

In recent political and international discourse and experience, three 'waves' of democratization are often distinguished (Huntington, 1991). During the nineteenth century, democracy took root in Europe and North America. Paradoxically, this period was accompanied by the rise of European colonization and North American hegemony across the developing world into the 20th century, effectively delaying the endogenous emergence of democracy in Africa, Asia, and Latin America until the second half of the century. After World War II, several countries became democracies. The end of the military dictatorships in southern Europe and Latin America in the 1970s and 1980s, and particularly the end of the Soviet Union, marks the beginning of the 'third wave' that lasted from 1974 to 1995, with the number of democracies leaping from 39 in 1974 to 76 in 1990, and then, dramatically, to 117 in 1995 (Plattner, 2005: 5).

Democracy promotion and security

Democracy is traditionally seen as a panacea to many ills, providing security and civil liberties to citizens and avoiding armed strife provoked by un-redressed grievances (Mani, 2006: 6). The oft-cited theory of democratic peace holds that democracies do not wage war against each other (Doyle, 1983; Russett, 1993). With the end of the Cold War, the concept of democracy promotion became closely linked to notions of security and development. The UN's 'Agenda for Peace' (UN, 1992) officially introduced the term peacebuilding into UN terminology and practice. The report identified 'an obvious connection between democratic practices—such as the rule of law and transparency in decision-making—and the achievement of true peace and security in any new and stable political order' (*ibid*) (see also the chapter on rule of law).

The subsequent 'Agenda for Democratization' (UN, 1996) emphasized the importance of effective democratic institutions to channel conflict in a peaceful manner and to prevent the recurrence of violent conflict. It argued that the authority of the UN system to act in the field of peacebuilding needs to rest on the consensus that 'social peace is as important as strategic or political peace' (*ibid*). The promotion of democracy has been recognized as an important priority by most states as well as many international organizations, including the European Union (EU), the UN Development Programme (UNDP), and a plethora of international and national non-governmental organizations (NGOs) have sought to promote democracy over the past decades.

Governance

The term 'governance' emerged around the same period. By itself the term refers to the manner in which the affairs of a state, civil society, and its structures were managed, going beyond government alone. It encompasses the various collective modes of regulating social matters in order to achieve certain standards in the area of political authority and rule making, security, welfare, and environment (Risse and Lehmkuhl, 2006: 4). The term gained additional currency after 1989 when it was applied in the context of 'global governance' to manage the affairs of the world community. In 1992, the Commission on Global Governance was established to address how to better manage the common affairs of the international community in the aftermath of the Cold War. Its final report, 'Our Global Neighbourhood' (Commission on Global Governance: 1995) was presented at both the UN and the World Economic Forum in Davos in January 2005, with recommendations on all dimensions of governance at the global level: peace and security, finance and development, environment and the UN. In this period, the concept of 'governance' was adopted within political and international terminology and the notion was popularized not only by governments and political parties at national and global level but also by a variety of other actors including civil society, business, and trade unions.

'Good governance'

In development circles, the term governance had been used from the 1980s onwards, as donors began to realize the importance of the efficiency and capacity of the recipient state's institutions to absorb aid and its effective translation into development (see the chapters on state-building and recovery). Democratization in many parts of the world had not been accompanied by better governance and service provision, resulting instead in notoriously corrupt and inefficient semi-democratic regimes breeding instability.

The term 'good governance' refers to a set of conditions and practices that recipient governments had to fulfil in order to receive aid. These include political participation, the rule of law, transparency, institutional responsiveness, equity, effectiveness, accountability, and a strategic vision for development (UNDP, 2006: 35). Demanding good governance practices enabled donors to impose minimal conditionality on governments receiving aid while avoiding direct political involvement such as promoting democracy, which for some donors like the World Bank lay outside their articles of agreement and hence their official practice. For their part, development actors began to realize that their promotion of good governance without the parallel legitimacy of nationally rooted democracy was proving to be normatively more and more inadequate and unacceptable.

Democratic governance, security, and peacebuilding

By the mid 1990s, as the political climate changed, the term 'democratic governance' had emerged, combining the security concern and democratization in the post-Cold War world with the developmental concern for good governance. It also implies a wider understanding of governance beyond governments to include non-state actors as well as concerns such as rights, development, and the environment.

The 2002 UNDP Report 'Deepening Democracy in a Fragmented World' linked democracy promotion to development and peace. From a development point of view, UNDP defined democratic governance as:

> a system of governance that incorporates into the notion of good governance, not only efficient processes, but also principles and institution that secure the civic rights and freedoms of all people, including the poorest of the poor and marginalized groups (UNDP, 2006: 35).

UNDP was also arguing that civilian control over the armed forces and democratic governance of the security sector were fundamental to ensuring sustainable peace in post-conflict environments (UNDP, 2002: 85–100) (see on this issue the chapter on security sector reform). Today, virtually all multilateral organizations in both the security and development fields (notably, the Organization for Security and Co-operation in Europe (OSCE), the United States Agency for International Development (USAID), UNDP, and the World Bank) have adopted democratic governance as a key policy objective to be promoted through their programming.

Linguistic and semantic difficulties

The linguistic and semantic difficulties of the term stem from its genesis as the coming together of two entirely disparate terms—democracy and governance—with distinct and differing genealogies and usages. This lends a degree of confusion to the recently compiled composite term of democratic governance. Further semantic difficulties are created because some organizations and academics use the term generically but do not provide a specific definition. While they define 'governance' succinctly in their policy statements, they eschew a clear definition of 'democratic governance', instead offering lengthy descriptions of principles, approaches, and components. This is true, for example, of USAID, France's Development Cooperation (2006) and UNDP, all of whom are leading proponents of the concept in practice and provide significant funds to support it. Moreover, many development agencies provide definitions and components of democratic governance that often overlap with the notion of good governance, as both concepts refer to political participation, the rule of law, equality, and accountability. Since both democracy and governance have very different usages and meanings, this lack of clear definition can lead to divergent understandings and misconceptions.

The definition of democratic governance that this chapter proposes reflects the changing international security discourse and practice of the last two decades. Democratic governance refers to the merging of two important concepts: democracy promotion as a security strategy, and the promotion of 'good governance' as a development concern. The concept thus acknowledges the fundamental interdependence of security and development. The definition incorporates both the procedural dimension of governing according to democratic principles and the standards of 'good governance' as well as the long-term objective of establishing an efficient democratic system and a functioning economy to ensure sustainable peace in societies wrecked by armed violence.

II. Content

Core components of democratic governance

In the context of post-conflict peacebuilding, democratic governance comprises several components:

1. *Election support:* This refers to organizing, running, and monitoring elections, including the promotion of a culture of democracy and the training of election officials.

2. *Bureaucracy and administration:* This area is of particular significance, as many countries emerging from conflict have no prior experience with democratic governance and have often lost many of their leading politicians and administrators. Thus an entire new generation of bureaucrats and administrators and parliamentary officers has to be trained.

3. *Decentralization and building local administrative capacity*: This overlaps closely with the topic above. Considerable importance is now given to the principle of subsidiarity and decentralization to reduce the pressure and demands of an overly centralized bureaucracy in a state emerging from debilitating conflict. Both processes are to foster a culture of democracy at the community level, promoting local governance through municipalities and communes, and supporting the central government in decentralizing powers and functions to provinces, districts, and municipalities.

4. *Justice and rule of law:* This involves reform of the judiciary, the police, and the prison system. It also includes re-equipping or rebuilding court houses, to rewriting or adapting laws, to training judges, lawyers, police officers, and prison officials in national law and human rights.

5. *Security sector reform/governance:* with a slight overlap with rule of law, security sector reform has emerged as a distinct field since the late 1990s, covering the

reformed governance of the military, police, and all armed personnel including paramilitaries, with an emphasis on bringing all such armed forces under democratic civilian control. This is of particular importance in the transition from conflict, where often the military dominated the police and operated in an undemocratic manner without any civilian or parliamentary oversight.

6. *Constitution writing:* This is a specific task that often arises in post-conflict societies, where an agreed component of peacebuilding involves the writing and adoption of an entirely new constitution acceptable to all sides of the conflict, or the revision of a prior constitution. In some cases this requirement may be written into the terms of the peace agreement.

7. *Human rights:* A major area of preoccupation within democratic governance is the protection and promotion of human rights. This would include human rights monitoring especially of vulnerable groups (such as women and children) and sensitive/volatile regions, training and education, and support to national human rights commissions and domestic human rights NGOs. It may also include supporting specific transitional justice mechanisms such as truth commissions or national or hybrid tribunals established to investigate war crimes or prosecute war criminals.

Key actors

The main and most numerous and decisive actors in democratic governance are the local actors in each post-conflict country. These local stakeholders (other than the *élite*) are often excluded rather than included in processes of democratic governance. This is naturally detrimental, as without the full engagement of all sectors of national stakeholders, the processes of shaping and implementing democratic governance will lack legitimacy and sustainability. These processes and institutions cannot be externally designed and imposed but must emerge endogenously (see the chapter on local ownership).

Democratic governance promotion includes the full range of international actors involved in post-conflict peacebuilding, spanning the political, economic and human rights dimensions. The most salient are mentioned below.

The UN

A UN peacekeeping or peacebuilding mission is typically the most important single outside actor as it is involved in an ongoing and daily basis in the process of establishing democratic governance in a country recovering from conflict. While reporting regularly to the Security Council through the Secretary-General, the appointed head of the mission (usually in the form of a Special Representative to the Secretary-General (SRSG)) wields considerable autonomy and authority to make decisions in coordination with the heads of other multilateral agencies and leading countries.

The UN agencies most directly concerned include the Department for Peacekeeping (DPKO) and the Department for Political Affairs (DPA) (see the chapter on peace operations). Most missions are deployed by, and controlled out of, DPKO. There are, however, a small but growing number of peacebuilding missions directly managed out of DPA as well. The UN Peacebuilding Commission, established following the UN Summit Declaration in 2005, is entrusted with shepherding and overseeing the consolidation of peace and avoiding any possible relapse into conflict of a select number of countries at a time. Currently, Burundi and Sierra Leone are on the Peacebuilding Commission's agenda (for further discussion on the Peacebuilding Commission, see the introduction to this Lexicon).

UNDP has emerged as a central operational actor within the UN system in the area of democratic governance. In 2005, 46 per cent of UNDP's technical assistance was in the area of democratic governance. It established a trust fund specifically for democratic governance which, since 2001, has received more than US$68 million of which over US$12 million was received in 2005 alone. Several other UN agencies and departments are also involved in the component elements of democratic governance but UNDP is notable as it has taken on responsibility for democratic governance as a core issue. The Office of the UN High Commissioner for Human Rights (OHCHR) plays an important role in the rule of law and human rights components underpinning democratic governance.

Other international and multilateral organizations

The World Bank plays a significant role in the reconstruction elements of democratic governance. It has also prioritized fighting corruption and raising transparency, which are important pre-requisites for the successful establishment of democratic governance.

The OSCE's mandate highlights democracy, the rule of law, and human rights under the Paris Charter of 1990. The OSCE has played a leading role in democratic governance in the wide region within its ambit, particularly through the work of its Warsaw-based Office for Democratic Institutions and Human Rights.

While primarily concerned with the military aspects of peace operations in theatres such as Afghanistan or Kosovo, the North Atlantic Treaty Organization (NATO) does have a role and interest in some aspects of democratic governance. Peacebuilding and conflict management have now risen to the top of NATO's agenda with its involvement in Afghanistan, the Balkans, Iraq, and even Darfur. The Provisional Reconstruction Teams (PRTs) in Afghanistan were a hands-on experiment for NATO troops in elements of democratic governance as well as in engaging directly with civilian populations.

The European Commission has given high priority to democratic governance and is now a major actor in theatres of peacebuilding, often deploying a Special Envoy and having an office in the field of operation.

The African Union has taken a bold and increasing role in peacekeeping and peacebuilding. This has also led it to play its part in democratic governance. However, despite great strides taken by the African Union, sensitivities remain in Africa about intervention in the internal affairs of sovereign states, especially on issues of democracy, as has been demonstrated in the case of Zimbabwe.

The Development Assistance Committee (DAC) of the Organisation for Economic Co-operation and Development (OECD) has developed important standard and policy guidelines for the OECD community. OECD's DAC and the European Commission have played a normative role in defining democratic governance for their constituent members and in establishing criteria and best practices. These involve, for example, best practices in development assistance to countries in conflict and for security sector reform. Likewise, DPKO distils lessons learned and best practices after each mission, while the UN Institute for Training and Research (UNITAR) debriefs and distils the experiences of SRSGs after missions.

Bilateral agencies and governments

Western national donor agencies also contribute significantly to the promotion of democratic governance in post-conflict settings. The US government and USAID have made democratic governance a national security priority. The UK government and its Department for International Development (DFID) remains an extremely important player in democratic governance, particularly in the area of security sector reform. The French government and French Development Cooperation, and the German Gesellschaft für Technische Zusammenarbeit (GTZ) have all underscored democratic governance as their key policy goal in line with the EU framework. These are certainly not the only bilateral agencies involved. According to the post-conflict country in question, a plethora of concerned donor countries with particular historical and current relations to that recipient country are actively involved in promoting democratic governance or its component parts.

Driving forces for democratic governance

Peacebuilding missions have become state-building missions promoting democratic governance because fragile states are seen as a risk to both their own people's and international security. In 2001, the Security Council clarified the expansive notion of peacebuilding as being 'aimed at preventing the outbreak, the recurrence or continuation of armed conflict', and declared that it should 'therefore focus on a broad range of activities such as fostering sustainable development, the eradication of poverty and inequalities, transparent and accountable governance, the promotion of democracy, respect for human rights and the rule of law, and the promotion of a culture of peace and non-violence.' Democratic governance also became central to post-conflict peacebuilding due to the support of development agencies which invested heavily in post-conflict societies.

For national donors, the rationale and driving force to promote democratic governance lies close to their national interests. For instance, USAID states that democratic governance is a major foreign policy objective that is vital to the national security of the US, because 'the only way to prevent or reverse the threats that flow from bad governance is to foster stable, effective democratic governance' (USAID, 2002: 34). The concept of democratic governance has also received widespread attention because it provides legitimacy as peacebuilding missions seek to bring war-shattered states into conformity with the international system's prevailing standards of domestic governance (Paris, 2002: 638).

Challenges and dilemmas

Democratic governance in post-conflict peacebuilding contexts faces a number of practical challenges and conceptual dilemmas. Afghanistan and Iraq provide daily reminders of the lack of substantive progress in securing peace and democratic governance despite huge financial investments over six- and four-year periods respectively (Diamond, 2005; Goodson, 2005; Maley, 2006). Repeated failures or setbacks in Haiti, Liberia, and Serbia also provide evidence that, for several reasons, this is not an easy task, despite donor aid and noble intentions. Some challenges are common to democratic governance anywhere but take a more acute form in post-conflict contexts; others are specific to post-conflict peacebuilding. These include, most notably, the external imposition of state-building and democratic governance as well as undemocratic decision-making procedures among international actors and a lack of accountability to the local population. These directly contradict the normative dimension of democratic governance.

The dilemma of promoting democratic governance

Peacebuilding by international actors is a process of external social engineering that represents a profound rupture with domestic and local modes of governance (Krause and Jütersonke, 2005). It aims to radically transform all aspects of the state, society, and economy in a matter of months, thereby expecting war-torn societies to achieve a level of development that took Western states decades or even centuries (Barnett, 2006: 89.) The introduction of Western models of political order as represented by the concept of democratic governance often leaves the targeted population without any mechanisms of appeal. This is even more so when bottom-up processes of democratization, development and local ownership are neglected. For example, African scholars note that in view of the structures of group, clan, or ethnic loyalty and patronage, as well as of community allegiance, certain Western norms of democratic governance are difficult to inculcate and need to be adapted to African contexts and needs. Democratic institutions have often papered over situations of repression and exclusion, while at the same time local functioning structures have been destroyed in peacebuilding efforts (Chopra and Hohe, 2004). State institutions that do not take root among the population may over time lead to renewed conflict.

For democratic governance to take hold in a country, full engagement is needed across the spectrum from national stakeholders. These include a free and vibrant media, religious bodies, academia, civil society, women's groups, youth movements, among others. Supporting freedom of expression in society through the support of legitimate local organizations such as these would ensure that democratic governance is not perceived merely as externally imposed. In peacebuilding processes these cultural and social factors need to be fully considered in adapting and designing case-specific democratic governance institutions. Yet organizational challenges such as coordination among international actors, coordination within the donor community, the pressure to present quick results, and the generally short timeframe make adequate consultation of the targeted population and respect for local ownership extremely difficult. This has proven a serious operational challenge each time, with international peacebuilders acknowledging their errors in importing inappropriate systems from elsewhere (Mani, 2002).

Furthermore, decision-making procedures among international actors implementing the political dimension of post-conflict peacebuilding are often not democratic, and there is a lack of accountability to the local population. Reporting procedures to the Secretary-General and the Security Council or an established steering board present only weak accountability mechanisms for peacebuilders and do not replace accountability to the population concerned. The lack of democratic procedures is further aggravated when democratically elected local leaders are removed by international peacebuilders for the sake of protecting the development and reconciliation process, as has been the case in Bosnia and Herzegovina. Consequently, peacebuilders often act on the basis of a weak sense of legitimacy derived only from their mandate, given by the international community, and some sense of acceptance by the local population. In some post-conflict countries, local stakeholders have questioned the legitimacy of international institutions, while the high rate of relapse into violence, for example in Haiti, raises questions of effectiveness.

As a result, international actors have to abide by the highest standards to maintain their credibility and the trust of the local population. Misdemeanours, however sporadic, can destroy legitimacy built up over a long period, and the international community has been badly burnt by incidents of corruption, trafficking, and sexual abuse committed by peacekeepers and peacebuilders. Accountability towards those they serve is essential for peacebuilders (Barnett, 2006). Deep disaffection has also led academics and practitioners to reconsider seriously the fundaments of democracy and democratic governance. 'Democratic practice', which emphasizes equity, equality, and service delivery, has been proposed as a preferable alternative to democracy, which stresses only electoral processes and mechanisms but not the accountability to all citizens (Sisk and Large, 2006).

Institutional challenges to democratic governance

A further challenge is the expansive scope, and hence the lack of finite and measurable parameters, for a policy objective as all encompassing as democratic governance, with its multiple components, each of which has its own challenges. Unrealistically high expectations generate a sense of unwarranted failure and hide partial successes. Failures or setbacks are also partly due to the continuing violence, volatility, and competitive nature of ostensibly post-conflict societies. It is difficult in such conditions to promote democratic institutions, which require a modicum of security in order to flourish. Further, the democratic institutions and processes themselves engender further competition and divisiveness and exacerbate insecurity.

Another significant factor is the absence of genuine political will by national political actors beyond lip service, as in Angola. The presence of spoilers may also jeopardize the process, as with warlords in Afghanistan (see on this issue the chapters on non-state actors and peace process). While it was considered expedient by international peacebuilders and the US coalition to include warlords in all dimensions of democratic governance in Afghanistan, they have repeatedly scuppered these processes and continue to cause insecurity today, even at a time when the Taliban are re-emerging strongly (Mani, 2003).

The high cost of the process and the failure of the donor community to honour their pledges and sustain their investment in this lengthy process is a further challenge. A more accountable and less costly system is needed where donors are held to their pledges and commit themselves on a longer term basis. Accountability has too often been demanded from local actors in democratic governance practice, while donors and international peacebuilders have been largely exempt and acted with impunity, leading to discredit among the local populations.

The relevance of democratic governance in post-conflict peacebuilding

Peacebuilding is now firmly established on the international security agenda. But the problems of democratic governance in post-conflict environments have led scholars to propose two options. The first is to downsize expectations and ambitions, and to aim for much more limited democratic governance measures, as proposed by Ottaway (Ottaway, 2003). The second is not to reduce the vision and goal, but to set a longer and more realistic timeframe for their achievement, as proposed by Call and Cook (Call and Cook, 2003), and then to pursue them incrementally (Barnett, 2006).

There exist a wide variety of forms and models of pursuing democratic governance, through elections, constitutions, power-sharing arrangements, human rights institutions and processes, and local governance. The many alternative and innovative forms and their sequencing proposed by scholars and policymakers should be closely considered and adopted where opportune.

Despite these challenges and dilemmas, the promotion of democratic governance remains a primary objective of peacebuilding because weak states pose a major threat to their societies and to international security.

III. Implementation

Difficulties of implementation

The detailed discussions in this Lexicon of the challenges and experiences in implementing free and fair elections, the rule of law, and security sector reform provide further insights into the difficulties of implementing democratic governance. Here are briefly presented the components of local governance, constitution making and human rights not dealt with elsewhere in the Lexicon.

Local governance

The promotion of local governance consists of assistance and other measures to build and improve local governance, promote e-governance, and decentralization of power, to give support to parliamentary institutions, and to rebuild public administration. (E-governance is defined by UNESCO as the public sector's use of information and communication technologies with the aim of improving information and service delivery, encouraging citizen participation in the decision-making process, and making government more accountable, transparent, and effective.) The main difficulty is the weakness or non-functioning of institutions and practices of local governance after years of conflict. Governance interventions may also be perceived as an external imposition, especially at local levels, where local and traditional power holders may feel sidelined.

While e-governance seems a simple and obvious way to bring governance to the ordinary people away from the capital, in devastated post-conflict settings computers are rare in rural areas, as are the persons remaining in the country with sufficient literacy to use them. While local governance is extremely important to instil the local ownership that is deemed one of the most important elements for sustainable peacebuilding, it is imperative to design and adapt suitable mechanisms and approaches in each situation, as needs can differ vastly and localized or decentralized governance may not be equally appropriate in different contexts.

Constitution-making processes

Constitution-making processes can provide an ideal forum for overcoming divides between groups and communities, and coming to a common understanding of state and governance. Constitutions themselves are ideal templates of a common vision of society and a social contract between citizens and their governments. A variety of processes and models of constitutions exist and should be chosen according to the needs of each context. If ill-chosen, constitutions can fail to provide these benefits and even exacerbate divisions and contestation (Samuels, 2006).

Human rights

In early peacebuilding missions, human rights were not accorded much importance. They were even seen as an obstruction, or an ill-advised luxury, during volatile and still often insecure post-conflict environments. Afghanistan was the clearest case where the political leadership of the UN Assistance Mission in Afghanistan believed that human rights could only be addressed once security had been definitely ensured (Mani, 2003). However, such attitudes are changing. It is becoming standard practice for OHCHR to have a presence in UN peacekeeping and peacebuilding missions through a senior advisor and supplementary field staff (see the chapters on peace operations and rule of law). In many post-conflict countries human rights actually played a more central role than the political mission. Already in 1992, Haiti had a joint UN/Organization of American States human rights monitoring mission, as does Nepal today. The UN's Verification Mission in Guatemala was primarily a monitoring mission as well as having a strong human rights mandate. National human rights commissions are often created by the peace agreements themselves and are supported by international peacebuilders.

Gender

Crosscutting all aspects of democratic governance is the issue of gender, and this has been one of the most difficult in implementation. Women's rights require particular attention, as high numbers of women are raped, trafficked, enslaved, and otherwise violated during most conflicts. Understandably, they are reluctant to come forward to report or seek redress, on account of social stigmatization. A deliberate and systematic focus on including women not just as victims or voters but as elected and nominated representatives at all levels of governance is a key priority. In some cases it will be necessary to provide protection to women candidates in the face of intimidation, as in the *loya jirga* in Afghanistan (Mani, 2003).

Democratic governance, whether in post-conflict societies or in developed peaceful societies, will only thrive if women are equally or significantly involved in all its component parts. In designing and implementing each component element of democratic governance, it is important for peacebuilders to focus on the specific needs of women and to build women's peacebuilding capacities. It should also be ensured that women who were often active in peacemaking efforts do not get sidelined from the processes of shaping and implementing democratic governance once a peace agreement is in place.

Children

The implementation of children's rights also represents a great challenge in post-conflict environments. Children may have been voluntarily or forcefully associated with armed forces as fighters, cooks, porters, or sexual slaves. As children, they may have committed serious crimes and stand between the juvenile and the adult justice system. In post-conflict environments, birth certificates and identification documents are often missing, making adherence to child protection standards difficult. Children's rights to special protection in the context of peacebuilding missions have received more attention over the last years as child protection advisors are increasingly deployed to UN missions to ensure the implementation of international child rights standards.

Worst practices

Regarding the effectiveness of the international community, the results are quite mixed. Neither Cambodia nor Bosnia and Herzegovina can be called successes, despite the commitment of massive international resources. For example, in Liberia, the international community acquiesced to rigged elections in the first attempt at peacebuilding, but peacebuilders are now assisting Africa's first democratically elected woman-President to stabilize the state. Over time, El Salvador and Mozambique have proven resilient although the initial elections had weaknesses (Ottaway, 2003). In Afghanistan and Iraq, it has been acknowledged that elections have played an important role in local perception. Although the overall peacebuilding processes in both countries are still not clearly successful, and high rates of violence and the risk of further escalation remain, the local and general elections in both countries played a positive role in creating a sense of participation and democratic spirit in the local populations (Ottaway, 2003; Maley, 2006). Yet many of the other aspects required for genuine democratic governance, including the establishment of a democratic culture, are still lacking (see also the chapters on peace process; free and fair elections; reconciliation).

Elections

In Cambodia, the SRSG succumbed to pressure from defeated Hun Sen to accord him the title of 'Second Prime Minister'. By 1997, Hun Sen had led a coup to oust the winning candidate, and remains in power today. Despite regular elections, democratic values have still not fully taken root in either Serbia or Bosnia and Herzegovina, despite unprecedented levels of European assistance. In July 2008, following the election of a pro-western government led by President Boris Tadic, the war criminal Radovan Karadzic was finally arrested. Yet thousands protested and threatened the government if they handed over this 'war hero' to The Hague, demonstrating that the notion of human rights and justice as core parts of democratic governance has not yet replaced the nationalism of the war years. In Bosnia and Herzegovina, thirteen years after the Dayton Peace Process, the system of power sharing, albeit 'democratic', has deepened division among the three main ethnic groups, and fostered deep political rivalry and continuing corruption (field visit of Rama Mani to Bosnia and Herzegovina, July 2008) (for further discussion see the chapter on free and fair elections).

Security sector reform

In Afghanistan, the international community tolerated Marshall Fahim as both Minister of Defence and head of the largest armed militia, while simultaneously undertaking a major security sector reform process led by the US. The US military openly admitted that Fahim was the biggest obstacle to security sector reform, and yet this concept was recognized as the best chance of restoring stability and spreading President Karzai's authority beyond Kabul.

Rule of law

In Haiti, in 1994–1995, international experts lauded returning President Aristide for entirely abolishing the 'Security Forces', and called it the single most positive step towards restoring the rule of law. They also praised the newly created Haitian National Police. By 2005, the same international experts claimed that the abolition of the Security Forces had been a singularly counter-productive decision that had caused a power vacuum, and recognized that the new Haitian National Police were the main cause of high insecurity.

Human rights

Both the Srebrenica massacre and the Rwandan genocide occurred under UN mandate and surveillance, deeply tarnishing the UN's image. The international community has engaged in soul-searching examinations of these grievous failures. A host of factors were responsible, including the lack of political will and resources in both cases to provide a forceful enough mission and mandate to protect citizens. The new norm of 'Responsibility to Protect' adopted by the UN in its sixtieth summit aspires to obviate such tragedies in the future through timely protective action. Human rights abuses in Abu Ghraib, human trafficking, rape and corruption by US and UN personnel have added to the deep discredit of the international community.

Power sharing

In Angola, although it was public knowledge that he had used diamonds and oil revenues to fuel his rebellion, Jonas Savimbi, leader of the Unita movement, was offered the post of Minister of Mines, as though to legitimize his continued pillage of national resources. Despite this, he dragged the country back to war in 1998.

Best practices

The peacebuilding failures during the 1990s have generated much debate in academic and policy circles as to how to avoid such pitfalls in future intervention. The following is a brief discussion on best practices.

Elections

Despite failures in countries such as Angola, there are some 'best practice' examples too. El Salvador is perhaps the most enduring case. Former guerrillas have been willing to acquire through the ballot box the social justice and equity they were unable to acquire after twelve years of war and a long-negotiated peace process. In Nicaragua, the recent election of its former president Daniel Ortega, who led the bloody Sandinista war against US-supported armed rebels, on a platform of market-friendly democratic governance, could signal a final turn-around in that country.

Mozambique and South Africa are also often cited as exemplifying best cases. However, while the resilience of democracy in both countries is praiseworthy, it is worrying that social inequality and exclusion continue in both cases due to skewed development patterns and to the social unrest and criminality which they have spawned. Also, South Africa has suffered from corruption and malpractice by politicians and political parties, and from recent riots by impoverished black residents of townships against refugees and immigrants from Africa's wars.

Human rights

In Afghanistan, despite many weaknesses in other aspects of the peacebuilding process, the Afghan National Commission for Human Rights played a positive role and managed to establish its presence and solicit input from locals across the country on key issues such as transitional justice. The Commission stands out as one that has survived despite the odds.

Security sector reform and the rule of law

The El Salvador peace agreement has provided an excellent model delineating the basis for the clear separation of police and military forces. The ad hoc Commission created to vet senior military officers and weed out abusers was particularly successful and should be tried in other cases.

Selected Bibliography

Barnett, M (2006), 'Building a Republican Peace: Stabilising States after War', *International Security*, 30/4: 87–112.
Call, C, & Cook, S (2003), 'On Democratisation and Peacebuilding', *Global Governance*, 9/2: 233–46.
Cheema, S (2005), *Building Democratic Institutions: Governance Reform in Developing Countries*, Westport: Kumarian Press.
Chopra, J, & Hohe, T (2004), 'Participatory Intervention', *Global Governance*, 10: 289–305.

Commission on Global Governance (1995), *Our Global Neighbourhood*, Oxford: Oxford University Press.

Dervis, K (2006), 'Governance and Development', *Journal of Democracy*, 17/4: 153–9.

Diamond, L (2005), 'Lessons from Iraq', *Journal of Democracy*, 16.1: 9–23.

Doyle, MW (1983), 'Kant, Liberal Legacies, and Foreign Affairs', *Philosophy and Public Affairs*, 12/3, 205–35.

European Commission, 2003, *Governance and Development*, communication from the Commission to the Council, the European Parliament and the European Economic and Social Committee, com(2003) 615 final, Brussels: Commission of the European Communities, 20 October 2003, available at: <http://europa.eu/eur-lex/en/com/cnc/2003/com2003_0615en01.pdf>.

Franck, T (1992), 'The Emerging Right to Democratic Governance', *American Journal of International Law*, 86/1: 46–91.

French Development Cooperation (2006), *Governance Strategy for French Development Assistance*, Paris: Ministry of Foreign Affairs.

Gershman, C, & Allen, M (2006), 'The Assault on Democracy Assistance', *Journal of Democracy*, 17/2: 36–51.

Goodson, L (2005), 'Bullets, Ballots, and Poppies in Afghanistan', *Journal of Democracy*, 16.1: 24–38

Huntington, S (1991), *The Third Wave: Democratization in the Late Twentieth Century* (Norman: University of Oklahoma Press).

Krasner, S (2005), 'Building Democracy after Conflict: The Case for Shared Sovereignty', *Journal of Democracy*, 16/1: 69–83.

Krause, K, & Jütersonke, O (2005), 'Peace, Security and Development in Post-Conflict Environments', *Security Dialogue*, 36/4: 447–62.

Linz, JJ, & Stepan, A (1996), 'Toward Consolidated Democracies', *Journal of Democracy*, 7/2: 14–33.

Luckham, R, & Bastian, S (2003), *Can Democracy Be Designed? The Politics of Institutional Choice in Conflict-Torn Societies*, London: Zed.

Maley, W (2006), 'Democratic Governance and Post-Conflict Transitions', *Chicago Journal of International Law*, 6/2: 683–701.

Mani, R (2002), *Beyond Retribution: Seeking Justice in the Shadows of War*, Cambridge: Polity Press.

—— (2003), 'Ending Impunity and Building Justice in Afghanistan', Issues Paper, Afghanistan Research and Evaluation Unit, December 2003.

—— (2006), 'The Relationship between Security and Democracy in Combating Terrorism', Background Paper No 6, presented to the 6th International Conference of New or Restored Democracies, Doha, Qatar, 29 October–1 November 2006.

Nzongola-Ntalaja, G (2004), 'Democratic Governance and Human Rights in an International Framework', Keynote Address for Joint Monthly Assembly of Finnish Advisory Board for Human Rights and Finnish Development Policy Committee, Helsinki, 15 June.

Ottaway, M (2003), 'Promoting Democracy after Conflict: The Difficult Choices', *International Studies Perspectives*, 4: 314–22.

Pai Panandiker, VA (ed) (2000), *Problems of Governance in South Asia*, New Delhi: Konark Publishers, 1–27.

Paris, R (2002), 'International peacebuilding and the mission civilisatrice', *Review of International Studies*, 28: 637–56.

Plattner, M (2005), 'Building Democracy after Conflict: Introduction', *Journal of Democracy*, 16/1: 4–8.

Risse, T & Lehmkuhi, U (2006), *Governance in Areas of Limited Statehood—New Modes of Governance?* SFB-Governance Working Paper Series, No. 1, December 2006, available at: <http://www.sfb-governance.de/publikationen/sfbgov_wp/wp1_en/sfbgov_wp1_en.pdf>.

Rosenberg, SW (2004), *Reconstructing the Concept of Democratic Deliberation*, Paper 04–02, Irvine: Centre for the Study of Democracy, University of California, available at: <http://repositories.cdlib.org/csd/04–02>.

Russett, B (1993), *Grasping the Democratic Peace*, Princeton University Press.

Samuels, K (2006), 'Post-Conflict Peacebuilding and Constitution-Making', *Chicago Journal of International Law*, 6/2: 1–20.

Santiso, C (2002), 'Promoting Democratic Governance and Preventing the Recurrence of Conflict: The Role of the UNDP in Post-Conflict Peacebuilding', *Journal of Latin American Studies*, 34/3: 555–86.

Sisk, T, & Large, J (2006), *Democracy Conflict and Human Security*, Stockholm: IDEA.

Sobhan, R (2000), 'Problems of Governance in South Asia: An Overview', in VA Pai Panandiker (ed), *Problems of Governance in South Asia*, New Delhi: Vedams.

Stewart, F (2006), *Policies towards Horizontal Inequalities in Post-Conflict Reconstruction*, Research Paper No 2006/149, UNU-WIDER.

UNDP (2002), *Deepening Democracy in a Fragmented World*. Human Development Report 2002.

UNDP (2004), *Strategy Note on Governance for Human Development*, New York.

UNDP (Democratic Governance Thematic Trust Fund) (2006), *2005 Annual Report*, New York.

UNDP (Management Development and Governance Division) (undated), *Governance in Post-Conflict Countries*, available at: <http://mirror.undp.org/magnet/Docs/crisis/monograph/Monograph.htm>.

UN (1992), An Agenda for Peace. Preventive diplomacy, peacemaking and peace-keeping. Report of the Secretary–General pusuant to the statement adopted by the Summit Meeting of the Security Council on 31 January 1992, A/47/277–S/24111, 17 June 1992.

UN (1996), An Agenda for Democratization. A/51/761;DPI/1867.

UN (2005), *Support by the United Nations System of the Efforts of Governments to Promote and Consolidate New or Restored Democracies*, Report of the Secretary-General, A/60/556, General Assembly, 15 November.

USAID (United States Agency for International Development) (2002), 'Promoting Democratic Governance', in USAID, *Foreign Aid in the National Interest*, Washington, DC: USAID, Chapter 2, 33–53, available at: <http://www.usaid.gov/fani/ch01>.

• Online resources

United Nations Development Programme Democratic Governance <http://www.undp.org/governance>.

United Nations Development Programme UNDP Oslo Governance Centre <http://www.undp.org/oslocentre>.

World Bank Institute (2004) <http://www.worldbank.org/wbi/governance>.

Disarmament, Demobilization, and Reintegration

Robert Muggah

Definition

Disarmament, demobilization, and reintegration ordinarily includes activities that focus on weapons collection and control, the cantonment and demobilization of ex-combatants and veterans, the provision of reintegration and reinsertion assistance and support, and incentives to assist former soldiers and persons associated with fighting forces in their transition to civilian life. Regularly introduced in the wake of a peace agreement DDR is aimed at bridging security and development concerns.

I. Term

Origin and context

Disarmament, demobilization, and reintegration (DDR) is a comparatively new concept. It was adopted by the development and security sectors in the context of so-called 'post-conflict recovery' and 'peace support operations'. As in the case of security sector reform, DDR emerged in conjunction with growing awareness among international donors, agencies, practitioners, and scholars of the linkages between insecurity and under-development in 'transitional' environments (Berdal, 1996).

Prior to the 1980s, initiatives involving disarmament, demobilization and reintegration were conceived and executed virtually exclusively by and for formal military entities and structures. Initially focused on veterans and in rare cases rebel combatants, these early DDR operations were expected to reduce defence expenditures and promote internal stability in the aftermath of an armed conflict. At best, it was expected that DDR might prevent armed conflicts from re-emerging and reduce the possibility of contagion across borders. Early DDR initiatives such as those promoted by the United Kingdom (UK) in Zimbabwe in 1979 and 1980 were confined to bilateral cooperation between ministries of defence. In the process, they brought together an assortment of objectives, such as ensuring ceasefires were adhered to as well as the down-sizing, decommissioning, and reform of formal military institutions. The outcomes of these early initiatives were mixed.

By the late 1980s, the UN and its associated agencies were increasingly requested by UN member states to support DDR activities. Investment in DDR and related small arms control activities was routinely pursued in conjunction with peace operations. The first official UN Security Council-sanctioned DDR operation was launched in Namibia (1989–1990) with support from the UN Transitional Assistance Group (UNTAG). Designed to support the country's overall transition to independence, the DDR programme was expected to ensure that South African and South West African People's Organization (SWAPO) troops were cantoned and that South African military forces and other 'ethnic and paramilitary units' were eventually disbanded. Analogous initiatives in southern Africa, Central America, and the Balkans followed soon after.

International optimism in humanitarian, state-building, and peacebuilding missions in the wake of the Cold War spurred on renewed commitment to UN-sponsored peace operations and post-conflict reconstruction efforts. In certain cases, states such as Ethiopia and Eritrea pursued DDR without formal support from the UN during the early 1990s (as has the Philippines since the late 1990s and Colombia since 2003). UN-supported DDR programmes—implemented with support from the Department for Peacekeeping Operations (DPKO) among others—were the norm, however, and rapidly emerged in Angola, Mozambique, El Salvador, Cambodia, and elsewhere. Throughout the 1990s, the DDR concept rapidly diffused into international security and development discourse and practice and emerged in a growing array of UN Security Council resolutions and declarations by regional organizations.

More fundamentally, during the latter 1990s the concept surfaced in a growing array of contexts. For example, DDR was applied to regular soldiers in post-conflict environments following a ceasefire or peace agreement, as well as to irregular ex-combatants originally part of a guerrilla group, and even gangs and 'at-risk' youth in urban slums and areas with high concentrations of extractable resources. A loose doctrine began to emerge: though every DDR operation was expected to be 'context-specific', approaches to DDR adopted common characteristics. For example, provisions for DDR were increasingly grafted into peace agreements and UN Security Council resolutions. DDR operations were regularly overseen by an enabling national mechanism so that it might be 'owned' by the hosting state. The process was also necessarily guided by a normative framework prescribing the division of labour and the precise role of the international community to 'assist'.

Many of the early missions in the 1990s were test cases for the viability of DDR. But even while the popularity for DDR grew amongst donors, the outcomes of these processes in preventing a return to conflict were not always positive. Indeed, in certain cases—notably the Democratic Republic of Congo, Haiti, the Philippines, and elsewhere—DDR did not prevent a return to war or war-like circumstances. Likewise, while disarmament and demobilization appeared to yield short-term dividends in terms of temporary improvements in security, the effectiveness of large-scale investments in 'reintegration' were much less evident. These shortcomings were noted in a 1998 report of the UN Secretary-General wherein the 'reintegration of ex-combatants and others into productive society' was declared one of the priorities of 'post-conflict peacebuilding'. Though still lacking a firm doctrine and minimum standards, expectations of DDR nevertheless continued to grow.

By the end of the 1990s DDR was widely considered to be a central plank of virtually all military–civilian transition operations. Financial and operational inputs into aspects of disarmament, demobilization, reinsertion, reintegration, and even repatriation of foreign combatants were provided by over fifteen UN agencies including DPKO, the UN Development Programme (UNDP), the International Organization for Migration (IOM), the UN Children's Fund (UNICEF), and the Office of the UN High Commissioner for Refugees (UNHCR), as well as international financial institutions (World Bank, regional banks), donor governments and a host of multilateral agencies, and non-governmental organizations (NGOs). At the same time, UNDP, as well as IOM, the European Union (EU), German Technical Cooperation (GTZ), the UK Department for International Development (DFID), and others began investing in a variety of analogous activities—including weapons reduction interventions focused on civilians—in more than fifty countries since 1995. These activities, while related to DDR, were expected to enhance and supplement more 'conventional' DDR, which remained the preserve of DPKO.

Meanings and official definitions

As expectations continued to grow, DDR operations themselves also began to expand. For example, in addition to a core focus on formal and informal ex-combatants, they started to emphasize specialized components for the repatriation of 'foreign' ex-combatants and focused interventions on behalf of child and female soldiers, dependants of soldiers, HIV/AIDS-affected combatants, and other so-called 'vulnerable' groups. Owing to the rapid proliferation of DDR activities around the world, a bewildering array of expressions and concepts emerged that are now regularly deployed by academics, policy-makers and practitioners. A short-list of expressions used regularly by UN agencies, the World Bank, donors, and research institutes includes:

- Disarmament, Demobilization, and Reintegration (DDR);
- Disarmament, Demobilization, and Reinsertion (DDR);
- Demobilization, Reinsertion, and Reintegration (DRR);
- *Réinsertion et Ramassage d'Armes* (RRA);
- Demobilization, Reintegration, and Rehabilitation (DRR);

- Disarmament, Demobilization, Reintegration, and Rehabilitation (DDRR);
- Disarmament, Demobilization, Reinsertion, and Reintegration (DDRR);
- Disarmament, Demobilization, Repatriation, Resettlement and Reintegration (DDRRR).

Despite the introduction of more robust definitions of DDR in the late 1990s, concepts were often confused and used synonymously. In some cases, for example, 'reinsertion' (defined by the World Bank as a short-term 'safety-net' lasting under six months following demobilization) was equated with 'reintegration' (considered by the UN and the World Bank to be a much longer-term exercise involving sustainable livelihoods and enduring for several years). Certain policy-makers and practitioners combined 'demobilization' and 'disarmament' while others kept them conceptually and operationally separate. The merging of expressions with different policy connotations led to a certain level of confusion and even tension between implementing agencies.

The development sector's premier agencies, the World Bank and UNDP, waded into the DDR sectors comparatively early on. Since the early 1990s, the World Bank has provided a combination of soft loans, credits, and grants to promote Demobilization and Reintegration Programmes (DRP)—often through multi-donor trust funds—to no fewer than 20 countries. The World Bank collaborated with the UN in the design and financing of many of these interventions—often in close partnership with UNDP or DPKO who typically handled disarmament, weapons destruction, mine action, and security sector reform. Even so, the World Bank was and continues to be unable to address 'disarmament' owing to mandate restrictions. Nevertheless, the World Bank (2003) was one of the first institutions to develop a robust analytical capacity in this sector and:

> broadened its response from a focus on providing financial capital and rebuilding physical infrastructure, to a comprehensive approach also including initiatives to support the demobilization and reintegration of ex-combatants . . . [as they are] an especially vulnerable group in the post-conflict setting.

The UN Secretary-General sought to clarify the terms in 2005 ('Defining DDR' (IDDRS, 2006; UN Doc A/C.5/59/31, 2005: para 1), defining DDR as follows:

> Disarmament is the collection, documentation, control and disposal of small arms, ammunition, explosives and light and heavy weapons of combatants and often also of the civilian population. Disarmament also includes the development of responsible arms management programmes.
>
> Demobilization is the formal and controlled discharge of active combatants from armed forces or other armed groups. The first stage of demobilization may extend from the processing of individual combatants in temporary centres to the massing of troops in camps designated for this purpose (cantonment sites, encampments, assembly areas or barracks). The second stage of demobilization encompasses the support package provided to the demobilized, which is called reinsertion.

Reinsertion is the assistance offered to ex-combatants during demobilization but prior to the longer-term process of reintegration.... reinsertion is short-term material and/or financial assistance to meet immediate needs, and can last up to one year.

Reintegration is the process by which ex-combatants acquire civilian status and gain sustainable employment and income. Reintegration is essentially a social and economic process with an open time-frame, primarily taking place in communities at the local level. It is part of the general development of a country and a national responsibility, and often necessitates long-term external assistance.

II. Content

Underlying ideological, normative, and institutional issues

While considered a mainstay of the development, security, peace-support, and peacebuilding lexicon, there is still no agreed doctrine for DDR. Owing to the sheer diversity and heterogeneity of actors involved, their competing epistemic and bureaucratic perspectives, and the absence of any agreed approach to financing, designing, executing, and managing DDR, it is hardly surprising that there are unacknowledged, if deeply ingrained, disagreements over its objectives.

Most actors concede that DDR is fundamentally concerned with the promotion of security and stability in the post-conflict period so that social and economic recovery can resume. But even at this basic level, concepts such as 'security', 'stability', and 'post-conflict' are variously defined and measured. For example, should security promotion be targeted at the international, national or human level? Should both objective and subjective metrics of stability apply? Likewise, as with definitions of 'war', 'conflict' and 'crime', there is no consensus on when a country is officially 'post' conflict or not. Basic agreement on definitions and core concepts is a *sine qua non* of effective communication and coordination.

One recent effort to standardize and professionalize approaches to DDR is the DPKO's Integrated Disarmament, Demobilization and Reintegration Standards (IDDRS, 2006). Established between 2004 and 2006, the IDDRS is a comprehensive set of policies, guidelines and procedures covering separate aspects of DDR. The guidelines focus on concepts, policy and strategy, structures and processes (including management and verification), and operations and programming support. They also touch on cross-cutting themes relating to gender, youth, children, migration, food security, HIV/AIDS, and public health more generally. Ultimately, the IDDRS consolidate policy guidance on DDR, and aim to provide an 'integrated' approach to undertaking it. They are described by DPKO as 'the most complete repository and best practices drawn from the experience of all United Nations departments, agencies, funds and programmes involved in DDR' (IDDRS, 2006).

Despite considerable international pressure to improve the coherence and predictability of DDR, there are nevertheless competing visions of its goals and objectives, the means by which it should be accomplished and even the target groups. Specifically, there are ideological differences between implementing agencies and donors on whether DDR should be narrowly or broadly conceived. Moreover, despite the growing commitment to 'integrated' approaches to DDR, there are still real challenges to making systems and institutions work effectively on the ground. Finally, there are lingering concerns over how to 'target' the beneficiary and, indeed, who is included as a beneficiary at all (Muggah, 2009).

DDR can be viewed on a continuum that extends from a minimalist (improving security) to a maximalist (as an opportunity for development) perspective (see also on this problematic, the chapters on conflict transformation and human security). Certain agencies such as the DPKO adopt the former view in that they focus instinctively on removing weapons and cantoning ex-soldiers. Others, such as UNDP, UNICEF and the World Bank tend to endorse programmes that envision DDR as an opportunity to redress distortions in defence and social welfare spending, to fully rehabilitate ex-combatants and provide for dependents, and to re-orientate attention to longer-term developmental support. It is important to acknowledge competing ideational approaches to DDR for they carry very different assumptions and biases. Though recent efforts have been made to promote shared understandings, certain implementing agencies note the benefits of retaining 'flexible' definitions.

Reconciling the minimalist and maximalist perspectives and articulating clear targets is important for a variety of reasons. On the one hand, clear unambiguous goals focusing on achievable targets such as collecting a specified number of weapons or demobilizing a certain number of ex-combatants are important. But objectives emphasizing tangible and subjective improvements in safety and sustainable reintegration are arguably even more crucial. Likewise, achievements in relation to poverty reduction are increasingly expected of DDR. Indeed, donors are increasingly keen to endorse the maximalist approach with all of its 'development' aspirations. Unsurprisingly, then, DDR activities are increasingly wide-ranging in their parameters and approach—incorporating, inter alia, armed violence prevention and reduction, community security promotion, and provisions for transitional justice. Some critics argue that these latter activities could be described as interim stabilization and second generation security promotion initiatives and not DDR (Colletta and Muggah, forthcoming).

The World Bank is an ardent supporter of maximalist DDR programmes. For example, DRP interventions supported by the World Bank in Uganda (1994), Ethiopia (2001–2003), and Eritrea (2001–2003) were designed to exert fundamental transformations in national budget priorities (downsizing of recurrent defence expenditures and increase in social spending) while also reintegrating ex-combatants and promoting specialized programmes for dependents as well as HIV/AIDS-infected or disabled veterans. In some cases, DRPs were linked with ongoing safety-net and food security initiatives and urban/rural renewal schemes. Likewise, at the micro level, DDR initiatives launched in the Republic of Congo, Haiti, Mozambique, the Philippines, Sierra Leone, the Solomon Islands, Sudan, and elsewhere also adopted maximalist approaches—both expanding the caseload to accommodate more beneficiaries (eg ex-combatants and non-combatants), but also investing in culturally and socially appropriate community-based 'incentives' as the basis of DDR rather than strict rational choice models focused exclusively on individual preferences.

Challenges and dilemmas

While few proponents dispute the desirability of integrated DDR in principle, many practical constraints limit its actualization on the ground. Policy makers, managers, and practitioners complain that the parameters of inter-agency collaboration remain unclear and that few guidelines have been issued to inform the process. Tensions are also surfacing between UN agencies over mandates and priorities when it comes to DDR, particularly in resource-scarce environments. In two countries where integrated approaches to DDR are being piloted—the UN Stabilization Mission in Haiti (MINUSTAH) and the UN Mission in Sudan (UNMIS)—interventions stalled soon after they began.

Another set of challenges relate to defining who is and who is not included as a 'combatant' and the ethical implications of 'rewarding' them for past atrocities. On the one hand, anthropological and sociological contributions to the DDR literature emphasize the porous line distinguishing a combatant from a civilian—some may be 'hard-core' fighters and rank and file, while others may be 'part-time warriors' or simply porters and associated forces (Jensen & Stepputat, 2001). An additional difficulty in registering ex-combatants lies in the large diversity of militias and para-military groups—many of whom are often deliberately excluded from formal peace agreements, and thus denied access to conventional DDR programmes. A narrowly defined focus on weapon holders at the expense of other 'high risk groups' not explicitly covered by DDR mandates often constitutes a major flaw in DDR, especially in countries where pervasive weapons cultures persist. At the same time, even after being identified as combatants, there are often tremendous stigmas accompanying their return and reintegration back to their original communities or another area.

These challenges notwithstanding, concrete and durable achievements are now regularly expected from DDR and weapons reduction. This is the case whether they are construed narrowly as interventions designed to reduce the number of firearms in a given post-conflict context and to improve safety or more broadly as programmes intended to contribute to community and economic development, to reconfigure national spending priorities and to diminish the prospects of renewed conflict. In reality, the effectiveness of DDR in any of these areas is still only beginning to be understood (Muggah, 2009). Ultimately, unless the objectives of DDR are more clearly articulated at the outset and their capacity to enhance security is irrefutably demonstrated, DDR may yet prove to be little more than another passing fad.

It is important to recognize that DDR is not the only type of security-promoting intervention in the post-conflict period. In fact, there are multiple activities that frequently overlap or run in parallel with DDR. These include armed violence prevention and reduction, child DDR (see below), micro-disarmament and weapons for development programmes, and community or citizen security promotion (see for instance the chapters on security sector reform, mine action, and even more generally recovery; conflict economies). There is a growing recognition that linkages between DDR and these other types of programmes need to be made more emphatically if genuinely comprehensive and sustainable solutions are to be realized on the ground.

'Armed violence prevention and reduction' is a relatively new concept pursued by the Inter-American Development Bank (IADB) in the context of crime reduction and recently endorsed by UNDP and the World Health Organization (WHO). The World Bank and the IADB have long provided soft loans and grants to governments in Latin America and the Caribbean to promote reduction of crime and violence—including urban renewal schemes, education schemes for high-risk groups, street lighting and temporary alcohol and weapons restrictions, and support for community policing. UNDP and WHO are also increasingly supporting national and municipal initiatives designed to provide alternatives for 'high-risk' groups, but also adopt other forms such as family planning, awareness, and sensitization programmes; anti-narcotics interventions; slum development schemes; gun-free zones and sanctuaries; and other forms of local-level reconciliation activities.

Though sharing many common features with conventional DDR, 'child DDR' is distinct from initiatives designed for adults. Such activities emphasize demobilization (or 'release') and reintegration of children, especially girls, on a continuous basis even during a conflict. Children 'associated' with armed forces are also considered child soldiers, and interventions focus on ensuring that they are released by the groups that recruited them and that they receive reintegration support without conditions for disarmament. Child DDR also shields related structures and mechanisms from setbacks in national DDR or security sector reform programmes, whether lack of funding or relapses of armed conflict. Equally, child-specific DDR mechanisms often endure longer than conventional DDR programmes—often long after the reintegration of adult soldiers is complete.

Disarmament focused exclusively on civilians is often referred to as 'practical' or 'micro-disarmament.' Micro-disarmament and weapons reduction has a much lengthier history than DDR (Muggah, 2006b). As with DDR, it is important that such programmes are carried out in a fair, efficient, and controlled fashion, with transparent monitoring and verification procedures to ensure public awareness of the purposes of disarmament, the safe handling, storage, and management of weapons, and, ultimately, their disposal. Importantly, micro-disarmament is expected to both physically remove (illegal) weapons, but more importantly, to eliminate or reduce the psychological or attitudinal predisposition for weapons acquisition and misuse.

III. Implementation

Lessons learned, good practice, and operational aspects

The UN defines DDR as proceeding along a 'continuum' that is aligned to a given peace process (UN Secretary-General, 2005; UN Security Council, 2000). Effective DDR is expected to substantially reduce the possibility for armed violence to re-emerge and to assist the foundations for social and economic development to proceed. Though a tendency toward linear sequenced approaches persists, there is also growing acceptance that the design and implementation of DDR should be informed by a context-specific strategic evaluation (for a similar conclusion see notably the chapter on security sector reform).

As noted above, disarmament was traditionally considered to be the preserve of military actors concerned with the management of arms and ammunition in order to create a secure and stable environment. Even so, the UNDP and other development actors have increasingly become involved in aspects of disarmament. Disarmament generally includes the collection, control, disposal, and destruction of small arms and light weapons, explosives, unexploded ordnance, and ammunition held by the organs of regular and irregular combatants and, in some cases, civilians.

Since the 1990s, disarmament processes have been carried out in at least three ways. First, they are administered coercively by the army, police, or a peacekeeping force—often through cordon and search operations and with severe penalties associated with non-compliance. Second, they are carried out with the threat of force, through amnesty initiatives and public collection/surrender campaigns administered by the army, police, peacekeeping forces, or other designated actors such as UNDP or IOM (see civil-military interface). Third, since the mid-1990s, weapons have been gathered via a public and transparent exchange for another good—either cash or other incentives, and administered by a combination of the abovementioned actors. Examples of 'voluntary' exchanges include 'weapons for development programmes', 'weapons lotteries', voluntary amnesties, and 'weapons free zones', and voluntary amnesties, as in Cambodia, Colombia, Haiti, Liberia, Mozambique, Sierra Leone, and the Solomon Islands.

Demobilization is typically conceived as a short-term process aiming at reducing the size of the armed forces or rebel groups through their integration into a formal entity, downsizing, or complete disbandment as part of a broader transformation from war to peace (UN, 2000). Demobilization includes the formal and usually controlled identification, registration, and discharge of active combatants from regular or irregular forces. Demobilization is therefore a temporary initiative targeted at regular soldiers serving in the military (or para-military) and/or combatants in irregular forces such as guerrilla or militia.

The demobilization process itself ordinarily includes the efficient massing of ex-combatants together in encampment or 'cantonment' sites that are specifically designed for this purpose and their socio-economic profiling. Demobilization may also include disarmament, though this is not always the case. Demobilization, then, is primarily concerned with the registration of formal soldiers as part of a security sector reform initiative or ex-combatants in post-conflict situations—and involves the distribution of non-transferable identification cards, the collection of relevant demographic and socio-economic information into a database, and, where appropriate, the health screening, orientation and facilitation of transport to a new site.

Reintegration is a complex, long-term process through which ex-combatants and their dependants are assisted to (re)settle in post-war communities, become part of the decision-making process, and engage in sustainable civilian employment and livelihoods, as well as adjust attitudes and expectations and/or deal with their war-related mental trauma (psychological) (Kingma, 2001). In this way it is a process with measurable outcomes. Reintegration is often conflated with 'reinsertion.' As noted above, reinsertion is generally considered to be a short-term 'entitlement' to ex-combatants—usually cash or a temporary safety-net—over a defined period. Importantly, reintegration assistance is expected to build on existing capacities (or endowment sets) of ex-combatants and take into consideration the absorptive capacity of the receiving or host community in order to avoid market distortions and for the purposes of equitable allocation of assistance (Colletta and Muggah, forthcoming).

The key objective of reintegration is therefore to support ex-combatants in their efforts to integrate into social, economic and even political networks. Combatants are expected to achieve parity with local communities, and become productive and self-reliant. Reintegration theoretically proceeds after demobilization, though this is not always the case. It can include, but is not limited to, the identification of capacities and needs among ex-combatants, vocational training and apprenticeship programmes (eg agricultural production, the service sector, etc), micro-projects (eg micro-enterprise development and micro-credit facilities), targeted health and education/vocational services, and/or basic implements for re-starting civilian livelihoods. Where appropriate, reintegration assistance may also include psycho-social and professional counselling and outreach services, referral mechanisms to the private sector, sensitization campaigns and the strengthening of 'community services.' Reintegration, then, is social engineering 'par excellence' (CERI, 2004).

DDR is an intensely political activity. Taken together, DDR includes a cluster of interventions explicitly designed to break the command and control of warring parties and promote their long-term integration into civil society. Traditionally the preserve of governments and their militaries, a range of development agencies and bilateral aid departments have waded into the DDR sector in the last decade. This is partly because of growing expertise of such agencies in post-conflict environments, but also due to external pressure from donors to engage more pro-actively in war-torn societies. But despite their growing technical competencies in supporting DDR, it should be recalled that DDR is not (or at least should not be considered) a substitute for political solutions. In fact, the acutely 'political' dimensions of DDR are often poorly-read and under-estimated by development agencies, as will be discussed in more detail below.

The challenges of implementation

There are a host of challenges confronting the smooth execution of DDR. In the early 1990s, DDR was largely conceived within a 'one-size-fits-all' framework and interventions in one country frequently mirrored those undertaken elsewhere. More recently, there has been growing recognition that DDR, as a politico-legal process and cluster of concrete activities, must be carefully tailored to match the particular 'context' for which it is intended. Indeed, several contexts can be considered in which DDR might be introduced—each of which will shape the design, target group and outcomes of the process. These include, but are not limited to:

- pre-conflict scenarios (for formal demobilization and reintegration of armies);
- following a cross-border conflict in which warring parties return to their respective countries;
- immediately following a ceasefire following an internal conflict;
- in the transition period between power-sharing negotiations following an internal conflict; and
- following a peace accord to end an internal conflict in which power-sharing arrangements have been negotiated.

The nature of any DDR activity in any of these scenarios will depend significantly on the extent to which external parties (including sponsors) were active in contributing to war and/or peace as well as the dynamics of combatant mobilization and their relationships to home communities.

The UN is increasingly involved in especially complex DDR operations—whether as part of a peace operation or in other contexts. The dramatic increase in scale, scope, and type of UN work in DDR has required constant adjustments in order to avoid incoherent programming, poor coordination and competition between and among peace operations, agencies and funds. A host of basic lessons are now emerging that form a kind of orthodoxy for DDR. These include the supposed importance of integrated missions; enhancing support for reintegration; nurturing political will and local ownership; ensuring that approaches are people-centred and rights-based; and encouraging a culture of creativity and flexibility.

There is growing support for integrated missions in transitional or post-conflict contexts. Proponents of the integrated model are convinced that a system-wide approach to programming in post-conflict contexts can reduce the likelihood of conflicts resuming. An integrated approach to DDR requires the deliberate positioning of core activities into the overall post-conflict stabilization and recovery process. Put another way, DDR can not be implemented in isolation from broader state and peacebuilding and recovery activities and should be integrated into national development frameworks. Integration of DDR with parallel humanitarian, development, peacekeeping and other priorities is gradually being encouraged in Common Country Assessments (CCA), UN Development Assistance Frameworks (UNDAF), and Poverty Reduction Strategies Papers (PRSP). Early experimentation has reinforced the conclusion that the 'form' of integration should follow 'function' and that standardized templates are to be avoided.

As observed above, the reintegration component continues to represent the most difficult element of DDR programmes both in terms of financing and implementation. UN agencies and donors that are technically equipped to address reintegration are increasingly encouraged to participate in the planning and design of DDR programmes at the earliest stage so as to ensure that the requisite resources are in place. This is considered to be especially important given that key aspects of the reintegration programme are expected to be established well before demobilization takes place. Despite the temptation to envision DDR as a narrow sequence of discrete activities, the sheer scale and complexity of reintegration demands a forward-looking strategy, with reintegration adequately aligned to market demand and the endowment sets of ex-combatants themselves.

DDR cannot be considered a technical substitute for a political process. Rather, it is fundamentally about negotiating politics. Many DDR programmes stall or are only partially implemented because the political climate has not yet ripened—parties to the conflict lack the confidence to engage in the process transparently. The success of DDR fundamentally depends on the presence of sufficient political will of core parties to enter into a meaningful collective enterprise. A key means of ensuring that DDR is supported by relevant actors is by ensuring that key provisions for DDR are included in peace agreements and that confidence building and verification measures are introduced soon after. Operationally, DDR planners often focus on first disarming, demobilizing, and reintegrating children, women, and the disabled as a 'confidence-building measure' before larger-scale demobilization begins.

It is also relevant that the DDR process should be nationally or locally administered (for a similar conclusion see notably the chapters on capacity-building and local ownership). UN agencies are expected to support national actors in the DDR process, including the strengthening or re-building of national capacities to undertake the process and related follow-on activities. In some cases, post-conflict governments may be weak, lack means and legitimacy, and not exercise full control of a country. There may also be little DDR expertise in programme development and management among national staff. In such situations, technical assistance, training and financial support, as well as the involvement of local authorities, affected communities, and ex-combatants and their dependents, becomes a priority. Institutionally, DDR should be overseen by a national enabling mechanism—a commission or department with clear authority and discretion and with civil society representation—so that the process is widely regarded as transparent and credible.

Non-discrimination and fair and equitable treatment are envisioned as core principles in the design and implementation of DDR. A people-centred and rights-based approach is also held to be inextricably linked to international law and the promotion of human rights and humanitarian law more generally, including the Rome Statute of the International Criminal Court and the Operational Protocol on the Convention of the Rights of the Child. DDR programmes tend to focus on several categories of people: (1) male and female adult combatants; (2) children associated with armed forces and groups; (3) those working in non-combat roles; (4) ex-combatants with disabilities and chronic illnesses; and (5) dependents and family members. A particular focus on women and girls—and specialized care and support for victims of sexual and gender-based violence—during the cantonment period is strongly encouraged. Regular consultation with ex-combatants, but also support for communities of return, is crucial so that sustainable rehabilitation and reintegration can proceed.

DDR has taken place in more than sixty countries since the 1980s, with some eighteen operations running concurrently in 2007 and 2008. Ultimately, to be effective, any approach to DDR must be flexible, responsive, and tailored to the country or region in which it is implemented. There is no formulaic or universal template for DDR—and all programmes adopt new innovations and approaches carefully tailored to the local context. Moreover, as the context changes—which often occurs in fragile post-conflict countries—so too must the strategies (including DDR); it is vital that planners and practitioners do not adopt too rigid an approach. While transparent mechanisms for independent monitoring, oversight, and evaluation are crucial, these must take account of changes over time. While the risks of engaging in DDR are high, the perils of not effectively dealing with spoilers are potentially higher still.

Selected Bibliography

Berdal, M (1996), *Disarmament and Demobilisation after Civil Wars*, Adelphi Paper 303, Oxford: Oxford University Press.

CERI (2004), *The Politics and Anti-Politics of Contemporary Disarmament, Demobilisation and Reintegration Programmes*, Paris: Sciences-Politiques/CERI.

Colletta, N, Kostner, M, & Wiederhofer, I (1996), *Case Studies in War-to-Peace Transition: The Demobilisation and Reintegration of Ex-Combatants in Ethiopia*, Namibia and Uganda, Washington, DC: World Bank.

——, & Muggah, R (forthcoming), 'Promoting Post-Conflict Security From the Bottom-Up', *Security Sector Management Journal*, Winter Edition.

Collier, P (1994), 'Demobilisation and Insecurity: A Study in the Economics of the Transition from War to Peace', *Journal of International Development*, 6/3: 343–51.

DPKO (1999), *Disarmament, Demobilisation and Reintegration of Ex-combatants in a Peacekeeping Environment: Principles and Guidelines*, New York: Lessons Learned Unit, Department of Peacekeeping Operations, United Nations.

German Technical Cooperation (2003), *Activity Area—Demobilisation and Reintegration of Ex-combatants*, available at: <http://www.gtz.de/en/>.

Humphreys, M, & Weinstein, J (2004), *What the Fighters Say: A Survey of Ex-Combatants in Sierra Leone: June-August 2003*, New York and Stanford, CA: Colombia University and Stanford University/PRIDE.

IDDRS (2006), *Integrated Disarmament, Demobilization and Reintegration Standards*, New York: DPKO.

Jensen, S, & Finn, S (2001), *Demobilising Armed Civilians*, CDR Policy Paper, Copenhagen: CDR.

Kingma, K (2001), 'Demobilisation, Reintegration and Peacebuilding in Africa', *International Peacekeeping*, 9/2: 181–21.

—— (ed) (2001), *Demobilisation in Sub-Saharan Africa: The Development and Security Impacts*, Basingstoke: Macmillan.

Meek, S (1998), 'Buy or Barter: The History and Prospects of Voluntary Weapons Collection Programmes', *ISS Monograph Series*, No 22, London: Institute for Strategic Studies.

Muggah, R (2004), 'The Anatomy of Disarmament, Demobilisation and Reintegration in the Republic of Congo', *Conflict, Security and Development*, 4: 21–37.

—— (2005), 'Securing Haiti's Transition: Prospects for Disarmament, Demobilisation and Reintegration', Occasional Paper No 14, Geneva: Small Arms Survey.

—— (2006a), 'Reflections on Disarmament, Demobilisation and Reintegration in Sudan', *Humanitarian Practice Exchange*, 33, London: ODI.

—— (2006b), 'Emerging from the Shadow of War: A Critical Perspective on DDR and Weapons Reduction in the Post-Conflict Period', *Journal of Contemporary Security Policy*, 27/1: 190–205.

—— (2007), 'Great expectations: (Dis)integrated DDR in Sudan and Haiti', *Humanitarian Practice Exchange*, 37, London: ODI.

____ (ed) (2009), *Security and Post-Conflict Recovery: Dealing with Fighters in the Aftermath of War*, New York: Routledge.

Swarbrick, P (2007), 'Avoiding Disarmament Failure: The Critical Link in DDR: An Operational Manual for Donors, Managers and Practitioners', Working Paper No 5, Geneva: Small Arms Survey.

UN (2000), *Report of the Panel on UN Peace Operations*, New York: DPKO (A55/102).

UNDP (2003), *UNDP Support for Disarmament, Demobilisation and Reintegration of Ex-Combatants (DDR): A Brief Stock-take of Experiences and Lessons Learned*, New York: UN Development Programme.

UN Secretary-General (2005*), Note to the General Assembly on the Administrative and Budgetary Aspects of the Financing of the United Nations Peacekeeping Operations*, A/C.5/59/31, 24 May.

UN Security Council (2000), *Report of the Secretary-General: The Role of the United Nations Peacekeeping in Disarmament, Demobilisation and Reintegration*, S/2000/101, 11 February.

World Bank (2003), 'Position paper: Linkages between Disarmament, Demobilisation and Reintegration of Ex-combatants and Security Sector Reform', MDRP Secretariat Paper, Washington, DC: World Bank and MDRP Secretariat.

Free and Fair Elections

Victor-Yves Ghebali

Definition

Free and fair elections—be they presidential, general, or local elections or referenda—are popular consultations, which, in peacetime, crisis situations, or post-conflict settings, aim to establish a legitimate and representative government. In addition to fairness and freedom, the election process must meet the demanding standards of periodicity, universality, and equality of the vote; secrecy of ballots; and transparency and accountability.

I. Term

Origin and context

The concept of free and fair elections was developed in the wake of decolonization. It seems to have been used first in a 1956 UN report devoted to Togo's independence from colonial rule (Ebersole, 1992: 94). However, the term still has no internationally accepted definition for the simple reason that universal and regional organizations, as well as non-governmental organizations (NGOs), use the adjectives 'free' and 'fair' as synonymous with 'honest', 'genuine', 'impartial', 'sincere', 'democratic', or 'transparent'. In fact, the notion of freedom is related to participation and choice, while fairness aims at equal participation in the poll, impartiality, and non-discrimination (Goodwin-Gill, 2006: 73). Indeed, elections may be considered as 'free' if they take place in the absence of any significant pressure, intimidation, or violence against voters; they can be labelled 'fair' when all candidates are treated in a non-discriminatory manner (Elklit & Svensson, 1997: 33–5).

It is easier to meet and assess the criteria of freedom than that of fairness. An election may meet the standards of freedom without offering equal opportunities to all candidates or parties—regardless of the challenges posed for transparency and accountability by e-voting, absentee ballots, or early voting ballots (Goodwin-Gill, 2006: 86). In any case, free and fair elections are a matter of general interest for both long-standing democracies and countries undergoing transition from authoritarian regimes to democratic rule, or from war to peace.

International observation of elections was first inaugurated in 1857 by a Commission of European powers which oversaw a plebiscite organized in Moldavia and Wallachia (Beigbeder, 1994: 78). But it developed as a trend only after World War II under the aegis of the UN in relation to decolonization, democratic transition, and peace operations. After the end of the Cold War it became standard practice. However, since the late 1990s, the UN has started to focus on electoral technical assistance, upon request from its member states, and now rarely conducts direct monitoring on the ground, leaving that to a host of regional intergovernmental organizations and NGOs.

For many years, international observation of elections was implemented in the absence of any uniform, or even commonly agreed, standards or guidelines. It was only in October 2005 that a Declaration of Principles for International Election Observation and a Code of Conduct for International Election Observers were framed, at the joint initiative of the UN Electoral Assistance Division and two American NGOs: the Carter Centre and the National Democratic Institute. The texts were immediately endorsed by the intergovernmental organizations most concerned with this issue, that is, the UN, the African Union, the Organization of American States (OAS), the Commonwealth Secretariat, the Council of Europe Parliamentary Assembly and Venice Commission, the European Union (EU) Commission, and the Office for Democratic Institutions and Human Rights (ODIHR) of the Organization for Security and Co-operation in Europe (OSCE). Nevertheless, there have been two major exceptions: the OSCE Parliamentary Assembly and the Commonwealth of Independent States, both of which have challenged the leadership of the ODIHR in this field. However, the Declaration has also received endorsement from specialized NGOs in the different regions of the world, as well as the Inter-Parliamentary Union. In order to avoid rivalries and overlapping roles, all of the endorsing entities now have an obligation to cooperate with each other in the implementation of joint or separate International Election Observation Missions (IEOMs), and any departure from the terms of the Declaration must be accounted for publicly.

Official definitions

The 2005 Declaration offers the first ever universal definition of international election observation in the following terms:

the systematic, comprehensive and accurate gathering of information concerning the laws, processes and institutions related to the conduct of elections and other factors concerning the overall electoral environment; the impartial and professional analysis of such information; and the drawing of conclusions about the character of electoral processes based on the highest standards of accuracy of information and impartiality of analysis (para 4).

Regrettably, the definition does not clarify the morass of election terminology in that it avoids referring to the related notions of 'monitoring', 'supervision', and 'verification' with which observation is confused. These terms are often treated as synonyms by international organizations and NGOs alike. According to the Code of Conduct for Ethical and Professional Observation of Elections, which was published in 1997 by the Swedish International Institute for Democracy and Electoral Assistance, monitoring and supervision entail direct involvement in the management of the electoral process and, hence, entrust monitors and supervisors with greater powers than observers.

While observation is a more passive activity limited to 'gathering information and making informed judgments from that information' with no interference in the election process, monitoring involves the authority 'to intervene in [an electoral] process if relevant laws or standard procedures are being violated or ignored' and supervision that to '[certify] the validity of all or some of the steps in an election process' (eg Namibia in 1989 and Bosnia and Herzegovina in 1996). In practice, though, the OSCE draws no distinction between observation and monitoring. This is not the case for the UN. Within the UN, monitoring simply gives rise to an internal final report; observation assesses the different stages in the election process; verification is the comprehensive observation of an election as well as the certification of the election's outcome; and, finally, supervision is the certification of the different stages in the election process. Ultimately, the real purpose of the 2005 Declaration is to codify not only the preconditions for observation of elections, but also the way it should be carried out and assessed.

II. Content

Guidelines and legal framework

Free and fair elections are governed by international law. Although a domestic matter, the conduct of elections is addressed in the 1948 Universal Declaration of Human Rights (Art 21), the 1966 International Covenant on Civil and Political Rights (Art 25), the 1954 Additional Protocol No 1 to the European Convention on Human Rights (Art 3), the 1969 American Convention on Human Rights (Art 23), the 1981 African Charter on Human and Peoples' Rights (Art 13), and the 1990 Document of the Copenhagen Meeting of the Conference on the Human Dimension of the CSCE (§§ 5.1 to 7.9). It is also referred to in a number of other texts, among them the Inter-Parliamentary Union 1997 Universal Declaration on Democracy (§ 12), the OAS 2001 Inter-American Democratic Charter (Art 3), and the OAU/African Union 2002 Declaration on the Principles Governing Democratic Elections in Africa (Sections I and II). Based on the premise that only periodic free and fair elections can allow the true expression of the people's political will and the establishment of a legitimate government, all texts recognize the rights to vote, to be elected and to participate (directly or through elected representatives) in public affairs—rights which cannot be effectively exercised in the absence of freedom of association, expression and assembly.

Although international law does not formally recognize the right to a representative democratic government, it requires that elections reflect the true will of the people by complying with a number of well-defined fundamental human rights that are in accordance with the basic election standards mentioned in the concept definition given above—periodicity, universality, equality of vote, secret ballot, transparency, and accountability. These standards are embodied in texts such as the Document of the Copenhagen Meeting of the Conference on the Human Dimension of the Commission on Security and Cooperation in Europe (CSCE) (1990), the Inter-Parliamentary Union Declaration on Criteria for Free and Fair Elections (1994), the Council of Europe's Code of Good Practice in Electoral Matters (2002), the Convention on the Standards of Democratic Elections, Electoral Rights, and Freedoms in the Member States of the Commonwealth of Independent States (2002), and in the Principles and Guidelines Governing Democratic Elections of the Southern African Development Community (2004).

The Declaration of Principles for International Election Observation (2005) has set up guidelines related to the preconditions, as well as the operational conduct and the assessment of observation. There are four prerequisites for observation of elections to be possible.

First, the country holding an election must issue a formal invitation sufficiently in advance to allow adequate observation planning. If such observation has not been provided for in a peace agreement or the mandate of a UN peacekeeping operation, standard practice is that observation of elections is triggered by an optional invitation, except in the case of OSCE states which, under § 8 of the Copenhagen Document, have the obligation to invite international observers as well as NGOs.

Second, the host state must guarantee (where possible in a memorandum of understanding) the safety and full freedom of IEOM agents at the different stages of the election process: official accreditation, unimpeded access to all persons and technologies involved in the election process, freedom of movement around the entire country, freedom to publish findings and recommendations, etc.

Third, all major contenders in an election must also approve the presence of the IEOM ahead of time.

Fourth, minimum standards guaranteeing free and fair elections must exist before the IEOM's visit. If this is not the case, international observation will not take place for fear that the IEOM presence may be interpreted as legitimating an undemocratic election process. The OSCE has developed a tried-and-tested approach worth mentioning here. Once the necessary guarantees have been obtained from the host State, the ODIHR establishes a Needs Assessment Mission to appraise whether the conditions are met to enable the conduct of credible free and fair elections. The mission's findings are crucial: in case of positive assessment, a full-fledged IEOM is deployed to observe the whole election cycle; if major inconsistencies are detected, a limited-size mission is sent but leaves the country before Election Day; if the conditions for free and fair elections are obviously not met in the host country, no observation will take place.

Challenges and dilemmas

At the operational level, the 2005 Declaration states that an election must not be considered a single event (Election Day), but instead a process that also includes pre-election and post-election phases. Put differently, the idea is not to end up with a snapshot or a short movie, but rather to shoot an entire feature film encompassing the whole election process, including candidate and voter registration, the campaign, public and private media coverage, Election Day, vote counting, resolution of litigation, and the elected representatives taking office. Accordingly, observation has to be carried out by long-term observers deployed in the capital of the host country some months prior to election, as well as short-term observers arriving just before polling and leaving a day or two after Election Day. Observers must comply with the instructions from IEOM leadership. They must also report any conflict of interest that may arise. In case of a serious violation of the Code of Conduct accompanying the 2005 Declaration, they may lose their accreditation or be dismissed from the mission altogether.

Furthermore, their special duties towards the host country include respect for its sovereignty and domestic laws, as well as cooperation with the authorities, all stakeholders in the election, and national observers. It is also their duty to collect accurate and impartial data. Regrettably, the 2005 Declaration says nothing about harmonization of criteria as regards the selection and training of observers (professional skills, expertise, nationality, gender equality, etc). Thus, while the UN has a roster of electoral experts at its disposal, OSCE short-term observers are seconded by governments. The same applies to the European Union, whose observers are selected by governments but are nonetheless recruited from the pool of UN volunteers.

Finally, regarding assessment, the 2005 Declaration confirms standard practice. It gives IEOMs authority to produce three categories of documents: pre-election statements, preliminary election findings, and a final report. Pre-election statements provide information on voter and candidate registration, the work of the election administration, media coverage and related matters. Preliminary election findings are issued the day after Election Day, sometimes even prior to the official proclamation of the outcome by the election authorities. They offer a rough assessment based on the combined information gathered by long-term and short-term observers. Final reports are published after all complaints and appeals have been settled, often several weeks or months after the poll, and are comprehensive stage-by-stage analyses of the election process. They must point out any occasional or systematic technical flaws or administrative misconduct observed during the process. The purpose of such reports is not to give the election process a pass or a fail, but to provide the most accurate account of the elections and make practical recommendations to improve future consultations. This means that observation does not rule out electoral assistance, such as technical and/or material support to help domestic election commissions and civil society organizations to better manage voter registration and civic education, to overhaul electoral laws, and to train election officers and national observers.

Since the basic aim of observation is to assess all relevant factors that affect the electoral process in order to assess how well it complies with international standards and domestic law, a major challenge facing the monitoring process relates to assessment reports. Such reports often lead to controversy for at least two main reasons.

First, regardless of whether an electoral consultation is conducted in peacetime, in a tense situation or in a post-conflict context, it is political in nature. As such, elections involve crucial stakes for which an IEOM's findings may have far-reaching consequences for both the government and the opposition parties of the concerned state. This can be illustrated by the strong criticisms against the ODIHR voiced by the Putin administration and a number of members of the Commonwealth of Independent States (CIS) close to Russia. They have accused the ODIHR of making findings that are partial to Western states with regard to elections held within the CIS and have criticized its methodology as being inconsistent. The reason for such virulent criticism is not just that ODIHR assessments of elections in CIS countries have been at loggerheads with those from Russian-controlled observer groups, but also that such assessments tarnish the image of the states under observation and undermine Moscow's policy in its self-proclaimed backyard (Ghebali, 2005).

Second, existing international standards for assessing democratic elections are too general to allow for a perfectly accurate, and hence unchallengeable, evaluation. Generally, experts think of these standards as 'broad aspirations' (Bjornlund, 2004: 79), which are 'always and necessarily relative' (Goodwin-Gill, 2006: 79). In reality, final assessment reports quite often come to the conclusion that observation has 'demonstrated the credibility of the election process' or that elections were simply 'acceptable'.

III. Implementation

Objectives and functions

Free and fair elections are an important part of peacebuilding programmes, alongside disarmament, demobilization, and reintegration of former combatants into civil society, recovery, socio-economic reconstruction, return and reintegration of refugees and displaced persons, democratic governance, and transitional just-ice. As such, free and fair elections serve three main functions.

First, given that elections can be tainted by multiple forms of fraud (ballot-box stuffing, voter intimidation, etc), the presence of international observers can deter electoral misconduct, encourage voter participation and guarantee the establish-ment of a legitimate government.

Second, after a violent conflict, free and fair elections are expected to trigger a process of sustainable peace by paving the way for democratic governance and by fostering national reconciliation.

Third, such elections announce the closing phase of the democratization com-ponent of peacebuilding, just as disarmament, demobilization, and reintegra-tion normally constitute its starting point, while also providing an 'exit strategy' which serves as a convenient alibi for a hasty international disengagement.

Since the end of the Cold War, the UN has deployed many peace operations that have included an electoral component mandated to observe, in the general sense of the word, the conduct and regularity of free and fair elections. This has occurred mainly in Africa (Namibia, Angola, Burundi, Central African Republic, Côte d'Ivoire, the Democratic Republic of Congo, Liberia, Mozambique, and Sierra Leone) and the Americas (El Salvador, Haiti). The OSCE performed a similar role in relation to post-conflict consultations in Albania, Croatia, the former Yugoslav Republic of Macedonia, and Tajikistan. In exceptional cases where the UN or the OSCE has assumed responsibility for the direct organiza-tion of elections, (Cambodia, Croatia, and Timor Leste for the UN, and Bosnia and Herzegovina and Kosovo for the OSCE), they have abstained from supervi-sion in favour of third-party intergovernmental actors to avoid being both judge and party.

Lessons learned

A number of these exercises have contributed, in varying degrees, to restoring civil peace and stability. This was the case in Albania, El Salvador, the former Yugoslav Republic of Macedonia, Mozambique, and Namibia. Other experiences, such as those in Cambodia, Liberia, and Kosovo, resulted in only superficial or short-term normalization. Initial post-conflict free and fair elections are only a preliminary step to putting democracy and stabilization on the right track. They are a sym-bolic starting point that can neither generate democracy where it does not already exist nor guarantee its sustainability. Subsequent periodic elections bear much more significance, but their success depends on real assimilation of democratic rules by major political stakeholders and, more importantly, on the existence of a state performing its traditional functions. However, in the absence of a reason-ably functioning state, first-generation post-conflict elections can lead to what the specialized literature labels 'qualified', 'semi', 'formal', 'electoral', 'façade', 'weak', 'partial', 'illiberal', or 'virtual' democracies (Carothers, 2002: 10). In essence, the positive potential of free and fair elections has real natural limits. In some cases, elections even have the ability to jeopardize national reconciliation and revive armed conflict.

In this connection, two major lessons can be drawn from the experience accumulated so far. As regards unrealistic timing, the first lesson has to do with prematurely held elections (see also in this sense the chapter on peace operations). Early consultation in the aftermath of a formal peace settlement may be justified by the need to fill the unhealthy political vacuum of a war-torn society by the election of a government accepted as being legitimate by the local population as well as the international community. However, if elections are organized prematurely, before effective completion of the disarmament, demobilization, and reintegration process, they have the potential to re-ignite armed conflicts. This happened in Angola in 1992. The second lesson has to do with the nature of the electoral system. Post-conflict societies are certainly too fragile to be exposed to a zero-sum game type of political competition. On the contrary, they need an electoral system that distributes political power amongst former enemies.

To take the example of Angola again, the technicalities of majority rule led to a winner-takes-all outcome which was challenged by the losers. The ensuing relapse of violence could have been prevented by a system based on proportional representation that made room for some kind of power-sharing arrangement. In the same vein, the electoral system used in Bosnia and Herzegovina for the different elections has also produced unwelcome effects: from the start in 1996 it has regularly given legitimacy to radical parties hostile to democracy (the same political parties responsible for the ethnic cleansing that occurred during the war in 1992–1995) and, hence, precluded the emergence of an operational government with a normal decision-making capacity. In short, free and fair elections are an indispensable instrument that nevertheless may have a limited impact and, if not carefully handled, may produce unexpected and devastating effects.

Selected Bibliography

Balian, H (2001), 'Ten Years of International Election Assistance and Observation', *Helsinki Monitor*, 12/3: 197–209.

Beigbeder, Y (1994), *International Monitoring of Plebiscites, Referenda and National Elections. Self-Determination and Transition to Democracy*, Dordrecht: Nijhoff, 329.

Bjornlund, EC (2004), *Beyond Free and Fair. Monitoring Elections and Building Democracy*, Baltimore: Johns Hopkins University Press, 383.

Carothers, T (2002), 'The End of the Transition Paradigm', *Journal of Democracy*, 13/1, 5–21.

Clark, ES (2000), 'Why Elections Matter', *The Washington Quarterly*, 23/3: 27–40.

Ebersole, JM (1992), 'The United Nations Response to Requests for Assistance in Electoral Matters', *Virginia Journal of International Law*, 13: 91–122.

Elklit, J, & Svensson, P (July 1997), 'The Rise of Election Monitoring: What Makes Elections Free and Fair?', *Journal of Democracy*, 8/3: 32–46.

Ghebali, V -Y (2005), 'Debating Election and Monitoring Standards at the OSCE. Between Technical Needs and Politicisation', *OSCE Yearbook 2005*, 215–41.

Goodwin-Gill, GS (2006), *Free and Fair Elections*, Geneva: Inter-Parliamentary Union, 233.

Guerrero, JC, & Del Mar, B (2001), 'Les élections dans les opérations internationales de pacification: un instrument de réconciliation? Une réflexion sur la Bosnie', *Cultures et conflits*, 40/1: 129–62.

Lyons, T (2005), *Demilitarising Politics. Elections on the Uncertain Road to Peace*. Boulder: Lynne Rienner, 232.

Manning, C, & Antic, M (2003), 'The Limits of Electoral Engineering', *Journal of Democracy*, 14/3: 45–59.

Human Security

*Keith Krause**

Definition

Over the past decade, many definitions of the term 'human security'—both broad and narrow—have been proposed. Although no consensus definition exists, a reasonable and pragmatic definition of human security in the context of post-conflict peacebuilding would be 'protecting individuals from existential and pervasive threats to their personal safety and physical well-being'.

I. Term

Origin and context

The concept of human security, today widely used by a wide range of governments, international organizations, and non-governmental organizations (NGOs), is the latest in a long series of attempts to broaden traditional conceptions of security. These include such ideas as global security, societal security, common security, comprehensive security, and cooperative security. Aside from being the most recent attempt to redefine the concept of security, the human security approach is significant for two reasons. First, unlike most other previous reformulations, it stands in tension with, or even opposition to, a state-centric conception of security. Second, policymakers have adopted the discourse of human security, and have used it to generate important and interesting foreign and security policy initiatives and to influence specific kinds of programmes and practices, especially in the context of post-conflict peacebuilding.

The concept of human security was born in the policy world. It was first used in the 1994 UN Development Programme (UNDP) 'Human Development Report', although arguably its roots are deeper. As Fen Hampson has noted,

* This article draws upon three previous publications: (2005) 'Human Security: An Idea Whose Time Has Come?', *Security and Peace*, 23/1: 1–6; (2005) 'Peace, Security and Development in Post-Conflict Environments', *Security Dialogue*, 36/4: 447–62; (2007) 'Human Security, States and Citizens: Reciprocal and Inextricable Relations', unpublished paper.

'since the founding of the International Committee of the Red Cross (ICRC) in the 19th century, the notion that people should be protected from violent threats and, when they are harmed or injured, that the international community has an obligation to assist them, has gained widespread acceptance' (Hampson *et al*, 2002: 17) (see also the chapter on responsibility to protect). Ultimately, the concept of human security itself, at least in its more focused formulation, arguably originated with the work of the ICRC and the humanitarian community.

By contrast, the UNDP's vision of human security in its 1994 report was very broad: it encompassed seven different dimensions, including economic, food, health, environmental, personal, community, and political security. The overall goal was to expand the concept of security, which had 'for too long been interpreted narrowly: as security of territory from external aggression, or as protection of national interests in foreign policy or as global security from the threat of nuclear holocaust'. Human security was thus meant to change the referent object of security 'from an exclusive stress on territorial security to a much greater stress on people's security', and, somewhat more problematically, to advocate for 'security through sustainable human development' (UNDP, 1994: 22–4). This conception was paralleled by the work of the Commission on Global Governance, whose 1995 report also advocated an expanded concept of human security that included:

safety from chronic threats such as hunger, disease, and repression, as well as protection from sudden and harmful disruptions in the patterns of daily life...The Commission believes that the security of people must be regarded as a goal as important as the security of states (Commission on Global Governance, 1995: 80–1).

The idea behind the UNDP report was both political and practical. UNDP argued that human security (in its political dimension) meant that 'people should be able to live in a society that honours their basic human rights' (UNDP, 1994: 32). It also noted that military governments, countries experiencing political unrest, and countries in which there were high levels of military spending were not likely to be politically secure, 'since governments sometimes use armies to repress their own people' (UNDP, 1994: 33). Practically, the hope was that an emphasis on human security would make it possible to capture the so-called peace dividend, and to ensure that resources devoted to the military through the Cold War were directed towards more productive ends. The direct aim of the 1994 'Human Development Report' was to influence the outcome of the 1995 Copenhagen Social Summit, and from the outset the concept of human security had clear strategic goals.

Evolution and understandings

Since the mid-1990s, variants of this concept of human security have been used by a wide array of NGOs, states, and international institutions. For example, the definition of human security used by the Commission on Human Security was 'to protect the vital core of all human lives in ways that enhance human freedoms and human fulfilment' (Commission on Human Security, 2003: 4). In practice, this included such things as food, environment, population, and human rights under the umbrella of human security. Others, such as the 'Human Security Report', have used human security more narrowly to describe 'violent threats to individuals' (Human Security Centre, 2005: 4).

It has also become a cornerstone of policy for states such as Canada, Japan, Norway, and Switzerland, and has been formalized in a multilateral setting within the Human Security Network, a loose grouping of fourteen states that have agreed to pursue a common human security agenda on a wide range of issues (<http://www.humansecuritynetwork.org>; Krause, 1996).

Within the UN system, the phrase 'human security' has become a regular feature of UN and multilateral discourses, being used by officials such as the UN High Commissioner for Refugees or the UN Secretary-General. This process reached its height with the '2005 World Summit Outcome' document, when the concept of human security received a 'subheading' and was treated in paragraph 143:

Human security

143. We stress the right of people to live in freedom and dignity, free from poverty and despair. We recognize that all individuals, in particular vulnerable people, are entitled to freedom from fear and freedom from want, with an equal opportunity to enjoy all their rights and fully develop their human potential. To this end, we commit ourselves to discussing and defining the notion of human security in the General Assembly (UN General Assembly, 2005: 31).

These states, NGOs and institutions were attracted to the idea because 'human security' was a nice slogan. But there was more to it than that: human security was a way of describing or framing what they were doing that allowed a number of disparate policy initiatives to be linked and to be given greater coherence. The concept of human security helped to catalyse a broader reframing of how analysts and practitioners thought of the different relationships between security, development, and human rights in world politics. By shifting the referent object of 'security' from that of the state to that of the individual, human security highlighted the tension that exists between promoting state security and promoting the security of individuals, which, historically, has often been jeopardized by the state.

Overall, the use of the concept of human security by states and decision-makers has not been just a matter of labelling, and the promotion of human security has not just been a conceptual or academic exercise. The discourse and practice of human security has led states and policymakers to focus on different issues, to ask different questions, and to promote different policies—policies that are having an impact on the post-conflict peacebuilding agenda.

II. Content

There were, however, two competing visions of the content of human security that emerged out of the various contributions to the debate, and that have been reflected in two different policy approaches. The first, broad vision drew upon the original UNDP formulation and could be summarized by the phrase 'freedom from want': human security was about ensuring basic human needs in economic, health, food, social, and environmental terms. It was directly conveyed in the 2003 report of the Commission on Human Security, and in the funding activities of the Japanese Trust Fund for Human Security. The commission report focused not just on situations of conflict, but also on issues of fair trade, access to healthcare, patent rights, access to education, and basic freedoms, while the Trust Fund has sponsored projects in areas as diverse as food security for farmers in East Timor or fishermen in Southern Sudan, health security in Tajikistan or Mongolia, or the rebuilding of schools in Kosovo.

The second, more tightly focused, vision was linked more closely to the activities of the Human Security Network, and its key slogan was 'freedom from fear': human security was about removing the use of, or threat of, force and violence from people's everyday lives. Examples of policy initiatives included the campaigns to ban anti-personnel mines and cluster munitions, international action to deal with the proliferation and misuse of small arms and light weapons, the promotion of the International Criminal Court, and the broad area of security sector reform. Some of these specific initiatives will be elaborated upon below.

Although it is possible to pursue both the 'freedom from fear' and 'freedom from want' agendas simultaneously (as the 'World Summit Outcome' document implies), the narrow conception of human security as 'freedom from fear' has proven to be intellectually and programmatically more coherent in the context of post-conflict peacebuilding and reconstruction, for two reasons. The first reason is a negative one: the broad vision of human security as 'freedom from want' is ultimately nothing more than a shopping list; it involves labelling as threats to human security a wide range of issues that have no necessary link to each other, and at a certain point, human security seems to capture almost everything that could be considered a threat to well-being. It falls into the trap that Daniel Deudney aptly describes: 'If everything that causes a reduction in human well-being is labelled a security threat, the term loses any analytical usefulness and becomes a loose synonym of "bad"' (Deudney, 1999: 192). At this point, the concept no longer has any utility for policymakers—and incidentally for analysts— since it does not facilitate priority setting or policy coherence and it obscures the distinctive entailments of the idea of 'security', inextricably linked to existential threats, conflicts, and the potential or actual use of violence.

It is not clear that anything is gained by putting the label 'human security' on issues such as the right to education, fair trade practices, or public health challenges. Scholars such as Ole Wæver have described this process as 'securitization', as 'the move that takes politics beyond the usual rules of the game', and as a process that involves political actors declaring that specific issues warrant exceptional attention, efforts, or even sacrifices (Wæver, 1998). Examples such as the 'war on drugs' or the 'global war on terror' well illustrate this process. But does it change our understanding of the right to basic education when we describe illiteracy as a threat to human security—does it facilitate more effective action? Does it help us solve problems? Or does it actually lead us down the wrong path in some cases, to treating certain problems, such as migration, the use of illegal drugs, or HIV/AIDS, as threats to security when they would better be considered as simple public policy challenges?

The example of the international response to the HIV/AIDS pandemic illustrates the tensions involved in securitizing issues. A high-level UN Security Council meeting in January 2000 examined the impact of HIV/AIDS on peace and security in Africa, and declared in July 2000 that 'the HIV/AIDS pandemic, if unchecked, may pose a risk to stability and security' (UN Security Council, 2000; Peterson, 2002/03). But what does this mean in practice? Does the prevalence or spread of HIV/AIDS actually 'decrease[s] security by undermining social and economic conditions, which in turn increases instability, crime, domestic violence, protest, and civil and international war', or are these simply postulated relationships without empirical foundation (Pharaoh & Schönteich, 2003; Singer, 2002)? More importantly, are the conventional responses to security threats (exclusionary, militarized, and linked to emergency measures) appropriate to public health challenges?

The narrow vision of human security has also been more directly and practically linked to post-conflict peacebuilding, and to a coherent policy agenda that is embedded in a particular understanding of liberal state-building. In practical terms, it has led policymakers to focus on basic questions about how to make people safe and secure in their daily lives—in their homes and on the streets, within their communities, and in their regions. In programmatic terms, human security as 'freedom from fear' gives coherence to a set of policy issues that urgently need to be addressed, including such issues as the challenge of post-conflict disarmament, demobilization, and reintegration; the situation of vulnerable groups in conflicts; the role of small arms and light weapons in armed violence; and effective security sector reform. Finally, in conceptual terms, the question of controlling the institutions of organized violence and evacuating force from political, economic, and social life has been central to the whole modern understanding of politics and the struggle to establish legitimate and representative institutions: the concept of human security shines a spotlight on the links between violence and insecurity, on the one hand, and underdevelopment and poverty, on the other.

Given these concerns, a reasonable (if not consensus) definition of human security in the context of post-conflict peacebuilding would be 'protecting individuals from existential and pervasive threats to their personal safety and physical well-being'. This definition has three distinct advantages. First, it is not restricted exclusively to 'violent' threats, but it does not go as far as some of the broader definitions that implicate psychological states or perceptions. Second, it includes 'thresholds': threats have to be existential *and* pervasive, that is, not random or accidental, but more systematic and pressing. Third, it allows such issues as food, health, and certain kinds of environmental or even political threats to be included (such as large-scale violations of human rights by state agents, or major and foreseeable risks of environmental disasters), but, again, only if they are existential and pervasive (see in the same perspective the chapter on responsibility to protect).

III. Implementation

Specific policy initiatives

The influence of a concept cannot be measured simply by the discourse that surrounds it, but by whether or not it informs, or is linked to, a set of concrete practices that are either new, or that represent a significant departure from previous practices. In the case of human security, there was at least one specific set of political initiatives that emerged in the late 1990s, and that represented a partial departure from existing 'ways of practising diplomacy' for a number of states. This was the creation of the Human Security Network, established in 1999 as a loose grouping of states led by Canada, Norway, and Switzerland, whose goal is the pursuit of common policies on human security in a variety of international and regional institutions. The members meet annually at the Foreign Minister level, as a forum for the coordination and shaping of the international security agenda, and throughout the year pursue their initiatives in a variety of formal and informal ways. As a result, many of the participating states have also devoted significant financial resources to promoting human security initiatives, often hand-in-hand with NGOs or with other member states of the network (see the chapter on civil society).

With respect to post-conflict peacebuilding, one can also identify a concrete agenda for political action on a range of issues such as eliminating the scourge of anti-personnel mines, stopping the use of child soldiers, promoting respect for international humanitarian law, and the work of the International Criminal Court, combating proliferation and misuse of small arms and light weapons, enhancing efforts to protect civilians in conflict, and working towards reform of the armed forces, the police and criminal justice systems (see notably the chapters on mine action; disarmament, demobilization, and reintegration; security sector reform; transitional justice; and rule of law). It is impossible to summarize all of the individual initiatives that have been pursued under this wide-ranging and ambitious agenda. Three examples, however, can be offered to show how the human security agenda has evolved from its earliest focus on relatively narrow and self-contained issues, to incorporate some of the policies and programmes that are implied by the 'deeper' state-remaking agenda of human security.

The first example is the evolution of the issue of anti-personnel mines. Earliest efforts in the mid-1990s focused on negotiating a ban (or partial ban) within the context of existing humanitarian law instruments. By 1996, when these efforts had proved fruitless, a coalition of like-minded states and NGOs committed to negotiating a total ban in an ad hoc forum, the result being the 1997 Ottawa Treaty, which entered into force in 1999 (Cameron, Lawson & Tomlin, 1998; Price, 1998). The initial focus was on banning the use (including development, production, transfer, and stockpiling) of anti-personnel mines. Within a short time, however, attention focused as much on assistance to mine victims, and, in the most recent period, on exploring the synergies between mine action and broader social and economic development issues. What began as an 'arms control' issue evolved into a humanitarian or human security issue, and then continued towards a concern with state capacity and the development needs of affected communities (see the chapter on capacity-building). This logical progression was not really foreseen by anyone, but it did reflect a learning process by which concerned states deepened their engagement with a human security issue. For example, in 2006 the Geneva International Centre for Humanitarian Demining launched a project to examine 'linking mine action and development'.

In a related fashion, one can demonstrate that an early concern among Human Security Network states with the high-profile issue of child soldiers evolved into a wide-ranging agenda for protection of children (and other vulnerable groups) in armed conflict. At the outset, the goal was simply to ban the recruitment of children below a certain age (usually 18) into armed forces, whether regular or irregular. But, as advocates and researchers pointed out, this captured only a small percentage—and arguably not the most important one—of the children profoundly affected by armed conflict. Attention turned then, through a series of UN Security Council resolutions (Resolutions 1460 and 1539), to the broader issues of protecting the rights of children (especially girls) in conflict situations, and to dealing with such phenomena as the deliberate use of rape as a strategy of war and the treatment of sexual violence as a war crime (see, for example, <http://www.child-soldiers.org>; Children and Armed Conflict Working Group, 2004).

Perhaps the policy arena in which this linkage is most visible is that of small arms and light weapons, which began, like the campaign to ban anti-personnel mines, with a focus on traditional arms control or supply-side measures. These included, for example, efforts to increase regulation of international arms brokering, the establishment of a mechanism for the international tracing of illicit weapons, concern over the security of weapons stockpiles, and codes of conduct on small arms transfers. Within a few years, however, the agenda had broadened to focus on post-conflict disarmament, demobilization, and reintegration efforts, on integrating small arms work into broader development strategies, as well as broader armed violence prevention and reduction (including demand reduction) strategies (Small Arms Survey 2003: 277–321). This was coupled with a growing recognition that the sources of most weapons in conflict or high-crime zones were local, and that reducing the availability or misuse of weapons depended crucially on whether or not individuals and communities felt that their security needs would be met by other means—by state institutions. The link between small arms and violence reduction and security sector reform is also therefore slowly emerging on the international agenda.

Although human security may be an idea whose time has come, this does not make it immune from critical scrutiny. Three main issues can be raised here. First, and as noted above, there is a potential paradox in the promotion of policies that can lead to a strengthening of the state at the same time as the state is diagnosed as the source of much human insecurity. Disarming the weak without controlling the strong, for example, will not enhance human security in the long run. Encouraging democratic governance with lower military spending may actually, in some cases, leave a state prey to lawlessness and anarchy. Of course, the goal is to contribute to the construction of strong and legitimate states, but the potential dilemmas or unanticipated consequences that human security policies may trigger must be recognized.

Second, the fact that much of the conceptualization of human security and the elaboration of concrete policy initiatives has emerged from states, rather than from civil society, poses a problem. States inevitably face systemic and competitive pressures that lead them to revert to more traditional foreign and security policy stances when they are perceived as getting too far ahead of the broader international community. Within every foreign policy bureaucracy there are traditionalists alongside the policy entrepreneurs, and the balance shifts between them, depending on the perceived advantages and disadvantages that either approach gives to the state (or to its Minister for Foreign Affairs). This sort of bureaucratic pulling and hauling is not surprising, but it can undermine the commitment to promoting the real concerns of human security. In Canada and Norway, two of the founders of the Human Security Network, traditionalists have certainly at different points reasserted their weight against the enthusiasts for human security.

The third problem relates to the role of civil society and non-state actors in the promotion of human security. In order for 'freedom from fear' to be achieved, individuals have to be empowered to take control of their environment and to become stakeholders in political, economic and social processes that affect them (see more generally on this issue the chapter on local ownership). Yet associating a number of prominent Western scholars or NGOs with the idea of human security, and soliciting their input on a variety of policy questions, is not in itself going to advance this bottom-up process of social change. Obviously, a more inclusive dialogue between states and civil society is desirable, but in the realm of human security, as in so many other realms, the 'new multilateralism' does not penetrate deeply, nor is it necessarily the case that non-governmental actors are equal contributors or partners. It is still the case that the people to whom 'freedom from fear' matters are mostly passive subjects in the human security discourse.

Limits and opportunities for human security: some observations

Although these sketchy observations and examples do not completely explain the resonance and importance of the concept of human security, they do show how states, NGOs, and international organizations, responding in a pragmatic and practical manner to perceived policy challenges of the post-Cold War period, opened the door to a wider agenda that involved a rethinking of the meaning of security—for whom, against what, and by what means. A coherent and consensual vision of the human security agenda, however, does not exist.

The development of the 'freedom from fear' agenda was ad hoc, based on the experience of middle-power states working together (and occasionally in partnership with NGOs), in particular on the International Campaign to Ban Landmines. Although the states and international organizations that adopted the human security agenda did so in many cases with their own baggage of policies that they wished to promote, and although political entrepreneurship by states, NGOs, and international organizations was a crucial feature shaping the rapid development of the practice of human security, it would be a mistake to consider that the crystallization of the concept of human security was a sort of afterthought; nor does its use as a label to describe policies that states were already pursuing make the concept itself irrelevant. In fact, most important concepts in international politics (such as sovereignty, diplomacy, international law) emerge as a result of changes in state practice, and of the recognition that disparate threads of policy and practice constitute a new sort of policy domain, or new form of political practice, that requires a specific label.

The important question to ask is therefore: how does what states are 'doing' today depart from conventional understandings of the international security agenda of ten or twenty years ago? Seen in this light, the main issues that come under the heading of human security—security sector reform, protection of civilians in conflict, regulating small arms and light weapons, child soldiers, etc—were almost completely absent from the international scene twenty years ago. Although concrete achievements have not emerged in all these areas, it is reasonably clear that these issues will remain preoccupations of policymakers for years to come.

The use of the concept of human security to unite disparate policy initiatives parallels post-1945 developments, when the concept of 'national security' itself crystallized in international discourse and practice. The concept of human security is entering international discourse in much the same way. Like all concepts, its meaning is constructed through the efforts of institutions and individuals, and in today's world, it is a powerful concept around which practical policies and concrete initiatives have been, and can be, developed and promoted.

Ultimately, though, promoting an agenda of human security—promoting 'freedom from fear'—draws our attention to a number of essential challenges around the world. It goes well beyond the traditional conflict prevention or conflict resolution agenda, and leads us to ask some basic questions about how to make people safe and secure in their daily lives—in their homes and streets, within their communities, and in their regions. It also shines a spotlight on the links between violence and insecurity, on the one hand, and underdevelopment and poverty, on the other hand, and perhaps can help give new direction or energy to some parts of the development community. For political actors and activists, human security is an excellent mobilizing slogan. It gives coherence to a set of policy issues that urgently need to be addressed, including the problems of post-conflict return and reintegration, the situation of vulnerable groups in conflicts, the role of small arms and light weapons in both war and non-war situations, and the effective and legitimate operation of the institutions that we have built to provide security and safety in the modern state. More than that, it provides an intellectually strong foundation for innovative and focused policy initiatives.

This analysis of the contemporary promotion of human security demonstrates that the idea represents the culmination of the liberal project of building strong, legitimate, and representative political institutions. It has its roots in Enlightenment ideas of the importance of individual rights and personal freedoms, and is inextricably linked with our modern understanding of the state, and of state-society relations.

Selected Bibliography

Cameron, M, Lawson, R, & Tomlin, B (eds) (1998), *To Walk Without Fear: The Global Movement to Ban Landmines*, Toronto: Oxford University Press.

Canada, Department of Foreign Affairs and International Trade (1999), *Human Security: Safety for People in a Changing World*, Ottawa.

Children and Armed Conflict Working Group (2004), *The Responsibility to Protect Children: An International Policy Priority*, Ottawa: Canadian Peacebuilding Coordinating Committee, available at: <http://action.web.ca/home/cpcc/attach/Responsibility%20to%20Protect%20Children-English.pdf>.

Commission on Global Governance (1995), *Our Global Neighbourhood*, Oxford: Oxford University Press.

Commission on Human Security (2003), *Human Security Now*, New York: Commission on Human Security.

Deudney, D (1999), 'Environmental Security: A Critique', in Deudney, DH, & Matthew, RA (eds), *Contested Grounds: Security and Conflict in the New Environmental Politics*, Albany: SUNY Press, 187–219.

Hampson, FO *et al* (2002), *Madness in the Multitude: Human Security and World Disorder*, Toronto: Oxford University Press.

Henk, D (2005), 'Human Security: Relevance and Implications', *Parameters*, 35/2: 91–106.

Human Security Centre (2005), *Human Security Report 2005: War and Peace in the 21st Century*, New York: Oxford University Press.

Krause, K (1996), 'Building the Agenda of Human Security: Policy and Practice within the Human Security Network', unpublished paper prepared for UNESCO.

MacFarlane, SN, & Foong Khong, Y (2006), *Human Security and the UN: A Critical History*, Bloomington: University of Indiana Press.

McRae, R, & Hubert, D (eds) (2001), *Human Security and the New Diplomacy: Protecting People, Promoting Peace*, Montreal: McGill-Queen's University Press, 231–5.

Owen, T (2004), 'Human Security – Conflict, Critique and Consensus: Colloquium Remarks and a Proposal for a Threshold-Based Definition', *Security Dialogue*, 35/3: 373–87.

Peterson, S (2002/03), 'Epidemic Disease and National Security', *Security Studies*, 12/2: 43–81.

Pharaoh, R, & Schönteich, M (2003), *AIDS, Security and Governance in Southern Africa: Exploring the Impact*, ISS Paper 65, Pretoria; Cape Town, Institute for Security Studies (ISS).

Price, R (1998), 'Reversing the Gun Sights: Transnational Civil Society Targets Land Mines', *International Organisation*, 52/3: 613–44.

Singer, PW (2002), 'AIDS and International Security', *Survival*, 44/1: 145–58.

Small Arms Survey (2003), *Small Arms Survey 2003: Development Denied*, Oxford: Oxford University Press.

Thomas, C (2001), 'Global Governance, Development and Human Security: Exploring the Links', *Third World Quarterly*, 22/2: 159–75.

UNDP (1994), 'New Dimensions of Human Security', in UNDP, *Human Development Report 1994*, New York: Oxford University Press, Chapter 2, 22–46.

UN Security Council (2000), *Resolution 1308 (2000)*, S/RES/1308 (2000), Security Council, 17 July.

UN General Assembly (2005), *2005 World Summit Outcome*, A/RES/60/1, General Assembly, 24 October.

Wæver, O (1998), 'Security Analysis: Conceptual Apparatus', in Buzan, B, Wæver, O, & de Wilde, J, *Security: A New Framework for Analysis*, Boulder, CO: Lynne Rienner Publishers, 21–47.

International Crimes

Louise Doswald-Beck

Definition

An international crime is a violation of international law which entails individual criminal responsibility. International crimes are perceived as being a threat to peace and security, and a lack of accountability for such crimes frequently prevents a lasting peace. The fact that these crimes are international, and not only national, enables their investigation and prosecution, as well as provision for reparation to the victims, whatever the state of national law may have been before the conflict.

I. Term

Origin and purpose

The notion of international crimes became well established in 1945 with the Charter of the International Military Tribunal in Nuremberg. This charter provided for the trial of persons not only of war crimes, which existed before this date, but also of crimes against peace and crimes against humanity committed during the Second World War. The same set of crimes was prosecuted by the Tribunal for the Far East, established in 1946.

The purpose of trying persons for international crimes after an armed conflict or other serious disturbance is to help rebuild a society based on justice. To this end, it is important that persons who have committed the most egregious offences are seen to face justice. Not to do so reinforces the perception of a society based on impunity; the frustrations felt by the victims of the crimes will continue to impede a genuine and long-term recovery of the society concerned. It is also hoped that knowledge of the existence of international crimes will deter their commission, thus making peacebuilding a less stressful exercise.

Definition and understandings

An international crime is a violation of international law which entails individual criminal responsibility. Apart from this general understanding, there are differences of opinion as to which violations fall within the term 'international crime'. Some limit it to crimes listed in the statutes of international criminal tribunals; typically, genocide, crimes against humanity, and war crimes. The crime of aggression (also referred to as a 'crime against peace') is also often included in this context as it is listed, together with the other three, in the Statute of the International Criminal Court (ICC Statute). The preamble to the statute states that 'such grave crimes threaten the peace, security and well-being of the world'.

Another understanding of the term is based on a special type of jurisdiction for national courts, namely 'universal jurisdiction'. Most national systems limit their jurisdiction to crimes committed on their territory (which can include national carriers such as aircraft and ships) or committed by their nationals. A number of nations also give themselves jurisdiction for crimes committed against their nationals (so-called passive nationality principle). For certain crimes, international law allows states to exercise 'universal jurisdiction', that is, they may exercise their criminal jurisdiction over an alleged perpetrator, irrespective of the nationality of that person or place of commission of the crime. Such universal jurisdiction clearly exists for war crimes and for piracy (an attack for private ends by the crew or passengers of a private ship or aircraft against a ship, aircraft, persons, or property on the high seas or in a place outside the jurisdiction of any state), although piracy is rarely cited these days as an 'international crime'.

Finally, the term 'international crimes' has been applied to violations of specific treaties which require the perpetrator of named offences to be tried by a national court in accordance with certain principles. There are many treaties to this effect. They include the crime of torture, forced disappearance, hijacking, offences against diplomatic staff, hostage taking, and the suppression of various types of terrorism. Another and more common term used for these crimes is 'crimes under international law'. Typically, the treaties concerned require states to include the crimes in their criminal codes. They then require any state, where the perpetrator is to be found, to try that person if the offence took place in that state, if the perpetrator is a national of that state or, if the state has such jurisdiction, if the victim of the crime is its national. These treaties also require a state where a perpetrator is to be found to extradite the person for trial to another state if it cannot or does not wish to try that person itself.

A common factor between 'international crimes' in the narrow sense and 'crimes under international law' is that individuals are guilty of these crimes by virtue of international law. Beyond this common factor there are variations, most notably in relation to rules regulating jurisdiction, although all of these crimes allow or require a perpetrator to be tried or extradited for trial. Most notably, most of the relevant treaties specify that extradition for these crimes cannot be refused on the basis that they are political. The treaties also specify that there needs to be a certain amount of cooperation between countries in order to ensure a proper investigation and prosecution.

For the sake of completeness, it should also be mentioned that a number of treaties require states to prevent violations of those treaties through appropriate legislation, including their national criminal law. However, these treaties are not seen as creating 'international crimes' or 'crimes under international law' because the violations are neither subject to universal jurisdiction, nor to a compulsory try-or-extradite regime. Examples of such treaties include the Ottawa treaty that bans anti-personnel mines and a number of environmental law treaties.

II. Content

Legal description of 'international crimes'

'Crimes against peace' or 'aggression'

'Crimes against peace' were defined under the Charter of the International Military Tribunal at Nuremberg as follows: 'planning, preparation, initiation, or waging of a war of aggression, or a war in violation of international treaties, agreements, or assurances, or participation in a common plan or conspiracy for the accomplishment of any of the foregoing' (Art 6a).

This definition was included in the charter in the context of an 'Agreement for the Prosecution and Punishment of the Major War Criminals of the European Axis' by the three main Allied Powers, the United Kingdom, the United States, and the Soviet Union. The same definition was used by the International Military Tribunal for the Far East, held in Tokyo.

Since the trial of persons for offences committed in the context of World War II, this crime has not been prosecuted by either a national or an international tribunal. After a great deal of discussion, states included the crime of 'aggression' in the ICC Statute. However, the statute specifies that the court cannot actually prosecute this crime until states parties have agreed on a definition. This issue was very controversial during the negotiations for this treaty, some states wanting a fairly wide definition such as that adopted for the Nuremberg tribunal or that adopted by the UN General Assembly in 1974, whereas others wanted a much narrower one or preferably none at all so that the court could not prosecute this crime.

Crimes against humanity

This crime was in effect created by the Charter of the International Military Tribunal at Nuremberg and has since then been incorporated into the tribunals created by the UN Security Council, in particular, the International Criminal Tribunal for the former Yugoslavia, 1993 (ICTY), the International Criminal Tribunal for Rwanda, 1994 (ICTR) and the Special Court for Sierra Leone, 2000 (SCSL).

The most comprehensive definition is that set forth in the ICC Statute:

any of the following acts when committed as part of a widespread or systematic attack directed against any civilian population, with knowledge of the attack:

(a) Murder;
(b) Extermination;
(c) Enslavement;
(d) Deportation or forcible transfer of population;
(e) Imprisonment or other severe deprivation of physical liberty in violation of fundamental rules of international law;
(f) Torture;
(g) Rape, sexual slavery, enforced prostitution, forced pregnancy, enforced sterilisation, or any other form of sexual violence of comparable gravity;
(h) Persecution against any identifiable group or collectivity on political, racial, national, ethnic, cultural, religious, gender ... or other grounds that are universally recognized as impermissible under international law, in connection with any act referred to in this paragraph or any crime within the jurisdiction of the Court;
(i) Enforced disappearance of persons;
(j) The crime of apartheid;
(k) Other inhumane acts of a similar character intentionally causing great suffering, or serious injury to body or to mental or physical health (Art 7(1)).

This definition differs from some others in the following respects:

• The Nuremberg and Far East tribunals as well as the Statute of the ICTY required such acts to be committed in the context of an armed conflict for them to be considered 'crimes against humanity'. This requirement has been dropped since the creation of the ICTR in 1994.

• This definition includes some acts not mentioned as such in the statutes of the other tribunals, in particular, enforced disappearance, apartheid, and various forms of sexual violence other than rape.

• The definition of persecution includes two types of groups not found in the statutes of the other tribunals, namely, 'national' and 'gender'.

The ICC Statute also includes a helpful list of definitions of various terms included in this definition. The definition of 'crimes against humanity' in the ICC Statute is a better basis for understanding the term than the definition in the other statutes for two reasons: first because the other definitions were influenced by the needs of those particular tribunals, and second, because this definition was carefully negotiated by the vast majority of the world's nations, rather than being adopted by the fifteen member states of the UN Security Council.

Genocide

This crime was not included in the charter of the Nuremberg tribunal and only appeared at a later date with the drafting of the 1948 UN Convention on the

Prevention and Punishment of the Crime of Genocide. This crime is defined as follows:

any of the following acts committed with intent to destroy, in whole or in part, a national, ethnical, racial or religious group, as such:

(a) Killing members of the group;
(b) Causing serious bodily or mental harm to members of the group;
(c) Deliberately inflicting on the group conditions of life calculated to bring about its physical destruction in whole or in part;
(d) Imposing measures intended to prevent births within the group;
(e) Forcibly transferring children of the group to another group (Art 2).

This definition is undisputed and has been reproduced *verbatim* in the Statutes of the ICTY and ICTR and in the ICC Statute (genocide is not included in the Statute of the SCSL). It should be noted that a significant difference between this definition and that of crimes against humanity is that 'genocide' requires proving a specific intent alongside the list of actions such as killing, etc, namely, the 'intent to destroy, in whole or in part, a national, ethnical, racial or religious group, as such'.

War crimes

Unlike the crimes defined above, war crimes have a very long history. It has been understood for centuries that state officials (which includes the military) may be tried for violations of the laws of war in national courts. There have been many national criminal cases involving violations of the laws of war, committed either by a state's own nationals or by the nationals of another state.

It should be noted that the term 'war crimes' is generally understood as referring to individual responsibility for violations of a body of law that has different names. International rules relating to what can or cannot be done during an armed conflict were traditionally called 'the laws and customs of war'. This is because such rules in the past only had to be respected in international armed conflicts that were recognized as 'wars'; hence the term 'war crimes'. However, with the abolition of 'war' as an acceptable instrument of national policy, the term 'law of armed conflict' began to be used. Still more recently, the terms 'international humanitarian law of armed conflict' or simply 'international humanitarian law' have been increasingly used. Despite this, the expression 'war crimes' is maintained without the need to show the existence of a 'war'.

In the various statutes of the international tribunals, we find a reference to some of these terms. Hence, the Statute of the ICTY refers to 'violations of the laws or customs of war', whereas the Statute of the SCSL refers to 'serious violations of international humanitarian law'. Some provisions in the statutes of international tribunals simply refer to violations of specific treaty texts regulating armed conflicts.

A definitional distinction exists between a list of particularly serious war crimes, known as 'grave breaches', and the other 'war crimes'. The term 'grave breaches' was first used in the 1949 Geneva Conventions for the introduction of compulsory universal jurisdiction for these serious war crimes. More violations have been classified as 'grave breaches' by Protocol I of 1977 Additional to the 1949 Geneva Conventions. As Protocol I has not yet been universally ratified, only the lists of grave breaches in the four 1949 Conventions are seen as applicable to all states. These lists have been streamlined in the ICC Statute as follows:

grave breaches of the Geneva Conventions of 12 August 1949, namely, any of the following acts against persons or property protected under the provisions of the relevant Geneva Convention:

(1) Wilful killing;
(2) Torture or inhuman treatment, including biological experiments;
(3) Wilfully causing great suffering, or serious injury to body or health;
(4) Extensive destruction and appropriation of property, not justified by military necessity and carried out unlawfully and wantonly;
(5) Compelling a prisoner of war or other protected person to serve in the forces of a hostile power;
(6) Wilfully depriving a prisoner of war or other protected person of the rights of fair and regular trial;
(7) Unlawful deportation or transfer or unlawful confinement;
(8) Taking of hostages (Art 8(2)).

The persons protected under the four Geneva Conventions are enemy sick, wounded or shipwrecked military personnel, prisoners of war, religious and medical personnel, as well as civilians in the power of the adversary, because they are either in enemy national territory or in occupied territory. Grave breaches apply only in international conflicts.

War crimes other than grave breaches are generally understood as any other serious violations of the law of armed conflict (law of war, international humanitarian law). States are required to prosecute such war crimes if committed by their own armed forces or civilians. They may prosecute other alleged offenders under the principle of universal jurisdiction, but, unlike grave breaches, they do not have to do so. Therefore in relation to these war crimes there is 'permissive universal jurisdiction'. War crimes are too numerous to be listed here; the majority are listed in the ICC Statute in the section relating to war crimes in international conflicts. In short, the law of armed conflict prohibits the murder and ill-treatment of persons in the power of the adversary and also limits who and what may be attacked during hostilities, in order to avoid any damage or injury not militarily required for the defeat of the adversary. This includes the prohibition of targeting civilians, attacking specially protected places, recruiting children under fifteen years of age into armed forces or using them in hostilities, and using certain weapons.

Until relatively recently, the notion of 'war crimes' was only applied to inter-national conflicts. However, since the adoption of the 1994 Statute of the ICTR, it is understood to also apply to non-international conflicts. The ICC Statute con-tains a list of war crimes, committed during such conflicts, which are subject to the jurisdiction of the court. In many respects the list is similar to, albeit shorter than, that for international conflicts.

War crimes may be committed by any person, whether civilian or military. The only limitation is that the act concerned must be not only a violation of the law applicable to armed conflicts, but also that there is a nexus between the act and the conflict. Thus an act such as murder, theft or rape, which is motivated by purely personal reasons and which would have occurred whether there was an armed conflict or not, would not be included in the expression 'war crimes'.

Special rules relating to criminal responsibility for 'international crimes'

The degree of seriousness of the four crimes listed above has led to some specific rules:

- *Refusal of refugee status:* the 1951 Convention relating to the Status of Refugees states that the treaty does not apply to any person if there are 'serious reasons' for considering that he or she has 'committed a crime against peace, a war crime, or a crime against humanity'. The same exclusion is specified in the 1960 Convention relating to the Status of Stateless Persons. Although the crime of genocide is not specifically listed, in practice it would be included, as genocide would also be a crime against humanity.

- *Command responsibility:* introduced during the trials by the Nuremburg and Far East tribunals after the Second World War, the principle of 'command responsibility' means that commanders and other superiors (whether military or civilian) are themselves criminally responsible for the international crimes that their subordinates commit if they knew, or had reason to know, that the subordinates were about to commit or were committing such crimes and did not take all the necessary and reasonable measures in their power to prevent such crimes. Such superiors are also responsible if, after the commission of such a crime by a subordinate, they do not take reasonable measures in their power or punish the persons responsible. The ICC Statute includes this rule for the four crimes within its jurisdiction.

- *Superior orders:* prior to the Second World War, it was generally accepted that a valid defence to a war crime was that the perpetrator of the crime was carrying out the order of a superior. This was changed by the Nuremberg and Far East tribunals. The general understanding now is that obeying a superior order does not relieve a subordinate of criminal responsibility if the subordinate knew that the act ordered was unlawful or should have known because of the manifestly unlawful nature of the act ordered. This rule is reflected in the ICC Statute which additionally specifies that 'orders to commit genocide or crimes against humanity are manifestly unlawful' (Art 33(2)).

The definition of international crimes, also referred to as 'crimes under international law'

As indicated above, there are a large number of treaties creating a regime of compulsory trial or extradition for trial for certain offences. Not all of these offences will be defined here but only those most pertinent to post-conflict peacebuilding. The offences listed below occur all too often during an armed conflict or other situation of violence. Victims, or families of victims, expect to see the perpetrators brought to justice (see the chapters on reparation and transitional justice).

Torture

The generally accepted definition is that contained in the 1984 UN Convention against Torture and Other Cruel, Inhuman or Degrading Treatment or Punishment. 'Torture' is defined as follows:

The term 'torture' means any act by which severe pain or suffering, whether physical or mental, is intentionally inflicted on a person for such purposes as obtaining from him or a third person information or a confession, punishing him for an act he or a third person has committed or is suspected of having committed, or intimidating or coercing him or a third person, or for any reason based on discrimination of any kind, when such pain or suffering is inflicted by or at the instigation of or with the consent or acquiescence of a public official or other person acting in an official capacity. It does not include pain or suffering arising only from, inherent in or incidental to lawful sanctions (Art 1(1)).

In short, this definition contains three conditions for an act to be considered to be 'torture':

- inflicting severe pain or suffering;
- intentionally done for a purpose; and
- by a state official or at the instigation or consent of a state official.

The last condition is peculiar to human rights law. The war crime of torture can be committed by any person (as long as it is in the context of an armed conflict) and the crime against humanity of torture can also be committed by any person provided that it is part of a systematic or widespread attack on a particular group.

An act of torture can also be simultaneously a violation of another rule of international law; thus international tribunals have found rape and enforced disappearance to also amount to acts of torture.

Hostage taking

Hostage taking in armed conflict or occupation was criminalized by the Fourth 1949 Geneva Convention and listed as a grave breach. It is also listed as a war crime if committed in non-international conflicts under the ICC Statute and the Statute of the SCSL.

The commonly accepted definition of hostage taking is that provided by the 1979 International Convention against the Taking of Hostages, as follows:

Any person who seizes or detains and threatens to kill, to injure or to continue to detain another person (hereinafter referred to as the 'hostage') in order to compel a third party, namely, a State, an international intergovernmental organization, a natural or juridical person, or a group of persons, to do or abstain from doing any act as an explicit or implicit condition for the release of the hostage commits the offence of taking of hostages (Art 1(1)).

Like genocide, this definition requires a specific intent, that is, compelling someone or a body to do or not do something specific and to make that an explicit condition for the release of the hostage.

Enforced disappearance

Enforced disappearance is subject to the try-or-extradite regime as a result of a specific UN treaty adopted in December 2006. The International Convention for the Protection of All Persons from Enforced Disappearance defines the term as follows:

'enforced disappearance' is considered to be the arrest, detention, abduction or any other form of deprivation of liberty by agents of the State or by persons or groups of persons acting with the authorization, support or acquiescence of the State, followed by a refusal to acknowledge the deprivation of liberty or by concealment of the fate or whereabouts of the disappeared person, which place such a person outside the protection of the law (Art 2).

Although this is a recent treaty, enforced disappearance was already defined as a crime against humanity under the 1998 ICC Statute if committed as part of a widespread or systematic attack against a particular group. Prior to this date, any act of enforced disappearance was subject to a try-or-extradite regime under the 1994 Inter-American Convention on Forced Disappearance of Persons. Finally, it should be noted that this composite crime can also fall within the definition of other international crimes, such as torture and the war crime of unlawful confinement.

Crimes against UN and associated personnel

The Convention on the Safety of United Nations and Associated Personnel was adopted in 1994 in order to provide protection for persons carrying out activities in support of a UN operation.

The convention defines the crimes as follows

The intentional commission of:

(a) A murder, kidnapping or other attack upon the person or liberty of any United Nations or associated personnel;

(b) A violent attack upon the official premises, the private accommodation or the means of transportation of any United Nations or associated personnel likely to endanger his or her person or liberty;

(c) A threat to commit any such attack with the objective of compelling a physical or juridical person to do or to refrain from doing any act;

(d) An attempt to commit any such attack; and

(e) An act constituting participation as an accomplice in any such attack, or in an attempt to commit such attack, or in organizing or ordering others to commit such attack (Art 9(1)).

It may also be noted that attacking such persons or objects (provided that they are not directly taking part in combat operations) is listed as a war crime in the ICC Statute if such attacks take place during, and in connection with, an international or non-international armed conflict.

Terrorism

'Terrorism' is a term that is used extensively, together with pressures to deal with alleged 'terrorists' in a way that may not be in accordance with obligations under international law, in particular international humanitarian law, refugee law and human rights law. The use of the term 'terrorism' is therefore a potential trap. It should be noted that despite numerous efforts, there is no generally agreed international definition of the term 'terrorism'. There are instead a number of treaties that create crimes under international law, each of which is precisely defined. Examples are treaties relating to hijacking, the use of nuclear material, and attacks on diplomatic agents, maritime navigation and platforms on the continental shelf.

There are in addition some international and regional treaties that contain the term 'terrorism' in the title, but which relate to specific actions which are defined in the treaty concerned. An example is the 1997 International Convention for the Suppression of Terrorist Bombing, which contains the following definition:

Any person commits [the offence of terrorist bombing] if that person unlawfully and intentionally delivers, places, discharges or detonates an explosive or other lethal device in, into or against a place of public use, a State or government facility, a public transportation system or an infrastructure facility:

(a) With the intent to cause death or serious bodily injury; or

(b) With the intent to causes extensive destruction of such a place, facility or system, where such destruction results in or is likely to result in major economic loss (Art 2(1)).

This treaty does not apply to acts committed during an armed conflict by armed forces, governmental or otherwise, or to activities undertaken by the military forces of a state when exercising official duties at any time. It would therefore only be relevant to activities undertaken by civilians. A further restriction is that the treaty does not apply if the offence, the offender and the victims are all within the territory of a single state.

The 1999 International Convention for the Suppression of the Financing of Terrorism similarly provides for a try-or-extradite regime for a person who:

provides or collects funds with the intention that they should be used or in the knowledge that they are to be used ... in order to carry out:

(a) An act which constitutes an offence [under a list of treaties in the annex]; or
(b) Any other act intended to cause death or serious bodily injury to a civilian, or to any other person not taking an active part in the hostilities in a situation of armed conflict, when the purpose of such act, by its nature or context, is to intimidate a population, or to compel a government or an international organization to do or to abstain from doing any act (Art 2(1)).

This convention also only applies if there is an international element to the offence and specifies that it in no way changes the rights and obligations of states and individuals under international law, including international humanitarian law.

Ethnic cleansing

'Ethnic cleansing' is another term that is frequently used to describe a phenomenon but for which there is no official definition under international law. This is because it is not a separate international crime. It will need to be prosecuted under other headings, most notably, the crime against humanity of 'deportation or forcible transfer of population'.

III. Implementation

There are legal and practical issues that may adversely affect the pursuit of these international crimes. The legal ones relate to issues of immunity and jurisdiction, and the practical ones relate to perceptions of the appropriateness of prosecuting persons accused of international crimes as well as to difficulties relating to the securing of evidence.

Legal difficulties

Immunities

There is a general rule under international law, called 'sovereign immunity', to the effect that a state official may not be subjected to the national courts of another state for acts carried out in his or her official capacity. An important exception is that this is not applicable to officials accused of international crimes. This exception began with army personnel (who are by definition officials of a state) being held accountable for war crimes and was then applied to the other international crimes prosecuted after the Second World War.

There are, however, several caveats to this exception which need to be kept in mind:

- Heads of state and foreign ministers before a national court: international tribunals accord no immunity for heads of state. However, in a case brought before the International Court of Justice by the Democratic Republic of Congo against Belgium, the court stated that although international tribunals have their own specific rules, national courts must respect the immunity of a head of state, a prime minister, and a foreign minister of another state.

- Diplomatic immunity: the 1961 Vienna Convention on Diplomatic Relations repeats the long-standing customary rule that diplomats stationed in another country cannot be pursued by national courts unless the sending country waives the immunity. There is a direct clash between this rule and the ones requiring the exercise of jurisdiction over international crimes and crimes under international law. The situation is not entirely clear, in particular in the light of one provision in the ICC Statute which specifies that the International Criminal Court may not request the surrender of an accused person if this would make the requested state act inconsistently with the diplomatic immunity of the accused. However, this rule, which relates to cooperation of states with the International Criminal Court, does not necessarily undermine the rules that require persons guilty of international crimes to be tried by a national court or extradited for such trial, and certainly does not absolve the sending state from its duty to prosecute.

- Special agreements: military and other official personnel stationed abroad are typically protected from possible prosecution by the local courts by virtue of special agreements between the sending and the receiving states. Such agreements are also referred to in the ICC Statute. The same comment as that made above under 'Diplomatic immunity' is applicable here.

Exercise of jurisdiction

It should be noted that cases may be heard by the ICC if the state concerned has ratified the treaty or if the case is referred to it by the UN Security Council. However, the court will not be able to proceed with the case if an alleged offender is being properly investigated and prosecuted by a state which has jurisdiction over that person. This means that during peacebuilding efforts, it should be kept in mind that if it is decided not to prosecute an alleged perpetrator of genocide, a crime against humanity or a war crime, then such person may find him or herself before the ICC.

Another problem may be that the national system has not properly given itself jurisdiction over international crimes. This has particularly been the case for crimes against humanity as, unlike genocide, grave breaches and crimes under international law, there has been no treaty requiring states to criminalize in their national law crimes against humanity as such. Therefore there have been cases of persons accused of genocide, where the elements of that offence could not be proved, whereas the prosecution for a crime against humanity would have been more appropriate. Another reason for a lack of appropriate national legislation is a lack of understanding by national parliaments of the need to prosecute persons accused of international crimes or a lack of diligence by the executive to implement its treaty obligations in national law. It should be noted, however, that prosecuting a person for an international crime where the state has not formally included the crime in its national law would not be a breach of international human rights law.

Practical difficulties

Perception that prosecution would not be the best solution

During peacebuilding efforts, it is often considered that in order to achieve peace, it is indispensable to negotiate with leaders involved in the armed conflict. This is because they may well have the support of a substantial part of the population, but they often only agree to such negotiation on the understanding of being granted immunity from prosecution (see on this issue the chapters on peace process and reconciliation). However, it should be noted that there is an important difference between prosecution under national law for taking part in hostilities (which is not an international crime and therefore can be 'forgiven' without breaching international law) and individuals guilty of international crimes which require prosecution. Peacemakers may feel that they are in the presence of a dilemma but possible short-term agreements granting immunity for certain leaders need to be weighed up against whether such agreements solve the long-term problem, including the perception and needs of the victims and the importance of creating a society based on the rule of law. Various measures taken in this context are typically referred to as transitional justice.

Another problem is one of double standards in relation to who is prosecuted for international crimes in another country and who is not. The choice is often based on political factors. A lack of prosecution will, depending on the circumstances and the crime concerned, be a violation of the treaty concerned. It is unlikely that this problem will disappear. However, a choice not to prosecute alleged offenders during peacebuilding efforts will only exacerbate a perception that the crimes are not to be taken seriously and will hinder the dissuasive effect that the existence of criminalization should have.

Securing sufficient evidence: ensuring protection of witnesses and problems relating to gender

In any criminal trial securing sufficient evidence for conviction is important. All individuals are to be considered innocent until proved guilty 'beyond reasonable doubt'. In this context, evidence from witnesses is of great importance but many potential witnesses may, with good reason, fear for their safety if they testify. This is particularly the case where a portion of the population is not sympathetic to the criminal responsibility of certain leaders. Insufficient witness protection in both the short and long term may frustrate effective trials.

Another major difficulty can be the prosecution of offences relating to sexual violence. In many societies, victims of such offences are shunned by their families and communities. In addition to the humiliation involved in relating the occurrence of such offences, victims are often cast as 'willing' or otherwise somehow responsible for what happened to them. Victims of rape, sexual slavery, etc, thus face the dilemma of whether to become a witness in the hope of securing a prosecution, but knowing the ostracism that this will bring; or whether to stay silent, thus ensuring continued impunity. The fact that many societies also consider such crimes as not important, because of the poor status of women, adds to the problem (see also on the issue of sexual abuse the chapter on peace operations).

Best practices

Incorporation of international crimes into national legislation

As far as implementation is concerned, the most important factor is for states to correctly incorporate these crimes into their national law so that they have the necessary jurisdiction to try alleged offenders. Although some states' constitutions provide that international treaties ratified by the state are automatically part of national law, many states need to adopt specific national legislation for national prosecutors and courts to be able to apply the rules of the treaties. Thus during peacebuilding it is imperative that the state undertakes such incorporation through the appropriate legislative process. It is also important that the wording of the new legislation is such that it is easily understood and applied in the national context as international treaties often use generic terms which may not be meaningful in a local context, for example, the war crime of 'wilful killing' will need to be incorporated as 'murder', 'homicide', or whatever term the national lawyers are used to. As already mentioned, crimes against humanity also need to be incorporated into national law, as Canada has recently done, despite the fact that there is no treaty that positively requires such national legislation.

Training

In addition to appropriate legislation, it is indispensable to ensure that persons who teach law at universities, law schools, etc, both are aware of such legislation and include international crimes in the curriculum of all professional legal courses. A proper training of prosecutors, judges, police, and all persons in authority is indispensable. The military need to have training in the law of armed conflict which does not consist only of lectures and booklets, but which is incorporated in all battle training exercises so that correct behaviour in the heat of battle becomes automatic. It is imperative in the short term to ensure that proposed peacekeeping/peace-support personnel are properly trained and fully aware of what acts amount to crimes under international law. To the degree possible, awareness by the general public of the existence of such international crimes would be appropriate in order to prevent, to the degree possible, such crimes being perpetrated at a later date and in order to ensure that the society being built is based on the rule of law and respect for international law. The most effective method, of course, in any peacebuilding exercise will be the national prosecution of such crimes together with sufficient publicity. A good recent example is the prosecution of international crimes by a Serb court which showed to the local population, for the first time, a video of the actual crimes being committed. In this way, the local population does not feel that it is simply being targeted by hostile forces.

Witness protection

As explained above, witness protection is particularly essential for the successful prosecution of international crimes in certain contexts. It is important to be aware of which persons are potential key witnesses and, if there are problems of security or problems relating to gender, to take measures to protect witnesses. Most states have measures of witness protection (safe houses, etc) which might be (re)introduced, but another alternative, possibly more effective in the long term, is the anonymity of witnesses who are particularly at risk. This is not a violation of the human right of the accused to a fair trial if the witnesses can be questioned (without revealing their identity) and provided that the conviction is based also on other evidence.

Selected Bibliography

Cassese, A (2008), *International Criminal Law*, 2nd edn, Oxford: Oxford University Press.

——, Gaeta, P, & Jones, J (2002), *The Rome Statute of the International Criminal Court: A Commentary*, Oxford: Oxford University Press.

David, E, Klein, P, & La Rosa, A -M (eds) (2000), *Tribunal pénal international pour le Rwanda/International Criminal Tribunal for Rwanda*, Bruxelles: Bruylant.

Dörmann, K (2003), *Elements of War Crimes under the Rome Statute of the International Criminal Court: Sources and Commentary*, Cambridge: Cambridge University Press.

Gutman, R, & Rieff, D (eds) (1999), *Crimes of War: What the Public Should Know*, New York; London: WW Norton & Company Ltd.

Human Rights Watch (2006), *Genocide, War Crimes and Crimes against Humanity: A Topical Digest of the Case-Law of the International Criminal Tribunal for the Former Yugoslavia*, USA: Human Rights Watch.

Kittichaisaree, K (2001), *International Criminal Law*, Oxford: Oxford University Press.

Laucci, C (2006), *Digest of Jurisprudence of the Special Court for Sierra Leone, 2003–2005*, Leiden: Martinus Nijhoff Publishers.

Ratner, S, & Abrams, J (2001), *Accountability for Human Rights Atrocities in International Law: Beyond the Nuremburg Legacy*, Oxford; New York: Oxford University Press.

Robertson, G (2002), *Crimes against Humanity: The Struggle for Global Justice*, London: Penguin.

Triffterer, O (ed) (2008), *Commentary on the Rome Statute of the International Criminal Court*, 2nd edn, Baden-Baden: Nomos.

Local Ownership

Béatrice Pouligny

Definition

Local ownership refers to the capacities of political, social, and community actors in a particular country (referred to as 'insiders') to set, and take responsibility for, the peacebuilding agenda and to muster and sustain support for it. Insiders need to develop their own capacity to significantly influence the conception, design, implementation, and review of peacebuilding strategies. Implementing bodies should be firmly rooted in the recipient country and represent the interests of ordinary citizens, while 'outsiders' have a responsibility to support the progressive development of these capacities in a constructive dialogue with 'insiders'.

I. Term

Origin and context

The idea of ownership in development is hardly new, but since the mid-1990s local ownership and its variants have taken on particular prominence in the publications of bilateral and multilateral development agencies. Well-known examples provide reference points for ongoing debates. The Development Assistance Committee (DAC) of the Organisation for Economic Cooperation and Development (OECD), in its seminal 1996 statement 'Shaping the 21st Century', asserted that sustainable development 'must be locally owned' and that development cooperation has to be shifted to a partnership model, where donors' programmes and activities operate within 'locally owned development strategies' (DAC, 1996). Donors should 'respect and encourage strong local commitment, participation, capacity development and ownership' (DAC, 1996: 14). The DAC linked these positions to a series of specific targets for poverty reduction, which formed the basis of the Millennium Development Goals adopted by the UN General Assembly in 2000.

In a landmark proposal to the World Bank three years later, James Wolfensohn emphasized that developing countries 'must be in the driver's seat and set the course', owning and implementing their development strategies. Both the OECD and the World Bank progressively developed the two notions of 'engaged society' and 'effective states' to express the way in which local ownership should be understood (World Bank, 2005). The UN Development Programme (UNDP) has also developed a series of analyses on ownership and technical cooperation. Major bilateral donors and non-governmental organization (NGO) consortiums have done the same, sometimes connecting ownership and conditionality as a main theme. However, the prominence of the phrase is not matched by a corresponding depth of analysis, explanation, or scrutiny in policy statements.

The notion of local ownership is newer but equally polysemic and ambiguous in the field of post-conflict peacebuilding. Because of its focus, it is commonly seen to be important and progressive. Few, if any, challenge its value *per se*. Disputes turn on what it looks like in practice and its real or rhetorical importance. *De facto*, it covers a host of different meanings, often used abstractly.

Local, national, or insiders?

In most of the references, the adjective 'local' is used, more occasionally 'national', to distinguish the sphere of the country in which the intervention occurs from the outside world. But these adjectives are often problematic in particular settings. A national actor coming from the capital city or another social group may well be considered as an outsider when he enters a specific community; therefore, some literature would distinguish a 'national' and a 'local' level but the criteria for distinction between the two are unclear. The notion of 'insiders'/'outsiders' may be of greater heuristic value. Some analysts have defined insiders as:

those vulnerable to the conflict, because they are from the area and living there, or people who in some other way must experience the conflict and live with its consequences personally. [...Outsiders are those] who choose to become involved in a conflict [and who] have personally little to lose (Anderson & Olson, 2003: 36).

For others, the dichotomy may be more flexible as it is subjectively constructed by the actors concerned and mainly reflects the power relationships in a particular setting (Culbertson & Pouligny, 2007).

(Local) involvement

The idea of an increasing involvement of local actors in peacebuilding and development processes is a common catch-phrase in the relevant discourse (see also civil society). But very few answers are given to who those actors should be, how they could be concretely involved, when, and for what purpose. This explains, for instance, the criticisms made by many development NGOs regarding the ambivalence of international financial institutions. They often champion local ownership, but only insofar as local actors—whoever they are—follow up a project entirely designed by outsiders. This also applies to the peacebuilding agenda.

When donors call for 'national appropriation', they indirectly acknowledge the fact that projects—peace agreements, but also constitutions, codes of law, or judicial institutions—have been largely designed and imposed by outsiders.

(Local) participation

The participative discourse covers a similarly narrow understanding of what local ownership is supposed to be. Participation is generally understood in a restricted way, as 'participative management'. It is an old notion in the development field and appears in expressions such as 'community participation', 'people participation', or 'popular participation'. Lately, these categories have tended to be rephrased in terms of 'intended beneficiaries', 'indirect beneficiaries', 'unintended beneficiaries', and so forth. In fact, the participation of local civil societies, and even more of communities, in elaborating development strategies is often more ceremonial—if not ornamental—than real. Participatory project launches for instance are used to show the commitment of stakeholders to the project and 'ease' its implementation, in a way very similar to some of the ceremonies or quick-impact projects conducted by UN peacekeepers in peace operations. The whole terminology is often misleading and generations of anthropologists have shown that this use of participation may actually hamper the achievement of a project.

Less attention has traditionally been paid to the idea of giving proper credit to the worth of local resources. Recently, the idea has come to the fore through the concepts of 'social capital' and capacity-building. In the past few years, they have become the new credo of the donor community and have also penetrated the fields of security and post-conflict management. Capacity development is now presented as a key to ensuring a smooth transition from relief to development and, ultimately, the withdrawal of international presence (UN, 2005, 2006).

(Local) empowerment and accountability

Within developing and post-conflict countries, the themes of democratic governance and capacity-building also focus attention on participation and voice in public decision-making. They highlight the openness and accountability of governments to their own citizens, as well as the tension between this internal accountability and a competing external accountability to donors, a contradiction regularly denounced by political actors. Most donors insist on the involvement of civil society organizations and local communities in the process as a requirement for establishing national ownership. At issue are the depth of organizational resources and autonomy in citizens' organizations and their own responsiveness, as they seek to represent their members or communities, provide much-needed services, and challenge their governments to be transparent and accountable.

Here, local ownership may be conceived as a form of local empowerment. It is most often phrased as 'community empowerment' to make the distinction with the first use of the concept in relation to gender issues. Fully embedded, the notion supposes that beneficiaries are given some power, which means a certain leverage capacity in the local socio-political arena, as well as representative mechanisms at the community level to influence and even have some control on the application of the different components of the peacebuilding agenda. In rural villages and city neighbourhoods, security issues (including disarmament, demobilization, and reintegration of former combatants into civil society) and those directly related to the return and reintegration of displaced people and refugees are generally the top priorities in which local communities ask for empowerment. So far, with very few exceptions, this has not been put into practice.

II. Content

If we consider the different dimensions mentioned above, it is possible to distinguish four key issues that help map the main components and functions of the concept applied to peacebuilding: the identification of the key local partners; the identification of and support to local resources; the choice of the instruments of intervention; and the ideological contradictions.

Local partners and actors of the processes

Defining who the local partners are, how they are identified, how their stake (in terms of ownership) is negotiated, and who takes the lead in the whole process, is essential. For a long time, there was scant reflection on these issues. The concept of 'peace constituencies' has developed within the conflict transformation field, mainly led by NGOs, referring to alliances and networks that strengthen local capacities for peace. Most international organizations distinguish three categories of actors: governments, civil society, and communities. These receive unequal attention from the different international actors intervening in a post-conflict situation. In practice, however, all three levels need to be addressed to ensure genuine ownership. The choice of local partners generally reflects the principles, interests, and priorities of the outside party. This entails a decision, often taken abroad, as to who will be the main interlocutors of a specific mission and who should be the beneficiaries of funds and support, creating a certain power shift in the conflict setting (Reich, 2006: 13). When a peace operation is deployed, negotiations held outside the country (in preparation of peace agreements or drafting of a Security Council resolution) will be decisive in defining who will be the main interlocutors of the international community.

Among the political actors, the interests and alliances move constantly and call for a dynamic understanding of the local political arena (Pouligny, 2006: 44–67). Peacemakers rarely work only with a local government—which sometimes does not even exist. The issue of 'leadership capacity' in transitional societies has taken increasing policy attention in that context, in particular with regards to the role and conversion of the so-called 'warlords'. Some have argued that in looking for 'positive leadership' outsiders may be searching for a chimera as this particular model of leadership rarely exists in the context of violent conflict. Moreover, in an increasingly internationally overseen world, local leaders may actually have very little power over grand issues of conflict and peace. Peace, when it finally comes, is not inspired by local leaders but ushered in by international political and military strength. Local political leaders may ultimately have little agency or control over the peace process (Peake, Gormley-Heenan & Fitzduff, 2004: 13, 57).

Engagement with civil society may be seen as a three-level strategy. First, in most cases (in particular as far as peace operations are concerned), it may be seen merely as a way to increase the ultimate acceptance of an intervention. Second, and more substantially, the work with local civil societies in a peacebuilding effort is designed to complement other components of the democratic governance programme. Local NGOs are often seen to carry the best hopes for a genuine democratic counterweight to the power-brokers, economic exploiters, and 'warlords' who tend to predominate in conflict-ridden, weak, or 'failed' states. They also serve as alternative implementing agencies (Pouligny, 2005: 496). Third, NGOs may also be seen as a bridge to other forms of social institutionalization, in particular at the community level, which is sometimes simply aggregated to the civil society sector.

The definition and content of the notion of 'community' differs and evolves according to the local context and history. From one situation to another the notion contains highly variable forms of organization and mediation. In a country's recent history, the modalities of organization and projection in the public space have often undergone a profound transformation stemming from several factors: first, contacts with national and international NGOs intervening in the area of humanitarian aid or development, according to a project-oriented approach that implies the existence of a certain type of 'organized' partner on the ground; second, the effects of repression and war, leading in particular to major displacements of people to refugee and displaced person camps, or to cities, which hastens the breakdown of former community ties according to the imperatives of survival; third, the effects of violence within the group, especially when this violence has been used and heightened by political entrepreneurs; and fourth, transformation of identities and frameworks of reference (Pouligny, 2005: 507; 2006: 67–68). Some experiences have shown that community consultation and engagement is, for instance, critical to successful and sustainable disarmament, demobilization, and reintegration programmes. Among the few success stories are experiences which have aimed at introducing normative compliance through local informal 'peace agreements' with voluntary disarmament and reintegration clauses, or with the declaration of weapon-free areas where civilian as well as combatant weapons are collected.

Even more than in the development field, pursuit of some sense of local ownership is hampered by significant asymmetries of resources, access, and influence at different stages of the design and implementation of peacebuilding agendas. Who sets these strategies is a critical question. Internationally, the imposition of a certain solution to a conflict, as well as donors' insistence on policy conditionality, are seen to limit the policy choices of local political leaders. Domestically, those leaders, implementing agencies, and NGOs are seen to shape peacebuilding initiatives for their own purposes, excluding nominal beneficiaries such as women, people with disabilities, ex-combatants (in particular former child soldiers), remote rural communities, displaced and repatriated persons, and the urban poor. This does not mean that local actors do not have the capacity to develop all kinds of strategies—the fact is that they do—but the less powerful they are, the more they will tend to protect themselves from outsiders as they consider that they have very little to gain in the encounter. This attitude, very common at the community level, is often wrongly perceived as a signal of 'indifference' or 'apathy', but it clearly limits the chance for any sense of ownership on the part of ordinary people (Pouligny, 2006).

Local resources for peacebuilding

There is an old debate about the project to import (or even impose) values alien to a specific culture, which is often the case in a post-conflict environment, in particular with regard to the liberal political agenda. Some liberal theorists suggest that such attempts are misguided and that, if forced, they will be perceived as a form of aggression or paternalistic colonialism. Since the most enduring forms of liberalization are those that result from internal reform, the primary focus for liberals outside the group should be to provide this sort of support. If for no other reason than an attempt to prevent resistance, some agencies try to infuse local values and elements of existing community activities into planned projects. In the mediation context, theorists have suggested that rather than imposing alien standards in resolving conflict, what they call the 'elicitive' model seeks to discover and solidify the resources that exist in a specific post-conflict setting. By empowering individuals to speak for their own cultural traditions, it allows a voice to under-represented or oppressed groups. In seeking resources within the specific contexts in which it is applied, it also demonstrates respect for the value and integrity of the local culture (Lederach, 1995).

In peacebuilding strategies, it is probably more a matter of creating a dialogical exchange between insider and outsider knowledge (Culbertson & Pouligny, 2007). It saves the relevant actors spending endless time and effort in searching for and pre-testing solutions that may already be held by local communities. Whatever is done, on the ground, locally, on the streets and in the apartment blocks and villages, some form of regularized social interaction will begin to emerge, whether imposed or not. This is community, not as a utopian

Béatrice Pouligny

or communitarian goal, but community in reality. In that context, local and traditional resources as well as outside references are used by the populations. For that reason, these resources must be known, at least minimally studied, and understood. They provide alternative modes of participation and inclusion of the majority. Another important dimension is that such an approach pays more attention to the radical transformations in the political cultures and codes of conduct of the individuals and communities who have experienced mass violence, and to the way in which these basic values and beliefs affect the manner in which a state is conceived and governed. As much as possible, the aim should be to supply external support to local processes rather than imposing external methods (Pouligny, 2005: 502–3). In too many cases, ignoring indigenous coping strategies may increase civilian jeopardy and make those vulnerable segments of the population even more so (Boyden, 1994: 25).

Instruments of intervention

Adequate—probably tailor-made—procedures need to be agreed on and implemented to ensure that local actors considered as key stakeholders in the peace process will have both the means and the capacity to be actively involved at all stages. This demands that (1) the focus should be on processes as much as on results of peacebuilding initiatives; (2) quality 'pre-assessments' are essential in order to identify the capacities and gaps of the different actors; and (3) a supporting partnership of diverse groups in a designated community needs to be built (Culbertson & Pouligny, 2007; Boyce, Koros & Hodgson, 2002). Ultimately, what is required is also a political process, support for democratic governance and participatory decision-making in public life, and support for the creation of new space for a more demanding civil society to hold governments accountable for their performance. All these elements will support the renewed social contract at the heart of successful capacity development and stronger institutions. This also requires adequate resources to develop local skills, including among the leadership. The lack of democratic governance and deficiency in leaders' administrative skills is a common pattern (Peake, Gormley-Heenan & Fitzduff, 2004: 59).

Ideological contradictions

The local ownership discourse is developed around two rather contradictory ideological visions which actually coexist in the peacebuilding field. In identifying and making use of local resources and capacities, potential peacebuilders address post-conflict situations with an implicit assumption of the value and abilities of other cultures. But the peacebuilding agenda is also inspired by a clear liberal messianism (Boyce, Koros & Hodgson, 2002). In this model, individuals are empowered by being freed from dependence on government. Identically, civil society needs to be 'liberated' from the orbit of the state and subsequently given a free hand in reconstruction. This approach clearly follows a highly ideological vision of what politics and the state-society relationship are about, whatever the local political cultures.

Another ideological ambiguity is that most peace agreements and subsequent interventions intend to 'stabilize' a situation, if not to 'freeze' the *status quo*, instead of aiming to 'change' the local situation, which is what is actually needed if there is a will to support any lasting and sustainable peace (Fisher, 1993: 249; Pouligny, 2006: 506) (see on this issue the chapter on conflict transformation). There is actually a double contradiction: first, this agenda may be perceived very negatively by social and community actors who want change; second, to create much-needed stability in a region, international leaders need to work with the very same actors deemed to be a major cause of past instability (Peake, Gormley-Heenan & Fitzduff, 2004: 11).

III. Implementation

Most observers and analysts agree that, so far, donors do not seem to be much guided by their own rhetoric. 'Local ownership' is a catch-phrase in every document but it is very little implemented in peacebuilding programmes. The handbooks developed by some UN agencies very clearly show the limits of its practicality (UNHCR, 2005). Some analysts would even argue that actual implementation of literal 'local ownership' is impossible, if not counterproductive, given the current asymmetrical structures of international cooperation (Reich, 2006: 3–4). However, the analysis of actual practices helps understanding of the main operational challenges and the potential of an actual implementation of the local ownership agenda in peacebuilding. The main principle to remember is that there is no blueprint for infusing local ownership. Approaches should be context-specific, determined by and tailored to the diversity of political, social, and economic factors (Boyce, Koros & Hodgson, 2002; Leonhardt, 2000).

Managing outsiders' invasion

The first important obstacle to local ownership is constituted by outsiders themselves. When a 'crisis' is discovered by the 'international community' and comes to the front through different channels, the country may then experience a real 'invasion'. Hundreds if not thousands of representatives of international organizations—intergovernmental and non-governmental—will arrive in the capital city, occupying a space no longer available to local actors. They also often have a detrimental effect on local economies—large increases in salaries, prices in the stores, and house rents—impeding local organizations from functioning properly. Because they intervene in an unknown, often still highly insecure environment, outsiders tend to actually collaborate with other outsiders, in a largely closed circle, partially isolated from the 'real world' (Pouligny, 2005: 501).

Outsiders also need to radically transform their operational culture. Contrary to what they may be inclined to feel or believe, they are not the main actors of the peacebuilding process, but should think of themselves as facilitators in a leverage process. Individuals need to be modest, flexible, patient, and unobtrusive: this is almost the opposite of what actually typifies most current practice. It may also contradict what any organization needs in order to ensure its visibility, self-promotion, and fund-raising, or what any staff member may seek to get a good performance report. Therefore, the role of facilitator, the leverage effect, and the actual objectives of these processes need to be better conceptualized, including in their various interactions with local political processes, so that they accurately inform programme and job descriptions as well as monitoring mechanisms. This also requires a true ethical reflection about what it is to be an outsider in a conflict/post-conflict environment (Pouligny, 2002).

Managing timing constraints

If one looks at local ownership principles at a practical implementation level, achieving true local ownership may be messy and time-consuming, and may not conform nicely to donors' needs for visible, easily verifiable, and quick results, and even sometimes for an exit strategy. The importance of promoting self-reliance is also sometimes overshadowed by the importance of urgent delivery. Interventions aimed at emergency relief are less inclined to focus on local ownership than those seeking to promote local capacity-building and the resultant self-sufficiency and sustainability. Practitioners may experience that there is a trade-off to be made between the immediacy of the required results and the process of delivering these results. But if peacebuilding is to achieve its true purpose of societal transformation, there may be no alternative.

There is another frequent contradiction: in many assistance programmes, the local ownership agenda is also conceived as the main way to ensure that outsiders can soon withdraw. Mine action and the return and reintegration of displaced persons and refugees are clear areas in which international agencies actually conceive local ownership first as a way to ensure that their intervention can be stopped as soon as possible after the immediate emergency phase (UNHCR, 2005). But reality does not generally work in that way. While everybody understands the importance of outside support during the first years after a war, the following period is generally even more critical. Local institutions, formal and informal, remain fragile and need to face new challenges, but they may also be in a better position to deliver and actually implement the agenda for peace. This is typically the precise moment at which the amount of aid given to the country is drastically reduced. Paying more attention to the local contexts and processes also implies fine-tuning the terms of scheduling outside support (Pouligny, 2005: 503–4).

Developing a dynamic micro-analysis of local socio-political contexts

An important step is also to open up to the local society and understand how it functions. Too often, outsiders act blindly, without adequate knowledge of the context of their intervention, and 'end up committing the dual sin of ignorance and arrogance', to take the words of a senior UN official. The development of such analytic capacity requires outsiders to look beyond the impression of disorganization, or even anomie, often given by societies at war or just emerging from conflict. Some projects, such as the Local Capacities for Peace project undertaken by Mary Anderson and the Collaborative for Development Action Inc., have shown that a better understanding of the underlying social and cultural values of a local community could be blended into projects designed to enhance ownership, participation and sustainability (CDA; Anderson, 1999; Anderson & Olson, 2003).

Such an approach implies fundamental changes in the outsiders' intelligence capacity, in order to better understand local contexts and identify the local actors likely to be the major motors for change. So far, one of the main reasons why practices do not change and improve fast enough is that the approach tends to be superficial, 'toolkit' oriented, and ad hoc. One avenue to bypass these limitations is to articulate research-action at each stage of peacebuilding programmes.

Monitoring interventions

Whereas some progress has been made in the pre-assessment, internal monitoring and evaluation of development aid programmes—considered a key factor to induce a shift towards actual ownership (UNDP Initiative)—much remains to be done in the peacebuilding field. Most programmes have no comprehensive monitoring and verification system of the socio-political and economic dynamics they engender (or hinder). Particularly when using any kind of conditionality programme, outsiders absolutely need to micro-monitor and manage the impact of their actions and the way in which local actors (especially the most powerful ones) adapt themselves rather quickly to new outside demands. If not analysed and addressed properly, there is a strong tendency for third-party interventions to perpetuate and even to reinforce existing asymmetries, making the voice of the 'weaker party' even less audible in the process of conflict transformation. In each programme, field staff should have at their disposal concrete guidelines to help them identify their interlocutors in contexts where actors may no longer play the same role as before the war, and where hierarchies and values may have been

transformed or new ones may have emerged; they also should have key indicators
for monitoring and reporting on the way in which they actually work and may
impact insiders' lives (Pouligny, 2005, 2006). This also means increasing efforts
to actually communicate with a large spectrum of local societies and to make
more information available to local public opinion (Pouligny, 2006: 147–54).

Managing 'clientele' relationships

Relationships between outsiders and insiders are very asymmetrical and, almost
by essence, have the nature of patronage. In the civil society sector, the mushrooming of all kinds of NGOs, often disconnected from any social base, is a well-
known phenomenon; they may spring up overnight in response to donor agendas
and outsiders' institutional needs, and vanish just as quickly (Carl, 2003: 3).
There is always a strong temptation to create or instigate the creation of 'home-
grown' NGOs, who may be more malleable and easier to work with (Pouligny,
2005: 501). This power asymmetry also goes with cultural domination, generally
qualified as 'conflict management imperialism', most of the models being decided
and imposed from outside. If international action replaces local decision-making
processes or substitutes for the role of local institutions such as parliaments, it will
continue to be difficult to make the rules of the game understood and assimilated,
even less discussed locally, all elements decisive in a local accountability process.
In that context, it is particularly important to consider the role of all actors who
are in a position of brokerage, performing all kinds of intermediary functions
between outsiders and insiders. Local employees of international structures play
an important role in that perspective and, depending on the way in which they
are selected, managed, given recognition, and controlled, they may either contribute to developing a sense of local ownership, or not (Pouligny, 2006: 87–95).

Re-enforcing local legitimacy and accountability

A specific difficulty posed by this patronage pattern is that local structures—
governmental and non-governmental—created or instigated by outsiders are generally oriented first towards the outside world and not their own society. Outside
interventions even tend to reverse the legitimization process. Legitimacy does not
arise from any social basis but must be granted by outsiders, by providing access
to crucial symbolic as well as material resources. International and local legitimating mechanisms may actually contradict one another. Local leaders do not
answer to their people but to the international authorities and norms; the great
advantage of this situation for local leaders is that they can easily manipulate it
if they are smart enough to appear to conform to the expectations of the international community. Yet local legitimacy is crucial to guarantee the sustainable
rebuilding of a state, and it is also crucial if any kind of conditionality is to play a
positive role.

There is a genuine risk of playing against the grounding of any democratic governance and accountability. The outsiders' actual accountability towards local peoples and partners also needs to be drastically improved; for the moment, it is close to zero and generates all kinds of frustrations. This should go together with an effective performance assessment and sanction system in the organizations themselves (Pouligny, 2005: 499–500) (see also on the need for outsiders' accountability the chapters on rule of law; peace operations and transitional administration).

Supporting knowledge and skills transfer to promote self-help skills

Acknowledging and fully considering the extent of knowledge and experience that local people have of their own situation is clearly difficult. One concrete illustration of this is the fact that the UN or other international organizations will more commonly cite reports of Northern human rights NGOs rather than local ones, although local organizations may possess a more profound knowledge of the situation. There has been clear progress in this area, but much more needs to be done. Similarly, a foreign 'expert' or 'academic' is more easily chosen over a local one to brief outsiders on the local situation. Local staff tend to be hired mainly as low-cost workers in subordinate roles, and rarely as main actors in a strategic process (Pouligny, 2005).

Lessons learnt in the development field show that the involvement of a greater proportion of national consultants and experts and, where appropriate, the development of South-South cooperation are among the major modalities of inducing a shift towards local ownership (UNDP Initiative). Comparative opportunities to encounter and learn about the various possibilities for governance in other diverse and conflict-ridden societies are also important contributions to local ownership at the leadership level (Peake, Gormley-Heenan & Fitzduff, 2004: 59).

These principles are even more important when working with social and community actors. As in the Canadian model of community-based rehabilitation programmes, there may be a need for a large-scale transfer of knowledge and skills, for instance to people with disabilities, their families, and members of the community, so that resources become available at the community level and rehabilitation is 'democratized' (Boyce, Koros & Hodgson, 2002; Boyce & Lysack, 1997; Helander *et al*, 1989). But such a transfer needs to be based on a consistent analysis of the existing skills and knowledge already available in the community. Local training institutions need to be involved in the process, as well as organized networking and seminars designed to facilitate the local exchange of knowledge and best practices.

It is obvious that these approaches, though helpful, cannot alone achieve more appropriate ownership. As is justly emphasized in the development field, the overriding requirement is a commitment to inclusion, on the part of all stakeholders—on the part of the donors, to include national governments, and on the part of national governments, to include other stakeholders. All of this requires a political decision so that local ownership is genuinely considered a priority.

Selected Bibliography

Anderson, M (1999), *Do No Harm: How Aid Can Support Peace—or War*, Boulder, CO: Lynne Rienner Publishers.

—— & Olson, L (2003), *Confronting War: Critical Lessons for Peace Practitioners*, Cambridge, MA: The Collaborative for Development Action, Inc.

Boyce, W, Koros, M, & Hodgson, J (2002), 'Community Based Rehabilitation: A Strategy for Peace-building', *BMC International Health and Human Rights*, 2/6.

—— & Lysack, C (1997), 'Understanding the Community in Canadian CBR: Critical Lessons from Abroad', *Canadian Journal of Rehabilitation*, 10/4: 261–71.

Boyden, J (1994), 'Children's Experience of Conflict Related Emergencies: Some Implications for Relief Policy and Practice', *Disasters*, 18/3: 254–67.

Carl, A (2003), *Supporting Local Capacities for Handling Violent Conflict: A Role for International NGOs?*, Occasional Paper, London: Conciliation Resources.

Chambers, R (1997), *Whose Reality Counts?*, London: Intermediate Technology Publications.

Culbertson, R, & Pouligny, B (2007), ' "Re-imagining Peace" after Mass Crime: A Dialogical Exchange between Insider and Outsider Knowledge', in Pouligny, B, Chesterman, S, & Schnabel, A (eds), *After Mass Crime: Rebuilding States and Communities*, Tokyo; New York: United Nations University Press, 271–87.

DAC (Development Assistance Committee) (1996), *Shaping the 21st Century: The Contribution of Development Cooperation*, Paris: Organisation for Economic Co-operation and Development.

—— (2006), *The Challenge of Capacity Development: Working Towards Good Practice*, DAC Guidelines and Reference Series, Paris: Organisation for Economic Cooperation and Development.

Fisher, RJ (1993), 'The Potential for Peacebuilding: Forging a Bridge from Peacekeeping to Peacemaking', *Peace and Change*, 18: 247–50.

Helander, E, Mendis, P, Nelson, G, & Goerdt, A (1989), *Training in the Community for People with Disabilities*, Geneva: World Health Organization.

Lederach, JP (1995), *Preparing for Peace: Conflict Transformation across Cultures*, New York: Syracuse University Press.

Leonhardt, M (2000), *Conflict Impact Assessment of EU Development Cooperation with ACP Countries: A Review of Literature and Practice*, Geneva: International Alert; Saferworld.

Peake, G, Gormley-Heenan, C, & Fitzduff, M (2004), *From Warlords to Peacelords: Local Leadership Capacity in Peace Processes*, Londonderry: INCORE (International Conflict Research), University of Ulster.

Pouligny, B (2002), 'An Ethic of Responsibility in Practice', *International Social Science Journal* (UNESCO), 174: 529–38.

——(2005), 'Civil Society and Post-Conflict Peacebuilding: Ambiguities of International Programmes Aimed at Building' 'New' Societies', *Security Dialogue*, 36:4, 495–510.

—— (2006), *Peace Operations Seen from Below: UN Missions and Local People*, Bloomfield (CT): Kumarian Press.

Reich, H (2006), *'Local Ownership' in Conflict Transformation Projects: Partnership, Participation or Patronage?*, Berghof Occasional Papers, No 27, Berlin: Berghof Research Centre for Constructive Conflict Management.

UNHCR (2005), *Handbook for Self-Reliance*, Geneva: UNHCR.

UN (2005), *The Transition from Relief to Development*, Report of the Secretary-General, A/60/89-E/2005/79, General Assembly and Economic and Social Council, 23 June.

—— (2006), *UNICEF Post-crisis Transition Strategy in Support of the Medium-term Strategic Plan*, E/ICEF/2006/17, Economic and Social Council, 10 April.

World Bank (2005), *Building Effective States, Forging Engaged Societies*, World Bank Task Force on Capacity Development in Africa, Washington, DC: World Bank.

• **Online resources**

The Collaborative for Development Action, Inc (CDA) <http://www.cdainc.com>.

UNDP Initiative Reforming Technical Cooperation for Capacity Development <http://www.capacity.undp.org/index.cfm?module=ActiveWeb&page=WebPage&s=reformingtechnical>.

Mine Action

*Davide Orifici and Suzanne Damman**

Definition

Mine action comprises five complementary groups of activities: (1) mine risk education; (2) demining, that is, surveying, mapping, marking, and clearance of mines and explosive remnants of war (ERW); (3) victim assistance, including rehabilitation and socio-economic reintegration; (4) stockpile destruction; and (5) advocacy against the use of anti-personnel mines and cluster munitions. A number of enabling activities are required to support these five components, including: assessment and planning; the mobilization and prioritization of resources; information management; human skills development and management training; quality management; and the application of effective, appropriate, and safe equipment.

I. Term

Origin and context

The definition of mine action has evolved over time together with the operational activities in mine-affected countries. The use of the term 'mine action' to describe the discipline was formally endorsed by the United Nations in its policy document issued in 1998 (UNMAS, 1998), although it was already used the previous year in a groundbreaking study of indigenous mine action capacities.

The term was first used in the early 1990s in Cambodia where Canadian military engineers named the body set up to administer and coordinate mine-related activities in the country the 'Cambodian Mine Action Centre'—to stress the multi-dimensional nature of the enterprise. The term 'mine action' is now in general use, although a number of countries, for example the US, which has not yet endorsed a total ban on the use of anti-personnel mines, still prefer to use the term 'humanitarian demining' (GICHD, 2007: 24).

---

* This chapter is drawn from material developed by the Geneva International Centre for Humanitarian Demining, particularly *A Guide to Mine Action and Explosive Remnants of War.*

From the late 1980s until the mid-1990s 'humanitarian demining' was a term used to distinguish this activity from military demining, and was understood to mean not only the removal of emplaced mines but also information and education activities to prevent injuries. The term 'demining' was used to denote mine clearance for humanitarian purposes and to distinguish it clearly from the military activity of 'breaching', which cleared paths through minefields to attain military mission objectives.

Official definition

According to the current UN definition, as contained in the International Mine Action Standards (IMAS), mine action refers to 'activities which aim to reduce the social, economic and environmental impact of mines and [ERW].'

The relevant IMAS provides that mine action:

is not just about demining; it is also about people and societies, and how they are affected by landmine contamination. The objective of mine action is to reduce the risk from landmines to a level where people can live safely; in which economic, social and health development can occur free from the constraints imposed by landmine contamination, and in which the victims' needs can be addressed (UN (IMAS), 2003).

According to the definition, mine action comprises five complementary groups of activities, known as pillars:

- mine risk education;
- demining, that is, surveying, mapping, marking and clearance of mines and ERW;
- victim assistance, including rehabilitation and reintegration;
- stockpile destruction; and
- advocacy against the use of anti-personnel mines.

The definition further notes that several other enabling activities are required to support these five components of mine action, including: assessment and planning; the mobilization and prioritization of resources; information management; human skills development and management training; quality management; and the application of effective, appropriate and safe equipment.

Translation work done by the Geneva International Centre for Humanitarian Demining (GICHD) indicates that mine action terms are not easily translated into French and Spanish, and translations into Russian, Arabic and Chinese cause even more difficulties. However, the International Mine Action Standards (IMAS) have been successfully translated into several of the official languages of the United Nations in recent years. This will allow a greater understanding of the technical terminology across languages, particularly amongst field practitioners, who apply the IMAS in their daily work.

A recent trend, supported by the United Nations and the GICHD, together with the National Mine Action Centres (MACs), Non-Governmental Organizations (NGOs) and commercial companies, is the development of National Mine Action Standards (NMAS) in the national languages of mine-affected countries. The NMAS will allow the guidelines to be translated into Standard Operating Procedures (SOPs) for national civilian and military personnel involved in mine action activities.

II. Content

Origin of mine action

The origin of the discipline of mine action can be traced back to October 1988, which was the first time the UN appealed for funds for a humanitarian response to the problems caused by landmines on behalf of Afghanistan. Prior to this period, activities intended to reduce the impact of mines, especially mine clearance, were largely the domain of national militaries. Afghanistan was a different case, though, as there was no functioning Afghan army, and the Soviet troops were not willing or able to clear mines before their departure from the country. The UN decided to support the creation of a number of Afghan NGOs to survey, map, mark, and clear mines and unexploded ordnance (UXO), and to conduct mine awareness (now called mine risk education) for the civilian population. More than ten years later, these NGOs are still performing well, and a number of them have conducted operations abroad.

The year 1988 also saw the birth of the world's first international humanitarian mine clearance NGO—the Hazardous Area Life-Support Organisation (HALO Trust). The following year the Mines Advisory Group (MAG) was set up and it conducted the first survey of the impact of landmines in Afghanistan in 1989. In 1992, Handicap International, which had already been operating for ten years as a humanitarian NGO implementing projects in favour of the disabled, including mine amputees and other victims, made an alliance with MAG to set up its first two demining programmes in Cambodia and northern Iraq, and took part in the creation of the International Campaign to Ban Landmines. Norwegian People's Aid has also been involved in mine action since 1992.

Following the 1991 Gulf War, Kuwait spent hundreds of millions of dollars on mine and UXO clearance by a number of commercial demining companies and military engineering units. The 1991–1993 clearance programmes saw a significant use of mechanical devices, and stimulated the development of such equipment. Commercial companies were cheaper than the alternatives in some cases and easier to set up than charities. Subsequently, a number of commercial companies, such as BACTEC, Mechem, and Mine-Tech have played a major role in demining (Smith, 1998).

Mine action since the early 1990s—three phases

The international community has roughly divided the development of mine action into three distinct phases that will be briefly discussed below.

In a first phase of mine action, following Afghanistan and Kuwait, the next major landmine challenge for the international community was in Cambodia. In January 1992, the UN Security Council expanded the mandate of the UN Advance Mission in Cambodia (UNAMIC) to include mine clearance and training (UN Security Council Resolution 728, New York). In June 1992, the Cambodian Mine Action Centre (CMAC) was set up (Eaton, 1997).

Planning for mine action in Mozambique began in 1992. The experiences in Mozambique represented a turning point for UN-supported mine-related activities as criticisms mounted against the slow pace of action and the direction the UN chose to take. A subsequent study of the programme suggested that an indigenous capability should not be seen merely as a mine clearance capacity: 'Empowering national authorities to regulate, coordinate and sustain all mine action objectives should be a key objective'.

Major problems were also encountered in Angola, where planning for mine action began in March 1993, although a Central Mine Action Office was not set up until August 1994. Angola proved to be problematic because of 'interminable bureaucratic in-fighting on overall programme objectives and approach and to disputes over assigned division of labour and responsibilities' (Eaton, 1997).

A second phase of mine action evolution was marked by a drive to understand the reasons for past successes and failures and to develop common ground that could underpin any new mine action programme. With a wide range of actors by then involved in mine action activities in one way or another, and multiple experiences on which to draw, it was both natural and desirable that the international community should move towards the standardization of mine action.

In July 1996, international standards for humanitarian mine clearance programmes were proposed by working groups at an international conference in Denmark. Criteria were prescribed for all aspects of mine clearance, standards were recommended and a new universal definition of 'clearance' was agreed. In late 1996, the principles proposed in Denmark were developed by an UN-led working group into International Standards for Humanitarian Mine Clearance Operations. A first edition of these standards was issued by the UN Mine Action Service (UNMAS) in March 1997.

In 1997, the UN published a report on the early successes and failures of UN mine action in four key mine-affected countries. It documented a serious lack of organization, commitment and vision, and many missed opportunities. At about the same time the UN launched its reform process which resulted in the creation of the Mine Action Service—UNMAS—within the Department of Peacekeeping Operations as the focal point for all mine-related activities in the UN (see the chapter on peace operations). Since then, considerable progress has been made and almost all of the many recommendations listed in the 1997 report have been, or are currently being, addressed by the UN.

As part of its reform process, the UN defined its roles and responsibilities related to mine action in 'Mine Action and Effective Coordination: The UN Policy' (1998). The overall mandate of the UN is to: (1) provide effective coordination in mine action; (2) provide assistance to mine action; (3) foster the establishment of mine clearance capacities. A revised and updated policy was adopted in 2005: 'Mine Action and Effective Coordination: the United Nations Inter-Agency Policy'. The new policy places responsibility for allocating roles to the various concerned UN agencies and bodies to the UN Country Team in each case (UNMAS, 2005). In all early UN demining plans, mine action was designed to become increasingly national and to pass to the UN Development Programme (UNDP) as soon as possible for later transition to full national control. UNDP therefore has an important role as an adviser to governments on the management of mine action programmes in such a context.

A third phase of mine action, which continues to this day, is characterized by an increased 'professionalization' of the discipline. Professionalization means first and foremost the development and regular review of quality management systems, including the IMAS but also SOPs of the main demining organizations, including NGOs.

Following the experiences in Kosovo and northern Iraq, together with the lessons of more mature programmes, such as in Afghanistan, Cambodia and Mozambique, the first edition of the fully fledged IMAS was issued in 2001. IMAS reflected changes to operational procedures, practices, and norms which had occurred since the publication of the International Standards for Humanitarian Mine Clearance Operations in 1997.

The UN has a general responsibility for enabling and encouraging the effective management of mine action programmes including the development and maintenance of standards. UNMAS is the office within the UN Secretariat responsible for the development and maintenance of the IMAS, most of which are drafted by the GICHD on its behalf. The work of preparing, reviewing and revising the standards is conducted by technical committees with the support of international and governmental organizations and NGOs. The latest version of each standard, together with information on the work of the technical committees, can be found at <http://www.mineactionstandards.org>.

Finally, in addition to regular review of international standards, the twin issues of capacity development and support for reconstruction and development have been steadily growing in importance. Sustainability in mine action—and maximizing its effectiveness—means strengthening the inter-relationship between mine action and other relief and development activities, and developing and exploiting indigenous capacities (see the chapters on capacity-building and local ownership).

III. Implementation

Over the past twenty years, mine action has evolved into an established component of the relief, reconstruction, and development sectors, and of peace operations. It benefits from an accepted international definition that comprises five main pillars. These activities are underpinned by international law, especially the 1997 Anti-Personnel Mine Ban Convention, the 2003 Convention on Certain Conventional Weapons (CCW) Protocol V on ERW, and the 2008 Convention on Cluster Munitions. In addition, internationally agreed standards, as well as a model legal and institutional frameworks, exist to guide the effective coordination, management and implementation of national mine action programmes. Today, the mine action sector recognizes that several challenges exist for the implementation of effective and efficient mine action programmes by national authorities of mine-affected countries. Activities falling under the mine action term need to be linked to the different phases of a country's transition from conflict, to peacebuilding, to development. Finally, the gender perspective should be taken into account in implementing mine action activities.

Responsibility of mine-affected countries

Ultimate responsibility for mine action remains with the government of the affected country. This responsibility is normally vested in a National Mine Action Authority (NMAA), which is charged with the policy, regulation, and overall management of a national mine action programme, as well as resource mobilization, particularly from the government. Typically an inter-ministerial body, the NMAA is primarily responsible for all phases and facets of a mine action programme within its national boundaries, including the national mine action strategy, national mine action standards, and instructions.

The operational arm of an NMAA is generally the Mine Action Centre (MAC). This body is the focal point for mine action activities on the ground. It carries out the policies of the NMAA and coordinates the daily activities of the various organizations and agencies conducting mine action operations. Together, the NMAA and the MAC should comprise the principal organs managing and coordinating mine action in a mine/ERW-affected country.

In some cases, the MAC coordinates a large number of operators and controls relatively large amounts of money while in others it has more modest functions. In Angola and Cambodia, the MAC controlled its own operational demining teams. This approach proved to be less successful, though, as the MAC became too focused on the work of its own teams and was not able to undertake effectively its national coordination functions. It also led to a conflict of interest, whereby the MAC, as the regulatory body, was acting as both 'referee' and 'player' (Mansfield, 2002).

It is normally desirable that the government of a mine or ERW-affected country enacts enabling legislation in support of its mine action programme. This enabling legislation focuses, among other things, on the mandate for the management and coordination institutions. In a few cases, national mine action legislation has been combined with domestic legislation to implement the provisions of the Anti-Personnel Mine Ban Convention, which requires the adoption of penal sanctions for violations of the core obligations.

Sound national mine action legislation

Mine action should be conducted by qualified operators. Mine action legislation should require that operators be accredited prior to beginning activities in the country. This ensures that international agencies, NGOs and commercial companies are capable of planning and managing mine action activities and competent to carry out particular mine action tasks. Requiring the accreditation of mine action operators helps ensure that mine action is conducted in accordance with accepted standards and national priorities.

Mine action legislation should authorize the national MAC to establish the criteria for accreditation and identify it as the body responsible for making such decisions. The process of accreditation should include the opportunity of an appeal to the NMAA in the event of an adverse decision. Accreditation generally applies to organizations involved in demining and mine risk education and, in some cases, stockpile destruction.

Quality management is vital to the ultimate success of mine action. Thus, the MAC must also ensure that ongoing work and completed projects have been conducted according to national standards and in accordance with the priorities of the national mine action plan. In the process of mine clearance the monitoring of organizations before and during the clearance process and inspection of cleared land prior to its formal release ensures that the operation has been conducted safely, in accordance with the contractual obligations, and that the land is safe for its intended use. The risk management strategy in use within a MAC will form a significant part of maintaining an auditable trail of decision-making throughout the process of survey, clearance, and handover of land.

The evolving context of mine action—from conflict to development

Most mine and ERW contamination is caused by conflicts. In many cases, and increasingly over the past two decades, these have been internal conflicts, creating what have been termed 'complex emergencies': situations where the legitimacy of the state is challenged in large parts of the country and may even have collapsed altogether; where peace can reign for long periods in some parts of the country while conflict persists in some areas and is intermittent in others; where civilians and their livelihoods are often targeted by the warring factions.

Frequently, warring parties will ask the international community to provide assistance in the form of peacekeeping or broader peacebuilding missions. Where such efforts appear to be successful—or where major countries deem their national interests are at stake—the peacekeeping phase will lead to a major reconstruction effort, financed by donor countries and multilateral financial institutions (World Bank and regional development banks).

Although in many cases 'traditional' development work (eg 'new' investments in infrastructure, social services, private sector development) does not stop entirely, the government and the major donors may focus initially on peacekeeping/peace-building only, and subsequently on the reconstruction programme. However, as the restoration of key infrastructure (roads, railways, ports, electrical utilities, and water systems) and basic public services (education, health, policing, etc) progresses, increasing attention shifts to more traditional development programmes.

Thus we can define up to four main stages in a country's transition:

- conflict;
- immediate post-conflict stabilization (including peacekeeping/peacebuilding);
- reconstruction; and
- traditional development with assistance from international donors and finan-cial institutions.

However, this description of the transition from conflict to development is a stylized one. In some cases, a dormant conflict will resume, halting the transi-tion to the reconstruction and development phases. Other countries will suffer from simmering conflict for prolonged periods, perhaps becoming a forgotten emergency, receiving little attention from the international community. Thus, the transition from conflict to development is uncertain and prone to reversals, and may proceed at different rates in different parts of the country. Moreover, the start and end points of the different phases are not clear-cut; instead, the phases tend to overlap.

What is important is not the detail of an individual country's transition, but rather the dynamics of such transitions in general, and the implications of these dynamics for those planning and managing mine action programmes. In particular:

- the country's social, political, and economic environment will evolve over time; in some aspects, quite rapidly;
- the size and relative importance of the different types of international assist-ance programmes—humanitarian, peacebuilding/immediate post-conflict, reconstruction, and development—will evolve over time;
- the international actors present in the country, their primary objectives, and their relative power to influence local affairs, will change over time.

The implications for mine action

The principal outputs of mine action (ie safe land and facilities, awareness of the dangers posed by landmines and ERW, amputees fitted with prostheses) are not ends in themselves; each mine action output is a means to an end. Therefore, mine action is (or should be) at the service of the mine-affected country and its citizens and should be focusing most of its resources in support of the most strategically important efforts underway in the country at that time.

Thus, mine action priorities and the allocation of resources should also change as the emphasis shifts from humanitarian assistance through stabilization through reconstruction and finally to development. Typically, these will be relative shifts over time rather than abrupt changes, so there may be periods when the mine action programme is working in support of, say, three types of programmes: humanitarian, reconstruction, and development.

In general, planners should expect three broad trends over time:

- increasing levels of local ownership over the mine action programme (eg the national government may assume responsibility for the MAC) which implies an increase in the power of the national government relative to the group of donors in setting priorities for the country's progress;

- increasing input from sectoral agencies (government departments; para-statals etc) as planners in the various sectors (agriculture, transportation, utilities, environment, etc) begin to grapple with the problems created by contamination for their sector development plans;

- increasing input from different levels of government as capacities of provincial and local governments are rebuilt following the conflict and they gradually assume the responsibilities mandated by the constitution and legislation.

Mine action in support of peacebuilding

Increasing attention is being given to the role of mine action in support of efforts to achieve or maintain peace within and between countries. A study by the Peace Research Institute of Oslo, published in 2004 concluded that:

Mine action can play an important role in peacebuilding. Emerging mine action initiatives may help foster confidence between parties to a conflict, as it has in recent years in Sri Lanka (prior to the recent upsurge in violence) and Sudan. Organizational structures that are set up for mine action, such as Sri Lanka's district committees, may eventually take on a larger role of sustaining interaction between former adversaries. Engagement in mine action may also support reconciliation at various levels, as illustrated by the relationships between former fighters in Afghanistan's Mine Action for Peace programme. Ultimately, mine action breeds general support for the peace process through its direct impact on people's daily lives—eliminating risks, reopening transport routes or freeing up scarce resources, such as land and water sources. Carefully designed, implemented and coordinated mine action interventions provide a flexible and robust tool for peacebuilding.

Preliminary research by the GICHD has identified a number of specific areas in which mine action can potentially support peacebuilding. These include:

- reducing unemployment (particularly among groups who might resort to violence in the absence of alternative livelihoods);
- building social capital at local community level; and
- confidence-building at regional level.

Reducing unemployment

Unemployment tends to be exceptionally high at the end of any prolonged armed conflict. In these economies, mine action has comparative advantages over many other sectors in providing employment through its ability to employ, train, procure, deploy, and partner quickly, thus delivering an early peace dividend. In Afghanistan, for example, the mine action programme was, for a time, the largest civilian employer in the country. This puts money in the hands of ordinary people who need it to survive and such (relative) economic security can encourage grass-roots support for a peace process.

Moreover, employment can be targeted to ex-combatants who may otherwise potentially play a negative role in the recovery of a country. Further support for peacebuilding may be achieved by integrated teams of ex-combatants that bring together former enemies with a common goal of clearing the explosive relics of the conflict. Positive experiences in this regard have been registered in Mozambique and Sudan, among others.

However, large-scale employment within a mine action programme is not without risks. Deminers in Afghanistan earn much higher wages than Afghan civil servants. The national staff (including the drivers) in the UN-supported Mine Action Centre earn more than most Afghan deminers. Care should therefore be taken to avoid distorting labour markets and thus contributing to wage inflation, as this can be counter-productive to a peace process.

Building social capital at local community level

Mine risk education, especially through community liaison work, can not only help to identify local concerns and priorities and communicate them up the chain, it can also help mobilize communities to take greater responsibility for managing their mine and ERW threat. This support for building social capital at community level can help sustain MRE initiatives long after the specialist teams have left, and bring subsequent benefits to community mobilization in the difficult tasks of building trust and cooperation in the post-conflict period.

Confidence-building at regional level

But confidence building can also take place at the regional level. For example, South East Europe, which has been the scene of some of the most violent fighting on the continent since the 1939–1945 War, has pioneered moves towards the regional coordination of mine action. The South East Europe Mine Action

Coordination Council (SEEMACC) is a regional cooperation body for mine action programmes in the Balkans.

The Council consists of the Directors of the Mine Action Centres of Albania, Bosnia and Herzegovina, Croatia, and Serbia, and has even extended invitations beyond the region, for example to the Azerbaijan National Mine Action Agency. UNMIK, the Mine Detection Dog Centre in Bosnia, the Regional Centre for Underwater Demining in Montenegro and the Centre for Testing, Development and Training in Croatia are also involved. The Council meets on a quarterly basis to share information and provide a forum for the resolution of common demining problems, particularly the coordination of clearance projects that cross national boundaries of the affected countries.

Gender and mine action

The issue of gender and mine action has gained greater attention in recent years. Already in 1997, through the Economic and Social Council, UN member states requested the Secretary General to ensure that all UN programmes pursued strategies of gender mainstreaming and gender balance. For the UN gender mainstreaming is 'the process of assessing the implications for women and men of any planned action'. It focuses attention on ensuring that the concerns and experiences of individuals of both sexes are taken into consideration in the design, implementation, monitoring and evaluation of programmes.

In February 2005, the UNMAS issued 'Gender Guidelines for Mine Action Programmes.' These guidelines are intended to help United Nations mine action policy makers and field personnel incorporate gender perspectives in all relevant mine action activities and operations. The guidelines highlight a range of gender considerations that ought to be taken into account in four of the five main areas of mine action: mine clearance; mine risk education; victim assistance; and advocacy. While the fifth area, stockpile destruction, might offer opportunities to advance the goal of gender balance, no relevant gender considerations have emerged for inclusion in the guidelines. The 2005 guidelines were intended to serve as a working document that would be revised, but as of 2008 this had not occurred.

Selected Bibliography

Eaton, R, *et al* (1997), *The Development of Indigenous Mine Action Capacities*, Study Report, New York: UN DHA.
GICHD (Geneva International Centre for Humanitarian Demining) (2005), *Mine Action: Lessons and Challenges*, Geneva, available at: <http://www.gichd.org>.
—— (2006), *A Guide to International Mine Action Standards*, Geneva.
—— (2007), *A Guide to Mine Action and Explosive Remnants of War*, Geneva.

Harpviken, BK, & Roberts R (2004), Preparing the Ground for Peace: Mine Action in Support of Peacebuilding, PRIO Report 2/2004, Oslo.

International Campaign to Ban Landmines (2007), Landmine Monitor Report 2007: Toward a Mine-Free World.

Mansfield, I (2002), 'Building National Mine Action Capacity: It Is No Myth', *Journal of Mine Action*, Issue 6.1, Mine Action Information Centre, Harrisonburg: James Madison University, Va, US.

Smith, A (1998) 'The Future of Humanitarian Demining', *The Journal of Humanitarian Demining*, Harrisonburg: James Madison University, Va, US.

UN (2001), *International Mine Action Standards*, First Edition, 1 October 2001.

—— (2003), *International Mine Action Standards*, Second Edition, 1 January 2003, available at: <http://www.mineactionstandards.org>.

UNMAS (1998) 'Report of the UN Secretary General on Assistance in Mine Clearance', Document Source, A/53/496, New York.

—— (2005), *Gender Guidelines for Mine Action Programmes*, New York: UNMAS.

—— (2005), *Mine Action and Effective Coordination: the United Nations Policy*, New York, available at: <http://www.mineaction.org>.

Non-state Actors

Andrew Clapham

Definition

The concept of non-state actors is generally understood as including any entity that is not actually a state, often used to refer to armed groups, terrorists, civil society, religious groups, or corporations; the concept is occasionally used to encompass inter-governmental organizations. In the specific context of post-conflict peacebuilding, the expression 'non-state actor' is being used in specialized literature to refer to a range of armed groups that operate beyond state control.

I. Term

A subjective term: an expansive definition

The expression 'non-state actors' suggests different things to different people. On various occasions I have taken the chance to ask a group of diplomats, UN officials, and others to say what they understand by the term non-state actors in the context of a training seminar on human rights. The responses range wide. Most groups of interlocutors cover a spectrum: from rebels, terrorists, and Al-Qaeda, through to business, non-governmental organizations, and religious groups. For some it is 'bad guys'; for others it is 'civil society'. Perhaps most tellingly one person once responded: 'all of us'. And here lies the problem with any attempt to give a lexical meaning of 'non-state actor' in the context of post-conflict peacebuilding: the phrase conjures up different entities depending on context and coincidence.

Those who have dealt with sanctions aimed at preventing nuclear weapons and *matériel* falling into the hands of non-state actors, have a certain image in their heads when they refer to non-state actors ('bad guys' does not really capture it). On the other hand, those who have been working on cross-cultural dialogue with religious groups apparently find the term useful to group together various key players in society. Furthermore, those concerned with the human rights impact of the policies of international organizations such as the World Bank and the International Monetary Fund (IMF) have addressed these entities under the rubric of 'recommendations to non-state actors'.

A dictionary definition of non-state actor can be made simple. Non-state actor implies any entity that is not actually a state. From a legalistic or 'technical' point of view, UN experts Biró and Motoc (2005: 7) report that: 'a non-state actor can be any actor on the international stage other than a sovereign state.' But as we have already seen, the expression non-state actor quickly conjures up a particular type of entity depending on the context and the speaker. How did we get to this point? Why do we have a term which covers such a diverse range of entities as to be almost unhelpful? The answer is partly the fault of public international law and international lawyers. As Philip Alston (2005: 3) points out:

Apart from its ability to obfuscate almost any debate, this insistence upon defining all actors in terms of what they are not combines impeccable purism in terms of traditional international legal analysis with an unparalleled capacity to marginalise a significant part of the international human rights regime from the most vital challenges confront-ing global governance at the dawn of the twenty-first century. In essence, these negative, euphemistic terms do not stem from language inadequacies but instead have been inten-tionally adopted in order to reinforce the assumption that the state is not only the central actor, but also the indispensable and pivotal one around which all other entities revolve.

There are multiple reasons why lawyers and governments want to exclude non-state actors from the state-centric regime of international law in general, and human rights law in particular. First, with regard to armed groups (terrorists for some, in some contexts), it is argued that suggesting that such groups have human rights obligations under international law lends them a state-like status which renders them somehow 'legitimate'. This enhanced legitimacy is considered by some governments to be undesirable. Second, in some circumstances governments are wary of allowing international organizations to assume state-like features by taking on international obligations, such as those relating to human rights. This is the case for example with regard to the attitude of some governments towards the European Union playing a greater role as the bearer of human rights obligations. Third, turning to organizations such as the World Bank or to the corporate world, it is not hard to understand the motivation for suggesting that such entities should not be subjected to the same obligations as states. The organizations themselves are usually not keen to take on a raft of responsibilities that they see as properly the responsibilities of states. And it is often suggested that there is a danger, in the pro-posed extension of all human rights obligations to corporations, of undermining or diluting the responsibilities of state actors. For example, John Ruggie (2006: 17) advised the UN Commission on Human Rights that:

Corporations are not democratic public interest institutions and that making them, in effect, co-equal duty bearers for the broad spectrum of human rights ... may undermine efforts to build indigenous social capacity and to make governments more responsible to their own citizenry.

We have then two perceived problems: a 'legitimacy' problem and a 'dilution' problem. These problems can be quite easily overcome. We can suggest that armed groups and their members are increasingly accused of violations of humanitarian law and even convicted of war crimes. This has not led to an upsurge in legitimacy. Holding them to account for human rights violations might be similarly successful. The problem of legitimizing armed groups evaporates if we decouple the supposed essential link between governments and their citizens, and see human rights as rights rather than solely stemming from governmental duties. With regards to dilution, we can suggest that international financial institutions have to respect human rights in ways that complement the responsibilities of states, rather than replacing such obligations.

It is suggested here that we are already moving in this direction, so that, even if the term non-state actor was invented, as Alston suggests, to occlude these entities from the framework of international legal responsibilities, non-state actors are now increasingly seen as having responsibilities on the international plane. We can recall the Report of the High Level Group of 13 November 2006 on the 'Alliance of Civilizations'. The High Level Group, established by the UN Secretary-General, fixes expectations on non-state actors (without seeming to be worried about legitimacy), and at the same time, the Group cautions about demonizing non-state actors and leaving states out of the picture (thus addressing worries about dilution):

2.3 A full and consistent adherence to human rights standards forms the foundation for stable societies and peaceful international relations. These rights include the prohibition against physical and mental torture; the right to freedom of religion; and the right to freedom of expression and association. The integrity of these rights rests on their universal and unconditional nature. These rights should therefore be considered inviolable and all states, international organizations, non-state actors, and individuals, under all circumstances, must abide by them.

...

3.12 Extremism and terrorism are not motivated solely by exclusivist interpretations of religion, nor are non-state actors alone in employing them. Indeed, secular political motives were responsible for some of the most horrifying reigns of terror in living memory, such as the Holocaust, the Stalinist repressions in the Soviet Union, and more recent genocides in Cambodia, the Balkans, and Rwanda, all perpetrated by state powers. In sum, a cursory look at the twentieth century indicates that no single group, culture, geographic region, or political orientation has a monopoly on extremism and terrorist acts.

We propose therefore to define non-state actor to include every entity apart from states. Although the expression 'non-state actor' is only rarely used to refer to international organizations, recent books on non-state actors do include chapters on certain international organizations, covering UN, the World Bank, the IMF, the European Union (EU), and the World Trade Organization (Clapham, 2006; Gianviti, 2005: 113).

According to Alston (2005: 29), there may be several reasons why international organizations are 'neglected' in discussions over the role of non-state actors in relation to human rights. First, because they are acting as surrogates for states;

second, they enjoy international personality and therefore their status under international law is not as different from states as other non-state actors; third, because their activities are seen as 'essentially benign'; and fourth, because it is difficult to fit them in with other groups as diverse as corporations and terrorists, who do not have a natural affinity with human rights, and cannot plausibly proclaim their adherence to the relevant norms.

All these assumptions make sense, but they may be breaking down. North Atlantic Treaty Organization (NATO) or UN action in Kosovo may not necessarily be attributable to particular states but rather be considered solely attributable to the organizations themselves (ECHR, 2007: 41, 44). International law increasingly addresses entities other than states (Institute of International Law, 2003). The advent of the international criminal tribunals has reinforced the notion that international law extends beyond inter-state relations. Protests at the policies and practices of entities such as the IMF suggest that being an international organization does not attract uncritical support from civil society; furthermore, sexual exploitation scandals concerning peacekeepers from international organizations have heightened awareness of the less-than-benign nature of certain aspects of the activities of international organizations (for further discussion on the accountability of UN staff and experts on mission see the chapters on peace operations; rule of law; and transitional administration). Lastly, as we shall see, corporations and armed groups do actually proclaim adherence to international norms, and are increasingly being held to these commitments.

We suggest therefore that anyone encountering the expression non-state actor be ready, according to the context, to see this term as referring to any entity that is not a state under international law. The range of possible entities includes: rebel groups, terrorist organizations, religious groups, civil society organizations, corporations, all kinds of businesses, and international organizations. Anything less comprehensive starts to suggest immunity from certain international responsibilities that are being generated and increasingly recognized in international relations.

This comprehensive definition is not meant to suggest that everyone will or should use the expression non-state actors in this expansive way. In the context of peacebuilding, the literature and research tends to use the term non-state actor (in its abbreviation NSA) as a shorthand for different types of armed groups including military security companies (see private sector and security sector reform chapters). Caroline Holmqvist (2005a) in 'Engaging Armed Non-State Actors in Post-Conflict Settings' approaches the issue as follows:

Armed non-state actors' (NSAs) are defined as 'armed groups that operate beyond state control', purposely casting the net wide. It includes, but is not limited to, the following groups:

– rebel opposition groups (groups with a stated incompatibility with the government, generally concerning the control of government or the control of territory);

- local militias (ethnically, clan, or otherwise based);
- vigilantes;
- warlords;
- civil defence forces and paramilitary groups (when such are clearly beyond state control);
- private companies that provide military and security services (hereafter private security companies, PSCs).

The categories offered here are fluid, and the same group may be differently classified over time. The splintering of rebel groups, inter-faction or inter-militia hostility, and the various roles played by warlords further add to the definitional conundrum, as illustrated by the recurrence of violence in Afghanistan, the Great Lakes, and the West African sub-region. The conflicts in Angola, Sierra Leone, and more recently, Iraq, are illustrative of the extent to which security relations both during and after conflict are shaped by a multiplicity of armed non-state actors (armed groups and the private sector alike), whereas the contracting of private security by other non-state entities, such as rebel groups (eg in Colombia), adds further complexity to the armed non-state actor picture.

Non-state actors defined in international texts

For completeness we mention here some examples of the use of the term non-state actor in texts adopted at the inter-governmental level. First, with regard to terrorist groups the Security Council adopted Resolution 1540 (2004), which created binding obligations on UN member states. It decided that 'all states shall refrain from providing any form of support to non-state actors that attempt to develop, acquire, manufacture, possess, transport, transfer or use nuclear, chemical or biological weapons and their means of delivery' and also that:

all States, in accordance with their national procedures, shall adopt and enforce appropriate effective laws which prohibit any non-state actor to manufacture, acquire, possess, develop, transport, transfer or use nuclear, chemical or biological weapons and their means of delivery, in particular for terrorist purposes, as well as attempts to engage in any of the foregoing activities, participate in them as an accomplice, assist or finance them.

The Council included an indefinite definition 'for the purpose of this resolution only ... Non-state actor: individual or entity, not acting under the lawful authority of any state in conducting activities which come within the scope of this resolution.' The context means that any entity lacking state authority to deal with these weapons of mass destruction is considered a non-state actor. In other contexts, however, one can imagine entities authorized by the state to carry out certain activities: say running a retirement home or hospice. Such entities could still be considered non-state actors in formal legal terms before national or international courts (Oliver & Fedtke, 2007). The Security Council's definition is therefore very context specific.

A second international text is the Cotonou Agreement between the Members of the African, Caribbean and Pacific (ACP) Group of States and the European Community and its member states. This treaty uses the term several times to refer to civil society organizations (which are to be identified in the relevant country strategy paper). Part 1, Chapter 2, Article 6 contains a definition:

1. The actors of cooperation will include:
    (a) State (local, national and regional);
    (b) Non-State:
    – Private sector;
    – Economic and social partners, including trade union organisations;
    – Civil Society in all its forms according to national characteristics.

2. Recognition by the parties of non-governmental actors shall depend on the extent to which they address the needs of the population, on their specific competencies and whether they are organised and managed democratically and transparently.

Specific roles are set out for such non-state actors in the treaty and are discussed in the next section.

II. Content

Obligations with regard to civil society non-state actors

Let us start with the Cotonou Agreement's provision on non-state actors. Part 1, Chapter 2, Article 4 reads in part:

...the parties recognise the complementary role of and potential for contributions by non-State actors to the development process. To this end, under the conditions laid down in this agreement, non-State actors shall, where appropriate:

• be informed and involved in consultation on cooperation policies and strategies, on priorities for cooperation especially in areas that concern or directly affect them, and on the political dialogue;

• be provided with financial resources, under the conditions laid down in this Agreement in order to support local development processes; be involved in the implementation of cooperation projects and programmes in areas that concern them or where these actors have a comparative advantage;...

• be provided with capacity-building support in critical areas in order to reinforce the capabilities of these actors, particularly as regards organisation and representation, and the establishment of consultation mechanisms including channels of communication and dialogue, and to promote strategic alliances.

The role of this type of non-state actor (the national civil society non-governmental organization) is dealt with elsewhere in this Lexicon. It is enough to note here two points. First, certain treaties (we could also mention the UN Convention against Corruption) oblige states to cooperate with relevant civil society organizations, otherwise known as non-state actors. This means in turn that we can speak of the rights of non-state actors to be consulted and to participate in certain development projects. Although this is strictly speaking a treaty obligation for EU and ACP states in a particular context, few would argue against a principle of involving civil society in peacebuilding projects where, in the words of the treaty, we are dealing with 'areas that concern them or where these actors have a comparative advantage'. Second, humanitarian organizations operating in post-conflict situations are realizing that there are expectations that they themselves should consider their own accountability and behaviour (Davis, 2007); and that these humanitarian organizations have not only rights but also responsibilities towards the victims of the conflict. But as prefigured above, civil society organizations are not the only set of actors with rights and obligations in such a context. Let us turn to the work of the human rights monitoring mechanism bodies.

Human rights recommendations with regard to non-state actors

One might suggest that the term non-state actor has become so ubiquitous in human rights discourse that no set of treaty body recommendations would be complete without a chapter on 'non-state actors'. What are the policy recommendations for this crucial group of entities? For example, General Comments prepared by the UN Committee on Economic, Social and Cultural Rights on topics such as the right to health, the right to food, the right to water, and the right to work, now not only refer to non-state actors but include the duty of states to protect individuals from non-state actors that might infringe on the enjoyment of these rights. For example, with regard to the right to work, the Committee stated:

Obligations to *protect* the right to work include, inter alia, the duties of States parties to adopt legislation or to take other measures ensuring equal access to work and training and to ensure that privatization measures do not undermine workers' rights. Specific measures to increase the flexibility of labour markets must not render work less stable or reduce the social protection of the worker. The obligation to protect the right to work includes the responsibility of States parties to prohibit forced or compulsory labour by non-State actors (UN Committee, 2005).

The Committee has a chapter at the end of its General Comments entitled 'Obligations of Actors Other than State Parties'. This includes, for example in the context of the right to work, recommendations for 'individuals, local communities, trade unions, civil society and private sector organizations'. Special attention is given to 'private enterprises – national and multinational'. The Comment goes on to address the role of 'the [International Labour Organization] ILO and the other specialized agencies of the United Nations, the World Bank, regional development banks, the International Monetary Fund, the World Trade Organization and other relevant bodies within the United Nations system'. So, despite the state-centric nature of the human rights treaty regime, the UN treaty monitoring bodies have been at pains to address their human rights recommendations to 'Actors Other than State Parties' (which is another way of referring to non-state actors). This is a general point which applies in all circumstances. Turning to conflict situations and post-conflict peacebuilding the inclusion of armed groups on the scene gives rise to multiple problems.

Monitoring armed groups

Other UN human rights monitoring mechanisms have recently started to address this other sort of non-state actor: the armed group fighting against state or other non-state forces. Most recently a group of Special Rapporteurs reported to the new Human Rights Council in the following terms:

Although Hezbollah, a non-State actor, cannot become a party to these human rights treaties, it remains subject to the demand of the international community, first expressed in the Universal Declaration of Human Rights, that every organ of society respect and promote human rights. The Security Council has long called upon various groups which member states do not recognize as having the capacity to do so to formally assume international obligations to respect human rights. It is especially appropriate and feasible to call for an armed group to respect human rights norms when it 'exercises significant control over territory and population and has an identifiable political structure' (UN, 2006: para 19).

We see here in these examples of UN practice the separation of non-state actors from state actors on very legalistic grounds. They are treated separately because they are not parties to the relevant international treaties. In fact, as the last example shows, they 'cannot' become party to the treaties, hence the need to find different legal and political regimes to hold them accountable for transgressing certain norms. Until the legal regimes adapt—or are adapted—to embrace the behaviour of non-state actors, such actors continue to be treated apart, in a separate chapter from states for the 'obvious' reason that they are outside the relevant treaty regime and its monitoring mechanisms.

This presents a problem for those working in conflict and post-conflict situations who want to engage with these armed groups in order to encourage compliance with certain norms. The reluctance of governments to include non-state actors as duty bearers in treaty regimes has led to innovative new monitoring mechanisms which negotiate 'commitments' from armed groups in fields such as the use of anti-personnel mines (see the mine action chapter) and the recruitment of child soldiers (Clapham, 2006: 286–99). It seems safe to predict that UN and civil society organizations will continue to expand their horizons by looking beyond the behaviour of states and state-centric monitoring mechanisms in order to develop new monitoring mechanisms for non-state actors.

This is particularly likely in situations of massive violations of human rights amounting to genocide, crimes against humanity and war crimes. As these violations amount to international crimes, engagement with such non-state actors is delicate. First, engaging with non-state actors may end up as evidence-gathering for a future prosecution. At this point, not only might those engaging with the armed non-state actor be putting themselves in danger, they also have to assess the implications for the rest of their work in the region. Second, to the extent that anyone is suppressing evidence of war crimes they could be accused of abetting an international crime and becoming liable for prosecution. But the international criminal law dimension is perhaps not the real problem here. The bigger obstacle is the concern of governments that engaging with armed non-state actors in the context of peacebuilding undermines the role of the state and empowers the 'terrorists'.

III. Implementation

Engaging with armed groups

Demands on non-state actor armed opposition groups for compliance with previous commitments can turn to accusations of criminality, and monitoring becomes the first stage of evidence gathering for potential international trials. Furthermore, the 'legitimacy' question resurfaces. For certain governments the non-state actor at issue is a terrorist outlaw group. Engaging, encouraging, or enticing such a group, even if it is with a view to ensuring a humanitarian objective, can be seen in some quarters as assisting terrorists. The problems here for civil society and inter-governmental organizations are legion. Certain governments will go to great lengths to target civil society groups and individuals as complicit with terrorism, and once anyone is listed in such a way it may be difficult to operate internationally or attract donors. This area merits a fuller discussion by the actors involved. Studies suggest that the repressive arrangements which came in the context of the 'Global War on Terror' (GWOT) are difficult to understand and frustrating for humanitarian organizations trying to operate in conflict zones (Thorne, 2007: 13). While reaffirming the principle of humanitarian assistance, there is an awareness that engagement with non-state actors needs a degree of political sophistication if one is to avoid the 'terrorist' tag.

By virtue of its mandate, the humanitarian mission is not contingent on whether certain (non-state) groups are deemed legitimate or not, or whether they are considered legal or illegal. At the same time, however, simply dismissing the GWOT and its concomitant policies as irrelevant is not enough. Non-governmental humanitarian agencies *will* be confronted with GWOT policies in the context of their operations. Governments, the public and beneficiaries themselves may all question agencies' interactions with certain armed groups, in particular if the latter are considered illegitimate or illegal (Glaser, 2007: 16).

Holding corporations accountable

The second problematic area is implementation of international norms with regard to the behaviour of corporate non-state actors. The growth of corporate social responsibility initiatives, as well as innovative mechanisms for holding corporations accountable in law, have focused attention on this area (Zerk, 2006; De Schutter, 2006). In particular, in the context of armed conflict and post-conflict reconstruction there have been serious allegations concerning the exploitation of natural resources, violence against the local population, and corruption (see also the chapters on private sector and conflict economies). A particular issue concerns the behaviour of private military companies and the inadequacy of the regulatory framework (Holmqvist, 2005b).

In many cases, the allegations will involve accusations of complicity in international crimes or other unlawful acts. This means that the corporation is essentially alleged to have knowingly substantially assisted a government or armed non-state actor to commit an unlawful act. While there are considerable obstacles to holding corporations accountable in a court of law (Joseph, 2004), the Organization for Economic Co-operation and Development (OECD) has been developing a mechanism for hearing allegations against corporations which allows for civil society organizations to confront corporations with complaints about their behaviour (OECD Watch, 2006). Such non-state actor confrontations reinforce the theme of this entry that, despite problems concerning legal accountability, non-state actors are increasingly seen, not as essential partners in conflict situations (Nelson, 2000), but as actors to be engaged with (or even evaluated) in order to ensure that their activities do not undermine efforts undertaken in the context of post-conflict peacebuilding.

A particularly interesting set of evaluations are undertaken by the Norwegian Council on Ethics for the Government Pension Fund—Global. This body carries out evaluations of companies (including arms manufacturers) for the purpose of excluding companies from receiving government investment where there is 'an unacceptable risk that the fund may contribute to unethical acts or omissions, such as violations of fundamental humanitarian principles, serious violations of human rights, gross corruption or severe environmental damages'. For example, in 2006 the Ponsgan Corporation was excluded on the grounds that its activities may include the manufacture of cluster munitions. The Council's list of excluded companies not only leads to disinvestment by the Norwegian Government's Pension Fund but also influences other governments and investors.

The problems and potential of engaging non-state actors

Non-state actors present multiple challenges in the context of post-conflict peacebuilding. First, the open-ended nature of the term defies a restrictive definition and as such gives rise to misunderstandings and tensions, as corporations find themselves branded in the same category as rebel groups, and the UN finds itself bracketed with paramilitaries. Second, there are the dual fears that engaging with non-state actors will legitimize the group and dilute the power of the state. Third, we have to realize that the international system remains state-centric and that working with non-state actors involves 'swimming against the tide', which is more concerned with state-building. Holmqvist (2005a: 63) has concluded that 'the goal of successful security governance in the context of post-conflict peace-building should be the establishment of effective, transparent and democratically accountable state institutions' (see more generally the chapter on democratic governance). But she is careful to leave a complementary role for engaging with non-state actors:

As measures complementary to the rebuilding of the state, efforts at constraining armed non-state actors, protecting vulnerable populations from abuse (or recruitment into non-state entities), and increasing respect for human rights, influencing armed non-state actors should be seen as an integral part of post-conflict peacebuilding.

Selected Bibliography

Alston, P (2005) 'The "Not-a-Cat" Syndrome: Can the International Human Rights Regime Accommodate Non-State Actors?', in Alston, P (ed), *Non-State Actors and Human Rights*, Oxford: Oxford University Press, 3–36.

Amnesty International (2000), *Respect, Protect, Fulfil—Women's Human Rights State Responsibility for Abuses by 'Non-State Actors'*, AI Index IOR 50/01/00.

Bianchi, A (1997), 'Globalisation of Human Rights: The Role of Non-state Actors', in Teubner, G (ed), *Global Law Without a State*, Aldershot: Dartmouth, 179.

Biró, G, & Motoc, A-I (2005), *Working Paper on Human Rights and Non-State Actors*, E/CN.4/Sub.2/2005/40, 11 July.

Bruderlein, C (2000), 'The Role of Non-State Actors in Building Human Security: The Case of Armed Groups in Intra-State Wars', Geneva: Centre for Humanitarian Dialogue, available at: <http://ihl.ihlresearch.org/>.

Clapham, A (2006), *Human Rights Obligations of Non-State Actors*, Oxford: Oxford University Press.

Davis, A (2007), *Concerning Accountability of Humanitarian Action*, HPN Network Paper No 58.

De Schutter, O (ed) (2006), *Transnational Corporations and Human Rights*, Oxford: Hart Publishing.

ECHR (2007), Decision of the European Court of Human Rights (Grand Chamber) in Application No 71412/01 *Behrami And Behrami v France* and Application No 78166/01 *Saramati v France, Germany and Norway.*

Fleck, D (2003), 'Humanitarian Protection Against Non-State Actors', in Frowein, JA, Scharioth, K, Winkelmann, I, & Wolfrum, R (eds), *Verhandeln für den Frieden— Negotiating for Peace: Liber Amicorum Tono Eitel*, Berlin: Springer, 69.

Gianviti, F (2005), 'Economic, Social and Cultural Rights and the International Monetary Fund', in Alston, P (ed), *Non-State Actors and Human Rights*, Oxford: Oxford University Press, 113.

Glaser, MP (2007), 'Engaging with Non-State Armed Groups in the Context of the "GlobalWar on Terror": Observations from Lebanon and Gaza', *Humanitarian Exchange*, 37: 16, available at: <http://www.odihpn.org/report.asp?id=2875>.

Harding, C (2001), 'Statist Assumptions, Normative Individualism and New Forms of Personality: Evolving a Philosophy of International Law for the Twenty-First Century', *Non-State Actors and International Law*, 1: 107–26.

Hessbruegge, JA (2005), 'Human Rights Violations Arising from Conduct of Non-State Actors', *Buffalo Human Rights Law Review*, 11: 21–88.

Hofmann, R (ed) (1999), *Non-State Actors as New Subjects of International Law: International Law–From the Traditional State Order Towards the Law of the Global Community,* Berlin: Dunker and Humblot.

Holmqvist, C (2005a), 'Engaging Armed Non-State Actors in Post-Conflict Settings', in Bryden, A, & Hänggi, H (eds), *Security Governance in Post-Conflict Peacebuilding*, Münster: Lit Verlag, 45–68.

—— (2005b), 'Private Security Companies: The Case for Regulation', Stockholm: SIPRI Policy Paper, No 9.

Institute of International Law (2003), *L'application du droit international humanitaire et des droits fondamentaux de l'homme dans les conflits armés auxquels prennent part des entités non étatiques: résolution de Berlin du 25 août 1999—The Application of International Humanitarian Law and Fundamental Human Rights in Armed Conflicts in which Non-State Entities are Parties: Berlin Resolution of 25 August 1999*, commentaire de Robert Kolb, Collection 'résolutions' No 1, Paris: Pedone.

Joseph, S (2004), *Corporations and Transnational Human Rights Litigation*, Oxford: Hart Publishing.

Kooijmans, PH (1998), 'The Security Council and Non-State Entities as Parties to Conflicts', in Wellens, K (ed), *International Law: Theory and Practice*, The Hague: Nijhoff, 333–46.

Nelson, J (2000), *The Business of Peace: The Private Sector as a Partner in Conflict Prevention and Resolution*, London: International Alert; Council on Economic Priorities; The Prince of Wales Business Leaders Forum.

Noortmann, M (2001), 'Non-State Actors in International Law', in Arts, B, Noortmann, M, & Reinalda, B (eds), *Non-State Actors in International Relations*, Aldershot: Ashgate, 59–78.

OECD Watch (2006), *Guide to the OECD Guidelines for Multinational Enterprises' Complaint Procedure: Lessons from Past NGO Complaints*, 2nd edn.

Oliver, D, & Fedtke, J (eds) (2007), *Human Rights and the Private Sphere*, Abingdon: Routledge-Cavendish.

Ruggie, J (2006) *Interim Report of the Special Representative of the Secretary-General on the Issue of Human Rights and Transnational Corporations and Other Business Enterprises*, UN Doc E/CN.4/2006/97, 22 February.

Thorne, K (2007), 'Terrorist Lists and Humanitarian Assistance', *Humanitarian Exchange*, 37: 13.

Türk, V (2002), 'Non-State Agents of Persecution', in Chetail, V, & Gowlland-Debbas, V (eds), *Switzerland and the International Protection of Refugees*, The Hague: Kluwer, 95.

UN (2006), *Report of the Special Rapporteur on Extrajudicial, Summary or Arbitrary Executions, Philip Alston; the Special Rapporteur on the Right of Everyone to the Enjoyment of the Highest Attainable Standard of Physical and Mental Health, Paul Hunt; the Representative of the Secretary-General on Human Rights of Internally Displaced Persons, Walter Kälin; and the Special Rapporteur on Adequate Housing as a Component of the Right to an Adequate Standard of Living, Miloon Kothari*, A/HRC/2/7, 2 October.

UN Committee on Economic Social and Cultural Rights (2005), *General Comment no. 18 (The Right to Work)*, E/C.12/GC/18, 24 November.

Wilde, R (2004), 'The Accountability of International Organisations and the Concepts of Functional Duality', in Heere, WP (ed), *From Government to Governance: The Growing Impact of Non-State Actors on the International and European Legal System*, The Hague: TMC Asser Press, 164.

Wilshire, D (2003), 'Non-State Actors and the Definition of a Refugee in the United Kingdom: Protection, Accountability or Culpability?', *International Journal of Refugee Law*, 15: 68–112.

Zerk, JA (2006), *Multinationals and Corporate Social Responsibility: Limitations and Opportunities in International Law*, Cambridge: Cambridge University Press.

Peace Operations

Nigel White

Definition

Peace operations involve the deployment of an organized team or teams of civilian, police and military specialists into post-conflict situations with the aim of performing two coordinated functions. The first function is peacekeeping—the provision of temporary post-conflict security by internationally mandated forces, normally consensually and impartially unless the peace requires restoration or civilians need protection. The second function is peacebuilding—those efforts (comprising coordinated humanitarian, development, and governance elements) undertaken by the international community to help a war-torn society create a self-sustaining peace in accordance with the principle of self-determination.

I. Term

Origin and context

The definition above builds on that provided by the Henry L. Stimson Centre (<http://www.stimson.org>). The term 'peace operations' emerged in the post-Cold War period, reaching its solidification in the Brahimi Report of 2000 (UN Doc A/55/505-S/2000/809). It has come largely to replace or rather subsume the older and narrower concept of peacekeeping as a key element of the UN's peace and security function. Whereas peacekeeping forces are mainly military in composition, peace operations consist of a variety of professionals and experts: soldiers, police, relief workers, election monitors, human rights workers, development advisers, and so on.

Historically, the UN has concerned itself in practice with defining and developing the concept of peacekeeping since the first full UN peacekeeping force in the Middle East in 1956. Peacekeeping was defined by the UN at the end of the Cold War in 1991 as an:

operation involving military personnel, but without enforcement powers, undertaken by the United Nations to help maintain or restore international peace and security in areas of conflict. These operations are voluntary and are based on consent and cooperation (UN, 1991).

Generally, peacekeeping operations consist of contributing states' military contingents under UN command and control, specifically the Secretary-General, acting under delegated authority from the Security Council, exceptionally the General Assembly. This should be contrasted with the enforcement model that emerged out of Chapter VII of the Charter under which a 'Coalition of the Willing' is authorized by the Security Council with command and control being vested in the contributing state(s).

In general terms, military enforcement action is taken against the sovereignty of a state, while peacekeeping operations are undertaken with the consent and cooperation of the state or states in question. Peace operations share a common heritage with peacekeeping; indeed in the above definition peacekeeping is one of the two key elements of the term. However, the addition of the broader function of peacebuilding to peacekeeping has necessitated the introduction of limited enforcement powers into peace operations, as discussed in section III.

Peacekeeping proved acceptable during the Cold War because it had limited objectives, normally assisting in the maintenance of a ceasefire and a separation of the belligerents, not by enforcement, but by consent and cooperation. Hence peacekeeping is still stated by the General Assembly's Special Committee on Peacekeeping to be based on a trinity of virtues—consent; impartiality; and restrictions on the use of force (UN, 2003: para 46). While the latter clearly includes a peacekeeper using force in defence of his own life, his comrades, and any person in his care, as well as his post, convoy, vehicle, or rifle (UN, 1995a), there has been a lack of clarity as to whether the force could also 'defend' its mandate (UN, 1958: para 179; UN, 1973). During the Cold War, with the exception of the Congo operation in the 1960s, rules of engagement were drawn up quite conservatively (Goulding, 1993: 455).

Evolution

Post-Cold War peace operations, where peacekeeping was combined with peacebuilding under the principles of consent, impartiality, and the limited use of force, started with the UN operation in Namibia in 1989. In the early 1990s the UN rapidly developed a multi-dimensional peacekeeping and peacebuilding model, a number of examples of which were successful in achieving their more ambitious mandates, for example in Nicaragua, El Salvador, Cambodia, and Mozambique in 1989–1995, though some struggled, most notably the operation in Angola, 1988–1997 (O'Neill & Rees, 2005: 139–68).

The crucial problem with the development of peace operations, from a practice and doctrinal basis in consensual and limited peacekeeping, is that while peacekeeping and peacebuilding can be perfectly compatible and complementary when both are based on negotiated peaceful solutions with the consent and cooperation of all the parties, difficulties arise if the peacebuilding element is, or becomes, undertaken in an environment that is 'non-consensual' or at best 'semi-permissive' (Hansen *et al*, 2004: 6), for example through the actions of factions (commonly referred to as 'spoilers'), who would undermine the process. Spoilers have been defined as 'factions who see a peace agreement as inimical to their interests, power or ideology, use violence to undermine or overthrow settlements' (UN, 2004: 222) (see also on this issue the chapters on non-state actors; peace process; and conflict transformation).

The need for coercive enforcement action in these circumstances becomes difficult to avoid, especially given the need to prevent repetition of the failures of the UN forces in Rwanda in 1994 and at Srebrenica in 1995. In such situations the traditional principles of peacekeeping cannot be fully upheld, though unless coercive action is taken against the sovereignty of a state, the military element of the peace operation would not normally become a full scale enforcement action, but a peacekeeping operation with enforcement elements. Nevertheless, the desire to do something in the face of large-scale human rights abuse has led to both conceptual problems with redefining peacekeeping (UN, 1992: paras 20–44; UN, 1995b: para 35); and serious practical problems in its implementation as evidenced by the failure of the operation in Somalia in 1995 (O'Neill & Rees 2005: 107–138) (see more generally the chapter on responsibility to protect).

The desire to improve the creaking peacekeeping function whose credibility had suffered greatly in the mid-1990s, led the then-UN Secretary-General Kofi Annan to establish the Panel on United Nations Peace Operations chaired by Lakhdar Brahimi. The aim was not simply to address the issue of how peacekeepers should approach human rights violations, but went much wider to try in effect to address the tension between the traditional values of peacekeeping and the need for greater effectiveness of the UN in post-conflict situations (Gray, 2004: 238).

Although the Brahimi Report included conflict prevention and peacemaking within its concept of peace operation, the two core elements were those identified above. First, 'peacekeeping', which has evolved from the traditional military model of observing ceasefires and forces separation best suited to inter-state conflicts, to 'incorporate a complex model of many elements, military and civilian, working together to build peace in the dangerous aftermath of civil wars.' Second, 'peacebuilding' consisting of 'activities undertaken on the far side of conflict to reassemble the foundations of peace and provide the tools for building on those foundations something that is more than just the absence of war.' It includes the disarmament, demobilization, and reintegration of former combatants into civilian life; strengthening the rule of law (for example reforming and training the police and judiciary); improving respect for human rights; providing technical assistance for democratic development; and promoting conflict resolution and reconciliation techniques (Brahimi Report, 2000: paras 10–3).

From Brahimi onwards the military (peacekeeping) element of peace operations has three aims: avoiding any failure to protect civilians; ensuring that there are 'adequate self-defence mechanisms for peacekeeping forces and UN staff', learning from Sierra Leone and East Timor in 1999 when UN staff were kidnapped and killed by mobs and militias; and finally preventing spoilers from undermining the peace process. Though Brahimi marked the turning point, the change to peacekeeping was also driven by the national defence academies of developed countries that had contributed to UN deployments in the 1990s, and who would 'no longer agree to send their military forces into conflict for which they were inadequately prepared and supported' (Hansen *et al*, 2004: 7).

With the increasing involvement of more powerful states there came demands for more effective operations. The UK is a leading proponent of more effective 'peace support operations' (PSO), which 'impartially' make 'use of diplomatic, civil and military means, normally in pursuit of United Nations Charter purposes and principles, to restore or maintain peace.' Such operations may include 'conflict prevention, peacemaking, peace enforcement, peacekeeping, peacebuilding and/or humanitarian' elements (UK Ministry of Defence, 2004: 7; Bellamy *et al*, 2004: 165–85). The military components of these are sometimes termed stabilization operations in recognition of the fact that they are the first component deployed to a semi-hostile environment to secure the peace before other elements of the PSO are sent. Arguably, PSO doctrine has been implicitly adopted by the EU in the development of its Petersberg tasks, namely 'humanitarian and rescue tasks, peacekeeping tasks and tasks of combat forces in crisis management, including peacemaking' (Art 17(2) of the Treaty on European Union), and in its practice in the deployment of the European Union Force (EUFOR), replacing the NATO-led Stabilisation Force (SFOR) in Bosnia and Herzegovina in 2004.

NATO has adopted this approach defining peace support operations as 'multifunctional operations, conducted impartially, normally in support of an internationally recognised organisation' and 'involving military forces and diplomatic and humanitarian agencies.' According to NATO such operations 'are designed to achieve a long-term political settlement or other specified conditions', and can include peacekeeping, peace enforcement as well as peacebuilding and humanitarian relief (NATO, 2001: para 202).

It must not be assumed that PSO doctrine is universally accepted. The NATO version suggests that such operations would not necessarily require UN authorization even though they included elements of enforcement, while the British version suggests such operations might not be undertaken in pursuit of UN purposes and principles. Both doctrines suggest that regional organizations could act autonomously from the UN, though normally they would act in support of it and its principles.

In contrast to this more interventionist PSO doctrine, the UN's Special Committee on Peacekeeping has, as recently as 2003, reiterated that the traditional virtues of peacekeeping 'such as the consent of the parties, impartiality and the non-use of force' are essential to its success. This was preceded in the report by the Committee emphasizing respect for the principles of the UN

Charter, especially sovereignty and non-intervention (UN, 2003: paras 45, 46). The failure by the Committee to develop the doctrine of peacekeeping to accurately reflect its role in peace operations is unsatisfactory, but may reflect the divisions within the UN with some states being unhappy about the increasingly interventionist nature of peace operations.

II. Content

The multi-dimensional peace operations that emerged in the immediate post-Cold War period, starting with the operation in Namibia in 1989, took the form of a combined military/civilian mission which supervized the end of the hostilities, and oversaw peacebuilding mainly in the form of an election process. The force consisted of a military component whose function was to 'serve in a supporting role: to guarantee and maintain a secure environment in which the civilian components' could work, by helping to maintain a ceasefire, and by the cantonment or withdrawal and disarmament of factions as provided by the peace agreement. Mine clearance and risk education was also included in most operations. Second, a police element with a role that was 'between the military and civilian actors' by assisting in maintenance of public order, by crowd control, law enforcement, and training local police officers. This was often accompanied by the development or reform of the judicial system. Finally there was a sizeable civilian component consisting of both intergovernmental organization (IGO) and non-governmental organization (NGO) actors with political, electoral, human rights, and humanitarian functions. The political function included overall guidance in the peace process and help with rebuilding or developing political institutions. The electoral function included advice, education, monitoring, and verification of the electoral process. The human rights function consisted of promoting, educating, monitoring, and investigating abuses. Finally, the humanitarian function included the delivery of aid, the return and reintegration of refugees, and the disarmament, demobilization, and reintegration of former combatants (Hansen *et al*, 2004: 5).

All of these elements are found and developed in the complex peace operations of the late 1990s and into the 21st century. Such developments have led to what has been labelled the 'civilianization' of peace operations whereby the still large military peacekeeping component is matched by the inclusion of a peacebuilding component in the form of 'civil administration, humanitarian assistance, policing, electoral, human rights monitoring, economic revival functions and personnel' (Cockayne & Malone, 2003: 18).

Current peace operations have an increasingly complex peacebuilding component as well as a more assertive peacekeeping element. Within the UN system this requires the coordination between the UN Department of Political Affairs (DPA) with responsibility for peacemaking, and the UN Department of Peacekeeping

Operations (DPKO). Other elements of the UN system may also be involved in peacebuilding, such as the UN Development Programme (UNDP) and in the longer term the World Bank, while peacekeepers will often operate alongside other UN actors and agencies such as the Office of the UN High Commissioner for Refugees (UNHCR), as well as regional organizations and agencies. Both peacekeeping and peacebuilding elements will be considered in some detail.

Peacekeeping component

Peacekeeping is clearly the well-established element of a peace operation. As recounted in the Brahimi Report, during the Cold War peacekeeping was the dominant function. Peacebuilding was a separate function, which meant that peacekeeping forces could be *in situ* for decades (for example the UN force in Cyprus since 1964). Although such forces have still been deployed in the post-Cold War era (for example the UN force emplaced between Ethiopia and Eritrea in 2000), they are difficult to justify unless accompanied by 'serious and sustained peacemaking efforts that seek to transform a ceasefire accord into a durable and lasting peace settlement' (Brahimi Report, 2000: para 17).

Such criticisms, plus the less restrictive atmosphere of the post-Cold War period, led the UN to combine peacekeeping with peacebuilding in 'complex peace operations deployed into settings of intra-State conflict' (Brahimi Report, 2000: para 28). Currently, we see these in place in the Democratic Republic of Congo, Côte d'Ivoire, Haiti, Kosovo, Liberia, and Sudan. In such operations the complexity of the task and the still volatile and hostile environment with any number of outside actors being involved or having an interest, as well as the allegiances, remaining structures, and the activities of those who would undermine the peace process within the post-conflict state itself, make it very difficult for the operation to fulfil its mandate, unless it has Chapter VII powers and uses them.

Overall peace operations commonly have the following elements: (1) they are based on an internationally brokered peace agreement; (2) they are normally mandated by the Security Council increasingly using Chapter VII enforcement provisions; (3) sometimes the operation draws on a number of organizations, such as the UN, EU, NATO, OSCE; (4) they do not simply observe the *status quo*, they also have the more ambitious aims of managing transitions—assisting in post-conflict rebuilding; (5) they are involved in the restoration of stability, law and order, the protection of civilians, and providing the basis for long-term recovery, development, and democratic governance; (6) to this end they are constructed around three functions involving differing actors—peacekeeping, development, and humanitarian actors; (7) because of the varied nature of the post-conflict situations in which such operations operate there should be no set template for such operations and the overall guide should be that 'form must follow function' (Eide *et al*, 2005: 10–2, 17); (8) normally such forces are made up of military contingents drawn from member states (known as troop contributing nations or

TCNs). However, there is a discernible trend towards the privatization of some peacekeeping functions. 'It is clear that the United Nations is moving towards a situation (particularly through DPKO) where private military companies (PMC) will be used in ever-greater capacities from their current existence as protectors and defenders of humanitarian aid operations in zones of conflict' (O'Brien, 2007: 45). It has been argued that suitably controlled and regulated use of PMCs by the UN and other organizations involved in peacekeeping would bring significant benefits: not only cost-savings but also a removal of the organization's dependence on voluntary and possibly poorly equipped contributions from member states (Bures, 2005) (see on this particular issue the chapters on non-state actors; private sector; security sector reform; and conflict economies).

Peacebuilding component

The Brahimi Report recognized that free and fair elections are just part of a process of building 'governance institutions', democratization, the protection of human rights, and the development of civil society (Brahimi Report, 2000: para 38). In a number of early peace operations 'hasty elections' took the 'place of finding legitimate interlocutors' (Challenges Project, 2005: 48). Thus there is no quick fix in which the international community supervizes elections and then leaves. There has to be a developed exit strategy based on a clear timetable under which a stable government and society is formed. Once it is clear that the people have exercised their right of self-determination (which does not mean simply holding elections), and secure institutions and processes are in place, then the sovereignty and independence of the people and the country should be respected and the operation withdrawn. The problems in Bosnia after the Dayton Accords of 1995 and Kosovo from 1999 in which peace operations struggle to establish such conditions are a salient reminder that these are ambitious projects. An essential element is that the process must engage the local population and ensure that they are the main stakeholders as well as the beneficiaries of the process. Fundamentally, the process should allow for the local population to shape the society, not for it to be shaped by outside actors (for further discussion see the chapter on local ownership). This is extremely difficult to achieve and is reflected in the human rights element of a peace operation.

Human rights promotion is a main function of the UN and this is reflected in peace operations. The promotion and protection of both civil and political rights, and economic, social, and cultural rights is essential in developing fair and effective governance. Peacebuilders should be careful to promote the different types of rights equally, and not see civil and political rights as a priority (whether for ideological or practical reasons). Only in so doing can the right to self-determination in both its political and economic aspects be promoted. Of importance for the economic aspect of the right to self-determination is the task of development and relief which will include at the lowest level the meeting of basic needs—the fulfilment of the basic human rights to life, food, water, and shelter (White & Klaasen, 2005: 465–6), and then the development of the economic and social infrastructure (see the chapters on human security and recovery). Clearly there is a danger here of interfering in the choices a society might make about its economic, social, and political development, and so the local population should have a clear say in these choices. 'The aim of any international support should not be to create replicas of their own home paradigms' (Challenges Project, 2005: 21), but should be to facilitate choices and decision-making by the local population (see the chapters on local ownership and civil society).

The reality, though, might not be so impartial. Roland Paris has argued that 'most international organisations', including the Bretton Woods bodies, 'engaged in peacebuilding have internalised the broadly liberal political and economic values of the wealthy and powerful industrialised democracies,' and have in effect 'transplanted' those values (elections, civil and political rights and market reforms) into weak countries in which peace operations have been located. This is most evident in cases of 'proxy government' by the UN in Kosovo and East Timor (UNTAET 1999–2002), though it is not only in these obvious cases, but in other multifunctional operations such as occurred in Cambodia and Mozambique. This process, he argued, amounts to the 'globalisation of the very idea of what a state should look like and how it should act' (Paris, 2002: 638–9).

III. Implementation

The challenges of enforcement

In the period after 2000 complex peace operations have regularly been given certain Chapter VII or enforcement powers to enable them to fulfil aspects of their mandates, tasks undertaken by the peacekeeping element, which is clearly a departure from traditional peacekeeping values (Zacklin, 2005: 91). In fact from the turn of the 21st century it has become normal practice for a Chapter VII mandate to be given to peace operations on the basis 'that even the most benign environment can turn sour when spoilers emerge to undermine a peace agreement and put civilians at risk' (UN, 2004: para 213).

Impartiality will also be justifiably impaired if peacekeepers are under a duty to protect civilians within their care, for they will sometimes have to use aggressive force to repel attacks on civilians as well as themselves. In such an environment the Brahimi Report recommended that peace operations be bigger and better equipped, to be able to deal with 'spoilers' and also protect civilians where necessary. The intent is that such forces would act as a credible deterrent, in contrast to traditional peacekeeping forces, which were more symbolic and non-interventionist. Contributing states in such peace operations should be prepared to allow their troops to operate under robust rules of engagement and run the risk of casualties. While still supporting the peacekeeping principles of consent, impartiality, and the use of force only in self-defence, the Report represented an attempt to draw the peacekeeping line nearer to Chapter VII than Chapter VI (Brahimi Report, 2000: paras 48–52). Impartiality has become lack of partiality in the carrying out of the mandate, as opposed to the traditional approach that interpreted impartiality as neutrality and non-intervention.

In 2006, the Security Council stated that peacekeeping and peacebuilding missions should, where appropriate, have a mandate that includes the 'protection of civilians, particularly those under imminent threat of physical danger, within their zones of operation' and stated its intention that such 'protections mandates' were to be implemented (UN Security Council, 2006). Certainly this is reflected in the more coercive mandates of recent UN peace operations. Arguments have been made that this reflects an emerging wider norm of a collective responsibility to protect in the event of genocide and other large-scale killings, ethnic cleansing, or serious violations of international humanitarian law which sovereign governments have proved powerless or unwilling to prevent (UN, 2004: para 203; UN General Assembly, 2005: para 139).

Though hitherto not the norm, the different elements and functions of peace operations should be integrated within the peace operation. Peace operations should ideally be 'integrated missions' namely an 'instrument with which the UN seeks to help countries in the transition between war and to lasting peace, or address a similarly complex situation that requires a system-wide UN response, through subsuming various actors and approaches within an overall political-strategic crisis management framework' (Eide *et al*, 2005: 14).

From multi-functional operations of the 1980s, to post-Brahimi peace operations, towards 'integrated' missions, each represent greater attempts to effectively coordinate 'security, political, human rights, rule of law, humanitarian and development components of the mission' (UN Secretary-General Note, 2006). The newly created Peacebuilding Commission should improve coordination and effectiveness of peacebuilding operations given its functions of bringing together the relevant actors, marshalling resources, and developing strategies for post-conflict peacebuilding (UN General Assembly, 2005). It is too early to judge the Commission's initial activities in Burundi and Sierra Leone, though improvements in coordination have been achieved in these two countries. However, it will be seen that, especially in 'hybrid' operations that involve two or more organizations, it is very difficult to achieve integration in practice.

The difference between peace support operations and peace operations is that the former emphasizes enforcement and de-emphasizes the cardinal principles of peacekeeping. Impartiality becomes the only remaining element and that is used in a way that would not be recognized in an orthodox peacekeeping operation. In practice, though, with an increasing use of Chapter VII by the Security Council in creating UN peace operations, the doctrines of 'peace operation' and 'peace support operation' are not clearly distinct. This reflects the increasing influence of powerful states in the shaping of modern operations.

First introduced to the discussion by Boutros-Ghali (UN, 1992: para 20), peace enforcement has become more central to peace operations after Brahimi (although not clearly included in the definitions in that Report). Peace enforcement does not mean military victory over the enemy, thereby distinguishing it from pure enforcement action under Chapter VII. Impartiality and consent are still the goals of any peace enforcement operation, though the former becomes the more important concept if factions indicate the withdrawal of their consent by attempting to undermine the peace. Furthermore, in such situations, according to the equivalent NATO peace support doctrine 'consent from the warring factions may be minimal and amount to nothing more than a phoney tolerance of the operation, whilst the rest of the population may be desperate for intervention and assistance'. According to NATO 'should the level of consent be uncertain, and the potential for opposition exist, it would be prudent to deploy a force capable of enforcing compliance and promoting consent from the outset' (NATO, 2001: para 508).

Peace support operations must be 'sufficiently flexible, robust and combat ready', exemplified by NATO-led force in Kosovo and the Australian-led force in East Timor, both deployed in 1999, and the role of British force in support of the UN force in Sierra Leone in 2000. 'PSO doctrine recognises that the military's role, while robust, must also be a limited one: its objective is to create and safeguard the secure space within which humanitarian and civilian components can work to re-establish peace' (Hansen *et al*, 2004: 7). In this regard they can be termed stabilization forces. Whereas pure Chapter VII enforcement action attempts to impose a solution by force, a peace support operation is engaged in preventing violence that will undermine the participation of the parties and the population as a whole in achieving peace. The aim of peace support operations is to achieve a political end-state, not victory over an enemy (NATO, 2001: para 204).

In general, better cooperation and coordination is needed between the UN and other organizations engaging in collective security. 'Increasingly, operations have taken on a hybrid character, with two or more organizations responsible for different elements of the international response'. However, it is difficult to standardize such practice due to different circumstances and political/military readiness. Thus 'the UN has sometimes deployed troops alongside those of other organizations with or without formal coordination, or preceded or followed a multinational, regional or bilateral force, with responsibilities and relationships changing as the mission matures' (Challenges Project, 2005: 12).

It would of course be better to have an 'integrated operation' with a 'single chain of command and control, if not a coordinated operation' where the UN and regional organizations have separate command structures but liaise closely, rather than a 'parallel operation' where there is no formal coordination. 'Sequential operations', when the UN precedes or follows a regional operation, are unlikely to be integrated but should be closely coordinated (Challenges Project, 2005: 36).

The role of regional organizations

The end of the Cold War has also allowed regional organizations to take up more active roles often in operations that have the characteristics of peace support (Bothe, 2002: 696–8), in that they have more coercive mandates than either the complex peace operation or the traditional peacekeeping force. The actions of the Economic Community of West African States (ECOWAS) in Liberia and Sierra Leone, NATO in Afghanistan, Bosnia and Herzegovina, and Kosovo, and the EU in the Democratic Republic of Congo and Bosnia and Herzegovina are based on them having enforcement powers when necessary. While there remains a peaceful situation on the ground these forces may have the appearance of traditional peacekeepers, supporting the job of peacebuilding, but when the peace breaks down they have the authority and capability of forcefully dealing with the 'spoilers' as well as protecting civilians.

In many ways, the stabilization forces in Bosnia and Herzegovina from 1995, Kosovo from 1999, Afghanistan from 2001, the EU's Operation Artemis in the Democratic Republic of Congo in 2003, and ECOWAS in West Africa in the 1990s share the characteristics of Coalitions of the Willing authorized by the Security Council under Chapter VII to undertake enforcement action. Coalitions of the Willing act under UN authority but they are not UN-commanded and controlled operations in the peacekeeping/peace operation sense. The Australian-led force in East Timor fits this pattern as well, though this was an ad hoc force. Coalitions of the Willing may fight a full-scale war as in Korea in 1950 and Iraq in 1991, but they can also be deployed to post-conflict situations where they have war-fighting potential rather than just a peacekeeping function. It is interesting to note that, with the exception of the West African forces, the regional forces are undertaken by the 'global north', in contrast to peacekeeping operations (either traditional or as part of a peace operation) which are undertaken by the 'global south' (Cockayne & Malone, 2003: 13), though the peacekeepers may be supported by separate enforcement elements drawn from the north.

The UN's Special Committee on Peacekeeping has recognized the significant contribution that regional organizations can make to peacekeeping, but has stressed that this must be in accordance with Chapter VIII of the UN Charter. The Committee put particular emphasis on Article 53 of the UN Charter which states that enforcement action undertaken by regional organizations requires the authorization of the Security Council (UN, 2003: paras 161–2). The High Level Panel endorsed this in 2004, and because of the propensity of modern peace operation to use force more widely, stated that all regional peace operations, including those undertaken by NATO must have the authority of the Council, except in urgent situations when it could be sought after the operation had started (UN, 2004: paras 272–3). This exceptional approach of retrospective authorization utilized in the past in relation to ECOWAS operations clearly presents difficulties if the Security Council is deadlocked. Arguably in these cases authority should be sought from the General Assembly under its exceptional competence for peace and security (White, 1997: 172–8).

The UN's Special Committee has stressed the need for enhancement of African peacekeeping by developing a close relationship with the African Union (AU) (UN, 2003: paras 165–9), perhaps in response to the constituent treaty of the new AU in 2000 that seemed, in Article 4, to permit enforcement action to combat crimes against humanity without the need for Security Council approval. The Committee's report, though, clearly did not accept that the AU could act autonomously in the field of enforcement action, even to combat grave and widespread breaches of human rights. Though the AU and the UN have cooperated and coordinated their efforts in response to the crisis in Darfur caused by the crimes against humanity (and arguably genocide) committed there since 2003, the hybrid UN/AU force (UNAMID) mandated in July 2007 had only deployed 7,000 troops by January 2008—far short of the 26,000 required.

The advantages of regional organizations becoming involved in peace operations is that they 'often enjoy a special legitimacy amongst local actors', they will be 'more familiar with local conditions' and in some ways they 'have a greater incentive to stay the course and implement long-term conflict prevention and monitoring strategies' (Cockayne & Malone, 2003: 11). However, they may be dominated by regional hegemons that will push them towards higher levels of enforcement than may be necessary (for example Nigeria's domination of ECOWAS). Alternatively, some organizations (for example the AU) may not have the resources to mount an effective peace operation. The better approach is to develop 'an interlocking system of peacekeeping capacities that will enable the United Nations to work with relevant regional organizations' (UN, 2005: para 112).

Lessons learned

The High Level Panel in 2004 stated that a credible and sustainable collective security system must be effective, efficient, and equitable. The latter means that such a system should 'promote security for all its members without regard to the nature of would be beneficiaries, their location, resources or relationship to Great Powers' (UN, 2004: paras 31, 40). To this end it would be good practice for all actors within peace operations to be coordinated under clear achievable mandates, perhaps leading to agreements between the UN and regional organizations on the command and functioning of peace operations. Greater work should be undertaken on bringing together the peace operations doctrines of the UN and key security actors such as NATO, the EU, AU, and ECOWAS. This should lead to a common peace operation doctrine respecting the traditional principles of impartiality, consent, and limited use of force, but recognizing that the dual needs to deal with spoilers and to protect civilians will require a coercive mandate and clear rules of engagement to that effect. In these circumstances the traditional principles must be returned to as soon as practicable.

Further work needs to be done on identifying the principles underlying peace operations. It is suggested here that fundamental human rights, including the right of self-determination, should be an important part of the framework within which peace operations operate. This is reflected in the recognition in practice that peace operations must be undertaken with the cooperation of the local peaceful population. The achievement of self-determination by the expression of the will of the people through stable democratic structures also provides a clear exit strategy for each operation (see also on this issue the chapters on capacity-building; local ownership; and free and fair elections). Self-determination must be exercised freely without outside interference in the substantive political and economic processes.

Peace operations should not only promote human rights but should respect them in their operations and activities. In this regard the UN and other actors should provide avenues and mechanisms of accountability for victims of human rights abuse by UN personnel. It is important that peacekeepers and peacebuilders are accountable for their actions, and cannot hide behind their immunities as has hitherto often been the case. Sexual abuse of women and girls by some individuals in the DR Congo operation is just a recent example (see UN, 2005b). Though actions before local courts may be counter-productive (but see UN, 2006), individuals (including private contractors engaged to fulfil certain aspects of the peace operation), guilty of criminal acts or human rights abuse should be punished and not simply repatriated. Agreements should be made between contributing states and the international organization dealing with the issue of punishment. In addition, it would enhance the legitimacy of the operation if each had an ombudsman to receive and process complaints of ill-treatment. The legitimacy of the operation is undermined if the international components are seen as above the law, while at the same time promoting the rule of law within the country itself (for further discussions on the crucial issue of accountability see notably the chapters on rule of law; local ownership; and transitional administration).

Selected Bibliography

Bellamy, AJ, Williams, P, & Griffin, S (2004), *Understanding Peacekeeping*, Cambridge: Polity.

Bothe, M (2002), 'Peacekeeping', in Simma, B (ed), *The Charter of the United Nations: A Commentary*, 2nd edn, Oxford: Oxford University Press, 648–70.

Bures, O (2005), 'Private Military Companies: A Second Best Peacekeeping Option?', *International Peacekeeping*, 12: 533–46.

Challenges Project (2005), *Meeting the Challenges of Peace Operations: Cooperation and Coordination*, Stockholm, available at: <http://www.challengesproject.net>.

Cockayne, J, & Malone, D (2003), 'United Nations Peace Operations: Then and Now', *International Peacekeeping: The Yearbook of International Peace Operations*, 9: 1–21.

Eide, EB, Kaspersen, AT, Kent, R, & von Hippel, K (2005), *Report on Integrated Missions*, Independent Study for the Expanded UN ECHA Core Group.

Goulding, M (1993), 'The Evolution of United Nations Peacekeeping', *International Affairs*, 69: 451–64.

Gray, C (2004), *International Law and the Use of Force*, 2nd edn, Oxford: Oxford University Press.

Hansen, W, Ramsbotham, O, & Woodhouse, T (2004), 'Hawks and Doves: Peacekeeping and Conflict Resolution', Berghof Research Centre for Constructive Conflict Management.

Miller, AJ (2006), 'Legal Aspects of Stopping Sexual Exploitation and Abuse in UN Peacekeeping Operations', *Cornell International Law Journal*, 39: 71–96.

North Atlantic Treaty Organization (NATO) (2001), *Peace Support Operations*, AJP 3.4.1.

O'Brien, KA (2007), 'What Should and What Should Not Be Regulated?' in Chesterman, S, & Lenhardt, C (eds), *From Mercenaries to Market: The Rise and Regulation of Private Military Companies*, Oxford: Oxford University Press, 29–48.

O'Neill, JT, & Rees, N (2005), *United Nations Peacekeeping in the Post-Cold War Era*, Abingdon: Routledge.

Paris, R (2002), 'International Peacekeeping and the "Mission Civilisatrice"', *Review of International Studies*, 28: 637–56.

Ramsbotham, O, & Woodhouse, T (1999), *Encyclopedia of International Peacekeeping Operations*, Santa Barbara: ABC-CLIO.

Shotton, A (2006), 'A Strategy to Address Sexual Exploitation and Abuse by United Nations Peacekeeping Personnel', *Cornell International Law Journal*, 39: 97.

UK Ministry of Defence (2004), *Peace Support Operations*, London: Joint Warfare Publication, JWP 3.50.

UN (1958), *Summary Study of the Experience Derived from the Establishment and Operation of the Force: Report of the Secretary-General Hammarsjkold*, A/3943.

—— (1973), Report of the Secretary-General Waldheim on the Implementation of Security Council Resolution 340, S/11052/Rev. 1.

—— (1991), *The Blue Helmets, A Review of United Nations Peacekeeping*, New York: United Nations Department of Public Information.

—— (1992), *An Agenda for Peace, Preventive Diplomacy, Peacemaking and Peacekeeping*, Report of the Secretary-General Pursuant to the Statement Adopted by the Summit Meeting of the Security Council on 31 January 1992, A/47/277–S/24111, 17 June.

—— (1995a), *General Guidelines for Peacekeeping Operations*, UN/210/TC/CG95.

—— (1995b), *Supplement to an Agenda for Peace*, Position Paper of the Secretary-General on the Occasion of the 50th anniversary of the United Nations, A/50/60–S/1995/1, 25 January.

—— (2000), *Report of the Panel on United Nations Peace Operations* (Brahimi Report), General Assembly and Security Council, New York A/55/305–S/2000/809.

—— (2003), *Report of the Special Committee on Peacekeeping*, A/56/767, 28 March 2003.

—— (2004), High Level Panel Report, *A More Secure World: Our Shared Responsibility*, A/59/565, 2 December.

—— (2005), Report of the Secretary-General (Kofi Annan), *In Larger Freedom: Towards Development, Security and Human Rights for All*, A/59/2005.

—— (2005b), *A Comprehensive Strategy to Eliminate Future Sexual Exploitation and Abuse in United Nations Peacekeeping Operations* (Zeid Report), A/59/710.

—— (2006), *Report of the Group of Legal Experts on Ensuring Accountability of UN Staff and Experts on Mission with Respect to Criminal Acts Committed in Peacekeeping Operations*, A/60/980.

UN General Assembly (2005), *World Summit Outcome*, A/RES/60/1, 24 October.

UN Secretary-General Note (2006), *Guidance on Integrated Missions*, 9 February.

UN Security Council (2006), *Security Council Resolution 1674 on Protection of Civilians in Armed Conflicts*, S/RES/1674, 28 July.

White, ND (1997), *Keeping the Peace: The United Nations and the Maintenance of International Peace and Security*, 2nd edn, Manchester: Manchester University Press.

—— & Klaasen, D (2005), *The UN, Human Rights and Post-Conflict Situations*, Manchester: Manchester University Press.

Zacklin, R (2005), 'The Use of Force in Peacekeeping Operations', in Blokker, N, & Schrijver, N (eds), *The Security Council and the Use of Force*, The Hague: Martinus Nijhoff, 91–106.

Peace Process

Bertrand G. Ramcharan

Definition

'Peace process' refers to the measures deployed to resolve differences, and to settle disputes or conflicts, through diplomacy or other methods of peaceful settlement rather than violence. It supports the implementation of peace agreements, and maintains the momentum in the consolidation of peace and the avoidance of future conflict. The peace process must strive, with the cooperation of the parties, to identify and head off pressure points and spoilers, and to tackle issues of development, equity, and justice related to the consolidation of peace.

I. Term

Origin and meaning

Dictionaries of language give several usages and contexts of the word 'peace' and many of these are undoubtedly relevant to an understanding of the term 'peace process' in a generic as opposed to a technical sense. The *Oxford English Reference Dictionary* refers to peace as a state of friendliness, establishing friendly relations, bringing about peace. A peacemaker is defined as one who brings about peace (Pearsall & Trumble, 1996: 1068). Littré's dictionary of the French language gives a long list of usages of the term *paix*, opening with *rapports réguliers, calmes, sans violence, d'un Etat, d'une nation avec un autre Etat, une autre nation* (normal relations, calm, without violence, of a state, a nation, with another state, another nation; 1974: 4403). From a generic point of view one could say that whatever is required to maintain, re-establish, or sustain peace is part of a peace process broadly considered.

A *Dictionary of the History of Ideas* published in 1973 has a rich discussion of the 'Ethics of Peace' in which the idea of peace and the requirements for it are traced in several religious and philosophical traditions and in the writings of philosophers such as Immanuel Kant (Wiener, 1973). The great religions all emphasize love, compassion and humility. 'Blessed', we are counselled, 'are the peacemakers; for they shall be called the children of God' (Matthew 5:9, in *ibid*: 1–12). Peace processes, rightly considered, might require us to go deeply into philosophy or religion! The *Dictionary of the History of Ideas* also has an article on 'International Peace', which discusses ideas on peace and war, the peace movement, peaceful settlement of disputes, peace through diplomacy, and peace through international organizations (*ibid*: 440–57). Many of these are closely related to peace processes generically or specifically.

However, we are not here concerned with these broader generic or historical dimensions of the term 'peace process' but rather with its specialized connotations in contemporary practice, which finds the term being used in relation to the peacemaking phase, the continuum between peacemaking and peacebuilding, and the post-conflict peacebuilding phase.

The peace process in the peacemaking phase

At the beginning of his book *Peace Process*, the author William B Quandt helps us trace the origins of one strand of the specialized usage of the term (Quandt, 1993). Quandt writes that sometime in the mid-1970s the term 'peace process' began to be widely used to describe the American-led efforts to bring about a negotiated peace between Israel and its Arab neighbours. 'The phrase stuck, and ever since it has been synonymous with the gradual, step-by-step approach to resolving one of the world's most difficult conflicts' (*ibid*: 1).

In the years since 1967, Quandt continues, the emphasis in Washington has shifted from the spelling out of the ingredients of 'peace' to the 'process' of getting there. This procedural bias, Quandt comments, reflects a practical side of American political culture. Procedures are less controversial than substance, more susceptible to compromise, and thus easier for politicians to deal with:

Whenever progress has been made towards Arab-Israeli peace through American mediation, there has always been a joining of substance and procedure. The United States has provided both a sense of direction and a mechanism. That, at its best, is what the 'peace process' has been about. At worst, it has been little more than a slogan used to mask the marking of time (*ibid*).

There have been great negotiations before and after those concerning the Middle East and one could apply the term 'peace process' to some of them, even if it might be difficult to pinpoint instances in which this label was actually used in respect of those efforts. The Congress of Vienna; the Hague Peace Conferences; the Versailles Peace Conference; the San Francisco Conference that drafted the UN Charter; the negotiations during the Cuban Missile crisis; the negotiations to end the conflicts in Vietnam, Afghanistan, Central America, the former Yugoslavia, Northern Ireland, and elsewhere—all of these certainly had elements of 'peace processes' in them.

The peace process in the continuum between peacemaking and peace implementation, and in the post-conflict peacebuilding phase

Another strand of practice sees the term 'peace process' being applied in the continuum between peacemaking and peace implementation and in the post-conflict peacebuilding phase. The 1992 UN milestone document *An Agenda for Peace* noted that, in order to be truly successful, peacemaking and peacekeeping operations must include:

> ... comprehensive efforts to identify and support structures which will tend to 'consolidate peace' and advance a sense of confidence and well-being among people. Through agreements ending civil strife, these may include disarming the previously warring parties and the restoration of order, the custody and possible destruction of weapons, repatriating refugees, advisory and training support for security personnel, monitoring elections, advancing efforts to protect human rights, reforming or strengthening governmental institutions, and promoting formal and informal processes of political participation (UN, 1992: para 55).

What is being described here, in essence, is the peace process in the phase of implementation of a peace agreement. In this context the concept 'peace process' encompasses all the procedures and events leading to the implementation of peace and the consolidation of peace.

The 1995 'Supplement to an Agenda for Peace' brought out well the relevance of a continuing peace process in the continuum between peacemaking and peacebuilding:

> International problems cannot be solved quickly or within a limited time. Conflicts the United Nations is asked to resolve usually have deep roots and have defied the peacemaking efforts of others. Their resolution requires patient diplomacy and the establishment of a political process that permits, over a period of time, the building of confidence and negotiated solutions to long-standing differences. Such processes often encounter frustrations and setbacks and almost invariably take longer than hoped (UN 1995: para 36).

The political process is at the heart of the peace process. Alvaro de Soto, former Special Representative of the Secretary-General in El Salvador, brought out well the continuum between peacemaking and peacebuilding when speaking at a conference in Berlin in 1996. One of the most difficult aspects of the negotiations, as well as of the implementation stage, he reflected, had been the issue of the institutions that would ensure the framework for the protection of human rights. During the implementation phase, they also had to deal with the general inability of Salvadorans to resolve conflict peacefully and the existence of the land transfer problem. Furthermore, it was necessary to address the issue of disarmament, demobilization, and reintegration of those who had taken up arms on both sides. And on the issue of impunity, namely, the need to bring military crimes to court, the parties had divergent approaches. Eventually an agreement was reached to create a commission on the truth, whose decisions would be binding. All of these issues had to be tackled in the negotiation as well as the implementation stages (Kuhne, 1996: 12–3).

A contemporary definition of 'peace process'

Bearing in mind the considerations and practice adduced above, it would be closer to the mark to consider a 'peace process' as one that entails efforts of a broad variety, tailored to each situation, to tackle the manifestations and root causes of differences that have led to dispute or conflict and to help re-establish and sustain peace. Elements of diplomacy, vision, substance, and procedure are drawn upon as considered by facilitators most likely to succeed. What is involved, as seen in the 'Supplement to an Agenda for Peace', is a political process that facilitates negotiated solutions to long-standing differences. This political process continues in the implementation and post-conflict peacebuilding phases.

Thus the peace process includes the peacemaking phase, the phase at which a peace agreement is being pursued, and the implementation phase, the phase at which an agreement is being implemented, as well as the post-conflict peacebuilding phase. In the last phase one might be required to go beyond the peace agreement itself and to enlarge the dimensions of the peace process, for the challenge then is to sustain the peace, to prevent the resurgence of conflict, and to tackle the root causes that gave rise to the conflict.

The peace process in the post-conflict peacebuilding phase might be envisaged in the peace agreement, or it might have to be injected after the peace agreement has been concluded, given that negotiators sometimes need to limit the issues included in a peace agreement to ensure it is accepted in the first place.

II. Content

The peace process in the post-conflict peacebuilding phase presents many of the challenges of peace processes generally. Studies have shown that the risks of a breakdown of the peace and a return to conflict are high (UN, 2006a). Therefore, even in the post-conflict peacebuilding phase it is important to have in view the different facets of peace processes generally, bearing in mind that one is dealing with the aftermath of conflict and also that each situation presents its own dynamics and challenges. At the same time, the peace process in the post-conflict peacebuilding phase needs to address additional challenges such as disarmament, demobilization, and reintegration, re-launching the economy and stimulating the development process, and addressing structural problems particularly in multi-ethnic countries (see notably the chapters on conflict economies; recovery; and rule of law).

Promotion: a culture of peace and halting hate media

Experience has taught us that both globally and in individual countries we must work to promote a culture of peace. International efforts to promote a culture of peace have sought to build on the precepts that emphasize respect, tolerance, human rights safeguards, and the peaceful settlement of differences. The promotion of a culture of peace is particularly essential in the aftermath of ethnic conflicts. One recalls conflicts such as those in Bosnia and Herzegovina, Rwanda, and Côte d'Ivoire where ethnic and group hatreds were high and propaganda media were active in fomenting hatred and dissension. In the aftermath of such conflicts the peace process must give high priority to ways of stopping and countering hate-media, and to promoting better relations and harmony between different population groups so as to attenuate past tensions and promote good neighbourly relations in the future (see the chapter on reconciliation).

Principles for peace

Three general principles need to be disseminated from the outset in order to underpin peace processes: the principle of the rule of law, the principle of the peaceful settlement of disputes, and the principle of universal respect for human rights and fundamental freedoms. General principles have a role to play in the negotiation, achievement and consolidation of peace. A 'hearts and minds' campaign should be waged to instil these principles into the soul of the society. Support for such a campaign can be drawn from the fact that all three of these principles are enshrined in the UN Charter, which emphasizes the importance of the rule of law, the peaceful settlement of differences, and the centrality of respect for human rights in the attainment and maintenance of peace. The Charter, together with the Universal Declaration of Human Rights, set a course towards a world of peace grounded in respect for human dignity and rights and economic and social progress. An appeal should be made to the people of the country to build their future on these precepts (see the chapter on local ownership).

The role of diplomacy and dialogue

The concept of diplomacy in conflicts has changed significantly over the past two decades. While the categories of official (traditional, bilateral) and unofficial (public, non-governmental) are still relevant, their meaning and function has evolved to match contemporary thinking on conflict transformation and peacebuilding. The emphasis has moved from the political arena to include a role for both bilateral and non-governmental actors.

It is now accepted that peace processes operate at various levels or tracks of diplomacy. Discussion on 'tracks' originated from Joseph Montville, then a US diplomat, who in 1981 made a distinction between official (Track 1) and unofficial efforts (Track 2) to resolve conflicts. While this distinction was seen as valuable and greatly promoted the role of non-governmental organizations (NGOs) in addressing conflict, Track 2 was still considered as only a means to indirectly focus on support for the formal, diplomatic avenues not as an approach on its own merits.

Building on the 'tracks' model, Diamond and McDonald identified other actors and activities and highlighted the relationships among them. They presented the 'multi-track diplomacy' model of nine tracks seen as essential during the peace process were: Government (Track 1); Professional Conflict Resolution; Business; Private citizen; Research, training and education; Activism; Religious; Funding; and last but not least Track 9, Public Opinion/Communication. The nine tracks of diplomacy were organized in a wheel, with 'Track 9—Public Opinion/Communication' at the centre (Diamond and McDonald, 1993). Until then, diplomacy had generally been presented as a hierarchal effort, with government at the top.

While implementers acknowledge the significance of all nine tracks, the most commonly documented Tracks in peacebuilding are arguably the following four (Search for Common Ground, undated):

- *Track I diplomacy:* 'This involves direct government-to-government interaction on the official level. Typical Track I activities include traditional diplomacy, official negotiations, and the use of international organizations. The participants stand as representatives of their respective states and reflect the official positions of their governments during discussions'.

- *Track 'One and a Half' diplomacy:* 'refers to situations when official representatives give authority to non-state actors (or official actors serving in an unofficial capacity) to participate, negotiate or facilitate on behalf of the official state actors. It also refers to non-state individuals who serve as intermediaries between official and non-official actors in difficult conflict situations. It is generally used to prepare key stakeholders before and during the official negotiation process by building consensus and support for agreements, both between parties in conflict and within their prospective constituencies'.

- *Track II diplomacy:* 'generally involves informal interaction with influential unofficial actors from civil society, business or religious communities, and local leaders and politicians who are considered to be experts in the area or issue being discussed. It generally seeks to supplement Track I diplomacy by working with middle and lower levels of society and often involves non-traditional methods, such as facilitating dialogue mechanisms and meetings that include participants from both government and non-government institutions'.

- *Track III diplomacy:* is essentially 'people to people' diplomacy undertaken by both individuals and private groups from international NGOs that are dedicated to promoting specific causes, universal ideals and norms, and enacting systematic social change. This type of diplomacy often involves organizing meetings and conferences, generating media exposure, and political and legal advocacy for people and communities who are largely marginalized from political power centres and are unable to achieve positive change without outside assistance (*ibid*).

Some experts prefer to use the term level instead of tracks, with Saunders (1999), using the concept of a 'multi-level peace process' to frame his analysis of governmental/non-governmental cooperation, describing citizen involvement as the 'public peace process'. He further identified five interconnected stages of a dialogue process that would lead to reconciliation and collaboration, as follows: (i) deciding to engage; (ii) mapping the relationship together; (iii) probing the dynamics of the relationship together; (iv) experiencing the relationship by thinking together; and (v) acting together (Saunders, 1999). These stages hold true to dialogue today, with acting together being promoted as crucial to the success of a process.

Prevention of conflicts

Having regard to the multiplicity of issues which, if not addressed appropriately could lead to a breakdown of the peace, it is important for any peace process that continues during the post-conflict peacebuilding phase to include in its purview problems that might cause a peace-breakdown. Both early warning and preventive diplomacy must be kept in mind.

Early warning

If we assume that, following a conflict, there has been a peace agreement which is in the process of implementation, possibly with a UN or regional peace operation in support, the question arises: who might be in a position to provide early warning about problems that, if not addressed properly, might lead to a return to conflict? If there is a peace support operation it is natural to expect that they will keep an eye on such issues. Civil society within the country might also be able to identify situations or issues and to provide the alert. Regional or international NGOs might do likewise, while regional or sub-regional conflict prevention mechanisms should also play a part. The UN Departments of Political Affairs, Peacekeeping Operations, and Humanitarian Affairs, can also contribute to early warning of a breakdown in peace. Where applicable, the special representative of the Secretary-General might also be able to play a role in sounding the alert.

This raises the question of the relevant roles of the UN Peacebuilding Commission and the Security Council. So far, the Peacebuilding Commission is operating in confidence-building mode, while the Security Council is expected to address the more overtly political issues and threats. One can contemplate situations in which it might be necessary for the Peacebuilding Commission to alert the Security Council to situations or issues that might threaten the peace and for the latter to bring its influence to bear upon the situation. This is a matter that will require reflection in the light of further experience.

Preventive diplomacy

Assuming that arrangements have been set in place to detect potential peace-breaking issues or situations, the next question that arises is, who might be in a position to engage in preventive diplomacy to head off a threatened rupture and a return to conflict? Where applicable, a special representative of the UN Secretary-General, or of the regional organization concerned, might play this role: likewise the Secretary-General of the regional organization or of the UN. The President or members of the UN Security Council could also engage in preventive diplomacy. Whoever does it, it is of the utmost importance that there are in place arrangements and actors for the exercise of preventive diplomacy, to ensure there is not a return to conflict.

In order to prevent the mistakes experienced in Angola, where fighting restarted after a peace agreement and elections, the international community has decided to spend more time from the beginning. The size of the peacekeeping force and the role of the international community, particularly that of the United States (US) and the UN, has been broadened to meet the needs of the situation. 'These features presented a unique opportunity' (Kuhne, 1996: 14–5).

The importance of early warning and preventive diplomacy in the peacebuilding phase can also be seen dramatically in the case of Timor Leste in 2006–2007. Following a UN peace operation that successfully saw the country emerge into independence in 2002, peacemakers and peacekeepers were withdrawn, some would say prematurely, and the country was left to its destiny. Four years later, open confrontation erupted in the streets of the capital and elsewhere in the country, and renewed conflict flared. Violence broke out in April and May of 2006, killing at least thirty-seven people and causing 15 per cent of the population (some 155,000 people) to flee their homes. It took Australian soldiers to calm the situation and to avoid the return to a bloodbath. In July–August, 2007, following elections in the country, violence again erupted. The lessons to be drawn from this were that the international community had left the country to its destiny far too precipitately: there was not an internationally sponsored, continuing peace process in the country to detect grievances or to deal with severe economic and social problems.

Continued peacemaking

Depending on the conflict in question, in many instances there may be a need for continued peacemaking efforts, even if a detailed peace agreement has been concluded. This may need to address problems not resolved in the framework peace agreement, or issues that emerge during the implementation phase. Cambodia is a case in point. Benny Widyono, Representative of the UN Secretary-General in Cambodia, noted that the Paris agreement was a good agreement that nevertheless failed to provide a design for peacebuilding. The agreement took the peace process to elections, but made no provisions for the period after. On the eve of the elections all political parties were still armed, and no attempt had been made to turn the military groups into political parties. The Khmer Rouge had refused to disarm and the other two groups consequently also did not disarm (Kuhne, 1996: 18–9). Continued peacemaking was thus indispensable in the implementation and peacebuilding phases.

This raises the question of who should address issues of continued peacemaking. The original peace negotiators can certainly continue, although this needs to be addressed case by case. Where applicable, a special representative of the Secretary General might be able to play this role, or there may be need for a different set of peacemakers.

From the outset of its consideration of the situations in Sierra Leone and Burundi, the UN Peacebuilding Commission has stressed the need for continued peacemaking efforts. The Chairman's summary of the Sierra Leone country-specific meeting on 12 October 2006, noted that the war in Sierra Leone had been largely the result of failures in governance and institutional processes in the country. The strengthening of the democratic governance institutions was an important prerequisite for sustaining peace and development, requiring capacity-building of governing institutions (UN, 2006f, Annex I: para 4).

As far as Burundi is concerned, the Chairman's summary of the Burundi country-specific meeting on 13 October 2006 recorded that participants acknowledged that Burundi was still in an early post-conflict phase and that its development and reconstruction challenges were immense in all areas. They emphasized the need for an intensive and sustained process of capacity-building to enable the state to perform its functions: 'The participants also called upon the countries of the Regional Peace Initiative on Burundi and the South African Facilitation to sustain their political support for the consolidation of peace' (UN, 2006f, Annex II: paras 4, 8).

The role of civil society in peace processes is worth mentioning. In the Bosnian and Croatian negotiations, the mediators dealt with the leadership of the various fighting forces. Quite often the case was made that instead of negotiating with war criminals, they should have negotiated with the leaders of civil society. As a practical matter there was no alternative but to negotiate with the leadership of the fighting forces (see, however, on this particular issue the chapters on international crimes and non-state actors). Nonetheless, there is an issue to be reflected upon, namely, how might mediators also, simultaneously, draw upon insights from the leadership of the forces for peace and civil society? In the peacebuilding phase it would be important to involve civil society from the outset of the implementation process and to build up their role progressively over time.

Human rights issues also need to be mentioned. We saw the importance of these issues earlier in relation to El Salvador and Angola. While the negotiations were taking place on Bosnia there were massive violations of human rights and major humanitarian emergencies. The UN/European Union (EU) mediators made representations to the Bosnian Parties and pleaded with them to cease the human rights violations. For the most part, this was to no avail. The UN High Commissioner for Refugees, Sadako Ogata, chaired the Humanitarian Working Group of the International Conference on the Former Yugoslavia and she made many plaintive submissions to the mediators about repeated violations of human rights and acute humanitarian emergencies. The UN/EU mediators responded as best they could, but the principal thrust of their efforts was to help bring about a negotiated end to the conflicts. They would subsequently be criticized for not centralizing human rights in the peace negotiations (Nystuen, 2005).

This was an unfair criticism, as all the draft peace agreements included extensive human rights provisions intended to safeguard human rights after peace was achieved. The Dayton Peace Accord, for example, built on the human rights provisions of the successive peace plans of the International Conference on the Former Yugoslavia. The fact of the matter, however, was that the UN/EU mediators gave priority to peacemaking and chose not to wreck the peacemaking effort by being outspoken on human rights violations. This is a difficult question. Should the mediators have taken a stronger stance on human rights violations? And had they done so, could they have continued their mediation efforts? Should they have considered denouncing the violations in any case and leaving it to others to take up the negotiating relay? Vance, Owen, Stoltenberg, and Bildt were all honourable men and this author witnessed their personal efforts to use their best endeavours on behalf of the protection of human rights (Bildt, 1998). The question that is posed for reflection is: as peacemakers should they have taken a more publicly critical stance?

Faced with the situation in which major powers had their clients in the different conflicts and the mediators were, in consequence, doomed to failure, it might have earned the mediators public plaudits had they denounced the violations. But they were statesmen in search of peace and they placed the emphasis on the search for peace. Still, the human rights issues carried over into the post-conflict peacebuilding phase, with the Prosecutor of the International Criminal Tribunal for the Former Yugoslavia (ICTY) pressing for the arrest and trial of suspected war-criminals.

Another question for reflection about the continuing peace process for Bosnia and Herzegovina concerns the human rights-related truth component of the process. The Dayton accord provided for the establishment of a highly successful human rights court for the country with a majority of international judges. It rendered great services but was prematurely shut down by the Steering Group and the High Representative, Paddy Ashdown (Ashdown, 2007). The costs of this court were modest and it surely would have been wise to continue it until the country's peace was truly established.

Furthermore, the Dayton accord did not provide for a truth and reconciliation process but instead relied on the ICTY. It would have been wise to have arranged for a parallel truth and reconciliation process to promote better relations between the constituent peoples (see more generally the chapter on transitional justice).

Peacekeeping and peace observation

While the peace process is underway in the post-conflict peacebuilding phase, the urgent deployment of observers or peacekeepers to dangerous situations can be particularly important in heading off the danger of a breakdown of peace and a return to conflict. Under a UN or regional peace operation, the rapid deployment of observers or peacekeepers to tense situations can have a calming effect. Even if there is no peace support operation in the country, there may still be the option of deploying international observers or peacekeepers to a situation of risk, provided that the international community is in a position to provide them (Ramcharan, 2005; de Rossanet, 1997: 117–24).

Development and equity

Coupled with efforts to create a secure environment for all human beings in a country that has come out of conflict, there is also a need to stimulate the development process (see the chapters on recovery and conflict economies). This can make the difference between a sustainable peace and a breakdown into conflict. People who see meaningful opportunities for themselves and their families will have a stake in the maintenance of peace. People who are lacking economic and social opportunities may be persuaded by opportunistic leaders to return to conflict.

In countries where there are horizontal inequalities, that is to say where some population groups have not fared as well as others, it will be essential to set in place policies and programmes to address such inequalities. If not, there will be continued friction inside the country that could degenerate into conflict if not attended to.

III. Implementation

Determining the existence of a peace process

Peace today is everywhere, its pursuit so active that when the phrase 'peace process', originally used in just a few cases, is pronounced, it has to be qualified with a national or geographical description so that the listener will know which of the literally dozens of such 'processes' is meant. Often it seems they resemble so many patients in a hospital ward: some are getting better, some 'improving', some serious, some sinking fast (Woollacott, 2000).

Bell goes further, posing the question: 'When is a process a *peace process*?' She suggests that:

the short and flippant answer might be, whenever it suits one of the parties to the conflict to so describe it. In other words, the term 'peace process' can be understood as a value judgement attached to efforts to resolve a conflict at a particular time. Just as one person's freedom fighter is another's terrorist, so one person's peace process is another's 'ceasefire agreement', or yet another's 'victory' and another's 'sell-out' or 'capitulation to terrorists' (Bell, 2000).

The above statement (though somewhat facetious, by the author's admission) has a certain validity. If we look at long-running conflicts such as the Israel–Palestine conflict, some look to the Security Council Resolution 242 passed in November 1967 calling for the withdrawal of Israeli armed forces from territories occupied in the conflict as the beginning of the process. Bell questions if perhaps the conflict was 'moving towards a peace process' in 1978 when the Camp David Frameworks for Peace were signed between Egypt and Israel leading to the Camp David Accords. Others view the shuttle diplomacy demonstrated by the Madrid Peace Conference of 1991 where Israel, Syria, Lebanon, Jordan and the Palestinians attended a conference jointly sponsored by the US and the Soviet Union, as a key milestone in the process. Still others look to 1993 when an Israeli ban on contact with the PLO was formally lifted, and the official recognition by Israel of the PLO's right to participate in the peace process, culminating in the signing of the Oslo peace accords.

What is certain is that peace processes are often long and convoluted processes. They are characterized by major highs and even greater lows, as negotiations falter or stall, intermediate agreements are reached and often breached, internal and external politicians move on and new faces emerge, and peace processes stop or move on to a new and invigorated phase.

The challenge of multiple peace processes

There may also be situations where there are multiple conflicts in the same country and an agreement in respect of one conflict might be at risk because of developments in another. The case of Sudan is instructive, where, after several years of conflict between north and south, a peace agreement was concluded in 2003 and a UN peace support operation put in place. Yet the conflict in the Darfur region of Sudan broke out around the same time and has been of such intensity that there has been a danger of that conflict adversely affecting the North/South peace agreement. A separate peace process was called for in respect of the Darfur situation with a different set of UN and African Union peace negotiators (see the chapter on responsibility to protect).

Similar complications were evident in the UN/EU peace negotiations in the Former Yugoslavia, which lasted from 1992 to 1996 and covered the following theatres of conflict or potential conflict: (1) the conflict in Bosnia and Herzegovina; (2) the conflict in Croatia; (3) the danger of conflict in Serbia; (4) the dangers of conflict in the Former Yugoslav Republic of Macedonia (FYROM); and (5) the danger of conflict between Greece and the FYROM. The UN/EU peace negotiators were active simultaneously in all five theatres. They

produced a number of notable successes, including the establishment of a preventive deployment of UN peacekeepers along the FYROM border; the negotiation
of a *modus vivendi* between the FYROM and Greece; and the peace agreement on
Eastern Slavonia in Croatia. Despite valiant efforts their quest for peace in Bosnia
and Herzegovina, Croatia, and Kosovo proved elusive.

Key factors influencing the success of a peace process

One thing was striking in the Yugoslav peace negotiations: however hard the
mediators tried to broker peace, if major powers were at cross-purposes with
them it was almost impossible to arrive at a successful result. The UN/EU mediators worked as hard as was humanly possible. For three and a half years they
worked around the clock. Notwithstanding the EU's political and economic
assets and the UN's political assets, success in the Bosnian negotiations eluded
them because the principal powers backed their favoured parties in the conflict. In the end it was not only negotiating skill but raw American power that
produced the Dayton Peace Accords. What lesson should one draw from this?
It is that without the support of the major powers the peace process cannot succeed either in the peacemaking, the peacekeeping, or the peacebuilding phases.
Thus, the US diplomat Harold Saunders, Assistant Secretary of State under
President Carter who participated in the 1978 Camp David Peace Accords, considers peace processes as a 'mixture of politics, diplomacy, changing relationships, negotiation, mediation and dialogue in both official and unofficial arenas'
(Saunders, 2001).

The case of Kosovo brings out dramatically the need for a continuing peace
process. The UN/EU mediators had sought to build confidence between the
leadership in Belgrade and Zagreb and had constructed their peace efforts largely
on this relationship. The reliance placed upon President Milosevic and President
Tudjman came at a cost. In Croatia, President Tudjman was insistent on incorporation of the Serb-held territories into Croatia and bargained hard against schemes
of autonomy. President Milosevic for his part supported the claims of the Serbs
in Croatia to be recognized as a distinct people, rather than as a minority inside
Croatia. In the end, the Serb population of Croatia would be expelled *en masse* by
Croatian forces with technical and intelligence support from the USA.

With regard to the situation in Kosovo, President Milosevic had ruled out any
conversation with the UN/EU mediators on it. In the end this would cost him a
North Atlantic Treaty Organisation (NATO) air campaign and would lead to his
arrest, incarceration, and death in prison in The Hague, while on trial before the
International Criminal Tribunal for the former Yugoslavia. It is not easy to see
what the UN/EU mediators could have done about the recalcitrance of President
Milosevic. Even at Dayton, the US chose to set aside the Kosovo problem for later
attention. This proved to have been disastrous. One could make the argument

that immediately after the Dayton conference a complementary peace process should have been initiated with respect to Kosovo.

Indeed, it is well recognized that violence often continues and sometimes even intensifies during peace negotiations. This has been the case in countries like Sudan, Sri Lanka, and Northern Ireland, to name but a few. This does not, however, mean the end of a peace process. Some might argue that it sometimes serves to put momentum back into the process when immediate wounds have been healed.

So what have we learnt about peace processes? Between 1990 and 2000, more than sixty peace agreements were signed as part of ongoing or new peace processes (Bell, 2000: Appendix). Reasons for failure in many of these are the following: misdiagnosis of the root causes; lack of inclusion of key stakeholders, lack of justice or compensation for affected populations; a settlement imposed by outsiders; and lack of external support during the recovery and reconstruction phase.

One of the greatest hurdles to be overcome during any peace process is the management of 'spoilers'. The 'phenomena' of 'spoilers' and 'spoiling' is defined by Newman and Richmond as 'groups and tactics that actively seek to hinder, delay, or undermine conflict settlement through a variety of means and for a variety of motives' (Newman and Richmond, 2006). There is often an assumption that spoilers are official rebels or factions thereof. They may in fact be not only rebel groups and insurgents, but also politicians, diasporas, governments, and other entities. Experience has shown that civil society 'peace constituencies' and social networks across conflict lines help to open space for negotiations and minimize the effects of spoilers in both camps (Kriesberg, 2001). Equally 'criminalization as a strategy to manage spoilers...has the potential of holding to account the entrepreneurs of violent economies' (International Peace Academy, 2003) (see also in this sense the chapter on international crimes).

In 2006, the International Crisis Group said of Sri Lanka's failed process that:

The initial peace deal was rushed through, with the government keen to capitalise on war-weariness among the population. Although it stopped full-scale military clashes, significant problems in the design of the process ultimately contributed to the renewal of conflict.

The peace process was exclusively focused on two parties: the government, then led by Ranil Wickremesinghe of the United National Party (UNP), and the LTTE. President Chandrika Kumaratunga and other key southern political elites were largely excluded from the process. Among Tamils, non-LTTE parties had no role; nor did the important Muslim community, which makes up some 7 per cent of the population. Much of the dynamic of the conflict is within ethnic communities, and the failure of the peace process to address this made a lasting peace more unlikely (International Crisis Group, 2006).

According to one commentator, 'there has been perhaps too much concentration on skilful ways of moving conflict from a violent phase to a non-violent phase and on military intervention to suppress the violence and not enough on tackling fundamental differences' (Woollacott, 2000). The Darfur peace process is a clear illustration of this. As Alex deWaal puts it:

In the early rounds of the Darfur peace talks, the armed movements repeatedly raised the issue of accountability for crimes committed and destruction caused during the conflict. Justice was high among their priorities and the Sudan Government's objection to the issue was one reason among many why so little progress was achieved... Until the very end of the peace talks, the question of compensation for lives lost, injuries inflicted and property destroyed or stolen, was treated within the framework of wealth-sharing, as a poor relation of the question of rebuilding Darfur after the war. It was not considered under the rubric of restitution and reparations, as a matter of justice and rights. The mediators misjudged the passion that the Darfurians brought to this issue (de Waal, 2008).

In conclusion, Carl Bildt, the mediator in the Balkans conflict, when analysing what had gone wrong in Bosnia and Herzegovina, reportedly said of the local leaders that 'for most of them peace was just the continuation of war by other means' (Woollacott, 2000). The challenge for any peace process is therefore to make peace a genuine, common aim of the warring parties, not just another cynical facet of military strategy.

Selected Bibliography

Anstee, MJ (1996), *Orphan of the Cold War. The Inside Story of the Collapse of the Angolan Peace Process*, 1992–1993, New York: St Martin's Press.

Ashdown, P (2007), *Swords and Ploughshares: Bringing Peace to the 21st Century*, London: Weidenfeld & Nicolson.

Bell, C (2000), *Peace Agreements and Human Rights*, Oxford: Oxford University Press.

Bildt, C (1998), *Peace Journey. The Struggle for Peace in Bosnia*, London: Weidenfeld & Nicolson.

Conciliations Resources (2006), 'Engaging Armed Groups in Peace Processes', Documents from Conciliation Resources, 19 April 2006, London: Conciliation Resources, available at: <http://www.c-r.org/index.php>.

Crocker, CA (1992), *High Noon in Southern Africa. Making Peace in a Rough Neighbourhood*, New York: W.W. Norton and Company.

de Waal, A (2008), 'ICC, Making Sense of Darfur, Peace Process: What Happened to Justice in the Darfur Peace Agreement?', available at: <http://www.ssrc.org/blogs/darfur/2008/06/25/what-happened-to-justice-in-the-darfur-peace-agreement/>.

Diamond, L & McDonald, J (2004), 'Multi-Track Diplomacy: A Systems Approach to Peace', Washington, DC: Institute for Multi-Track Diplomacy, in Nan, SA, & Strimling, A, 'Track 1—Track 2 Cooperation', January 2004, available at: <http://www.beyondintractability.org/essay/track_1_2_cooperation/>.

Gastrow, P (1995), *Bargaining for Peace. South Africa and the National Peace Accord*, Washington DC: United States Institute for Peace.

Hartzell, C (2006), 'Structuring the Peace–Negotiated Settlements and Construction of Conflict Management Institutions', in Mason, D, & Meernik, J (eds), *International Conflict Prevention and Peacebuilding in Post-War Societies*, London: Routledge, 31–52.

—— (1999), 'Explaining the Stability of Negotiated Settlements to Civil Wars', *Journal of Conflict Resolution*, 43: 3–23.

—— & Hoddie, M (2003), 'Institutionalising Peace. Power Sharing and Post-Civil War Conflict Management', *American Journal of Political Science*, 47/3: 318–32.

—— & Hoddie, M (2003), 'Civil War Settlements and the Implementation of Military Power-Sharing Arrangements', *Journal of Peace Research*, 40/3: 303–20.

International Crisis Group (2006), 'Sri Lanka: The Failure of the Peace Process', Asia Report No 124, 28 November.

International Peace Academy (2003), 'Transforming War Economies: Challenges for Peacemaking and Peacebuilding', Report of the 725th Wilton Park Conference, Sussex, 27–29 October.

Kriesberg, L (2001), 'Mediation and the Transformation of the Israeli-Palestinian Conflict', *Journal of Peace Research*, 38/3: 373–92.

Kuhne, W (1996), 'Winning the Peace. Concept and Lessons Learned of Post-Conflict Peacebuilding', Report of an International Workshop, Berlin, July 4–6, Ebenhausen, Germany: Stiftung Wissenschaft und Politik.

Littré, E (1974), *Dictonnaire de la langue française*, 4403.

Newman, E, & Richmond, O (2006), *Challenges to peace building: Managing spoilers during conflict resolution*, UN University Press.

Nystuen, G (2005), *Achieving Peace or Protecting Human Rights?: Conflicts between Norms Regarding Ethnic Discrimination in the Dayton Peace Agreement*, The Hague: Martinus Nijhoff Publishers.

Quandt, W (1993), *Peace Process: American Diplomacy and the Arab-Israeli Conflict Since 1967*, Washington, DC: Brookings.

Ramcharan, BG (ed) (2005), *Conflict-Prevention in Practice: Essays in Honour of Jim Sutterlin*, Leiden, Boston: Martinus Nijhoff.

—— (2007), *Preventive Diplomacy at the United Nations: The Journey of an Idea*, Bloomington: Indiana University Press.

Saunders, HH (1999) *Public Peace Process: Sustained Dialogue to Transform Racial and Ethnic Conflicts*, London: St. Martin's Press; as elaborated in 'Five Stages of the Public Peace Process', available at: <http://traubman.igc.org/pubpeace.htm>, developed in cooperation with former Russian diplomat Gennady Chufrin.

—— (2001), 'Prenegotiation and Circum-negotiation: Arenas of the Multilevel Peace Process', Turbulent Peace. Washington, DC: US Institute of Peace.

Search for Common Ground website, 'Commonly Used Terms', undated, available at: <http://www.sfcg.org/resources/resources_terms.html>.

Stedman, S, Rothchild, D, & Cousens, E (eds) (2003), *Ending Civil Wars: The Implementation of Peace Agreements*, Boulder: Lynne Rienner Publishers.

UN (1992), *An Agenda for Peace, Preventive Diplomacy, Peacemaking and Peacekeeping*, Report of the Secretary-General Pursuant to the Statement Adopted by the Summit Meeting of the Security Council on 31 January 1992, A/47/277–S/24111, 17 June.

—— (1995), *Supplement to an Agenda for Peace, Position Paper of the Secretary-General on the Occasion of the 50th anniversary of the United Nations*, A/50/60–S/1995/1, 25 January.

—— (2006a), Letter dated 2006/08/03 from the Permanent Representative of Ghana to the United Nations Addressed to the Secretary-General, S/2006/610, 3 August.

—— (2006b) Summary Record of the 1st Meeting of the Peacebuilding Commission Burundi Configuration held in New York on 13 October 2006 PBC/2/BUR/SR.1, available at: <http://www.un.org/peace/peacebuilding/docs>.

—— (2006c), Chairman's summary of the Peacebuilding Commission, 13 October 2006, available at: <http://www.un.org/peace/peacebuilding/docs>.

—— (2006d), Chairman's Summary of the Peacebuilding Commission 12 December 2006, available at: <http://www.un.org/peace/peacebuilding/docs>.

—— (2006e), Summary Record of the 1st Meeting of the Peacebuilding Commission Burundi Configuration PBC/2/BUR/SR.2.

—— (2006f), Letter dated 2006/12/20 from the Chairman of the Peacebuilding Commission addressed to the President of the Security Council, 2006S/2006/1050, 3 August.

UN Security Council (2006), 61st Year: Record of the 5509th Meeting, New York, S/PV.5509, 9 August.

—— (2007a), 62nd Year: Record of the 5627th Meeting, New York, S/PV.5627, 31 January.

—— (2007b), 62nd Year: Record of the 5627th Meeting, New York, S/PV.5627 Resumption 1, 31 January.

Wiener, PP (ed) (1973), *The Dictionary of the History of Ideas: Studies of Selected Pivotal Ideas*, New York: Charles Scribner's Sons.

Woollacott, M (2000), 'Why Peace Processes Are Breaking Down All Over', *The Guardian*, 22 December.

Private Sector

Gilles Carbonnier

Definition

The private sector usually refers to the sector of the economy which is not managed by, and does not belong to—or only as a minority holding—the state. In the context of post-conflict peacebuilding, the operational definition of the private sector includes all businesses which sell goods and services and which are active in the formal, informal, or illegal economy. The private sector includes strictly profit-making companies or those pursuing broader goals (eg cooperatives). As explained below, it may also include state-owned enterprises, even if they are not, by definition, privately owned.

I. Term

The concept of the private sector first appeared with the emergence of the market economy and liberal ideology, which emphasized the notions of private property and corporate freedom within a legal and institutional framework provided and guaranteed by the state. Thus the concept, far from being new, has long belonged to everyday parlance.

And yet no universally accepted definition exists of the private sector. The adjective 'private' indicates that what is referred to is the sector of the economy that is not managed by, and does not belong to—or only as a minority holding—the state. In essence, it is the opposite of the public sector, which is by definition mainly controlled and managed by the state.

In the context of international cooperation for development, the Canadian International Development Agency (CIDA) recently defined the private sector as:

a basic organizing principle for economic activity in a market-based economy where:

- physical and financial capital is generally privately owned;
- markets, competition, and profit drive allocation and production; and
- decisions are made and risks are taken as a result of private initiative (CIDA, 2003).

The choice of an operationally relevant definition raises different issues given the specificity of peacebuilding. Is privately owned capital a relevant criterion to deal with the role of economic agents and activities? Would it not be more judicious to choose another criterion based on the kind of activities involved (eg production *v* exchange activities, formal *v* informal activities, legal *v* illegal activities) or on the ultimate goal of these activities (eg profit *v* non-profit activities)? Three different definitions of the 'private sector' are now presented:

- A narrow definition includes only corporations and other commercial businesses which have been registered with a public authority and whose goal is to generate or maximize profits, that is, 'for-profit' entities. From an operational point of view, the scope of this definition is too limited as it excludes many relevant economic stakeholders in post-conflict settings.

- A midway definition also includes the informal sector, which consists of economic activities that take place outside social, tax, and penal legislation and which do not come under state regulation. This definition corresponds better to the characteristics of post-conflict settings in countries with weak governance structures where the bulk of economic activity takes place in the informal sector. In addition, this definition includes trading and productive activities undertaken by organizations that are not merely for-profit organizations, such as cooperatives or mutual benefit societies. Economic activities are not limited to profit-making businesses, especially given the solidarity networks that may develop during armed conflicts.

- A broad definition includes everything that is not part of the public sector, that is, all non-state actors: individuals, associations, foundations, non-governmental organizations (NGOs), etc. However, this definition is so broad that it is no longer operationally useful.

The general definition cited at the beginning of this chapter corresponds to the midway definition, which includes a majority of the private sector actors to be taken into account during peacebuilding. We further propose adding government-owned businesses to this general definition, since they often play an important part in armed conflicts and in post-war reconstruction (see below).

II. Content

There is no official definition of the 'private sector' in the context of peacebuilding. International organizations, government agencies and academia have carefully avoided giving a clear definition of what this concept covers. They often use terms indiscriminately such as private sector, private economy, business community or business world, businesses, private or commercial companies, firms, economic actors, etc.

For example, John Ruggie—the Special Representative of the UN Secretary-General appointed in 2005 and whose mandate is to identify and clarify standards of corporate social responsibility and transparency with regard to human rights—refers to 'transnational corporations and other business enterprises' without providing an explicit definition of the range of actors covered (UN, 2006).

In practice, debates about the role played by the private sector in peacebuilding processes often focus on a single specific aspect of the field covered by this concept, depending on the topic under study. Thus, subsequent recommendations rarely consider all the economic actors, but focus on a given subgroup such as transnational corporations, local businesses, private security companies, companies from the extractive industry, or actors in the criminal economy.

We suggest adding government-owned businesses into the general definition, as capital ownership is not a fundamental criterion when it comes to determining whether or not an economic entity should be considered an important stakeholder in peacebuilding. State-owned oil companies such as Ecopetrol in Colombia or Pertamina in Indonesia play as important a role as Exxon-Mobil or Shell, or even more so, given that they are responsible for the security of staff and facilities. Likewise, the issues at stake are similar whether we consider the activities of a European private oil company or of an Asian government-owned company in Sudan. In the report presented before the Human Rights Council at the end of his first term of office, John Ruggie highlighted the importance of government-owned businesses: 'Evidence suggests that firms operating in only one country and state-owned companies are often worse [human rights] offenders than their highly visible private sector transnational counterparts' (UN, 2007: 3).

The main difference between private companies and state-owned companies lies in the fact that publicly-traded companies are accountable to their shareholders. This is not the case for state-owned companies. If a company violates, or assists in violating, international law the accountability of the state owner of the incriminated company is more direct than for a state where an incriminated private business is merely headquartered.

This definition of the private sector encompasses many actors. Companies may be categorized in terms of their size (number of employees, turnover, number of branches and markets, etc), legal form (limited company, limited liability company, joint venture, sole proprietorship, state-owned company, etc) or sector (private security, extraction, finance, agro-processing, etc).

The private sector should not, however, be considered in isolation. The influence of state regulations, as well as market incentives, needs to be taken into account: international organizations and government agencies play a major role in providing the incentives and 'rules of the game' under which private companies operate. They also play a fundamental role by funding reconstruction programmes through grants, concessional loans, and guarantees offered to the private sector. They may set conditions that can support peacebuilding efforts, whether through transparency requirements, sound revenue management practices, or by fostering commercial relations between former enemies with reconciliation as an ultimate goal.

Market incentives may thus be the result of either consumer pressure or the conditional granting of loans or guarantees by international financial institutions or government bodies (eg export risk guarantee agencies).

Political economy of war

Why, then, has the 'private sector' become a relevant concept in the context of post-Cold War peacebuilding? Ever since the beginning of the 1990s, many studies have delved into the economic causes and consequences of civil wars. In 1996, *Economie des guerres civiles*, a book published under the guidance of François Jean and Jean-Christophe Rufin (1996), was one of the first publications to look in detail at the issue of funding in non-international armed conflicts, seeking to explain how armed groups finance warfare and what the economic functions of armed conflicts are. Other scholars such as David Keen (1998) or Mary Kaldor (1999) suggested analyzing armed conflicts and peace processes from a political economy point of view. This approach focuses on the impact of conflicts on the distribution of power, wealth, and income, as well as on destitution in a historical and institutional setting. Armed conflicts and peace processes both produce winners and losers while violence fulfils specific economic functions (see the chapters on conflict economies and conflict transformation). This approach has unquestionably offered a new perspective on civil war in the post-Cold War context.

In parallel, various researchers and institutions started to improve their understanding of the dynamics of conflict economies which, until then, had largely been ignored. Studies conducted by Paul Collier under the aegis of the World Bank (see Collier & Hoeffler, 2000) or by the World Peace Academy (Berdal & Malone, 2000) have highlighted that the economic agendas of the belligerents could take on a major role in conflict dynamics and peace processes. According to the 'rebel greed' theory, the prospect of financial gain may lure conflict parties into prolonging the war so that they may continue to reap benefits from it. Their impunity enables them to derive substantial profits from criminal activities. Those war 'winners' tend to oppose the peace process. Therefore, peacebuilding must rest on the transformation of a conflict economy into a peace economy. Such an effort requires the collaboration of all the economic actors, starting with the private sector.

This approach has given rise to a heated debate on whether grievance explains armed conflicts better than greed (the so-called greed *v* grievance debate). Some authors have pointed out that armed rebellions are not essentially motivated by greed but rather by inequalities in the distribution of wealth and income, alongside a strong feeling of injustice or relative deprivation. More recent studies tend to show that greed and grievance may actually be two sides of the same coin (Ballentine & Sherman, 2003; Collier & Sambanis, 2005) (see also the chapter on conflict economies).

Role and accountability of economic stakeholders

In light of this renewed interest in war economics, governments, international organizations, and other actors traditionally dealing with peacebuilding have started to look more closely at economic stakeholders, with a specific focus on the potential contribution of the private sector to peace and on corporate responsibility in armed conflicts, for example, through the way businesses deal with security.

The role of the private sector in post-war reconstruction has, of course, been studied and debated in the distant past. In the context of Western Europe's economic recovery at the end of World War II, the Marshall Plan already aimed at promoting private sector development and liberalizing the economy (De Long & Eichengreen, 1991). After the end of the Cold War, however, the role of the private sector was raised even more strongly. Some countries were going down the road of a double transitional process: from war to peace and from planned economy to market economy. With privatization and the shutting down of state-owned companies, it seemed essential to promote the private sector in order to foster growth, create jobs, and counter endemic unemployment, itself a root of political instability (eg in Bosnia and Herzegovina and Mozambique).

The emergence of the private sector as a partner in peacebuilding processes resulted also from other factors, such as a growing imbalance in global governance, as was evidenced by studies conducted under the aegis of the UN, the World Bank (Gerson, 2001) and the Organisation for Economic Co-operation and Development (OECD, 2001) at the end of the 1990s. The contributing trends were as follows:

- With the end of the East *v* West confrontation, governments had to undergo serious downsizing as a result of liberal reforms in Eastern European countries and structural adjustment programmes in developing countries, with a weakening or even sometimes a collapse of the state, especially in countries affected by civil war (see, further, on collapsed states the chapter on state-building).

- At the same time, privatization and successive waves of mergers and acquisitions strengthened transnational companies even further. The biggest of these companies generate added value that exceeds most developing countries' national income. Nowadays, more than 70,000 transnational companies are able to implement their decisions globally in real time, thanks to a network of approximately 700,000 branches, in addition to millions of suppliers and subcontractors with whom they do business (UN, 2006).

- As early as 1993, direct investment by multinational companies from the OECD region in developing countries—where most armed conflicts take place—exceeded the amounts invested by their governments under official development assistance.

- This trend has challenged the roles traditionally assigned to the public and the private sectors. NGOs have launched campaigns to raise awareness about the legal responsibility of private businesses. Most large transnational companies have voluntarily made commitments with regard to human rights and good corporate governance (see further the chapter on non-state actors). Governments, NGOs, and private companies have even initiated a number of multi-stakeholder initiatives.

Ideological and institutional issues

The emergence of the private sector as a major stakeholder in the peacebuilding process can be explained by the conjunction of four issues: (1) the promotion of a (neo)liberal agenda; (2) the eagerness to acquire new market shares in post-conflict settings and to reap benefits from reconstruction efforts; (3) the fight against the funding of terrorism; and (4) the promotion of public/private partnerships and of a new kind of governance.

The inclusion of the private sector as an integral part of the peacebuilding process is the result of 'liberal peace' (Duffield, 2001), which merges the development and security agendas (see also discussion in the chapter on human security). Poor development and poverty are a source of insecurity, crime, and armed conflicts. Hence, political leaders and scholars insist on the need to promote economic development based on an effective market economy. This often requires far-reaching economic reforms that encourage private investment as a means to achieve economic growth and create jobs. From this point of view, the private sector can be used to revive the economy and should contribute to fighting unemployment by offering work to demobilized combatants, refugees, and displaced people upon their return and reintegration (see the chapters on disarmament, demobilization, and reintegration and return and reintegration). The mission of international financial institutions is to support the emergence of the private sector. This has been particularly true of the World Bank which, at the end of the Cold War, was highly influential in the allocation of the financial boon of post-conflict reconstruction.

In this context, donor countries and their companies often compete to seize the opportunities offered by the opening up of new markets and by contracts related to post-conflict reconstruction, for example, in the construction and public utility sectors. Even prior to the US intervention in Iraq in 2003, and before the end of the sanction regime, the opportunity of participating in the country's economic recovery was a major foreign policy issue, particularly with regard to the oil industry. It is also worth noting that the partial privatization of both foreign assistance and the security sector is the subject of heated debate, especially as far as the role and responsibilities of private military companies are concerned (Singer, 2003) (for further discussion on the issue of privatized security, see the chapters on non-state actors; peace operations; and security sector reform).

Ever since 11 September 2001, a new issue linked to peacebuilding has been the fight against terrorism, and more specifically against the funding of terrorist groups via networks associated with conflict economies. This involves, in particular, struggling against certain criminal activities and obtaining better control of the financial flows generated by the informal economy. In November 2001, for instance, Washington ordered the closing down of Al-Barakaat, a Somali financial company, because it was suspected of being in touch with the *al-Qaeda* network. The company had become the main financial agent between Somalia and its diaspora.

The fourth issue related to global governance is that of public/private partnerships and fundraising (see below). Private sector participation in mechanisms that seek to manage global problems is a necessary and promising evolution. Yet the role and responsibilities of the corporate world alongside those of governments and NGOs remains vague and subject to debate. The coming years will show whether these voluntary commitments by companies and public/private partnerships can produce the stated outcomes, or whether it will be necessary to elaborate new normative frameworks.

III. Implementation

Challenges and dilemmas

The liberal peace agenda rests on a series of hypotheses about the institutional setting necessary for the private sector to thrive and contribute to economic recovery: democratic governance, respect for the rule of law, a credible legal system, together with the security forces serving these institutions. Yet studies on conflict economies give another picture whereby countries in transition from war to peace are often plagued by high levels of insecurity which discourage long-term investment due to high levels of crime, corruption, impunity, and a lack of transparency between the economic and political elites.

After a civil war, the role of the private sector should not therefore be limited to creating jobs or to fostering growth—even though this is a major contribution of businesses to peacebuilding. First and foremost the private sector must avoid inflaming the armed conflict or exacerbating tensions between the belligerent parties. It must also avoid contributing to conflict economies, whether by funding (directly or indirectly) armed groups or by reinforcing the political and economic power of leaders involved in criminal activities. In this respect, it is important to grasp the potential interaction between the private sector and conflict economies in a given context so as to make relevant operational recommendations. Businesses should systematically undertake peace and conflict impact assessments for each one of their operations in a post-conflict setting, in order to appraise the relative risks and opportunities (eg Bush, 2003).

In addition to the injunction to 'do no harm', the private sector is also supposed to contribute not only to the transformation of war economies, but also to peacebuilding and conflict prevention (Wenger & Möckli, 2002). International organizations and NGOs have identified the private sector as a strategic partner able to participate in peacebuilding. In 1999, during the annual World Economic Forum in Davos, a former UN Secretary-General actually invited global business leaders to sign the Global Compact under the aegis of the UN. Since 1999, thousands of businesses have voluntarily taken the non-binding commitment to abide by a series of principles related to human rights, labour law, environmental protection, and anti-corruption. In 2001, at the instigation of several chief executive officers, the Office of the Global Compact organized a first policy dialogue on the role of the private sector in conflict zones. This dialogue tackled issues such as transparency and good revenue management, security management, as well as public/private partnerships (see <http://www.unglobalcompact. org/Issues/conflict_prevention/index.html>).

Some international organizations and NGOs are interested in the skills and the material and financial resources that businesses can provide to them, as well as in the political influence that the business sector is able to exert in post-conflict settings. In the past ten years, public/private partnerships have grown in number (Forster & Schümperli Younossian, 2005). The same can be said of dialogues between public and private partners, for example, the signing of the Voluntary Principles on Security and Human Rights in the extractive industry (<http:// www.voluntaryprinciples.org>). Leading mining and oil companies have thereby committed themselves to respect and promote human rights and international humanitarian law in their relationships with public and private security forces (see the chapter on non-state actors).

In a study about the potential contribution of the private sector in peacebuilding, International Alert has suggested four different areas for intervention. Even though these recommendations are meant for local businesses, they are just as relevant for foreign businesses investing in post-conflict settings (International Alert, 2006), as follows:

- From an economic point of view, the private sector may tackle the causes of conflict by favouring in its recruitment policy groups that have been socio-economically ostracized, or by offering alternatives to criminal activities (eg growing food crops rather than poppy or coca).

- From a political point of view, the private sector is invited to use its influence to facilitate peace negotiations, especially by means of 'track two' diplomacy (eg unofficial or informal intermediaries). The private sector can contribute to reconciliation by fostering trade exchanges between former enemies, thus giving antagonistic groups incentives to work together.

- From a security point of view, businesses play an increasing role with the ongoing privatization of security services, which raises many political, legal, and social issues (Carbonnier, 2004).

The quality of the relationships between businesses and local communities plays a pivotal role in conflict dynamics, as was shown by the experience of the Corporate Engagement Project (CEP) with numerous multinational businesses in different contexts (<http://www.cdainc.com/cdawww/project_profile.php?pid=CEP&pname=Corporate%20Engagement%20Project>). CEP has made a series of recommendations about best practice with regard to interaction between various stakeholders, particularly between businesses and their employees, as well as with local communities and authorities. CEP highlights the need for all businesses to appraise carefully the impact their conduct and activities may have on conflict dynamics, and to establish a sustainable relationship with local partners based on trust, understanding, and respect. The attitudes of corporate executives and staff play a significant role in this respect.

Recommendations

The private sector has many different functions to carry out in the peacebuilding process. Yet the impact of the private sector depends, first and foremost, on the regulatory framework and the incentives provided by public authorities, commercial and financial intermediaries, as well as local, national, and global interest groups. It is therefore essential that current legislation and both positive and negative market incentives reinforce the business case so that it encourages private sector involvement in the transformation of conflict economies into peace economies.

The lessons learned over the last decade have shown that it is of the utmost importance to assess and support systematically the transformation of conflict economies. Thus, for example, the new UN Peacebuilding Commission could monitor on a regular basis the progress made in struggling against conflict economies. If necessary, it could make recommendations to the Security Council, advocating the setting up of mechanisms to monitor and support the transformation of conflict economies. Such mechanisms could be inspired by the experiences carried out by panels of experts instituted by the Security Council towards the end of the 1990s to assess the interactions between the exploitation of natural resources, the arms trade and wars in different African settings (<http://www.globalpolicy.org/security/natres/docsindex.htm#UN>).

Local and foreign entrepreneurs are hesitant to make long-term, productive investments in post-conflict countries in the face of the high levels of security risks and political instability. Peace is thus threatened by the lack of job opportunities given to former combatants and disenfranchised groups, apart from precarious jobs in the informal or criminal sectors (see also on this important issue the chapters on disarmament, demobilization, and reintegration and security sector reform). States and international organizations must work together to lay down framework conditions conducive to sustainable employment policies. With appropriate incentives, and together with private banks and insurers, development cooperation agencies and international financial institutions must encourage productive and responsible investment. A promising solution may be to set up mechanisms to underwrite specific risks which entrepreneurs face in the context of fragile transition processes from war to peace.

Recently, a set of tools inspired by environmental impact assessments has been developed to help businesses assess the consequences of their activities on conflict dynamics and peacebuilding. The aim of such peace and conflict impact assessments is, for instance, to analyse whether a specific investment may escalate the tension between antagonistic groups, reinforce the power of a given warlord, or contribute to funding a militia (Bush, 2003). However, few businesses take advantage of these tools. A possible approach could be, for instance, to train chambers of commerce and other umbrella organizations in the use of these tools. The priority target of such training should be corporate executives working in sensitive regions of the world. It is critical that private sector company officers be able to rely on sound impact analyses if they are to take appropriate decisions that will contribute to the peacebuilding process, rather than undermine it.

Selected Bibliography

Ballentine, K, & Sherman, J (eds) (2003), *The Political Economy of Armed Conflict: Beyond Greed and Grievance*, Boulder: Lynne Rienner Publishers for IPA.

Berdal, M, & Malone, D (eds) (2000), *Greed and Grievance: Economic Agendas in Civil Wars*, Boulder: Lynne Rienner Publishers.

Bush, K (2003), *Hands-on PCIA: A Handbook for Peace and Conflict Impact Assessment (PCIA)*, Ottawa: Federation of Canadian Municipalities; Canada-Philippines Local Government Support Programme.

Carbonnier, G (2004), 'Privatisations, sous-traitance et partenariats public-privé: charity.com ou business.org?', *Revue internationale de la Croix-Rouge*, 86/856: 725–43.

CIDA (2003), *CIDA's Policy on Private Sector Development*, Ottawa: Canadian International Development Agency.

Collier, P, & Hoeffler, A (2000), *Greed and Grievance in Civil War*, World Bank Policy Research Working Paper No 2355, Washington, DC: The World Bank.

—— & Sambanis, N (2005), *Understanding Civil War: Evidence and Analysis*, Washington, DC: The World Bank.

De Long, J, & Eichengreen, B (1991), *The Marshall Plan: History's Most Successful Structural Adjustment Programme*, NBER Working Paper, No 3899, Cambridge, MA: National Bureau of Economic Research.

Duffield, M (2001), *Global Governance and the New Wars: The Merging of Development and Security*, London: Zed Books.

Forster, J, & Schümperli Younossian, C (2005), *Annuaire suisse de politique de développement. Partenariats public-privé et coopération internationale*, 24/2, Genève: Institut universitaire d'études du développement.

Gerson, A (2001), 'Building Peace: The Private Sector's Role', *American Journal of International Law*, 95/202: 102–19.

International Alert (2006), *Local Business, Local Peace: The Peacebuilding Potential of the Domestic Private Sector*, London: International Alert.

Jean, F, & Rufin, J -C (eds) (1996), *Economie des guerres civiles*, Paris: Hachette.

Kaldor, M (1999), *New and Old Wars: Organised Violence in a Global Era*, Cambridge: Polity Press.

Keen, D (1998), *The Economic Functions of Violence in Civil Wars*, Adelphi Paper, No 320, Oxford: Oxford University Press.

OECD (2001), *Helping Prevent Violent Conflicts*, The DAC Guidelines, Paris: Organisation for Economic Co-operation and Development.

Singer, P (2003), *Corporate Warriors: The Rise of the Privatised Military Industry*, Ithaca, NY: Cornell University Press.

UN (2006), *Interim Report of the Special Representative of the Secretary-General on the Issue of Human Rights and Transnational Corporations and Other Business Enterprises*, E/CN.4/2006/97, Economic and Social Council, 22 February .

—— (2007), *Report of the Special Representative of the Secretary-General on the Issue of Human Rights and Transnational Corporations and Other Business Enterprises*, UN doc. A/HRC/4/35, General Assembly, 19 February.

Wenger, A, & Möckli, D (2002), *Conflict Prevention: The Untapped Potential of the Business Sector*, Boulder, CO: Lynne Rienner Publishers.

Reconciliation

Pierre Hazan

Definition

Reconciliation is a process that allows a society to move from a divided past to a shared future. It is a means by which former enemies can find a way to live side by side, without necessarily liking or forgiving each other, and without forgetting the past. Such peaceful coexistence between former enemies is achieved, in particular, by fostering an ability among the various parties to cooperate with each other.

I. Term

Origin

The term *'réconciliation'* first appeared in the French language around 1350, before being borrowed by English. According to the French dictionary *Petit Robert*, *réconciliation* is used to refer to the action by which friendship is restored (between persons who have fallen out) (Petit Robert, 2006). The *New World Dictionary*'s definition of reconciliation is: (1) to restore to friendship; (2) to settle a feud; (3) to restore to harmony. However, the definition of reconciliation has gradually changed. It is no longer applied only in the field of individual relationships but is used increasingly for collective situations, especially where peoples or communities are involved in peacebuilding, or in the aftermath of internal or international conflict.

Traditionally, in order to re-establish civil peace, reconciliation between enemy citizens has implied the adoption of amnesty measures—a word derived from the Greek *'amnistia'*, meaning oblivion. In the *Athenian Constitution*, Aristotle was the first to talk about a form of amnesty for the purpose of reconciliation: he cited a decree, promulgated in 403 BC after the victory of democracy over the oligarchy of the Thirty that banned anyone from 'recalling the evils of the past'. Anyone who did so would be cursed. Forgetting was thus seen as vital for the re-establishment of the city after the ordeal of division.

Paul Ricoeur has pointed out that amnesia and amnesty are more than just phonetically or semantically similar; there is a hidden connection between the words, both of which evoke a denial of memory (Ricoeur, 2000). Amnesty, or obliteration from memory by both the people and the judiciary, seemed necessary to unite a restored city or nation. Many contemporary authors have underlined the paradox of amnesty—that it often renders not subject to punishment the very crimes that most offend the national or international community and which therefore appear most deserving of punishment. But perhaps, as Hannah Arendt has suggested, mass crimes can never really be either punished or forgiven; instead, they may need to be separated from the notion of proportionality between the punishment and the gravity of the crime committed.

Contexts

In the modern political context the term reconciliation is used in a variety of situations:

National reconciliation

National reconciliation may be needed after an occupying power has been defeated, when part of the population has collaborated with the occupier. For example, this occurred in France after World War II, when, after a short period of violent retribution, amnesty laws marked the full reintegration into the life of the nation of those who had sided with the occupying German forces.

National reconciliation may also be called for after the end of a bloody dictatorship, such as those that occurred in Argentina, Chile, or Uruguay, or a racist regime, such as that of *apartheid* South Africa. In Uruguay, for example, the government adopted an amnesty law in 1986 that covered acts of repression by the military and police forces during the 1973–1975 dictatorship—a measure intended to restore national unity. On 16 April 1989, a majority of voters (60 per cent) rejected a referendum aimed at overturning the amnesty law. Most justified this apparent denial of the past as a means of protecting Uruguay's still fragile democratic institutions.

Inter-state reconciliation

In this context, reconciliation means bringing together and normalizing relations between countries that have been at war. For example, in July 1962, French President Charles de Gaulle and German Chancellor Konrad Adenauer met in the city of Reims to seal officially the 'reconciliation' between their two countries, signalling that friendly relations had been restored between these states after the suffering inflicted on France during World War II.

Reconciliation in the Post-Cold War period

After the end of the Cold War, the term 'reconciliation' started to take on even more importance in the political lexicon. The revival of the United Nations and the influence of a new discourse on human rights and political liberalism contributed to the emergence of a more ethical vision of international relations, replacing the pessimistic *realpolitik* of the Cold War. This shift in perspective provided the opportunity for reconciliation to play a more decisive role. In particular, it was no longer seen solely as a government-initiated process. Reconciliation began to be interpreted by the UN and human rights NGOs not only as a 'top-down' process, but also as a 'bottom-up' process, ie one that could be initiated by civil society (see the chapters on local ownership and civil society). This change in perspective can also be explained by an increasing number of internal conflicts—such as those in Burundi, Chechnya, Rwanda, Sierra Leone, and the former Yugoslavia—characterized by crimes committed on a massive scale, including the chilling new term, 'ethnic cleansing'.

At the beginning of the 1990s, new judicial and extra-judicial institutions were set up in order to undertake national or regional reconciliation:

- The International Criminal Tribunal for the former Yugoslavia (ICTY) in 1993 and the International Criminal Tribunal for Rwanda (ICTR) in 1994, the International Criminal Court (whose statute was adopted in 1998), and internationalized courts in Cambodia, Sierra Leone, and Timor-Leste.
- Truth and Reconciliation Commissions that aim to ensure seamless transition towards democracy in countries that have experienced bloody repression or internal strife, such as in South Africa (see below).

These two types of institutions—the former being institutions for criminal prosecution and the latter having a reparative function—are similar not only in terms of their purpose of reconciliation, but also in the methodology they use to achieve those aims. The silence required by amnesty laws is no longer considered indispensable for reconciliation; instead, value is placed on the revelation of truth about crimes committed (see the chapters on reconciliation and reparation).

In the post-Cold War period, the concepts of amnesty and amnesia have gradually diverged. Theoretically, this trend has marked a reversal in strategies for dealing with the past, even though many exceptions remain in practice. For instance, after the genocide against the Tutsis in Rwanda, the UN Security Council expressly gave the Rwanda Tribunal the purpose of contributing to 'reconciliation' (Resolution 955). In 1995, South Africa set up its 'Truth and Reconciliation Commission' (TRC). By adding the word 'reconciliation' to the 'truth commissions' as had been established in Argentina and Chile, the new South African authorities wished to express their will to unite the nation and create the necessary conditions for social peace and internal peacebuilding.

Reconciliation is now considered an essential feature of any post-conflict peace process. In theory, reconciliation goes hand in hand with other elements, such as democratic governance, establishment of the rule of law, free and fair elections, disarmament, demobilization, and reintegration of combatants, recognition of victims, and protection of human rights. The UN General Assembly was so convinced of the need to promote such an integrated approach to the peace process that it declared 2009 to be the international year of reconciliation (A/RES/61/17, 20 November 2006).

Definitions

It is difficult to define reconciliation because it refers *both* to the end *and* to the means to attain that end. In fact, there is no broad agreement about its definition, the social changes it entails, or the conditions necessary for reconciliation to be achieved.

In addition to the lack of precision of the concept, reconciliation carries moral and even religious connotations which, for some, imply purification or even restoration of the bond between an individual and God. Some authors argue that the term is so symbolically charged that it should be avoided. Thus, Eric Stover and Harvey Weinstein (2004: 13–8) have suggested replacing it with the more neutral term 'social reconstruction'.

Many organizations and researchers have tried giving an operational definition to the concept of reconciliation. However, whatever definition is used, the term reconciliation remains problematic.

First, the scope of the term is so broad that it leaves room for a wide range of interpretations with regard to its links to other key concepts of peacebuilding, such as transitional justice, democratic governance, and the rule of law.

Second, the concept of reconciliation is not measurable: there exists no standard by which we can assess the progress of reconciliation in a society.

Third, the concept has sometimes been entirely misappropriated. The term reconciliation has such an aura that it has been used by some regimes to justify impunity (such as the amnesties General Pinochet provided for himself in Chile) or to pressure victims into giving up their right to justice.

Yet despite (or perhaps because of) these ambiguities, the term reconciliation has become one of the key notions in the vocabulary of transitional justice as used by the UN and many non-governmental organizations (NGOs).

The reference handbook *Reconciliation after a Violent Conflict* (International Institute for Democracy and International Assistance (IDEA), 2004) essentially defines reconciliation as the process by which former enemies manage to coexist peacefully. This definition stresses the dynamic transformation of a society where enemy groups go from conflict to mutual recognition, as well as recognition of the new institutions. Thus, the IDEA lays the emphasis on coexistence, a concept that does not entail forgiveness.

In contrast, Archbishop Desmond Tutu, Chair of the South African TRC, insists on the need for forgiveness, as illustrated in the title of his book: *No Future without Forgiveness* (2000). There are a number of different ways to forgive, or pardon, as part of a reconciliation process. One is moral forgiveness, given unilaterally by the victim to the perpetrator. Another is strategic pardoning, resulting from a cool-headed analysis of the balance of power.

The International Center for Transitional Justice defines reconciliation in the negative, seeking to avoid misuse of the term:

- Legitimate reconciliation must be distinguished from efforts to use reconciliation as a substitute for justice.
- There cannot be significant inequities in the distribution of the burdens that reconciliation inevitably entails. It cannot involve transferring responsibilities from perpetrators to victims.
- Reconciliation efforts should not focus unduly on 'wiping the slate clean'. It is not reasonable to seek unqualified closure or a comprehensive ideal of social harmony.
- Reconciliation cannot be reduced to a state of mind, nor can it expect extraordinary attributes on the part of those being reconciled.
- Reconciliation must be articulated in terms that do not depend entirely on a particular set of religious beliefs.

It follows that reconciliation is linked to the notion of 'civic trust', which includes:

- Political reconciliation (so-called 'vertical' trust between citizens and their institutions), which requires the establishment or restoration of credible institutions recognized as such by the population.
- Social reconciliation, or the establishment of a 'horizontal' trust under which citizens can once again trust one another as citizens. That means that they are sufficiently committed to the norms and values that motivate their ruling institutions; sufficiently confident that those who operate those institutions do so also on this basis; and sufficiently secure about their fellow citizens' commitment to abide by these basic norms and values (<http://www.ictj.org/en/tj/784.html>).

The aim of social reconciliation is to change beliefs, values and attitudes within a given population. It seeks to redefine the relationship between former enemy groups, and, fundamentally, to re-humanize former enemies. Weinstein and Stover emphasize that identity and memory are social constructs of reality susceptible to modification. From their perspective, the politics of reconciliation consists of devising social, political, and memorial strategies that modify individual and collective identities and, subsequently, the representations of oneself and of others. This, in turn, makes it possible to move from an understanding based on exclusion and violence to one grounded in integration and recognition. Such a process, by which a new national identity is gradually elaborated, contributes to the consolidation of peace. The definition of reconciliation must of course be adapted to the specific characteristics of each society.

Without fundamentally challenging the idea that reconciliation is both a social and political process, some authors have emphasized specific issues:

Audrey Chapman has highlighted the way the authorities may intervene to improve ethnic, racial, economic and political relations (Van der Merwe, Baxter & Chapman, 2007). From this vantage point, reconciliation means restoring civic peace but without implying that society or the victims have 'healed' or that they have established a cordial relationship with the perpetrators. Mark Amstutz has adopted a similarly pragmatic approach in stating that reconciliation is never guaranteed, including in situations when justice has in fact been administered (Amstutz, 2005).

For James Gibson, who has studied the South African context, reconciliation is defined by the four following traits: inter-racial tolerance; political tolerance; legitimacy of the new political institutions; and protection of human rights (Gibson, 2004).

II. Content

Reconciliation is a multidimensional concept. It involves a range of actors, at both the local and national level (political authorities, political parties, victims' associations, NGOs, churches, the army, the police, the judiciary, etc), sometimes with the support of international actors (the UN, regional organizations, international NGOs). It also entails an integrated approach to peacebuilding that often includes free and fair elections, as well as reform of political institutions, the judiciary, security forces, the educational system, and the economic sector.

Reconciliation, understood today in the sense of transitional justice, includes two main principles. The first principle involves seeking the truth about the crimes committed. It translates into many different actions: drafting and circulating fact sheets about past abuses; exhuming victims from mass graves and organizing dignified burials; recognizing the suffering endured by the victims; and opening up government archives.

The second principle requires that justice be rendered through a process of stigmatizing the perpetrators, either through the administration of criminal justice or restorative justice, or a combination of both.

This second point raises the contentious issue of sanctions. Are criminal penalties or symbolic sanctions better able to achieve reconciliation in a society? The nearly simultaneous establishment of the international criminal tribunals for Rwanda and the former Yugoslavia and of the South African TRC gave rise to an intense debate between 1995 and 2000. Ultimately, those who supported the TRC and those in favour of the international criminal courts were able to see both the limits and the complementarity of the models they were advocating.

Put in economic terms, in such situations there is an excess supply of people who have committed crimes against humanity, whom neither national nor international justice systems have the means to process. The international criminal tribunals for the former Yugoslavia and for Rwanda illustrate this problem. Only a few dozen people have been put on trial whereas thousands, and in the case of Rwanda tens of thousands of people, committed abuses. It is also unacceptable to see impunity enjoyed by people responsible for the deaths of tens or hundreds of thousands of men, women, and children, and the promoters of Truth Commissions acknowledge this (see also the chapters on international crimes and transitional justice). In fact, the principle of complementarity between the Commissions and criminal proceedings has been established in order to achieve the ultimate goal of reconciliation.

III. Implementation

Challenges, operational aspects, and positive or negative experiences

The challenges associated with the reconciliation process are myriad. In the first place, an affected population must be convinced that political elites are actually determined to put democratization in motion and to end repression or civil war (local ownership). This presupposes the existence of new elites that are strong enough, from both a political and a military point of view, to restore respect for the rule of law and civil liberties. Second, the population must be persuaded that the chosen instruments of reconciliation, such as truth commissions and/or criminal courts, are serious and unbiased. The reconciliation process can only attain its goals if these preconditions are met.

The main obstacles are the following:

• Many countries experience major difficulties pursuing reconciliation after the end of an internal conflict, as their authorities have also to confront a plethora of other problems, without the necessary resources at their disposal. The UN Secretary-General's report on transitional justice (UN Secretary-General, 2004) highlights the accumulation of such difficulties. Such countries must simultaneously administer justice, undertake political and institutional reform, rebuild public services, and guarantee the existence of an independent ministry of justice, among other things. Further, while financial resources and qualified staff are in short supply, the people are divided, some are traumatized, and their fundamental human rights have often been violated over an extended period. But despite the fact that such an integrated approach is difficult to realize, it is the surest way to successful reconciliation.

• Governments may sometimes opt for a policy of impunity if the balance of power is not in their favour. By way of illustration, on 12 March 2007, the government of Afghanistan proclaimed an amnesty law for those commonly referred to as 'warlords', many of whom, in all probability, are guilty of war crimes and crimes against humanity. The reasoning behind this amnesty law is that it enables a weak central government in Kabul to fight against the Taliban without also prosecuting or fighting the warlords. Yet when the Afghan Independent Commission for Human Rights conducted a study involving thousands of Afghans it showed that the population wanted justice to be done in a country that, over recent decades, has experienced successive conflicts involving countless massacres and resulting in more than a million dead, and causing millions more to seek refuge abroad. The Commission's study highlights the fact that, instead of strengthening the government, such a law undermines both the government's authority and the reconciliation process, and may thus jeopardize the country's future.

- In other countries, national authorities have launched reconciliation processes that have not been fully implemented due to lack of political will on the part of government. In Serbia, the Truth and Reconciliation Commission set up in 2002 by President Kostunica was dismantled before the end of its mandate. In Haiti, the report drafted by the Truth Commission had very limited circulation at first, and in the end was distributed mainly to foreign diplomats. These two examples underscore the need to apply an integrated approach to reconciliation. The instruments that are set up—especially Truth Commissions and/or criminal courts—only have an impact to the extent that they are part of a broader process of political change that is owned by the population.

- One of the most acute challenges facing reconciliation processes is finding a balance between the search for peace and the search for justice. Some argue that peace without justice is an illusion, resulting in perpetuation of the conflict rather than true reconciliation. This is the opinion voiced by David Crane, Prosecutor for the Special Court for Sierra Leone, who published Charles Taylor's indictment on the same day the former Liberian President finally began peace negotiations. Later on, Mr Crane revealed his ulterior motive: he did not believe a man allegedly responsible for hundreds of thousands of deaths would be a credible partner to restore peace and, more importantly, to lead reconciliation. In contrast, others think that the search for justice through criminal prosecutions delays the peace process, allowing new abuses which, in turn, further undermine the peace process and hence reconciliation. The case of Sudan, where in July 2008 the chief prosecutor at the International Criminal Court sought a warrant for the arrest of Sudan's President for crimes committed in Darfur, is an obvious and highly contentious example. The objective here is not to limit debate, but to recognize recent approaches that have attempted to go beyond this dichotomy by pursuing peace and justice at the same time.

Lessons drawn from the past

With hindsight, what is the track record of Truth Commissions and ad hoc courts in terms of reconciliation? The issue is a complex one. Indeed, we have sought to show that reconciliation is a notion that is hard to grasp, and even harder to assess. In addition, justice mechanisms can only be effective if they are part of an integrated approach. Time is a crucial factor: reconciliation, and more specifically social reconciliation, is a slow process.

Let us first consider the two UN ad hoc criminal tribunals: for the former Yugoslavia and Rwanda. Established as part of an exit strategy for the UN, such tribunals are now widely considered a thing of the past (especially since the establishment of the International Criminal Court). They are too expensive (approximately US$100 million per annum per court); too slow (since 1994, the Rwanda tribunal has tried about 20 people); and they have not managed in the shorter term to gain the confidence of the concerned population.

For example, a majority of Serbs are hostile to the ICTY and a majority of Rwandans have access to very limited information about their international criminal tribunal (Stover & Weinstein, 2004). This is due not only to the political obstacles that these courts have had to overcome, but also to the weakness of their public communications strategies and the many setbacks their prosecutors have encountered. To this day, for instance, the Prosecutor for the Rwanda tribunal has been unable to indict any members of the Rwanda Patriotic Front suspected of war crimes, despite the UN Security Council Resolution 955 required to sanction authors of war crimes. Nonetheless, in the medium-to-long-term, the track records of these institutions, especially the ICTY, will probably attract less criticism and will at least prevent denial of the crimes committed by the different parties involved.

Like the UN ad hoc tribunals, truth commissions have also had mixed results. On the one hand, the report by the Truth Commission in Argentina has had a profound social impact, while the public hearings conducted by the TRC in South Africa have likewise resounded at both the national and the international level. On the other hand, commissions in countries such as Haiti, Serbia, and Uganda have met with less success. But in societies where criminal courts and Truth Commissions have worked fairly well, these institutions have triggered social and institutional change: they have opened new fora for dialogue within society, broken with impunity, supported change and democratic reform, and helped create institutional guarantees and a human rights culture aimed at preventing the repetition of such crimes. In such cases, they have been essential elements in the process of reconciliation.

The idea that revealing the truth can heal both the victims and the society—the slogan of the South African TRC was 'revealing is healing'—rests on an assumption that is yet to be proven. Limited studies have elicited a wide variety of attitudes and reactions among the victims who have testified. Some were extremely glad to have had the opportunity to testify publicly, but others regretted having testified because they had to relive painful and even traumatic experiences. In addition, the use of pseudo-medical and psychoanalytic terminology is problematic when it is applied on a collective scale: can 'coming to terms' with the past help 'heal' a nation by 'exorcizing' its past? There is, however, no supporting evidence to show that policies of impunity have helped the victims in any way, or contributed to reinforcing national cohesion.

At this time it remains difficult to make even a provisional appraisal of reconciliation processes. Civil peacebuilding takes place over a long period of time, sometimes over several generations, and the real impact of reconciliation institutions may not be known for some time. A good illustration is the Allies' International Military Tribunal in Nuremberg: it was only in the 1960s and 1970s that West Germans stopped considering the Nuremberg trial as a manifestation of victors' justice, and began to consider it as a mechanism through which Nazi crimes and the sanctions that punished them were integrated into Germany's collective memory. Without the necessary historical distance, it is difficult to appraise the impact of public reconciliation policies.

Recommendations

Since public reconciliation policies are fairly recent and have been, on each occasion, the object of intense political negotiation, they tend to lack conceptual precision. In addition, the range of different models, and the radically different contexts in which they are applied, make it difficult to make specific recommendations. However, past experience makes it possible to formulate some general principles.

Need to set up control mechanisms

At the national level, the first challenge is to ensure that people can understand and participate in a reconciliation process that determines responsibility for crimes committed. Unfortunately, there is often no such local ownership. In their role as observers, NGOs and the international community have a crucial mission to fulfil in assessing the validity of the reconciliation policies implemented. It is essential for them to denounce transitional justice mechanisms that are clearly dysfunctional or which serve only as an excuse for inaction.

Need to establish follow-up mechanisms

In their reports, truth commissions almost always include suggestions as to political and institutional reform. More often than not, state authorities do not follow these up. Once again, NGOs and the UN can play a role in pursuing these reform proposals.

Protecting existing standards

A further major challenge has been generated since 11 September 2001, through the erosion of legally binding norms and respect for international humanitarian law. This erosion has been justified by the so-called 'war on terror' and a heightened concern for international security. However, it is an approach that jeopardizes the entire reconciliation process. Afghanistan, as noted above, is the perfect example of a country where, despite the presence of national authorities, the UN, and the United States, not one of these actors has opened a single inquiry against the perpetrators of war crimes or crimes against humanity. In fact, in January 2005, the UN buried its own commissioned report that accused Afghan parliamentarians of responsibility for massacres and torture (Walsh, 2006).

The processes of reconciliation are fragile, and if they are not to be imperilled, the major international actors must not allow strategic concerns to place them in situations where they are seen to tolerate, let alone encourage, impunity.

Selected Bibliography

Amstutz, M (2005), *International Ethics: Concepts, Theories, and Cases in Global Politics*, Lanham, Md: Rowman & Littlefield.
Boraine, A, Lévy J & Scheffer, R (1994), *Dealing With the Past, Truth and Reconciliation Commission in South Africa*, Cape Town: Idasa.
Brody, R (2001), 'Justice: The First Casualty of Truth', *The Nation*, April 30.
Chapman, AR (2007) 'Approaches to Studying Reconciliation', in Van der Merwe, Baxter, V, & Chapman, A (eds), *Assessing the Impact of Transitional Justice: Challenges for Empirical Research*, Washington DC: USIP.
Derrida, J (1999), 'Le siècle et le pardon', Le Monde des Débats, 9.
Garapon, A (2001), *Des crimes qu'on ne peut ni punir ni pardonner*, Paris: Odile Jacob.
Gardner Feldman, L (1999), 'The Principle and Practice of "Reconciliation" in German Foreign Policy: Relations with France, Israel, Poland and the Czech Republic', *International Affairs*, 75/2: 333–56.
Gibson, JL (2004), *Overcoming Apartheid: Can Truth Reconcile a Divided Nation?*, New York: Russell Sage Foundation.
—— (2006), 'The Contributions of Truth to Reconciliation: Lessons from South Africa', *Journal of Conflict Resolution*, 50/3: 409–32.
Hazan, P (2006), *Morocco: Betting on a Truth and Reconciliation Commission*, Washington DC: USIP, Special Report No 165.
Kritz, N (ed) (1995), *Transitional Justice: How Emerging Democracies Reckon with Former Regimes*, 3 Volumes, Washington DC: USIP Press.
Ricoeur, P (2000), *La mémoire, l'histoire et l'oubli*, Paris: Seuil.
Stover, E & Weinstein, H (eds) (2004), *My Neighbour, My Enemy, Justice and Community in the Aftermath of Mass Atrocity*, Cambridge: Cambridge University Press.

Tutu, D, Foreword in Bloomfield, D, Barnes, T, & Huyse, L (2003) *Reconciliation After Violent Conflict, a Handbook*, Stockholm: Institute for Democracy and Electoral Assistance.

UN Secretary-General (2004), Report on the 'rule of law and transitional justice in conflict and post-conflict societies', UN Security Council, S/2004/616, 23 August.

United States Institute of Peace (2006), *Working Group on Social Reconstruction and Reconciliation, Defining Terms: Reconciliation, Transitional Justice, Social Reconstruction*, unpublished, Washington DC: USIP.

Walsh, D (2006), 'UN report accuses Afghan MPs of torture and massacres', *Guardian*, June 12.

Recovery

Riccardo Bocco, Pierre Harrisson, and Lucas Oesch

Definition

In the context of post-crisis transition situations (natural or man-made disasters, mainly conflicts), rather than merely coordinating 'relief' and 'development', the recovery approach currently being developed by the United Nations aims to integrate these two dimensions as well as, in the case of conflicts, peacebuilding and peacekeeping activities. The core principles of recovery are to restore, to improve, and to prevent. Recovery thus focuses on restoring the capacity of national institutions and communities after a crisis.

I. Term

Into the 1990s, the 'relief and development continuum' approach led mainstream discourses and practices in the international community related to post-crisis interventions. This concept was based on the understanding that relief and development should follow a logical and linear sequence of phases, where different types of interventions follow each other successively. Since the early 1990s, however, inspired by experiences of international agencies in the field, considerations about the need to integrate relief and development, and not merely to coordinate the two, have emerged in parallel. Since 2005, these concepts have started to crystallize within the UN system into what can be called the 'recovery approach'.

Meaning

The word recovery is often used to describe a person returning to a normal state of health after an illness or a medical problem, as well as to indicate the improvement of an economic situation after a period of stagnation or decline. Central to the notion is the idea of 'getting better'. In the context of post-crisis interventions, recovery 'focuses on restoring the capacity of national institutions and communities after a crisis' (UNDP, 2007a). This concept must be considered in parallel with the concept of 'transition'. Transition (from conflict to peace, from relief to development) has progressively replaced the notion of continuum among the international community. In 2002, the UN Development Group (UNDG) and the UN Executive Committee on Humanitarian Affairs (ECHA) established a joint working group on transition issues. In considering the absorptive capacities and economic growth in countries after a conflict or a disaster, the UN Development Programme (UNDP), the World Bank, and the UNDG are now using the following typology for the phasing of recovery: Stabilization/ Transition (12 months), Transformation (12–36 months), and Consolidation (36–120 months) (UNDP/UNDG/World Bank, 2004).

Furthermore, the following definition of transition, from conflict to peace, has been proposed:

> For the UN, transition refers to the period in a crisis when external assistance is most crucial in supporting or underpinning still fragile ceasefires or peace processes by helping to create the conditions for political stability, security, justice and social equity (UNDG/ ECHA, 2004: 12).

The UNDG/ECHA working group has also found that the terms 'rehabilitation' and 'recovery' tend to be used interchangeably within transition plans and appeals, thus reflecting 'the need to continue with the same activities in both the humanitarian period and in transition' (UNDG/ECHA, 2004: 16). An even broader definition of transition can be given:

> The term 'transition'... refers to a period in time immediately following a crisis, when pre-existing plans, strategies and programmes no longer reflect the most pressing priorities and needs in a given national setting. The aim of the UN system in transition should be to assist national authorities to initiate immediate priority crisis resolution and recovery activities, and to move from a post-crisis recovery short- or medium-term strategy into a longer-term strategy. Within the overall timeframe of transition, therefore, there are two distinct phases of transformation that the country undergoes: the early recovery phase, which is the period immediately following the onset of the crisis, where the priorities are to show immediate results for vulnerable populations and to promote opportunities for recovery. There is a second, longer phase of recovery following an increase in national capacity that is demonstrated by national leadership of the recovery process and the articulation of a national plan (CWGER/UNDG/ECHA, 2006, cited in Harrisson, 2007: 7).

Recovery is still a 'work-in-progress' notion, but the approach currently being developed by the UN aims to address post-crisis transition situations by integrating relief, development, and, in the case of conflicts, peacebuilding and peacekeeping activities. The recovery approach is mainly designed to bridge the gap, frequently identified, between the relief and development phases of post-crises interventions, often referred to as the 'grey zone'. This gap has been highlighted by many experiences in the field. The grey zone is characterized by mixed concepts and implementation mechanisms that often prevent a smooth handover from one phase to the next. In practice, humanitarian actors often leave the field as development actors enter the scene, without precise strategic planning and coordination for a transition period between the two aid systems.

A 2004 report of the International Strategy for Disaster Reduction (ISDR) (2004, Vol 2: 6) defined recovery as: 'Decisions and actions taken after a disaster with a view to restoring or improving the pre-disaster living conditions of the stricken community, while encouraging and facilitating necessary adjustments to reduce disaster risk.' The Cluster Working Group on Early Recovery (CWGER) of the UN's Inter-Agency Standing Committee (IASC) is considered today as the leading coordinator through its joint strategic planning and programming mechanism for agencies working on recovery. In 2007, it extended the notion of recovery to include conflict situations alongside natural disasters, and has adopted the wording of 'crisis' to refer to both natural and man-made disasters, mainly conflicts.

In addition, the CWGER (2007b: 3), in its 'Early Recovery Guidance Note' (the Guidance Note), has distinguished an 'early recovery' (ER) phase from a second longer phase or recovery in the full sense of the term. The Guidance Note (2007b: 5) defines ER as: 'Recovery that begins early in a humanitarian setting. It is a multi-dimensional process, guided by development principles, that seeks to build upon humanitarian programmes and to catalyse sustainable development opportunities'. The implementation of ER is considered indispensable in order to secure the foundations for sustainable recovery. It is to be implemented alongside 'life-saving' assistance, and it intends to influence the way humanitarian assistance is provided in order 'to avoid dependencies, and ensure relief efforts take into account longer term developmental considerations and 'do no harm' (CWGER, 2007b: 7). The core principles of recovery can be summarized as follows: to restore, to improve, and to prevent.

Genealogy

Suhrke and Buckmaster (2005: 739) mention that, since the end of the Cold War, there has been a 'progressive standardisation of international responses to post-war situations with increasingly agreed-upon formulas for the nature and sequencing of aid, improved coordination, and clearer division of labour among aid agencies.' One of those formulas is certainly the 'relief and development continuum' approach which preceded in the 1990s the notions of transition and recovery.

The 'relief and development continuum' concept emerged in the late 1980s in response to the need to fill the gap between short-term oriented emergency or relief assistance and longer-term oriented development cooperation work. It is based on the understanding that post-conflict peacebuilding and reconstruction follow a logical and linear sequence of phases (that is, emergency, relief, rehabilitation, and reconstruction) where different types of interventions follow each other successively. Since its inception the 'relief and development continuum' concept has been subject to a variety of criticisms directed against its linear nature.

In parallel, the general understandings of post-conflict peacebuilding and reconstruction have also developed in a different direction due to experiences gained and lessons learned since the early 1990s. Both developments have led to a wider, more holistic and sometimes more political understanding of the relevant concept.

A narrow understanding of the concept of continuum aims to fill the operational gaps between relief, rehabilitation and development assistance and emphasizes the use of coordination mechanisms as a means to bridge the gaps (EC, 1996). Critics of the linear sequencing understanding of the 'relief and development continuum' have introduced the 'contiguum' terminology in order to draw attention to the need to address the complexity of conflict situations and to acknowledge that the different phases do not follow each other in a linear sequence but can take place at the same time with many links in all directions. This understanding is nurtured by the reality on the ground showing that the transition from relief to rehabilitation or development is rarely a linear, chronological process, especially in conflict-prone countries (EC, 2001: 6).

A slightly wider understanding of the concept of continuum goes beyond improved coordination and supports the incorporation of elements of developmental thinking into both planning and implementing relief and rehabilitation assistance as a means to bridge the gap. This is often referred to as 'developmental relief or rehabilitation assistance'.

However, despite frequent criticism and a wider understanding of the continuum concept, a meta-evaluation of the UN and the international community's support in six conflict-affected countries (UNDP, 2006: viii) found that in all these countries, despite a 'contiguum' understanding of the linkages between relief, rehabilitation, and development of integrated approaches and missions since 2001 (UN, 2005), the international response continues to be structured mainly around a linear phase approach.

The current, more holistic, recovery concept is an outcome of the reform of peacebuilding/peacekeeping doctrine and practice, and of humanitarian and developmental responses by bilateral and multilateral agencies and non-governmental organizations (NGOs). It tries to integrate the reform currently under way at the UN concerning preparedness of the broad humanitarian response. Moreover, it has to be understood as an attempt to elaborate a new approach which addresses the criticisms made of the continuum notion. For example, in 2000, a UNDP document (2000: 5) mentioned that 'every stage of crisis and post-conflict has a development dimension. The "relief to development" or "continuum" concepts have been shown to be inadequate paradigms in capturing the complex reality of crisis and post-conflict situations.' In fact, reference to the recovery approach can be identified even earlier, for example in 1991 UN General Assembly Resolution 46/182 on 'Strengthening of the Coordination of

Humanitarian Assistance of the United Nations' (UN, 1991, cited in White & Cliffe, 2000: 316). In a section entitled 'Continuum from relief to rehabilitation and development', the Resolution states that:

Emergency assistance must be provided in ways that will be supportive of recovery and long-term development. Development assistance organizations of the United Nations system should be involved at an early stage and should collaborate closely with those responsible for emergency relief and recovery, within their existing mandates.

For its part the Development Assistance Committee (DAC) noted in 1997 that it was necessary to overcome the functional distinctions of the different agencies involved in post-crisis interventions, and to integrate, rather than merely coordinate, their different objectives within long-term strategies (White & Cliffe, 2000: 319).

The recovery concept also follows the broad debate of the international community on natural disasters, which developed in the 1990s. One of the main outcomes of the debate is that, in post-disasters interventions, it is necessary to concentrate on existing and potential risks and vulnerabilities, and not simply to focus on how to improve the operational capacities for relief assistance. Integrated disaster risk reduction approaches are thus required (ISDR, 2004). In addition, the post-crisis recovery approach currently being developed by the CWGER mirrors the coordination model adopted by Japan to address post-disaster situations (especially earthquakes in the case of Japan). This model is being adapted to the UN system and has been enlarged by the CWGER in order to include post-conflict situations and issues of peacebuilding and peacekeeping (see peace operations). The CWGER (2007b: 4) recognizes that, despite the differences in the way recovery interventions must respond to natural disasters compared with complex emergency settings (eg post-conflict situations), there are also many similarities.

Furthermore, the recovery concept has already been adopted by the UNDP, the CWGER's current lead agency, since at least 2000; specifically by its Bureau for Crisis Prevention and Recovery which works closely with different agencies at global level as well as with country teams and local governments in particular national situations for post-disaster and post-conflict responses. Predicting somehow the creation of the CWGER, UNDP even stated in 2005 that, if a new structure were to be created to address recovery efforts within the UN, 'it should have the major objective of achieving a strong level of cohesion, coordination and consensus amongst different stakeholders' (UNDP 2005: 11). The UNDP will publish regular 'Conflict Prevention and Recovery Reports'. The first one was published in 2008 (UNDP, 2008) (this article was completed before the publication of the report).

II. Content

Functions and objectives

The main goal of the recovery approach, and principally of the ER concept, is to overcome the 'mandate' functioning of the UN system, where for example the Office for the Coordination of Humanitarian Affairs (OCHA) is concerned with emergency and relief assistance and the UNDP with development assistance. As White and Cliffe (2000: 314) recall, the distinction between 'relief' and 'development' is to some extent artificial. It has been constructed from the point of view of aid programmers and has little meaning for beneficiaries. Rather than merely coordinating 'relief' and 'development', the recovery approach currently being developed by the CWGER aims to integrate the two dimensions. The challenge is then to create a unified understanding of the meaning of recovery and ER, as well as to develop common procedures and mechanisms. The CWGER Guidance Note is designed for that purpose. As the Guidance Note recalls:

Under the coordination of OCHA, there are well-known and applied procedures and mechanisms for the provision of immediate life-saving humanitarian assistance. No such established procedures and mechanisms exist yet in support of immediate early recovery planning in the aftermath of crises (CWGER, 2007b: 9).

The main objective of the actual reforms of humanitarian assistance, peace-keeping/peacebuilding, and development assistance in the UN and in bilateral agencies, is the improvement of predictability, timeliness, and effectiveness of responses to crises. The purpose of these objectives is to obtain more inclusive solutions (participatory approaches and governance) that are sustainable and which take into account vulnerabilities, capacities and resilience at local, national, and international level (OCHA, 2005; High Level Forum, 2005; UN, 2000). The main challenge in post-crisis intervention is to secure good coordination between international agencies and with national stakeholders, in order to elaborate a common needs assessment and joint strategic planning, programming and costing, not only in the immediate aftermath of crises, but also to establish sustainable reforms.

The IASC is a forum involving both UN and non-UN humanitarian actors, which was created in 1992 to respond to UN General Assembly Resolution 46/182 (UN, 1991), noted above. In 2005, the IASC highlighted the need to improve the humanitarian response, identifying nine 'critical gaps' within post-crisis interventions, which required new understandings and new strategies designed to address them effectively. It suggested the designation of a lead agency to coordinate strategies and actions for each specific cluster—understood as a sector of activity and a group of organizations and stakeholders. More precisely it said:

A cluster is a group comprising organisations and other stakeholders, with a designated lead, working in an area of humanitarian response in which gaps in response have been identified. These areas include some traditional relief and assistance sectors (water and sanitation, nutrition, health, emergency shelter); service provision (emergency telecommunications, logistics) and cross-cutting issues (camp coordination, early recovery and protection). Clusters are organised at both field and global level (CWGER, 2007a).

Challenges

The main challenge of the cluster approach is to 'bring together a broad range of organisations to work in a coordinated and cohesive manner to effectively support national actors' (CWGER, 2007b: 12). Led by the UNDP, the CWGER consists of nineteen UN and non-UN (other international agencies) members concerned with humanitarian and development issues. The UNDP has received the mandate to lead the cluster at an international level, reflecting the claim of the UNDP in the 1990s to have a leading role in relief as well as rehabilitation and development (White & Cliffe, 2000: 317).

The IASC/CWGER Guidance Note, mentioned above, was developed in cooperation with the UNDG/ECHA Working Group on Transition. It 'provides guidance on how to plan, implement and monitor early recovery activities from the beginning of the humanitarian phase to the recovery phase' (CWGER, 2007b: 4). As mentioned above, in situations of conflict or natural disaster, the main focus of the ER approach 'is on restoring the capacity of national institutions and communities to recover from crisis, build back better and to prevent relapses' (CWGER, 2007b: 5). More precisely the Guidance Note is designed to help practitioners understand the complexities of ER environments and the multiplicity of actors involved; to set some basic guiding principles and standards of interventions in ER situations; to provide tools and resources that may be used by practitioners; as well as to indicate means of effective handover to longer term recovery processes (CWGER, 2007b: 4).

The interventions of ER are multidimensional, ranging from services, infrastructure, livelihood opportunities, and governance capacities, to shelter, environment, and social dimensions, including the return and reintegration of displaced persons (CWGER, 2006: 1; CWGER, 2007b: 5). The main 'techniques of government' used by the CWGER (2007b: 7) are centred on 'capacity-building' and 'institution building' of national and local actors, in order to secure local ownership of the ER and longer-term recovery process. To determine the objectives and priorities of ER plans and implementation, reliable information gathering is considered by the CWGER to be a crucial element. To that purpose, the CWGER has reviewed the methodologies and tools used by UN and other agencies to carry out needs assessment, strategic planning, programme design, monitoring and evaluation, coordination and funding mechanisms, and knowledge management. The CWGER is currently developing new tools based on lessons learned from specific country interventions (CWGER, 2007a).

III. Implementation

'Following disasters and armed conflict, UNDP assists national governments and communities to lay the foundation for sustainable development' (UNDP,

2007b). UNDP supports the strengthening of national and community-based institutions for ER, economic recovery, recovery from natural disasters, security and social cohesion and reconciliation, with particular initiatives on disarmament, demobilization, and reintegration, mine action, natural disasters, security sector reform, small arms control, and transitional justice (UNDP, 2007b).

Lessons learned

Since late 2005, the cluster approach has been applied to all new major emergencies, for example, the Pakistan, Yogyakarta, and Indonesia earthquakes and the 2006 conflict in Lebanon (CWGER, 2006: 2). The cluster approach has also been rolled out within a limited number of existing post-conflict situations, for example the Democratic Republic of Congo, Liberia, Somalia, and Uganda. In Liberia and Uganda, needs assessments have been developed, as well as, in the case of Uganda, a results-based recovery framework (RBF) (CWGER, 2006: Annex 2). Specific common cluster websites for ER and reintegration clusters have been developed for Lebanon, Pakistan and Uganda.

Due to the novelty of the ER cluster approach and its implementation, it is difficult to find further examples, or to obtain details on how ER is being planned and implemented in the field, as well as to appreciate its main results or limits. The CWGER website gives reports of NGOs on the cluster approach at country level (eg ActionAid, 2006; ACFIN, 2006). CWGER is trying to involve more NGOs in this cluster division, and in coordination of labour in humanitarian responses, at both global and country level.

The Active Learning Network for Accountability and Performance (ALNAP) and the ProVention Consortium (2007) have published a synthesis of lessons learned from previous recovery operations for those working on recovery policies and strategies. A similar exercise has been done by the Tsunami Evaluation Coalition (2007). It is also of interest to note—albeit not a concrete example of implementation—that in 2005, the 'African Post-Conflict Reconstruction Policy Framework' of the Organisation of African Unity's New Partnership for Africa's Development (NEPAD) (2005) was largely inspired by the ER principles and the cluster functioning. The framework, for example, mentions the identification of gaps between peace, security, humanitarian, and development dimensions in post-conflict situations; the need for coherent overall country level strategic framework; the necessity of local ownership; the development of legitimate and sustainable internal capacity; and so on.

Operational guidelines

Although the ER approach is in its early stages, it is useful to describe in more detail its suggested implementation as proposed by the CWGER. The work of the CWGER is conceived as one that aims to support the UN Humanitarian Coordinator (HC) or the UN Resident Coordinator (RC) in a post-crisis situation at the level of planning and implementation of ER. It also aims to ensure that interventions of other 'humanitarian' actors or other clusters (eg health or nutrition clusters) present in the field also take into account and address ER issues (CWGER, 2006). As the Guidance Note (2007c: 13) mentions: 'In order to encourage the integration of early recovery issues into the work of other clusters, an early recovery network model is recommended.'

An early recovery network (ERN) and the deployment of recovery support can be activated after discussion and agreement between the cluster lead and the UN's RC/HC (CWGER, 2007b: 10–11). The cluster leader then informs the CWGER members and key partners that the network has been activated, and organizes information exchange systems and meetings. An ERN Action Plan has to be adopted before the deployment of CWGER support to the field. The main tasks of the CWGER's support are coordination, assessment, and strategic planning. And, as the Guidance Note indicates:

Planning must accord early priority to supporting the development of government capacity for aid coordination, policy setting and programme delivery;...[and] planning must be strategic, field-driven and guided by a common understanding, analysis and shared vision of the underlying causes of the crisis (CWGER, 2007b: 19–20).

After a monitoring and evaluation of ER responses, the cluster is then de-activated. As the Guidance Note (2007b: 14) mentions:

Early on, it is important to plan when and how early recovery will be transitioned from the emergency phase and into longer-term recovery, reconstruction and development processes. The early recovery cluster/network at the country level should define criteria for when and under which circumstances it will close down and hand over to another institution.

Finally, to illustrate the actual efforts to develop more inter-agency integrated responses within the UN system, it is worth mentioning the high-level Transition Workshop which took place in 2006 and gathered representatives of UN Resident Coordinator Offices coming from seventeen countries, resources personnel from thirteen UN agencies, and Special Representatives of the UN Secretary-General from the Democratic Republic of Congo Liberia, Sierra Leone, and Sudan. The main objectives were:

(1) to share experiences, network, and to build relationships amongst the coordination practitioners in post-crisis, as a foundation for a community of practice; (2) to review the tools and policy guidance currently being issued on transition, and to reassess the actual needs on the ground in terms of support; and finally to (3) get input on what DGO could better do to support UN Country Teams in transition, and to clarify roles and responsibilities amongst the major Agencies (UNDG/ECHA, 2006).

Selected Bibliography

Action contre la Faim (ACFIN) (2006), *Action contre la Faim International Positioning vis-à-vis the Reform of Clusters*, June, available at: <http://www.undp.org/cpr/iasc/content/docs/ACF_Cluster_positionnement_June_2006.doc>.

ActionAid (2006), The Evolving UN Cluster Approach in the Aftermath of the Pakistan Earthquake: An NGO Perspective, April, available at: <http://www.undp.org/cpr/iasc/pages/background_material.shtml>.

Active Learning Network for Accountability and Performance (ALNAP)/ProVention Consortium (2007), Slow-Onset Disasters: Drought and Food and Livelihoods Insecurity: Learning from Previous Relief and Recovery Responses, available at: <http://www.alnap.org/publications/pdfs/ALNAP-ProVention_lessons_on_slow-onset_disasters.pdf>.

Cluster Working Group on Early Recovery (CWGER) (2006), *Implementing Early Recovery*, Inter-Agency Standing Committee (IASC), New York and Geneva: UN, July, available at: <www.reliefweb.int/rw/lib.nsf/db900sid/LTIO-6SCLD2/$file/iasc-earlyrecovery-jul2006.pdf?openelement>.

—— (2007a), available at: <http://www.humanitarianreform.org/humanitarianreform/Default.aspx?tabid=80>.

—— (2007b), Transition Recovery: Early Recovery Guidance Note, Draft, Inter-Agency Standing Committee (IASC), New York and Geneva: UN, April, available at: <http://www.undp.org/cpr/iasc/content/docs/4th_Draft_Early_Recovery_Guidance.doc>.

—— (2007c) Guidance note on Early Recovery, Draft, Inter-Agency Standing Committee (IASC), New York and Geneva: UN, October 2007, available at <www.undp.org/cpr/iasc/content/docs/Nov07_Links/Doc_13.pdf>.

European Commission (EC) (1996), *Communication of the European Commission to the Council on Linking Relief, Rehabilitation and Development (LRRD)*, Brussels: COM, 153.

—— (2001), *Communication from the Commission to the Council and the European Parliament: Linking Relief, Rehabilitation and Development—An assessment*, Brussels: COM, 153 final, available at: <http://eur-lex.europa.eu/LexUriServ/site/en/com/2001/com2001_0153en01.pdf>.

Harrisson, P (2007), *Review of Existing Tools and Methodologies Proposed for Early Recovery: Analysis of their Applicability to Early Recovery and Preparing their Dissemination*, Geneva: UNDP/BCPR, February, available at: <http://www.undp.org/cpr/iasc/content/docs/report.doc>.

High Level Forum (2005), *Paris Declaration on Aid Effectiveness: Ownership, Harmonisation, Alignment, Results, and Mutual Accountability*, available at: <http://www.oecd.org/dataoecd/11/41/34428351.pdf>.

International Strategy for Disaster Reduction (ISDR) (2004), *Living with Risk: A Global Review of Disaster Reduction Initiatives*, 2 Volumes, New York and Geneva: UN.

New Partnership for Africa's Development (NEPAD) (2005), *African Post-Conflict Reconstruction Policy Framework*, Johannesburg: NEPAD Secretariat, June, available at: <http://www.nepad.org/2005/aprmforum/PCRPolicyFramework_en.pdf>.

Office for the Coordination of Humanitarian Affairs (OCHA) (2005), *Humanitarian Response Review: An Independent Report*, New York and Geneva: UN, available at: <http://www.reliefweb.int/library/documents/2005/ocha-gen-02sep.pdf>.

Suhrke, A, & Buckmaster, J (2005), 'Post-War Aid: Patterns and Purposes', *Development in Practice*, 15/6: 737–46.

Tsunami Evaluation Coalition (TEC) (2007), <http://www.tsunami-evaluation.org>, 8 November.

UN (1991), Strengthening of the Coordination of Humanitarian Assistance of the United Nations, A/RES/46/182, General Assembly.

—— (2000), *Report of the Panel on United Nations Peace Operations* (Brahimi Report), General Assembly and Security Council, New York A/55/305–S/2000/809.

—— (2005), *Report on Integrated Missions: Practical Perspectives and Recommendations*, Independent Study for the Expanded UN ECHA Core Group.

UN Development Group (UNDG)/Executive Committee on Humanitarian Assistance (ECHA) (2004), Report of the UNDG/ECHA Working Group on Transition Issues, New York and Geneva: UN, February, available at: <www.undg.org/docs/6870/3330-UNDG_ECHA_WG_on_Transition_Issues_Report_-2004_Final_Report.doc>.

—— (2006), UNDG-ECHA Workshop on Transition, Workshop Report, March, available at: < http://www.undg.org/?P=586>.

UN Development Programme (UNDP) (2000), *Sharing New Ground in Post-Conflict Situations: The Role of the UNDP in Support of Reintegration Programmes*, New York: UN, available at: <http://www.undp.org/eo/documents/postconflict_march2000.pdf>.

—— (2005), *Post-Disaster Recovery Guidelines*, New York and Geneva: UN, February, available at: <http://www.undp.org/cpr/disred/documents/publications/regions/america/recovery_guidelines_eng.pdf>.

—— (2006), *Evaluation of UNDP Support to Conflict Affected Countries*, New York: UN, available at: <http://www.undp.org/eo/documents/thematic/conflict/ConflictEvaluation2006.pdf>.

—— (2007a), 'Early Recovery', available at: <http://www.undp.org/cpr/we_do/early_recovery.shtml>.

—— (2007b), 'Recovery', available at: <http://www.undp.org/cpr/we_do/_recovery.shtml>.

—— (2008) *Post-Conflict Economic Recovery, Enabling Local Ingenuity*, Conflict Prevention and Recovery Report 2008, New York: Bureau for Crisis Prevention and Recovery (BCPR).

UNDP/UNDG/World Bank (2004), *Practical Guide to Post-Conflict Needs Assessment (PCNA)*.

UNDP (2008), Post-Conflict Economic Recovery, Enabling Local Ingenuity, Conflict Prevention and Recovery Report 2008, New York: Bureau for Crisis Prevention and Recovery (BCPR).

White, P, & Cliffe, L (2000), 'Matching Responses to Context in Complex Political Emergencies: "Relief", "Development", "Peacebuilding" or Something In-between', *Disasters*, Vol 24, No 4, 314–42.

Reparation

Marco Sassòli

Definition

Following damage and/or the violation of a rule, reparation restores the previous situation, either by returning things to their original state or by providing compensation for the damage sustained. In the context of post-conflict peacebuilding, it covers either all transitional justice measures in favour of the victims of previous violations of international humanitarian law or human rights, or, in a more narrow sense, only mass compensation programmes in favour of the victims.

I. Term

Origin

The term 'reparation' is not specific to post-conflict peacebuilding and reconstruction. Rather, it is a general concept dating from the beginning of time and existing in all cultures, which can be found in legal systems and social relations. Indeed, '[i]t is a principle of international law, that the breach of an engagement involves an obligation to make reparation in an adequate form. Reparation therefore is the indispensable complement of a failure to apply a [rule]' (Permanent Court of International Justice, 1927: 21). For traditional internationalist doctrine, responsibility for an unlawful act entails only the obligation to make reparation, whereas the International Law Commission adds the obligation to put an end to the unlawful act (which may also be understood as a kind of restitution) and, in some cases, to offer guarantees of non-repetition of the unlawful act (Draft Articles, 2001: Arts 31–9).

Meanings

In a more limited sense, the concept of reparation (especially when it is used in the plural) also refers to the compensation paid by the loser to the winner of a war. This is justified by the unlawful act of having triggered a war, or, in rare cases, by the commission of war crimes.

Beyond the obligation to make reparation that arises when there is a violation, all legal systems have also established special rules providing for the obligation to repair damages that do not result from a violation (this is referred to as 'responsibility without fault' under domestic law).

In the social sciences, the notion of reparation is sometimes used in a broad sense similar to the definition given under international law and which covers all aspects of transitional justice, perceived from the point of view of the victims. However, the term is usually used more narrowly to refer to mass compensation programmes in favour of victims of gross and systematic violations. Such programmes include material but also symbolic compensation (apologies, monuments, remembrance days), which also derive from the legal concept. The two forms of reparation may be collectively allocated. This is rather convenient in the event of mass violations, but strays from the legal concept of reparation. The difference between the narrow and the broad definition of reparation is said to be the direct benefit brought to the victim under the narrow definition of reparation (De Greiff, 2006: 453). One can nonetheless wonder whether erecting a monument is of more direct benefit to the victim than the conviction of a perpetrator (which results from the broad concept, but would not be part of a reparation programme which falls under the narrow definition).

The various definitions of reparation are used in discussions about peacebuilding. This contribution refers to the broad concept described under international law, which is the legal basis for different transitional justice measures, while placing the emphasis on mass compensation.

II. Content

Sources

Any armed conflict implies (at least for one of the parties) a violation of international or domestic law. Any armed conflict results in violations of international humanitarian law and human rights law. In addition, human rights violations are often at the root of armed conflicts. Thus, peacebuilding is always confronted with the issue of reparation of these violations. These violations are typically widespread and systematic and they affect a large number of victims. It was specifically to cope with such violations that states have adopted an instrument that is not in itself binding (Basic Principles, 2005), but which declares rules that identify mechanisms, modalities, procedures, and methods for implementation of existing legal obligations under either the treaties protecting human rights and codifying international humanitarian law, or under customary international law, particularly with regard to the international responsibility of a state for unlawful acts (see their codification in Draft Articles, 2001: Arts 31–39).

The goals of reparation

The goals of reparation (which may overlap) are the following:

- re-affirming (or acknowledging) the subjective rights of victims and objective law which have been violated;
- deterring future violations;
- preventing the perpetrator from enjoying the fruits of the violation;
- striking a balance between the victim and the perpetrator (by reintegrating both in society);
- helping the victim overcome the distress caused by the violation (this goal goes beyond the narrow definition, since it goes beyond fulfilling a legal right arising from a violation);
- expressing society's solidarity with the victim.

Forms of reparation

Traditionally, the legal obligation is to repair harm in full, that is, both the material damage (or property damage) and the moral damage (or emotional damage) resulting from the violation. Reparation includes restitution, compensation where restitution is not possible, and satisfaction. The priority given to restitution over compensation corresponds to the Latin etymology of the word ('*reparare*': restore, repair, recover). Even if restitution is possible, it must be replaced by compensation if, for the responsible state, the former involves a disproportionate burden compared with the benefit deriving from restitution instead of compensation (Draft Articles, 2001: Art 35b). In the specific context of peacebuilding, reparation, in its broad sense, may take different forms. Whatever the form, attention should be given to a specific gender issue: in many societies, only men are paid compensation or given property rights, thus excluding women from any effective reparation. A particular effort should therefore be made to correct this situation, or at least to compensate the women who have fallen victim to the system.

Restitution

Restitution is usually defined as 'restoring things to their original state' or 'reparation in kind'. It may include 'restoration of liberty, enjoyment of human rights, identity, family life and citizenship, return to one's place of residence, restoration of employment and return of property' (Basic Principles, 2005: No 19). But it may also include rehabilitation, which 'should include medical and psychological care as well as legal and social services' (*ibid*, 2005: No 21). The restitution of real estate is a particularly sensitive issue in post-conflict settings because, though it may repair forced displacement, it can trigger other displacements or at least violate the economic and social rights of the people to whom this real estate was given during the conflict.

Compensation

Compensation is reparation through an equivalent, usually money (Permanent Court of International Justice, 1927: 21), as it is the standard value measuring the usefulness of all things (Grotius, 1646: book II, chapter VII, section XXII). Compensation is calculated by adding the value of restitution in kind to the value of sustained losses (*damnum emergens*) and loss of earnings (*lucrum cessans*)— which must be established—and, when applicable, interest on arrears. However, international law does not recognize compound interest.

Compensation 'should be provided for any economically assessable damage, as appropriate and proportional to the gravity of the violation and the circumstances of each case' (Basic Principles, 2005: No 20). Damage can be either physical or psychological harm, lost opportunities, (including jobs and education), and costs incurred for legal assistance or experts' reports, drugs, health services, psychological care or social support. The Inter-American Court of Human Rights has a sophisticated, elaborate, and generous method of calculating compensation (Carillo, 2006: 510–25). History shows that when the number of victims overwhelms the administrative and financial capacities of the responsible state, gestures offering symbolic satisfaction and reparation that are proportional to current needs often prevail over the concern for (and the feasibility of) assessing material and moral losses. In any event, in the victims' eyes, damage to their lives, health or freedom will never be compensated proportionally to the damage done, whereas proportionality is a traditional requirement of reparation. Thus, it may even be preferable not to mention proportionality as a criterion in mass reparation programmes. While some victims may deem any amount of money insufficient, others may fear that such 'blood' money might cancel the debt of blood and, as a result, may reject all financial reparation.

Satisfaction

Satisfaction repairs immaterial harm. On the one hand, if a state sustains moral damage, it is usually content with the sole fact that the violation is acknowledged or that apologies are made. On the other hand, individuals are usually compensated to repair moral damage. Nevertheless, the jurisprudence of international human rights courts often limits itself to recording violations in order to satisfy individuals. 'Satisfaction should include, where applicable, any or all elements of a whole array of measures' (Basic Principles, 2005: No 22): verification of facts; public and full disclosure of the truth; the search for the disappeared; assistance in recovering, identifying, and reburying the bodies; an official declaration or judicial decision restoring the dignity, reputation, and rights of the victim; public apologies, including acknowledgement and acceptance of responsibility; legal and administrative sanctions against the persons liable for the violations; commemorations and tributes to the victims; and the inclusion of an account of the violations in teaching material.

Guarantees of non-repetition

Guarantees of non-repetition are, like reparation, one of the possible consequences of an internationally wrongful act. The 'Basic Principles' offer a wide
range of legal, judicial, administrative and social measures meant to prevent any
future violation.

The impact on peacebuilding

Compared with all other measures of transitional justice, reparation, in its narrow meaning, benefits individual victims in a more direct and visible way. It is
also tangible evidence that truth, justice, regret, and change are not just wishful
thinking or empty promises. The difficulty is to prevent victims from taking on
a passive role as beneficiaries instead of being pro-active in economic recovery.
Reparation (in the narrow sense) should consist in a real expiatory apology and
not just amount to an easy attempt at covering up crimes committed.

Reparation (in the broad sense) prevents revenge and fosters reconciliation.
It breaks the vicious circle of hatred, which is often the underlying cause of the
next conflict. However, it inevitably reopens past wounds, including those of the
victims. When either those who are supposed to be its beneficiaries, or those who
must finance it, perceive reparation as being unfair it may even contribute to
creating new tensions and conflicts. For the sake of those who are to finance
reparation, the process should go hand in hand with an educational account of
historical facts.

Mass compensation programmes unavoidably face:

difficult questions [including] who to include among the victims to compensate, how
much compensation is to be rewarded, what kinds of harm are to be covered, how harm
is to be quantified, how different kinds of harm are to be compared and compensated and
how compensation is to be distributed (UN, 2004: 24).

In practice, they also have to deal with the reality that: often victims are unable
to put forward sufficient evidence; frequently there are difficulties in identifying
victims and perpetrators; some crimes belong to the distant past; and that there
is a temptation to grant special favours to certain (famous) people or categories of
victims who are important stakeholders in the peacebuilding process, to the detriment of the anonymous masses (Bufford & van der Merwe, 2004: 286, 304).

III. Implementation

The obligation to make reparations

Traditionally, under international law, it is the state that has to make reparation,
because legally it was the state that violated the rules it was supposed to respect

(though in reality those rules have been violated by persons whose conduct is attributed to the state). International law rarely obliges individuals to provide reparation for a violation. Yet, according to international institutions implementing human rights, the obligation imposed on states to guarantee the respect of human rights instruments implies that the state shall provide for remedy and reparation to the victims of human rights abuses against the perpetrators of violations even when they cannot be imputed to the state. In all other cases, the obligation of an individual to make reparation is based on the applicable domestic law, which may refer to international law in its definition of unlawful acts.

The right to reparation

Under international law, it is usually the state injured by a violation that has the right to reparation. International law refers to 'diplomatic protection' for the damage sustained by nationals in foreign countries. This right is based on damage sustained by an individual, but from a legal point of view, it is the individual's country of origin that is injured. Article 3 of the 1907 Hague Convention IV as well as Article 91 of the 1977 Additional Protocol I to the Geneva Conventions state that a country violating these instruments 'shall, if the case demands, be liable to pay compensation'. According to a majority of writers and court decisions, these provisions should be understood in the light of the traditional inter-state context mentioned above.

Of course, this traditional implementation structure does not correspond to the context of internal armed conflicts or human rights violations, as in such cases victims of violations are often nationals of the responsible state. Thus, for a growing number of violations, international law requires that the state makes reparation for these violations directly to the beneficiary of the rule. For example, many human rights instruments confer on victims a right to domestic and international remedies if their rights under these instruments are violated. The state must then ensure the victims receive reparation for the acts or omissions attributable to the state itself. International human rights bodies finding violations may require or recommend the responsible state to pay compensation to the victims of those violations.

Legal limits to the possibility of waiving one's right to reparation

From a legal point of view, the right to reparation may be waived by its holder, though often states have also waived the rights of their nationals against other states and their nationals in bilateral treaties. Given that, when protecting its nationals, a state is exercising its own rights (according to the mechanism of diplomatic protection), such a waiver is valid (while individuals may not waive the state's obligation to protect them diplomatically). Waiving this right may even lead to the waiving state having to ensure that, in its domestic legal system, individuals may not bring claims which the state itself has already waived. However, it is possible for a state to become liable under its own domestic law to provide reparation for the harm caused to its nationals if it has chosen to waive their claims against another state or its nationals. Such liability could be based on human rights, such as the right to an effective remedy, the right to property, and the right to be heard by a tribunal which shall decide on civil rights and obligations.

A state may not waive reparation for the future violation of a peremptory norm (*jus cogens*), given that it cannot consent to the violation. However, after World War II, the common practice was for states to waive reparation for armed aggression and violations of fundamental human rights norms and international humanitarian law after a violation had occurred and the claim had arisen. And yet Articles 51, 52, 131, and 148 respectively of the first, second, third, and fourth 1949 Geneva Conventions state the following:

No High Contracting Party shall be allowed to absolve itself or any other High Contracting Party of any liability incurred by itself or by another High Contracting Party in respect of [grave] breaches [to the Conventions].

According to this text and the interpretation given by the ICRC, this excludes waiving reparation for grave breaches (Pictet, 1958: 603). According to the preparatory work, these provisions may have been intended only to exclude the possibility of war criminals being exempted from criminal liability (and states of their obligation to prosecute) in cases where the states had waived reparation (D'Argent, 2003: 771–4).

Statutory limitations

Like Anglo-Saxon legal systems, public international law does not recognize negative prescription resulting from sheer lapse of time. However, inaction may sometimes be considered as relinquishing one's right to reparation. As to individuals' claims to reparation based on domestic legal systems that have statutory limitations, some domestic courts have held that, for civil lawsuits regarding international crimes that are not subject to statutory limitations under conventional or customary law, such time limits will also not apply in domestic law.

Proceedings

A claim for reparation between two states may be brought through diplomatic channels, using either an existing international tribunal or an arbitral tribunal set up specifically to deal with a great number of claims resulting from a single event. In the latter case, victims may take part in the proceedings, sometimes even in their own names. Interstate negotiations often lead to an arrangement whereby the liable state pays out a lump sum to the state to which the victims belong. The money is then distributed by the country of origin to the persons concerned, in proportion to the material and moral damage sustained, using an ad hoc quasi-judicial process.

A state may claim reparation at the international level in favour of its nationals, or individuals may make claims at the international level on the basis of their human rights, only after they have exhausted domestic remedies within the responsible state. The exception is where such remedies are non-existent or ineffective.

There are different types of proceedings. On the one hand, there are diplomatic, legal, or administrative proceedings against a responsible state. On the other hand, there are legal proceedings against liable individuals. Administrative and legal proceedings may take place before different authorities, at the domestic level (in the responsible state; in the state where the liable individual or the victim is located; or in a third state), at the interstate level, or at the international level. They can also be brought before existing ordinary courts, or before special courts established to grant reparation in a given post-conflict situation.

At the international level, ordinary courts include the International Court of Justice for interstate proceedings and international human rights bodies for individual claims against a state. International law does not recognize individual plaintiffs' claims for damages in criminal proceedings, unlike the concept of 'partie civile' from the Roman-Germanic legal systems, which would allow victims to have their claims to reparation judged in a criminal proceeding against the defendant. The International Criminal Court (ICC) must nonetheless 'establish principles relating to reparations to, or in respect of, victims including restitution, compensation and rehabilitation.' It can issue a binding order making it compulsory for a convicted person to make reparations to a victim (Art 75, Rome Statute of the ICC). In September 2002, the Assembly of States Parties set up a Trust Fund in favour of victims, in accordance with Article 79 of the Rome Statute.

At the national level, a claim against a state must be brought before its tribunals or its administration. The normal means of claiming reparation from an individual is through a civil lawsuit before a civil court. In Roman-Germanic judicial systems, the criminal tribunal that tries the perpetrator of an infraction may also judge the victim's civil claims. Courts in third countries do not necessarily have jurisdiction over civil lawsuits brought before them. Unlike criminal law, under which the principle of universal jurisdiction is applicable to international crimes, private law is still not governed by such a principle. The United States (US) has enacted a law (Alien Tort Claims Act), which enables foreigners who are not located on US territory to sue other foreigners for reparation in cases of violations of customary international law.

In addition, lawsuits against a responsible state or individual brought before the courts of a third country may also face the problem of potential international immunities. Jurisprudence is not unanimous as to whether such immunities also apply to international crimes.

Obviously, proceedings that have been specially created are better adapted to deal with mass reparation in post-conflict situations. Such proceedings may take place before a national, mixed, or international judicial body. The UN Compensation Commission is an example of such an international body: it received 2.7 million claims amounting to US$500 billion, and paid more than US$18 billion to victims of the Iraqi invasion of Kuwait. It also found innovative solutions which broke from traditional international law criteria. Thus Iraq, which was liable, only had a limited right to be heard. For the category with the greatest number of victims, standard compensation scales were used. Computerized processing of the claims involved the use of statistical models; computer-based crosschecks were made between claims and independent sources; claims were brought together under broad categories; and verification of the cogency of only some claims was limited to cases that were typical of an entire category. In Bosnia and Herzegovina, even the restitution of houses and apartments to their pre-conflict owners or beneficiaries required long, painstaking work by a commission distinguished by a strong commitment from the international community.

Local proceedings are sometimes established by occupying powers to enable the people living in an occupied territory to lay claims for damage sustained because of the occupying forces, eg in the Allied occupation zones in Germany (Freeman, 1955: 375–89).

After World War II, Germany set up different procedures by means of which pre-determined amounts of money were given to victims of the Nazi regime, especially those of the Holocaust/Shoah. These procedures dealt with individual claims, but it was sufficient for the victims to present their claims in a plausible way. In some countries moving towards democracy, reconciliation and truth commissions have also distributed lump-sum compensations to the victims of previous regimes (Chile, Peru) or advised the new authorities to do so (eg South Africa and, to a lesser extent, Malawi).

Of course, there have been unilateral or *ex gratia* agreements or gestures providing for payment of compensation without any acknowledgement of either a legal obligation or any subsequent violations. Such agreements often require that the victim waive all future claims. They do not meet all the aims of reparation, especially that of recognizing that a right has been violated. However, they do spare victims long and costly proceedings, the outcome of which is never guaranteed.

Finally, in some cases, partial compensation or benefits, according to need, are paid by the state to which the victim belongs under social legislation, the sharing of expenses, or social insurance schemes.

Implementation difficulties

When it comes to making reparation for mass violations, the ideal of full reparation of the harm done—the aim of the legal concept of reparation—is never quite achieved. Some even go so far as to think that, in such cases, full compensation for each individual case is not appropriate and does not even correspond to the requirements of justice. In all legal systems the concept of reparation presupposes that violation is exceptional. Therefore, there is an argument that this concept of reparation cannot be applied when violation has become the rule. Dealing with claims on a case-by-case basis in legal proceedings can lead to even more injustice (lack of access to courts; difficulties in gathering evidence; more substantial reparation for affluent victims; the impossibility of achieving a global perspective on historical events). In addition, when there have been mass violations, reparation—in the narrow sense—must always be a political project involving the entire society concerned and which aims at recognition (of individuals, their rights, the facts, the harm done), restoration of mutual confidence and confidence in the judiciary and political system, and social solidarity (De Greiff, 2006: 454–66).

The broad definition of reparation nonetheless influences the solutions adopted in the framework of mass compensation programmes and the complementary measures of transitional justice. Yet, there is a great discrepancy between the reparation provided for by public international law and as laid out in the 'Basic Principles' for cases of mass violations, and the way reparation is practiced in peacebuilding situations. Often, no compensation at all is paid (Haiti, El Salvador). Even when compensation programmes exist, the procedures in which the compensation is adjudicated, the ways of calculating the compensation, the narrow definitions of those violations giving rise to compensation, and the frequent practice of linking compensation to need or suffering rather than to the violation committed, stray far from what international and domestic law prescribe for isolated violations. This leads many to think that such mass compensation is governed by principles that differ from those for isolated violations under public international law. It is very difficult to distil principles of international law or even best practices given the widely differing practices so influenced by non-legal factors specific to each context (the financial resources available; the historical distance of events; the political importance of victims; the existence of and links to other measures of transitional justice; and the economic and social situation of the victims and the society in which they live) (Falk, 2006: 485).

In international discourse, and to a lesser extent in reality, the trend is clearly moving toward reparation in peacebuilding situations. The main challenges this trend faces are: the lack of political will of national governing authorities; the fact that institutions are often inherited from a previous regime that was responsible for past abuses; and the likelihood that authorities may have other priorities oriented towards the needs of the majority of the population who will not benefit from reparation. Any reparation programme (in the narrow sense of the term) implies arbitration between the demands of sustainable development and coming to terms with the past. Such arbitration should be left principally to the national governing authorities, especially following internal conflicts, as long as these new authorities represent the victims as much as the perpetrators.

In addition, given that post-conflict situations are often characterized by great economic and humanitarian hardship for the entire population, the aim is to avoid escalating tension between the victims seeking reparation and the rest of the population experiencing the same economic and social problems.

Financial hardship is often used as an excuse. However, since international law does not recognize state bankruptcy, compensation may have to be paid by a generation of taxpayers that was not even born at the time the violation occurred.

Reparation for the victims of the Holocaust/Shoah has also proven that, for the great crimes in history, even a country as developed as Germany was not financially able to cope with the full compensation for the material harm resulting from such crimes. For other important crimes in history, financial claims (linked, for example, to the transatlantic trafficking of slaves and colonial rule) stem first and foremost from a need for political recognition expressed by given communities or states. These claims also raise a number of other issues, such as tracing the victims and identifying responsibilities, when time has erased direct traces of the crimes.

After World War I, Germany's situation revealed the negative consequences that reparations can have, not only on the country's economy, but also on the international financial system and the resurgence of armed conflicts more generally. In a similar way, reparations by Iraq through the UN Compensation Commission, financed through the 'oil-for-food' programme, have shown that reparations may have catastrophic humanitarian consequences for innocent people.

Selected Bibliography

Appiah, KA (2004), 'Comprendre les réparations, une réflexion préliminaire', *Cahiers d'études africaines*, 173–4: 25–40.
Bufford, W, & Van der Merwe, H (2004), 'Les réparations en Afrique australe', *Cahiers d'études africaines*, 173–4: 263–322.
Carillo, AJ (2006), 'Justice in Context: The Relevance of Inter-American Human Rights Law and Practice to Repairing the Past', in De Greiff, P (ed), *The Handbook of Reparations*, Oxford: Oxford University Press, 510–25.
D'Argent, P (2003), *Les réparations de guerre en droit international public*, Brussels: Bruylant.
De Feyter, K, Parmentier, S, Bossuyt, M, & Lemmen, P (eds) (2005), *Out of the Ashes, Reparations for Victims of Gross and Systematic Human Rights Violations*, Antwerpen: Intersentia.
De Greiff, P (ed) (2006), *The Handbook of Reparations*, Oxford: Oxford University Press.
Falk, R (2006), 'Reparations, International Law and Global Justice', in De Greiff (ed), *The Handbook of Reparations*, Oxford: Oxford University Press, 478–504.

Freeman, AW (1955), 'Responsibility of States for Unlawful Acts of their Armed Forces', in *Collected Courses of the Hague Academy of International Law*, vol 88, 1955-II, 267–415.

Gotius, H (1646), *De jure belli ac pacis. Libri tres, in Quibus Jus Naturae et Gentium*, Amsterdam: Johannes Blaev.

Hague Convention (1907), Convention IV concerning the laws and customs of war on land, Art 3.

Holtzmann, HM, & Kristjánsdóttir, E (eds) (2007), *International Mass Claims Processes, Legal and Practical Perspectives*, Oxford: Oxford University Press.

Jewsiewicki, B (2004), 'Héritages et réparations en quête d'une justice pour le passé ou le present', *Cahiers d'études africaines*, 173–4: 7–24.

Miller, J, & Kumar, R (eds) (2007), *Reparations, Interdisciplinary Enquiries*, Oxford: Oxford University Press.

Permanent Court of International Justice (1927), *Factory of Chorzów, Jurisdiction*, PCIJ, Series A, no 9.

Pictet, J (ed) (1958), *Commentary, Geneva Convention IV*, Geneva: ICRC, 645–6.

Stover, E, & Weinstein, HM (eds) (2004), *My Neighbour, My Enemy, Justice and Community in the Aftermath of Mass Atrocity*, Cambridge: Cambridge University Press.

UN (2001), *UN International Law Commission's Articles on Responsibility of States for Internationally Wrongful Acts*, A/RES//56/83, General Assembly, 12 December.

—— (2004), *Report of the Secretary General on The Rule of Law and Transitional Justice in Conflict and Post Conflict Societies*, S/2004/616, 23 August 2004.

—— (2005), *Basic Principles and Guidelines on the Right to a Remedy and Reparation for Victims of Gross Violations of International Human Rights Law and Serious Violations of International Humanitarian Law*, A/RES/60/147, General Assembly, 16 December.

Responsibility to Protect

Daniel Warner and Gilles Giacca

Definition

Sovereignty implies responsibility; accordingly, each state has the primary responsibility to protect its own population. When the state is unable or unwilling to carry out this fundamental obligation, the international community has the responsibility to respond, in full respect of the principles of the UN Charter and international law. As an umbrella concept, the responsibility to protect incorporates three distinct and interrelated dimensions: (1) the responsibility to prevent gross abuses of human rights; (2) the responsibility to react; and (3) the responsibility to rebuild, which entails comprehensive assistance with recovery, reconstruction, and reconciliation, as well as to address the causes of the harm that intervention sought to halt or avert.

I. Term

Origin and context

The concept of the responsibility to protect is a key element in any discussion of crises that entail massive violations of human rights. It is essential in the overall theme of human security because, rather than letting individual states be solely responsible for the well-being of their populations, the responsibility to protect introduces the notion that outsiders may be involved in protecting individuals or groups when a state fails, or is unwilling, to protect its population.

With more and more conflicts being intra-state, and internal violence persistently perpetrated on a massive scale, the importance of protecting populations within international borders has become crucial. This can be seen in prevention, during conflicts, and also in post-conflict peacebuilding where ensuring the human security of civilian populations is often beyond local capacities. This idea of duties beyond borders is closely associated with Western liberalism in the form of 'humanitarian intervention'. The term 'responsibility to protect' (R2P or RtoP, as it is commonly abbreviated) derives from, and is closely linked to, various policy and conceptual debates arising from the doctrine of humanitarian intervention developed in the course of past centuries.

From the perspective of international law, the concept of humanitarian intervention encompasses any unilateral use of armed force by a state (or a group of states) against another for the purpose of protecting the life and freedom of citizens of the latter state unwilling or unable to carry out this function (Beyerlin, 2003: 926–8). This has to be distinguished from an intervention by a state to protect its own nationals in another state. Thus, humanitarian intervention concept generally refers to three essential features. First, the term 'intervention' stipulates a high degree of coercion, which entails the use of military force. Second, it refers to a form of interference that takes place without the consent of the state in which intervention occurs. And third, the term 'humanitarian' highlights the aim of preventing or stopping widespread and grave violations of the fundamental human rights of the civilian population.

The concept dates back to the Middle Ages, and the founding fathers of international law. Samuel Pufendorf, Hugo Grotius or Emer de Vattel have referred to a natural right to resort to arms against the tyranny of the sovereign by neighbouring states. Grotius supported in *De jure belli ac pacis* (1625) legitimacy for resort to war to prevent or end acts of violence by a state against its own subjects. In the words of Hersch Lauterpacht, this is considered 'the first authoritative statement of the principle of humanitarian intervention—the principle that the exclusiveness of domestic jurisdiction stops where outrage upon humanity begins' (Lauterpacht, 1946: 46).

The issue gained prominence in the nineteenth century with what is referred to as *intervention d'humanité*, exercised as part of foreign policy of European countries as a measure of control over the internal affairs of the Ottoman Empire. Designed to further the political and diplomatic interests of the intervening powers, it was allegedly a means to guarantee a minimum standard of protection to citizens—especially religious minorities—under Turkish jurisdiction (Stowell, 1921: 51–62).

During the 20th century, and especially since the adoption of the UN Charter in 1945, the legal and political system of international relations has been built around, and still preserves many constraints imposed by, the classical concept of state sovereignty inherited from the Treaties of Westphalia of 1648. Article 2(1) of the Charter accordingly affirms the sovereign equality of all member states and Article 2(7) restates the principle of non-interference in matters within a state's jurisdiction, which binds organs of the UN and which is also applicable in interstate relations (see also UN General Assembly Resolutions 2131 and 2625).

However this framework has not impeded, especially in the 1970s, several regional powers from intervening abroad allegedly on the basis of humanitarian imperatives, notably the intervention of India in East Pakistan (1971), of Vietnam in Kampuchea (1978), and of Tanzania in Uganda (1979). In the 1980s, the concept of *droit d'ingérence* ('duty to intervene' or a 'right of intervention')—coined by Professor Mario Bettati and Bernard Kouchner—relaunched the debate by proposing a duty to restrict the traditional concept of sovereignty for the purpose of providing humanitarian assistance even without the state's consent (Bettati and Kouchner, 1987). Subsequently, various humanitarian catastrophes, including the chemical bombings and gassing of the Iraqi Kurds by Saddam Hussein, Somalia, Rwanda, the former Yugoslavia, especially the massacre at Srebrenica and the intervention of the North Atlantic Treaty Organization (NATO) in Kosovo, and East Timor, fuelled the debate between advocates and opponents of a 'right' to humanitarian intervention and the limits of state sovereignty.

This has led certain authors, such as Francis Deng, to reflect on how the notion of sovereignty could evolve. In light of various humanitarian crises in the 1990s in Africa, he developed the concept of sovereignty as responsibility. Deng challenged the legal and moral authority of sovereignty, arguing that a 'government that allows its citizens to suffer a vacuum of responsibility for moral leadership cannot claim sovereignty in an effort to keep the outside world from stepping in to offer protection and assistance' (Deng, 1996: 33).

This evolving notion of state sovereignty has been witnessed in other fora and especially within the UN. Several Secretaries-General have also intervened publicly in the growing debate. In 1991, Pérez de Cuéllar declared that there was an 'irresistible shift in public attitude towards a belief that the defence of the oppressed in the name of morality should probably prevail over frontiers and legal documents' (de Cuéllar, 1991: para 11). In the late 1990s, Kofi Annan set member states the challenge of finding a consensus around when and how humanitarian intervention might be acceptable in the current political environment (Annan, 1999: 50). In response to Annan's challenge, the Government of Canada, with a group of major foundations, established the International Commission on Intervention and State Sovereignty (ICISS or Evans-Sahnoun Commission). The concept of R2P was *formally* established by the report of the Commission which appeared in December 2001 (ICISS, 2001).

After its appearance in the ICISS, the concept of R2P was dealt with in three major UN documents, which represent the conceptual and political foundation of the concept. First, the Secretary-General's *High Level Panel on Threats, Challenges and Change* endorsed the concept in the report entitled 'A More Secure World: Our Shared Responsibility' at the end of 2004 (paras 201–9). Second, this theme was included in Kofi Annan's subsequent report *In Larger Freedom* in the section that addressed the 'freedom to live in dignity' (para 135). And third, by 2005, the heads of state and government at the General Assembly's World Summit—convened to address the possible reform of the UN—took a major step forward by endorsing the principle of a responsibility to protect, which thereby gained unprecedented political weight (UN General Assembly, 2005: para 138).

Official definition

As a basic principle, state sovereignty implies responsibility. The term 'responsibility' refers in its traditional liberal understanding to a charge, or a duty for which one is responsible, suggesting an authority or control over an object. The term 'to protect' is largely understood in international law as referring to the fundamental responsibility of the state to protect the population under its jurisdiction from egregious crimes and violations, a notion rooted in the relevant instruments of human rights law, criminal law, and humanitarian law, in both conventional and customary law.

Since this concept is relatively new, it is not surprising that no single, coherent understanding of its scope exists, given the variety of articulations of R2P as it is framed in the four major documents. Nevertheless, the R2P concept has enjoyed resonance among many governments as well as international and nongovernmental organizations, with widespread agreement coalescing around a number of key elements.

One definition is offered by the UN Terminology Database, which describes R2P as follows:

[A]n evolving concept about the duties of governments to prevent and end unconscionable acts of violence against the people of the world. Aims to provide a legal and ethical basis for humanitarian intervention. Responsibility to protect populations from genocide, ethnic cleansing, war crimes and crimes against humanity is an international commitment by governments to prevent and react to grave crises. The idea is that if a particular State were unwilling or unable to carry out its responsibility to prevent abuses, the responsibility would have to be transferred to the international community, which would then solve problems primarily via peaceful means (such as diplomatic pressure, dialogue, sanctions) or, as a last resort, through the use of military force (<http://unterm.un.org/>).

However, this definition does not fully encapsulate the core of the R2P as it is framed in the four major documents referred to above. Emphasis should be placed first and foremost on the principle that the state is the primary subject of responsibility. States individually are responsible to protect their citizens from genocide, war crimes, ethnic cleansing, and crimes against humanity, and their efforts should be complemented by the commitment of the collective international community to assist states in meeting these duties (Luck, 2008: 2).

This change in conceptual vocabulary from a right and possible duty of humanitarian intervention to a 'responsibility to protect' is significant. The conceptual foundation of the principle appears to have a far broader and more pragmatic notion than mere military intervention. In this sense, there is less focus on the role of state sovereignty and on the traditional debate between non-interference and intervention, and more on the state's responsibility to aid victims, namely a conceptual shift from control to responsibility.

As set out in the ICISS Report (XI), the R2P concept is, at its core, a system of shared responsibility. Thus, in the case where the state is manifestly unable or unwilling to avert serious harm to its population, the international community shares a collective responsibility to respond, fully respecting the principles of the UN Charter and international law (Luck, 2008: 2).

The other key element of the concept is its umbrella nature. The responsibility to protect involves a broad approach to humanitarian crises and uses a variety of tools of a non-coercive nature, including prevention, reaction, capacity-building, and rebuilding. (ICISS XI).

II. Content

Core components

Sovereignty as responsibility to protect the population from four egregious crimes

Since the signing of the UN Charter, there have been an increasing number of state obligations in the field of human rights and an expanding notion of the rights of individuals and groups. In such a context the R2P concept can be understood as part of the broader shift from sovereignty as a right of exclusivity, to sovereignty as responsibility (Thakur, 2002: 256). It is argued that it forms part of the evolution from an interstate, international system, to a global system based on human rights and human security, where states are 'instruments at the service of their people, and not vice versa' (Annan, 1999: 50).

In this way, the scope of protection has been limited to the four international crimes, namely genocide, war crimes, ethnic cleansing, and crimes against humanity (see the chapter on international crimes). These threats represent a narrow set of circumstances that can trigger the R2P, as established in the World Summit Outcome Document (para 138). Thus, the concept *per se* does not cover broader threats to development and the related rights to food, health, education, or gender equality; it does not deal with climate change and environmental degradation; nor does it cover pandemics such as HIV/AIDs or the effects of natural disasters (Evans, 2007).

The prevention-reaction-rebuilding continuum

The notion of a continuum of responsibility before, during, and after violent attacks on the vulnerable is inherent to the concept of R2P. Effective protection is inextricably linked to the responsibility to prevent, which remains, for obvious reasons, the most important feature of the concept. Thus, states included the following sentence in the Outcome Document:

We also intend to commit ourselves, as necessary and appropriate, to helping States build capacity to protect their populations from genocide, war crimes, ethnic cleansing and crimes against humanity and to assisting those which are under stress before crises and conflicts break out (para 139).

Prevention can take various forms, through early warning strategies of development assistance, efforts to provide support for local initiatives to catalyze democratic governance, to the promotion of human rights and the rule of law, and mediation to promote dialogue and reconciliation with the ultimate aim of addressing the root causes of potential conflict (ICISS, para 3.3).

A clear strategy for post-conflict peacebuilding is crucial in order to realize the benefits of intervention, which is defined by Roland Paris as 'longer-lasting and ultimately more intrusive forms of intervention in the domestic affairs of these states' (Paris, 2004: ix). This approach clearly entails a coordinated response of international organizations, non-governmental, and regional and sub-regional actors, civil society, and the private sector. However, the use of the R2P concept by states and decision-makers specific to the realities of a post-conflict peacebuilding agenda lacks clarity, a reality reflected in the academic literature.

Principles governing the use of force

Bearing in mind the political sensitivity that military intervention can entail, the ICISS, followed by the High-Level Panel (paras 204–9) and Kofi Annan's report (paras 122–6) have all addressed—with the notable exception of the Outcome Document—the question of principles governing the use of force in case of exhaustion of all non-coercive means to protect the vulnerable from being the subject of atrocities on a massive scale.

Two questions immediately arise: first, who determines that a state is unable or unwilling to carry out the function of protecting its populations; and second, who has the right to intervene? The international system is based on rules of legitimacy founded on the sovereignty of individual states. To say that individuals or groups within a state are threatened is to call into question the legitimacy of a particular state. Beyond this ongoing dilemma, a framework within which military action could possibly take place has been identified, following the recommendation of the Kosovo report (2000). This framework for humanitarian intervention has to bridge the gap between legality and legitimacy in a way that can guide future responses to imminent humanitarian catastrophes. Included are six principles (described below), derived in part from the 'just war' doctrine, each of which has to be satisfied. The first requirement is the 'right authority' which is designed around the notion of *legality* in light of the present system of collective security. The other principles are built upon the notion of *legitimacy:* the 'just cause' threshold and with special emphasis upon proportionality, reasonable prospects of success, and that the measures taken are as a last resort.

Emphasis should be put on the 'just cause threshold', which aims to reconcile state sovereignty with the imperative requirement of protection in a legitimate manner. As the ICISS recognized, a certain, high threshold of human suffering must be crossed, understood as a threat to international peace and security, since military intervention is an extraordinary measure:

A. large scale loss of life, actual or apprehended, with genocidal intent or not, which is the product either of deliberate state action, or state neglect or inability to act, or a failed state situation; or

B. large scale 'ethnic cleansing', actual or apprehended, whether carried out by killing, forced expulsion, acts of terror or rape (ICISS: 32).

The four precautionary principles can be summarized as follows:

A. Right intention: The primary purpose of the intervention, whatever other motives intervening states may have, must be to halt or avert human suffering. Right intention is better assured with multilateral operations, clearly supported by regional opinion and the victims concerned.

B. Last resort: Military intervention can only be justified when every non-military option for the prevention or peaceful resolution of the crisis has been explored, with reasonable grounds for believing lesser measures would not have succeeded.

C. Proportional means: The scale, duration and intensity of the planned military intervention should be the minimum necessary to secure the defined human protection objective.

D. Reasonable prospects: There must be a reasonable chance of success in halting or averting the suffering which has justified the intervention, with the consequences of action not likely to be worse than the consequences of inaction (ICISS: xii).

The thorny issues of who is to intervene, whether an intervention should occur, and under what circumstances this may take place without the Security Council's approval, remains unresolved. The potential impasse for interventions not authorized under the UN Charter was not directly tackled by any of the four documents. The ICISS does at least attempt, under the heading 'the implications of inaction', to raise the fundamental dilemma: 'It is a real question in these circumstances where lies the most harm: in the damage to international order if the Security Council is bypassed or in the damage to that order if human beings are slaughtered while the Security Council stands by' (ICISS: para 6.37).

Actors

In a broad understanding of the scope of R2P, there is inevitably a wide variety of competitive and complementary national, regional, and international actors. Here, the main actors are highlighted.

First and foremost, the domestic authorities of the state at the centre of the actual or potential mass human rights abuses are the primary subject of responsibility. As Cohen and Deng have noted: 'Since there is no adequate replacement in sight for the system of state sovereignty, primary responsibility for promoting the security, welfare, and liberty of populations must remain with the state' (Cohen and Deng, 1998: 275).

As discussed above, the subsidiary or residual role falls upon the international community to intervene when any given state is clearly unwilling or unable to fulfil its R2P. Although there is no precise meaning of 'international community', it could be defined alternatively in a narrow sense by the community of 'states'. As an expanded notion, international community in this context could include a range of actors whose actions influence and articulate the notion of R2P, from intergovernmental organizations, national and international non-governmental organizations (NGOs), the private sector, to an individual. Nonetheless, in this kaleidoscope of actors and activities the UN and the Security Council remain the legitimate authority for any potential role in this integrated approach based on the current system of collective security.

A notable instance occurred in 2006, when the UN Security Council in its country-specific Resolution 1706 (31 August 2006) applied the R2P principle to a particular crisis for the first time, calling for the deployment of UN peacekeepers to Darfur. '*Recalling* also its previous resolutions [...] and 1674 (2006) on the protection of civilians in armed conflict, which reaffirms inter alia the provisions of paragraphs 138 and 139 of the 2005 United Nations World Summit outcome document...' Despite the many difficulties witnessed in the implementation of this peace operation, it at least constitutes an attempt to intervene to maintain peace and security (Art 24, UN Charter).

With regard to the current system of collective security, the ICISS stated that 'the task is not to find alternatives to the Security Council as a source of authority but to make the Council work better than it has' (ICISS: para 6.14). However, in cases where the Security Council is at a stalemate, the General Assembly is legally able to call an Emergency Special Session to recommend possible enforcement measures (Resolution 377 (V) Uniting for Peace, 3 November 1950). Under Chapter IV of the UN Charter, the General Assembly has the legitimacy to discuss and make recommendations to the member states and the Security Council on matters including international peace and security, except when the issue in question is before the Security Council.

In addition to the UN, regional and sub-regional organizations can play a crucial role in implementing the R2P. In particular, the African Union's emerging peace and security framework is becoming an important regional tool for conflict prevention, management, and resolution. Although the African Union's Constitutive Act and the Protocol Relating to the Establishment of the Peace and Security Council (adopted at the Durban Summit in 2002) embrace the respect of sovereignty and the principle of non-intervention in domestic affairs, they build on the notion of a 'conditional sovereignty' which depends on the state's capacity or willingness to provide protection to its population.

Moreover, Article 4(h) of the Constitutive Act declares that the Union has 'the right to intervene in a Member State pursuant to a decision of the Assembly in respect of grave circumstances: namely war crimes, genocide and crimes against humanity'. The primary body charged with implementing this regional security system is the Peace and Security Council, which has the mandate to perform a variety of peace and security functions such as anticipating and preventing conflicts; promoting and implementing peacebuilding and post-conflict reconstruction; and promoting and encouraging democratic governance and the rule of law, through the protection of human rights and fundamental freedoms and international humanitarian law (Art 3, African Union Peace and Security Council Protocol; see also Art 14). This clearly sets out the responsibility to intervene in the internal affairs of a member state through military force if necessary, and represents the first international treaty to contain such an express legal responsibility.

Challenges and dilemmas

A vast body of academic literature has generated a broad spectrum of views on the concept of R2P: 'a duty of care', 'a moral perspective', 'a slippery concept', 'an emerging norm', 'a Trojan horse', 'a political rhetoric', 'an impossible mandate', 'old wine in new bottles', 'the limits of imagination', or the 'schizophrenia of R2P'. These are only a few of the opinions it has engendered since its formal conceptualization in 2001. Although there has been a growing interest in R2P, which witnessed an extraordinary effort on the part of many international actors and culminated in the political commitment of the Outcome Document of the 2005 World Summit, the concept still raises legitimate questions about its sustainability and operational application.

Irrespective of the conceptual change undertaken in the past years toward a 'human-being-oriented approach' to sovereignty, doubts over the practical application of R2P are based on two perennial facts. First, such a doctrine will not eliminate the setbacks, inconsistencies, and hypocrisies that come with practical decision-making driven by specific states' interests. Second, the present system of collective security based on the 1945 UN Charter still presents potential cases where the Council will be unable to achieve consensus to avert an immediate and overwhelming humanitarian crisis. Although the discourse has shifted from intervention to responsibility, reliance on state sovereignty continues to be more powerful than on human rights.

Interestingly, the ICISS, followed by the High-level Panel, referred to R2P as an 'emerging norm' of a collective responsibility to protect (para. 203), which was subsequently endorsed by the former UN Secretary-General Kofi Annan's report, *In Larger Freedom* (para 135). This led to a long debate between those who defend the R2P as an emerging norm (Arbour, 2008) and those who insist on the political nature of such a concept, devoid of any international obligation to act in the present state of international law (Alvarez, 2007).

On this question, many states, including the United States (US), clearly objected to any language at the World Summit that would imply any sort of legal obligation on the international community or the Security Council to act under Chapter VII. The US Ambassador to the UN, John Bolton, stated that the

US would 'not accept that either the United Nations as a whole, or the Security Council, or individual states, have an obligation to intervene under international law' (2005: 2). Thus, although there are well developed international legal aspects on which the concept builds (ie the Convention on the Prevention and Punishment of the Crime of Genocide and the Rome Statute of the International Criminal Court), it would be far too premature to refer to a crystallizing practice that would generate—under the classical sources of international law—a legal obligation (Stahn, 2007: 110–1). The R2P cannot *per se* deal with all the difficulties present in the actual state of international law, such as the liability for international organizations and their organs for failing to act (Alvarez, 2007: 11). R2P appears to remain at the level of 'soft law' and probably because of its nature; it has gathered a solemn, but rather fragile, moral commitment to reshape the debate over the limits of sovereignty. Further efforts to develop a solid legal framework and to elaborate its operational application will be needed in order to find wider endorsement.

The use of humanitarian intervention by certain policy makers to justify the 2003 invasion of Iraq as entailing a duty to protect people from tyrannical rule, after weapons of mass destruction were not found, is relevant. (Teson, 2005: 3). According to the criteria and principles, it is hard to believe there was *per se* any humanitarian justification for invading Iraq, especially when the human rights arguments has been put forward were an *ex post facto* explanation for 'regime change'. Pessimistically, on the use of humanitarian language, Kenneth Roth stated 'it will be more difficult next time for us to call on military action when we need it to save potentially hundreds of thousands of lives' (Roth, 2004: 2–3).

The recent controversy over whether R2P should apply to natural disasters such as Cyclone Nargis is helpful inasmuch as it highlights a typical example of the misconception on the interpretation and application of the concept (although R2P may nonetheless have contributed to raising global awareness to act). The cyclone created a broad humanitarian catastrophe in Myanmar, which needed international support due to the lack or inadequacy of its resources and domestic capacities. In that context, the government used sovereignty as a justification for resisting or obstructing international aid efforts, and many outside the country, in good or bad faith, called for an international response through R2P. Natural disasters do not fall within the ambit of the four listed crimes. As Luck recalled, '[w]e should take care not to undermine the historic but fragile international consensus behind the responsibility to protect by succumbing to the temptation to stretch it beyond what was intended by the heads of state and government' (Luck, 2008: 3).

Concerning the many invocations of R2P—whether justified or not—the armed conflict in Georgia in August 2008 is another case in point. Justifying the protection of Russian citizens abroad, a senior Russian official stated that there is a 'responsibility to protect – the term which is very widely used in the UN when people see some trouble in Africa or in any remote part of other regions. But this is not Africa to us, this is next door' (Global Centre for the R2P, 2008: 1). The misuse of the concept appears blatant. First, the concept does not confer authority on a state to take direct military action to protect its nationals located in another sovereign state. Second, in light of the principles mentioned above, the scale and intervention of the military operation went beyond the protection of the targeted population allegedly under threat (Global Centre for the R2P: 2). Third, in reference to the 'right authority' principle, the action was taken without Security Council approval (or, indeed, any attempt to secure it).

Whether or not it is the end of the road for the classical view on humanitarian intervention, R2P has been constantly shadowed by the military intervention debate, conveniently forgetting the programmatic framework the concept embodies: As Evans notes, it is 'an absolute travesty of the R2P principle to say that it is about military force and nothing else' (2007: 3).

III. Implementation

Challenges of implementation

The responsibility to protect doctrine, although not formally institutionalized, can be seen as influencing various activities by the international community. However, the operational capacity problems of establishing who should make the judgment, who should act, and what kind of actions should take place, have still not been resolved for many practical reasons.

First, most states are hesitant to say that another state has failed or is unwilling to protect its population, since other states may eventually make the same observation about them. Second, since there is no rapid deployment force or a multinational standby force, states are reluctant to send their troops and risk their lives for peace operations in other countries where there is no clear national interest to defend the intervention. And third, many of the interventions have not been successful since the rules of engagement, coordination of activities, and length of mission were not made clear at the outset. There have been various examples of mission creep and over-extension which make countries more hesitant today to intervene.

As an example, the ambassadors of the Philippines and the United Kingdom used the language of the responsibility to protect shortly after the UN Security Council passed Resolution 1556 on the crisis in the Sudanese province of Darfur. Early in 2004, the conditions in Darfur were generally described as meeting the threshold conditions—large loss of life and ethnic cleansing—which could justify invoking the responsibility to protect by outside forces. The Security Council did not choose to act, although Resolution 1556 was passed under Chapter VII of the UN Charter. An embargo was imposed with support for an African Union protection force and calls for the government of Sudan to disarm the rebels and facilitate humanitarian aid, but nothing more. It should be noted that the US Secretary of State, Colin Powell, even went so far as to say that the US believed that genocide had been committed in Darfur.

Thus, while the humanitarian emergency in Darfur was recognized and the language of the responsibility to protect was used, the major response has been in the form of humanitarian assistance, and a report to the new Human Rights Council—which was compromised because the members of a special committee had been unable to obtain visas to do on-site inspections in 2007. Neither the UN nor the European Union has proposed intervention. Resolution 1556 itself was a compromise in that it placed the responsibility to protect with the government of Sudan.

This example exemplifies the danger of the conceptual shift coming from the R2P concept. It could facilitate the efforts of anti-interventionists to argue against action by maintaining that the primary responsibility in certain situation still lies with the state itself and not with the international community (Bellamy, 2005: 33). That would clearly weaken the concept of its substance, and this issue makes it even more difficult to establish at what point one can determine that the state is unwilling or unable to protect. And on this question, the US Ambassador to the UN clearly stated that:

the responsibility of the other countries in the international community is not of the same character as the responsibility of the host, and we thus want to avoid formulations that suggest that the other countries are inheriting the same responsibility that the host state has (Bolton, 2005).

So, whereas the ICISS report and follow-up discussions focused attention on the importance of developing clear guidelines concerning the responsibility to protect, political and operational realities have stymied further clarification and implementation, especially in peacebuilding. The debate and hesitation over the crisis in Darfur, described above, is a clear example. The realization that state sovereignty should not be absolute has not been translated into institutional benchmarks for efficient action to protect human security within state borders.

The noted reluctance to operationalize the responsibility to protect has no doubt been influenced by both the end of the Cold War and the initiation of the so-called 'war on terror'. Although traditionally weak states from the South have always been wary of imperial ambitions from the North, the recent US-led actions in Afghanistan and Iraq have served to reinforce perceptions that humanitarian interventions are really hegemonic take-overs. In this sense, cynics argue that a call for humanitarian intervention in Darfur really masks ambitions for Sudanese oil, just as the invasion of Iraq can be seen as tied to geopolitical considerations. Doubts about the motives behind intervention and the true objectivity of peace operations have been further entrenched by the fact that Western countries, especially the US, have been extremely selective in their choices of intervention and have used force only in certain situations.

Responsibility to rebuild

R2P is much more complex than it seems, especially when it becomes strongly connected with the many facets of peacebuilding. As noted earlier, research on R2P has been constantly focused on the controversy surrounding military intervention, leaving aside the potential benefits of the R2P understood as an umbrella concept. This has created a serious gap between the interrelated phenomena of peacebuilding and the R2P. A coherent and theoretically driven approach that addresses this relationship is therefore needed. If durable peace is to be established and democratic governance and sustainable development are to be promoted, appropriate prevention and/or reaction of the international community should be followed by operationally sound and politically sustainable rebuilding measures. Thus, when the Security Council agrees to deploy personnel in a peace operation, there could be greater contribution of human and financial resources from states and a clear strategy to assess the needs on the ground for an effective peacebuilding mission.

In this context, capacity-building plays a pivotal role as a process that reinforces the ability of the various stakeholders to rebuild with the aim to prevent or reduce the commission of the four egregious crimes. This necessitates closer coordination and collaboration among relevant UN agencies, NGOs, donor countries, local and regional entities with the ultimate aim of creating a reliable political process to the point where the local actors find themselves in position to take over responsibility for rebuilding their own country.

Several core issues to be dealt with in post-conflict situations can be highlighted, which require a concerted and coordinated effort in three crucial areas: security; justice and reconciliation; and economic development:

- Security: ensuring security for the populations, regardless of ethnic origin or relation to the previous ruling power, is a major challenge facing both international and national stakeholders in war-torn societies. It is also the prerequisite for their stability. This implies many tasks, such as engaging in the disarmament, demobilization, and reintegration programmes of former combatants, ensuring the reform of the security sector through rebuilding of new national armed forces and police force, or developing mine action activities (ICISS: paras 5.8–5.12).

- Justice and reconciliation: a second peacebuilding responsibility lies in the need to make transitional arrangements for justice during an operation and to restore a judicial system (including both the courts and police) without delay. As a related issue, return and reintegration of refugees and internally displaced persons should be facilitated through effective long-term strategies (ICISS: paras 5.13–5.18).

- Economic development: commitments should be directed toward poverty reduction initiatives and democratic governance that advance the priorities of local ownership. Local actors working with the assistance of domestic and international development agencies should commit support to the state's community recovery programme and provide capacity-building to the national government in various sectors, such as education, health care or food production (ICISS: paras 5.19–5.21).

The international community during the World Summit of 2005 recognized the UN's responsibility to help states recover from devastation in a more coordinated and focused way with the establishment of the Peacebuilding Commission. Although the creation of the Commission was treated under a separate heading from the R2P, namely 'Peacebuilding', this institutional mechanism reflects the will to create an institutional tool to help States build the necessary structures to protect their populations and to strengthen the institutional and systematic links between peacekeeping operations and post-conflict peacebuilding efforts (UN General Assembly, 2005: para 139).

In addition to the Commission, another key component of the UN strategy for post-conflict peacebuilding was the Peacebuilding Fund, established 'with the objective of ensuring the immediate release of resources needed to launch peacebuilding activities and the availability of appropriate financing for recovery' (UN Security Council Resolution 1645, 2005: para 24). In this context, Burundi and Sierra Leone are the first two countries that the Peacebuilding Commission has focused on since October 2006, its key priorities being to promote democratic governance, to strengthen the rule of law, and to reform the security sector (UN Security Council, 2007: paras 13 and 21).

However, none of the aspects of prevention or rebuilding should blur the core principle that the responsibility to protect involves a responsibility to react to a catastrophic situation of compelling need for human protection to which the concerned state is unwilling or unable to respond. The emphasis on victims and on the responsibility to protect them is an important paradigm shift in viewing the world. But not surprisingly, in spite of the numerous Security Council resolutions enlarging its definition of what constitutes a threat to international peace and security, and recognizing the responsibility to protect, this shift has been largely intellectual. As a former senior adviser to the US State Department wrote: 'Universal adoption of the responsibility to protect has begun to remove the classic excuses for doing nothing in the face of mass atrocities. What is needed now is real capacity to back it up' (Lee Feinstein, 'The "Responsibility to Protect" Darfur', *International Herald Tribune*, 26 September 2006, cited in Clapham, 2007: 191).

Selected Bibliography

Abbott, C (2005), 'Rights and Responsibilities: Resolving the Dilemma of Humanitarian Intervention', briefing paper, Oxford: Oxford Research Group.

African Union (2002), *Protocol Relating to the Establishment of the Peace and Security Council of the African Union*, Addis Ababa.

Alvarez, JA (2007), 'The Schizophrenias of R2P', Panel Presentation at the 2007 Hague Joint Conference on Contemporary Issues of International Law: Criminal Jurisdiction 100 Years After the 1907 Hague Peace Conference, The Hague, The Netherlands, June 30, available at: <http://www.asil.org/pdfs/r2pPanel.pdf>.

Annan, K (1999), 'Two Concepts of Sovereignty', *The Economist*, 352: 49–50 (18 September).

Arbour, L (2008), 'The responsibility to protect as a duty of care in international law and practice', *Review of International Studies*, 34: 445–58.

Bellamy, AJ (2005), 'Responsibility to Protect or Trojan Horse? The Crisis in Darfur and Humanitarian Intervention after Iraq', *Ethics and International Affairs*, 19/2: 31–54.

Bettati, M & Kouchner, B (1987), *Le Devoir d'ingérence*, Paris: Denoël.

Beyerlin, U (2003), 'Humanitarian Intervention', in *Encyclopaedia of Public International Law* (published under the auspices of the Max Planck Institute for Comparative Public Law and International Law under the direction of Bernhardt, R), Amsterdam: Elsevier, 926–8.

Bolton, J (2005), Letter from Ambassador Bolton to UN Member States Conveying U.S. Amendments to the Draft Outcome Being Prepared for the High Level Event on Responsibility to Protect, available at: <http://www.reformtheun.org/index.php/issues/100?theme=alt4>.

Chandler, D (2004), 'The Responsibility to Protect? Imposing the "Liberal Peace"', *International Peacekeeping*, 11/1: 59–81.

Clapham, A (2007), 'Responsibility to Protect: Some Sort of Commitment', in Chetail, V (ed), *Conflits, sécurité et coopération/Conflicts, Security and Cooperation: Liber Amicorum Victor-Yves Ghebali*, Brussels: Bruylant, 169–92.

Cohen, R, & Deng, F (1998), *Masses in Flight: The Global Crisis of Internal Displacement*, Washington DC: Brookings Institution Press.

Deng, F, *et al* (1996), *Sovereignty as Responsibility: Conflict Management in Africa*, Washington, DC: Brookings Institution Press.

Evans, G (2007), 'Delivering on the Responsibility to Protect: Four Misunderstandings, Three Challenges and How To Overcome Them', SEF Symposium 2007, The Responsibility to Protect (R2P): Progress, Empty Promise or a License for "Humanitarian Intervention"', Bonn, 30 November, available at: http://www.crisis-group.org/home/index.cfm?id=5190&l=1.

—— (2008), *The Responsibility to Protect Ending Mass Atrocity Crimes Once and For All*, Washington DC: Brookings Institution Press.

—— & Sahnoun, M (2002), 'The Responsibility to Protect', *Foreign Affairs*, 81/6: 99–121.

Goldstone, R, *et al* (2000), *The Kosovo Report: Conflict, International Response, Lessons Learned*, Independent International Commission on Kosovo, Oxford: Oxford University Press.

Grotius, H (1625), *On the Law of War and Peace (translation of the 1625 Edition of the De Jure Belli ac Pacis Libri Tres)*, Carnegie Endowment for International Peace, London: Clarendon Press.

ICISS (2001), The Responsibility to Protect, Report of the International Commission on Intervention and State Sovereignty, Ottawa: International Development Research Centre.

Lauterpacht, H (1946), 'The Grotian Tradition in International Law', *British Yearbook of International Law*, 23/1: 1–53.

Luck, E (2008), Briefing on 'International Disaster Assistance: Policy Options', Subcommittee on International Development, Foreign Assistance, Economic Affairs and International Environmental Protection Committee on Foreign Relations of the United States Senate, 17 June, available at: http://foreign.senate.gov/hearings/2008/hrg080617p.html.

Paris, R (2004), *At War's End: Building Peace after Civil Conflict*, Cambridge: Cambridge University Press.

Roth, K (2004), *The War in Iraq: Justified as Humanitarian Intervention?*, Kroc Institute, Occasional Paper, 1–14

Stahn, C (2007), 'Responsibility to Protect: Political Rhetoric or Emerging Legal Norm?', *American Journal of International Law*, 101/1: 99–121.

Stowell, E (1921), Intervention in International Law, Washington, DC: J Bryne.

Teson, FR (2005), 'Ending Tyranny in Iraq', *Ethics and International Affairs*, 19/2: 1–20.

Thakur, R (2002), 'Intervention, Sovereignty and the Responsibility to Protect: Experiences from ICISS', *Security Dialogue*, 33/3: 323–43.

UN (2004), *A more secure world: our shared responsibility*, Report of the High-Level Panel on Threats, Challenges and Change, A/59/565, 2 December.

—— (2005) *In larger freedom: towards development, security and human rights for all*, Report of the Secretary-General, A/59/2005, 21 March.

—— (2006), Resolution 1674 (2006), S/RES/1674 (2006), Security Council, 28 April.

UN General Assembly (2005), 2005 World Summit Outcome, UN Doc A/RES/60/1, New York, 24 October.

UN Security Council (2005), *Post-conflict Peacebuilding*, UN Doc S/RES/1646, 20 December.

—— (2006), *Protection of Civilians in Armed Conflict*, UN Doc S/RES/1674 (2006), 28 April.

—— (2007), *Report of the Peacebuilding Commission on its first session*, UN Doc S/2007/458, 25 July.

Weiss, T, & Hubert, D (eds) (2001), *The Responsibility to Protect: Research, Bibliography, Background*, Supplementary Volume to the Report of the International Commission on Intervention and State Sovereignty (summary), Ottawa: International Development Research Centre.

Williams, PD, & Bellamy, AJ (2005), 'The Responsibility to Protect and the Crisis in Darfur', *Security Dialogue*, 36/1: 27–47.

• Online resources

<http://www.responsibilitytoprotect.org/index.php>
<http://globalr2p.org/>
<http://www.ir2p.org/>

Return and Reintegration

Vicky Tennant

Definition

Return and reintegration together constitute the process by which refugees and internally displaced persons return to their areas of origin (or new areas in their own countries), and are reincorporated into their communities. Reintegration involves the establishment of conditions which enable returnees to exercise basic social, economic, civil, and political rights and which provide the basic elements of life, livelihood, and dignity. While seeking to promote reconciliation and restitution for past interference with rights, it involves a repositioning of returnees as equal citizens and, in particular, the removal of any distinctions linked to their former displacement.

I. Term

Origin and context

The concept of return and reintegration is most commonly used with reference to people and communities who have been forcibly displaced as a result of conflict, war, persecution, or natural disasters. The right to return (and, conversely, the right not to be forced to return to a situation of danger or persecution) developed as a key component of international human rights law and refugee law in the mid-twentieth century. The related concept of reintegration has developed more recently, and encompasses the complex process by which returnees are gradually reincorporated within the social, economic and cultural fabric of their communities, and their rights as citizens restored to them.

The legal framework for return and the terminology used are linked to whether an international border has been crossed. Those outside their own countries as a result of persecution or war are generally categorized as refugees and under international refugee law have specific rights arising from their refugee status. These are set out in the 1951 Convention relating to the Status of Refugees and its 1967 Protocol, and in regional instruments such as the 1969 Organization of African Unity (OAU) Convention Governing the Specific Aspects of Refugee Problems in Africa. The return of refugees is generally referred to as repatriation, and both the 1951 Convention and the OAU Convention emphasize that this should be voluntary in nature. Both incorporate the principle of 'non-refoulement', which prohibits the forcible return of refugees to countries where their life or liberty would be at risk. The concept of voluntary repatriation is elaborated in Article 5 of the OAU Convention, which states that 'the essentially voluntary character of repatriation shall be respected in all cases and no refugee shall be repatriated against his will'.

The Office of the UN High Commissioner for Refugees (UNHCR) was established in 1950 with a specific mandate to provide international protec-tion to refugees and 'to seek permanent solutions to [their] problems by assist-ing Governments...to facilitate the voluntary repatriation of such refugees, or their assimilation within new national communities' (Statute of UNHCR, 1950, Chapter 1, para 1).

The terms 'deportation', 'expulsion', 'removal', and 'forced repatriation' describe the process by which non-citizens may be required to leave the territory of a state. The right of a state to restrict the admission and residence of foreign nationals is, however, subject to the prohibition on 'refoulement' of refugees referred to above and to other provisions of international human rights law.

There is no distinct legal regime for those who are forced to flee their homes as a result of events such as human rights violations, conflict, natural disas-ters, or war, but who, unlike refugees, have not crossed an international border. Such persons remain the responsibility of their own states, and are protected by relevant provisions of national law, international human rights law and inter-national humanitarian law. Nonetheless, in recognition of the particular risks to which internally displaced persons (IDPs) are exposed, a framework known as the Guiding Principles on Internal Displacement was developed in 1998 and endorsed by the UN General Assembly. This restates key provisions of inter-national human rights law, humanitarian law, and (by analogy) refugee law, all of which are pertinent to situations of forced displacement. Among these provisions is a requirement that competent authorities create the conditions and provide the means to enable IDPs 'to return voluntarily, in safety and with dignity, to their homes or places of habitual residence, or to resettle voluntarily in another part of the country'. The same authorities are enjoined to facilitate the reintegration of returned or resettled IDPs.

The right to return to one's country is enshrined in the 1948 Universal Declaration of Human Rights, the 1966 International Covenant on Civil and Political Rights, and other international and regional human rights instruments. While these do not explicitly incorporate the right to return to one's place of origin or former resi-dence, this may nonetheless be inferred from the rights to freedom of movement and to choice of place of residence, also enshrined in the same instruments.

Meaning

The uprooting of individuals and communities from their homes is just one mani-festation of the breakdown in the relationship between the citizen and the state in situations of armed conflict or widespread human rights violations. As such, most analysts now argue that the process of rebuilding this bond requires more than just geographical return, and also entails the restoration of civil, political, economic, social, and cultural rights to returnees on an equal basis with those who were never displaced. For return to be sustainable, former refugees and displaced persons must be fully reintegrated into their former (or new) communities. The process of reintegration has been defined by UNHCR as:

a process which enables former refugees and displaced people to enjoy a progressively greater degree of physical, social, legal and material security. In addition, reintegration entails the erosion—and ultimately the disappearance—of any observable distinctions which set returnees apart from their compatriots, particularly in terms of their socio-economic and legal status (UNHCR, 1997: 87).

More recently, analysts seeking to identify the key components of reintegration have argued that reintegration goes beyond the process of equalizing the conditions of returnees and other citizens, noting that this may include situations where key elements of life with dignity are not met. Others have noted the significance of restitution, including restoration of land and property and the reshaping of legal frameworks. There has also been a recent tendency to move away from a static concept of reintegration as 'anchoring' returnees back in their home communities, and to recognise that onward movement of returnees, for example, to take advantage of new economic opportunities in urban areas, does not necessarily signal a failure of the reintegration process.

The term 'reintegration' has also come to be applied more broadly in recent years, to a range of rehabilitation processes whereby persons who have become in some way separated or dislocated from their home communities are assisted in re-establishing themselves as members of society. In particular, it has come to be associated with the process of supporting former combatants or those associated with the armed forces or military groups, including abductees, child soldiers, and women associated with fighting forces, to re-establish themselves in civilian life, often in the context of disarmament, demobilization, and reintegration programmes. In some cases, this may also involve the return of prisoners of war or fighters who have sought refuge on foreign territory. While this entry focuses on reintegration in the context of refugee and IDP returns, there are nonetheless important linkages with the reintegration of other categories of persons who have become dislocated from their communities as a result of conflict or human rights violations.

II. Content

The impact on post-conflict peacebuilding

The return and reintegration of IDPs and refugees has important links with the broader processes of post-conflict peacebuilding and reconciliation. Forced displacement—both internal and across borders—is one of the most visible manifestations of armed conflict and human rights violations, and represents in a particularly stark manner a rupture of the bond between individuals, communities, and the state. Experience has shown that, as societies begin to emerge from violent conflict and repressive regimes, the voluntary return of refugees and IDPs and their reincorporation within their communities and within a reshaped national identity, are often seen as a crucial element of a comprehensive process of conflict transformation, particularly where forced displacement was used as a weapon of war (for example, in situations of ethnic cleansing or depopulation strategies).

The return and reintegration process is a crucial component of peacebuilding and has the potential to make a substantial contribution to the medium-to-long-term development of societies emerging from conflict. It is linked to the confrontation of inequality and other injustices at the root of displacement, and to the re-positioning of returnees as equal citizens endowed with rights and dignity. Nonetheless, the return of refugees and IDPs also has the potential to destabilize the peacebuilding process if reintegration support is not sufficient or the process is not skilfully timed and managed. The precipitous return of large numbers of refugees and IDPs may result in sudden shifts in ethnic composition and/or result in increased competition and conflict over scarce resources.

In a number of countries, refugees have played an important part in developing and sustaining peace processes, and provisions for the voluntary return of refugees appear in almost all peace agreements concluded since the early 1990s. Increasingly, peace agreements have tended also to specifically incorporate the right of refugees and IDPs to return to their homes or areas of origin, and have included provisions which acknowledge that return is only the first part of a complex process of reinsertion into the home community, making reference to the human rights of returnees, their social and economic reintegration and reconciliation processes. For example, the 2000 peace agreement for Burundi and the 2003 agreement for Liberia both contained provisions on reintegration and commitments to coexistence among returnees and receiving populations.

In some cases, refugees have played a direct part in the negotiation of peace agreements, as for example in the case of the 1994 Agreement on Resettlement of the Population Groups Uprooted by the Armed Conflict, one of a series of agreements which paved the way for the 1996 agreement on a definitive ceasefire in Guatemala and which incorporated extensive provisions on the return and reintegration of refugees and the development of areas for settlement by returnees. These provisions included guarantees of the right to return, freedom of choice as to place of residence, human rights protection, participation in decision making, and 'free and full integration into the social, economic and political life of the country'. Specific provision was made for issuance of personal documentation, recognition of the rights of indigenous communities, recovery of land and property, land allocation, investment in infrastructure, water rights, establishment of basic services, investment in agriculture, and strengthening of local ownership and governance.

Actors

The primary actors in the process of voluntary repatriation are refugees. Large-scale return frequently takes place without assistance, before formally negotiated frameworks are in place, as refugees decide to 'vote with their feet'. Approximately 800,000 refugees returned 'spontaneously' to Mozambique following the signature of a peace agreement in Rome in 1992. Similarly, approximately 200,000 refugees returned spontaneously to Afghanistan in late 2001 and early 2002 prior to the commencement of the assisted voluntary repatriation programme from Iran and Pakistan.

Within the UN system, UNHCR has a specific mandate for the protection of refugees and for facilitating their voluntary repatriation where conditions are conducive to return. Voluntary repatriation is considered one of three possible 'durable solutions' for refugees, along with local integration in the country of asylum and resettlement to a third country. UNHCR has been directed by its Executive Committee to 'promote measures, with governments and with relevant international bodies, to establish conditions that would permit refugees, on the basis of a free and informed choice, to return peacefully to their homes and to rebuild their lives' (UNHCR, 2005: 126). In many instances, this work needs to be preceded by political processes involving actors other than UNHCR, which address the root causes of flight and lead to sufficient stability and security to enable the return of refugees in a safe and dignified manner. The core components of voluntary repatriation have been identified by UNHCR as 'return in and to conditions of physical, legal and material safety, with full restoration of national protection [as] the end product' (UNHCR, 2005: 126).

Where return takes place within formal frameworks, the key institutional actors are generally national governments in the countries hosting refugees, and governments in countries of origin. Frameworks for the voluntary repatriation of refugees frequently take the form of tripartite agreements between the host country, the country of origin, and UNHCR. These typically establish institutional arrangements for the implementation of the voluntary repatriation programme, and include provisions on matters such as the voluntary character of repatriation, freedom of choice of destination, safe and dignified return, amnesties, access to land and property, recognition of personal documentation and academic and educational certificates, family unity, and waiver of customs duties and other taxes. In the Mozambique example, 378,000 refugees were assisted to return between 1994 and 1996 under tripartite agreements with six neighbouring countries. Similarly, more than three million refugees returned to Afghanistan under tripartite arrangements between 2002 and 2006.

There is no single UN agency with overall responsibility for internally displaced persons. In principle, IDPs are the responsibility of their own governments. In practice, however, this has led to significant protection and assistance gaps, and marked differences in standards of treatment for IDPs and refugees. Under the 'cluster approach' to humanitarian assistance developed in late 2005 by the UN, responsibilities for leading key components of the international humanitarian response have been assigned to specific agencies. Key responsibilities for the protection of IDPs have been assigned to UNHCR (for conflict-related IDPs), together with the UN Children's Fund (UNICEF) and the Office of the High Commissioner for Human Rights (for those displaced by natural disasters), while recognizing that the primary responsibility for the protection of IDPs lies with national governments. The assisted return of IDPs in general takes place within the framework of institutional partnerships between the government, the UN, NGOs, and (ideally) IDPs themselves. For example, the return of more than 800,000 IDPs to their areas of origin in Liberia from 2004 to 2007 was planned and managed through a body known as the IDP Consultative Forum, made up of government representatives, UN agencies, NGOs, donor states, and IDP representatives.

Security issues

One of the most complex aspects of the return and reintegration process is its link with security. As seen above, large-scale return may often take place, in practice, in contexts where the conflict transformation process is still under way and the state has yet to establish its legitimacy and authority. Refugees and IDPs may come under pressure to return from governments in countries of asylum or their own fellow-nationals. In such cases, the sustainability of their return may be particularly precarious. Analysts have highlighted a 'principle-reality gap' (Macrae, 1999: 28), pointing out that in practice, asylum fatigue on the part of host states and dwindling donor interest in protracted refugee situations have resulted in increased pressure on refugees to return, often to situations characterized by ongoing instability and, in some cases, complex political emergencies. In some instances, the security of returning refugees and IDPs may be guaranteed in practice only through the presence of peacekeeping forces or other external military actors. As pointed out in the civil-military interface chapter, this calls for communication and coordination between humanitarian and military actors, whether through integrated missions or other institutional arrangements. Such arrangements may nonetheless arguably compromise the neutrality of humanitarian action as the distinctions between humanitarian agencies and military and political actors become blurred.

Development component

From the outset, the concept of sustainable reintegration of returnees was viewed as inextricably linked with that of development, as reflected in the 'returnee aid and development' nomenclature used in the early 1990s. Ultimately, the successful reintegration of returnees is generally seen as dependent on the resumption of development processes in areas of return, and on the linking of short-term assistance activities to long-term, large-scale programmes led by national governments and international development agencies (for a similar problematique see especially the chapter on disarmament, demobilization, and reintegration). Linking reintegration to development implies the engagement of a range of institutional actors, in particular national governments, the World Bank, the UN Development Programme (UNDP) and the UN development-oriented agencies such as the Food and Agriculture Organization (FAO), the UNICEF, the UN Population Fund (UNFPA), and the International Labour Organization (ILO).

Nonetheless, the transition from reintegration to development has proven to be highly complex, owing to a range of contextual and structural factors. A seven-country evaluation conducted for UNHCR in 1997 concluded that many of the agency's reintegration interventions were not sustainable, highlighting boreholes and wells that had not been maintained and had fallen into disuse, schools and health posts not functioning owing to lack of staff or materials, and similar problems with agricultural projects. In the late 1990s, UNHCR and the World Bank embarked on a joint process (the 'Brookings Process') with the aim of addressing the barriers to an effective transition from humanitarian assistance to development in post-conflict contexts, and to ensuring a 'more predictable, coherent, flexible and timely response' (Crisp, 2001: 15). Two key gaps were highlighted: the 'institutional gap', which stemmed from differences in priorities, planning and programming cycles between agencies, particularly between humanitarian and development agencies; and the 'funding gap', stemming from reduced interest by donors in initiatives that do not fall easily into either of the categories of 'emergency relief' or 'development assistance' (see further the chapter on recovery).

Some commentators have sought to analyze this gap by questioning the 'post-conflict' concept and by pointing out that this is used to imply that situations have normalized when in reality they are still characterized by instability and insecurity. In such situations, high numbers of refugee and IDP returns may occur, but without the institutional and political conditions in place necessary to sustain nationally led development processes. One analyst has pointed to the pitfalls of a 'persistent glossing over of the very substantive distinction between post-conflict situations and complex political emergencies' (Macrae, 1999: 26). Whilst humanitarian aid is frequently delivered outside government structures, this is not so for development programmes, which seek to enhance capacity-building and to adhere to priorities set by the government. As one commentator has observed, 'All official development assistance agencies suffer from an inability to work effectively in "quasi-states"' (Macrae, 1999: 25). Some observers have been critical of UNHCR's expanded role in reintegration, arguing that when renewed displacement occurs, this is as a result of insecurity and political failures, not from economic hardship, and that the agency has no 'comparative advantage' when it comes to reintegration activities. Others have criticized the encroachment of donor government foreign policy goals into reintegration programmes and have highlighted the political factors which shape donor support for reintegration operations.

Human rights component

As well as its socio-economic dimensions, the sustainable reintegration of refugees and IDPs also has strong human rights components, at a number of different levels. The process of successful reintegration encompasses the reincorporation of those who have been failed by the state within a reshaped national identity, a reckoning with the past, and the elaboration of laws and reform of institutions such as the security sector, judiciary, and human rights commissions, which provide both the framework and the means to guarantee effective national protection to returnees and others affected by conflict and human rights abuses (see the chapters on security sector reform; rule of law; and reconciliation). Reintegration programmes developed by UNHCR and its partners have typically incorporated significant protection-related components. These have included human rights monitoring, legal assistance projects, support to victims, and community awareness on sexual and gender-based violence, capacity-building for the legal profession, police forces and judiciary, advice on land tenure and property rights, and training for NGOs on human rights.

The restitution of housing, land and property and other forms of reparation to refugees and IDPs have received particular attention in the last years, resulting in the development of the Principles on Housing and Property Restitution for Refugees and Displaced Persons (the 'Pinheiro Principles'), endorsed by the UN Sub-Commission on the Promotion and Protection of Human Rights in 2005. These elaborate key rights relating to the equitable restitution of housing and property, and provide guidelines to states and international actors on institutional and procedural mechanisms to ensure access to these rights.

III. Implementation

The changing context of refugee returns

The process of reintegration of returned refugees started to receive particular attention from international aid agencies from around 1990 onwards. Prior to that, particularly when the Cold War was at its height, the prospect of return of exiles from the Communist bloc appeared implausible, and asylum was generally granted on a permanent basis. Similarly, refugees fleeing wars of liberation in Africa in the 1960s and 1970s benefited from relatively generous asylum regimes in the region, and in general returned only once fundamental regime changes had occurred in their own countries, when they were able to avail themselves of the protection of national authorities enjoying a high degree of legitimacy. In these circumstances, the focus of UNHCR and other international actors was primarily on the facilitation of the return process, and on the provision of individual assistance packages (consisting for example of food rations, seeds, and agricultural tools), with only marginal involvement in the more complex process of reintegrating refugees in their home communities.

A significant shift in approach took place in the early 1990s, shaped in part by the changing context of refugee returns. Prompted to some extent by a decline in donor interest, states became less willing to host large refugee populations indefinitely, particularly where their own political interests no longer coincided with those of refugee populations. Large numbers of refugees returned over very short periods of time to countries such as Afghanistan, Bosnia and Herzegovina, Mozambique, Nicaragua, and Rwanda, which were characterized by high levels of insecurity, deep social divisions, destroyed infrastructure, and a legacy of violence and human rights abuses. In these circumstances, there was a real concern that, without adequate support, the return of refugees and IDPs to areas where they would be in competition for scarce resources with receiving communities, could rekindle conflict and might ultimately be unsustainable. There was a particular concern that this might result in renewed forced displacement, or onward movement of returnees from rural to urban areas. Nonetheless, in the immediate aftermath of violent conflict, the capacity of national authorities to support the reintegration process was often limited. There was also an increasing recognition of the links between reintegration and the restoration of rights, including restitution of housing, land and property, access to documentation, and transitional justice mechanisms.

As a result, by the mid-1990s, support for the reintegration of refugees had become a standard feature of voluntary repatriation operations, as a key component of UNHCR's mandate to seek durable solutions for refugees, including sustainable return. An early 'returnee aid and development' strategy, adopted by UNHCR, incorporated a number of key principles which still underpin approaches to reintegration today. It was posited that reintegration assistance was most equitable and effective when provided on an inclusive, community-wide basis that sought to foster reconciliation and coexistence; that it should be provided in a way which discouraged dependency and contributed to the development of local capacity-building; and that its success was closely linked to the resumption of development activities in areas of return. As such, the impact and sustainability of reintegration activities were seen as hinging on ensuring a smooth transition from short-term humanitarian assistance to longer term development programmes steered by national authorities and international development agencies (see the chapter on recovery). By the beginning of the new millennium, the principle of reintegration had also been firmly incorporated into the discourse on the rights of IDPs.

Reintegration programmes

UNHCR's reintegration programmes have typically focused on supporting the reestablishment of infrastructure, basic services and livelihood opportunities in returnee areas, using a community-wide approach which promotes reconciliation rather than differentiating between returnees and receiving populations. This approach often takes the form of 'quick-impact projects' (QIPs), which are generally small-scale projects involving a one-time allocation of resources identified following consultation with returnees and their communities. Examples of QIPs include construction of schools, clinics or community centres, irrigation, small crop production and forestry projects, road rehabilitation, animal restocking, and potable water projects. Key features of QIPs include a focus on community-wide involvement and on ensuring the participation of women. In some operations (eg in Afghanistan and Bosnia and Herzegovina) these have incorporated components aimed at promoting coexistence between affected communities, including the promotion of mediation and conflict-resolution skills.

Over time, and particularly in large-scale repatriation operations, UNHCR's reintegration interventions became more extensive. While QIPs were generally well received by returnee communities and were evaluated as having a positive impact on living standards and livelihoods in the early phases of voluntary repatriation programmes, questions were raised about technical standards and long-term impact. By the end of the 1990s, there was a partial move away from the QIPs approach. For example, from 2002 in Afghanistan UNHCR's reintegration programme focused on large-scale, low-cost shelter programmes and water projects in areas of return, with only a moderate QIPs component. There was also a shift towards community capacity-building through community empowerment projects (CEPs) rather than infrastructure projects (examples include Liberia and Sierra Leone from 2001).

There has also been a shift towards the involvement of a broader range of actors in reintegration programmes, with a particular focus on the engagement of national authorities. In the early stages of the large-scale return of refugees to Afghanistan in 2002, a reintegration unit was established under the Ministry of Rural Rehabilitation and Development (MRRD). It produced a national policy on the return and reintegration of displaced populations, and established a successful process for mainstreaming refugee and IDP priorities into major national development programmes. The unit provided training to MRRD staff on the return and reintegration of IDPs and refugees and placed reintegration advisors in provincial administrations. This contrasts with the approach adopted in Mozambique some ten years earlier, where reintegration was largely seen as the responsibility of the international community and there was limited government engagement.

The 4Rs approach

The range of international actors engaging in reintegration-related activities has also expanded. Following on from the Brookings Process, in 2003 UNHCR, UNDP and the World Bank launched the '4Rs' ('repatriation, reintegration, rehabilitation, and reconstruction') approach, which was piloted in Afghanistan, Eritrea, Sierra Leone, and Sri Lanka. This aimed to provide an 'overarching framework for institutional collaboration in the implementation of reintegration operations... [and to] address effectively the mainstreaming of reintegration into national development plans and programmes' (Muggah, 2006: 25). Nonetheless, an extensive review completed in 2006 (Buchanan) concluded that while there had been some progress in mainstreaming the needs and concerns of returnee communities into the transition, reconstruction, and development agenda, operational impact in the pilot countries had been limited, in part due to the fact that the process had not been sufficiently institutionalized by the UN and lacked structural arrangements, authority, resources, training, and technical guidance. While the process was conceived as being flexible and community and country-driven, the report concluded that it was only with substantial input from agency headquarters, and structural reforms, that institutional and funding discordances could be adequately addressed. As an 'approach' without sufficient authority, and without a structured and institutionalized programme, it was assessed—despite some success in Sierra Leone and Sri Lanka—as having had limited impact.

Nonetheless, the 4Rs approach provided important experience of institutional partnerships as key components of a reintegration strategy. This experience has been drawn on in Liberia, where a 2006–2007 Joint Action Plan for Community-Based Recovery and Restoration of Social Services was developed and implemented by UNDP, UNHCR, UNICEF, and the World Food Programme (WFP). Similarly, a study on youth employment conducted in December 2006 led to the development of a joint implementation plan involving UNHCR, ILO, UNDP, UNICEF, and the UN Educational, Scientific and Cultural Organization.

The humanitarian reform process

The humanitarian reform process launched in 2005 may provide new impetus to efforts to bridge the gap between relief and development (as highlighted in recovery). The 'cluster approach' to humanitarian assistance aims at improving delivery, coordination, and accountability in emergency situations and incorporates the establishment of an Early Recovery Cluster led by UNDP. A draft guidance note prepared by the Cluster Working Group on Early Recovery together with the UNDG-ECHA Working Group on Transition in April 2007 defines early recovery as:

recovery that begins early in a humanitarian setting. It is a multi-dimensional process, guided by development principles, that seeks to build upon humanitarian programmes and to catalyze sustainable development opportunities. Early recovery aims to generate to the extent possible self-sustaining nationally owned and resilient processes for post-crisis recovery. Early recovery encompasses livelihoods, shelter, governance, environment and social dimensions, including the reintegration of displaced populations. It stabilizes human security and where the opportunity exists begins to address underlying risks that contributed to the crisis (Cluster Working Group on Early Recovery, 2007: 5).

Two advantages of this most recent approach are, first, that it is embedded within a new institutional structure steered at a high level and, second, that it recognizes the need to incorporate strategies for the transition to development from the out-set of an emergency, and not sequentially. There have also been positive developments on funding mechanisms, and some donors have renewed their interest in sustainable return and in the link between relief, recovery and development. Nonetheless, there remain differences between key agencies in institutional mandate, field presence, priorities, and programmatic approach.

Selected Bibliography

Bell, C (2000), *Peace Agreements and Human Rights*, Oxford: Oxford University Press, Chapter 8.

Buchanan, J (2006), *Review of the 4Rs Approach*, Inter-Agency Independent Report.

Chetail, V (ed) (2004), *Voluntary Repatriation: Achievements and Prospects, Refugee Survey Quarterly*, Oxford: Oxford University Press, 23/3.

—— (2005), *Internally Displaced Persons: The Challenges of International Protection, Refugee Survey Quarterly*, Oxford: Oxford University Press, 24/3.

Cluster Working Group on Early Recovery (2006), *Implementing Early Recovery*, New York: Inter-Agency Standing Committee, available at: <http://www.reliefweb.int/rw/lib.nsf/db900SID/LTIO-6SCLD2/$FILE/iasc-earlyrecovery-jul2006.pdf?OpenElement>.

—— in cooperation with UNDG-ECHA Working Group on Transition (2007), 'Transition Recovery: Early Recovery Guidance Note', draft, New York: Inter-Agency Standing Committee.

Crisp, J (2001), *Mind the Gap! UNHCR, Humanitarian Assistance and the Development Process*, Geneva: UNHCR, available at: <http://www.unhcr.org/research/RESEARCH/3b309dd07.pdf>.

Dolan, C, Large, J, & Obi, N (2004), *Evaluation of UNHCR's Repatriation and Reintegration Programme in East Timor, 1999–2003*, Geneva: UNHCR, available at: <http://www.unhcr.org/research/RESEARCH/403f62e17.pdf>.

Fitzpatrick, J (2001), *Human Rights Protection for Refugees, Asylum-Seekers, and Internally Displaced Persons: A Guide to International Mechanisms and Procedures*, New York: Transnational Publishers.

Goodwin-Gill, G, & McAdam, J (2007), *The Refugee in International Law*, 3rd edn, Oxford: Oxford University Press.

Leckie, S (ed) (2003), *Returning Home: Housing and Property Restitution Rights of Refugees and Displaced Persons*, New York: Transnational Publishers.

Macrae, J (1999), *Aiding Peace... and War: UNHCR, Returnee Reintegration and the Relief-Development Debate*, New Issues in Refugee Research, Working Paper, No 14, Geneva: UNHCR, available at: <http://www.unhcr.org/research/RESEARCH/3ae6a0cc0.pdf>.

Muggah, R (2006), 'The Death-knell of "4R": Rethinking Durable Solutions for Displaced People', *Humanitarian Exchange*, 36: 25–7, Humanitarian Policy Network, London: ODI, available at: <http://www.odihpn.org/documents/humanitarianexchange036.pdf>.

OCHA (1998), *Guiding Principles on Internal Displacement*, New York: OCHA (reprinted 2004).

Perault, M, *et al* (2006), *Guide on Selected Good Practices in Reintegration*, Geneva: UNHCR.

Phuong, C (2005), *The International Protection of Internally Displaced Persons*, Cambridge: Cambridge University Press.

Refugee Studies Centre (2004), *Home for Good? Challenges in Return and Reintegration*, Forced Migration Review, 21, Oxford: Refugee Studies Centre, available at: <http://www.fmreview.org/FMRpdfs/FMR21/FMR21full.pdf>.

Sperl, S, & De Vriese, M (2005), *From Emergency Evacuation to Community Empowerment: Review of the Repatriation and Reintegration Programme in Sierra Leone*, Geneva: UNHCR, available at: <http://www.unhcr.org/research/RESEARCH/420b80384.pdf>.

UNHCR (1997), *The State of the World's Refugees*, Geneva: UNHCR.

—— (2004), *Handbook for Repatriation and Reintegration Activities*, Geneva: UNHCR.

—— (2005), *Conclusion on Legal Safety Issues in the Context of Voluntary Repatriation*, EC/54/SC/CRP.127, Executive Committee of the High Commissioner's Programme, 7 June 2004. Reprinted in *Refugee Survey Quarterly*, Oxford: Oxford University Press, 24/1.

—— (2006), *The State of the Word's Refugees*, Geneva: UNHCR.

Rule of Law

Vera Gowlland-Debbas and Vassilis Pergantis

Definition

The rule of law refers to a principle of governance upholding the supremacy of the law adopted through an established procedure, accountability of public authority under the law, equality of all before the law, and access to an impartial and autonomous system of justice. It is ideologically linked to constitutionalism, democracy, and human rights. Rule of law projects in a peacebuilding context focus on elimination of arbitrariness; institutional reform, including the administration of justice; and accountability.

I. Term

Origin and evolution

The rule of law concept was conceived as a constraining force against political power when *jus divinum* and natural law lost their legitimacy and binding force. It is inextricably linked to the liberal state and the idea of constitutionalism. Despite its frequent use, the term lacks conceptual clarity. While the idea of the rule of law has been characterized as a pleonasm or as an 'essentially contestable concept' (Fallon, 1997: 7), others consider it 'a key element of constitutional democracy' (Maddex, 2000: 305). Undeniably an open-textured notion, the rule of law can be better characterized as a normative standard, albeit a general, vague, and imprecise one, always to be attained (Salmon, 2001: 1049).

Whereas the emergence and evolution of the rule of law differ from one political system to another—as one can see in Table 5—some common traits can be discerned.

The rule of law calls for limitations to public authority. These limitations can have a procedural character (governmental power defined and exercised in accordance with known procedures, thus affording consistency and predictability of law-making and law enforcement), or a substantive one (establishing a normative hierarchy/recognition of a body of fundamental rights and freedoms).

Table 5 Origins and Evolution of the Rule of Law in National Legal Systems

	Context of emergence	*Evolution*
England	The common law of the land as the hierarchically superior body of law constraining Parliament's law-making power.	The notion (coined by Albert V Dicey) manifested through concepts such as supremacy of law, formal equality before the law, and 'jurisdictionalization'.
US	Effort to circumscribe the legislative discretion of the colonial power (Great Britain).	The notion manifested through concepts such as the wide power of judicial review of legislative action and the doctrine of separation of powers.
Germany	The term 'Rechtsstaat' as a response to arbitrary power and despotism, involving a constitution that guarantees civil liberties.	While initially focusing on protection of individual liberties and democratic representation, the notion later embodied formal elements such as the principle of legality and the doctrine of judicial review.
France	The term '*Etat de droit*' is linked to the idea of parliamentary sovereignty and the principle of legality (*habilitation*: power based on authority conferred by law).	Focus on the separation of powers. The idea of rule of law was never given the same importance as in Germany. French scholars remained suspicious of the idea of broad judicial review.

The rule of law is inextricably linked to the principle of 'no power without accountability'. This may include a system of checks and balances usually ensured by the separation of powers, transparency, justification of decisions, financial and administrative control, and political or judicial mechanisms reviewing governmental and administrative action to ensure observance of constitutional limits (although the latter is more controversial). The provision of remedies from governmental abuse is an important aspect of accountability.

References to the domestic law principle of the rule of law may be found at the international level, in particular in the framework of international human rights law which has promoted its core aspects. The International Court of Justice (ICJ) has also opposed the rule of law to arbitrary action, characterizing the latter as 'a wilful disregard of due process of law' (ICJ, 1989: 76; ICJ, 1950: 284).

The international principle of the rule of law is undoubtedly inspired by its domestic counterpart, but has emerged on the international plane through international law processes. However, it cannot operate in the same way as in the domestic law context, since the international system lacks a centralized legislative authority and is permeated by the idea of state sovereignty. Any effort to apply the domestic rule of law in inter-state relationships, where some states are more equal than others and where the consequent inconsistent application of rules is coupled with rule indeterminacy, has been considered illusory. Nevertheless, a trend towards the rule of law at the international level can be discerned. Voices against the abusive use of wide discretionary powers and in favour of transparency, consistency, and accountability are raised. The UN has spearheaded this concept, repeatedly affirming its commitment 'to an international order based on the rule of law' (UN, 2005b: para 134(a); UN, 2004b; 2006a; 2006b), while both the Council of Europe (CoE) and the Organization for Security and Co-operation in Europe (OSCE) refer to the rule of law in their constitutional documents.

The rule of law has undoubtedly become the catchphrase of peace operations, including peacebuilding components. In analysing its various conceptualizations, one can observe that the rule of law constitutes simultaneously the basis, the purpose, and the means of achieving sustained recovery in a state under duress. The recent expansion of international organizations' (IOs) peacebuilding activities (UN, 1992: para 55; UN, 2000c: para 13)—from consulting and assisting national authorities, to re-establishing the rule of law (Cambodia or Afghanistan), to imposing solutions, fully assuming sovereign powers, and replacing the failed governmental structures (Kosovo or East Timor) in the state-building process—brings rule of law projects to the heart of their mandates and has 'spawned a virtual rule of law industry' (Tolbert & Solomon, 2006: 55). At the same time, the usual absence of governmental structures and the subsequent anarchy in war-torn territories require types of action that prioritize a more pragmatic and flexible approach to the rule of law rather than the formalistic one of its domestic counterpart. Thus, the application of the rule of law in a peacebuilding context should involve a combination of the two distinct (domestic–international) dimensions of the rule of law.

Rule of law projects focus primarily on early recovery efforts for creating a secure environment for all human beings and setting the basis for prosperity and long-term development (UN, 2005a: paras 133–4). In this framework, they focus on: strengthening national justice systems and institutions through measures for institutional reform in the judicial, penal, and security sectors; training judges, lawyers, and policing personnel; disarmament, demobilization, and reintegration; restoration of order; protection of human rights; transparency of governmental institutions and strengthening of local participation therein; and transitional justice, namely the accountability of perpetrators for past human rights abuses and of the new (international or local) administration.

Meanings of the rule of law

Rule of law, ruled by law

One of the most common misconceptions with regard to the rule of law is its identification with the idea of being ruled by (international) law—of being law-abiding. In peace operations that include peacebuilding components, where civil disobedience is the prevailing mood, there is an almost natural tendency to equate the rule *by* law with the rule *of* law in order to avoid chaos and anarchy. Nevertheless, the two concepts must be distinguished. While according to the rule of law concept, law serves as a check to arbitrary power, rule by law 'can serve as a mere tool for a government that suppresses in a legalistic fashion' (Tamanaha, 2002: 101). Furthermore, in the case of failed states the state of law is often in disarray, and the existing legislative *corpus* is repudiated because of its links to the previous regime. In order to avoid possible frictions from the application of those laws, there is sometimes a massive importation of foreign rules/codes and international law standards. While these rules cover the legislative gap, the idea of being ruled by (international/foreign) law can alienate the local population and undermine rule of law projects.

Nevertheless, the rule of law and being ruled by law are not mutually exclusive. Law is a force restraining arbitrary power and absolute discretion. It is one of the basic premises of the rule of law that any 'government shall be ruled by the law and subject to it' (Raz, 1977: 196). It is thus for the rule of law to ensure that all actors of a state are equal before the law and that the law represents a reflection of multiple societal interests and not just a means for hegemony by one group (see democratic governance; civil society).

Formal v *substantive understandings*

The formal conceptions of the rule of law emphasize its procedural aspects, such as: the way laws are promulgated; the separation and independence of each of the three powers (executive, legislative, judicial); and the question of the equal application of laws and its consequences (governmental accountability/judicial review).

The formal constraints of the rule of law, however, offer a weak substantive constraint on the will of the rulers. A rigidly formalistic reading of the rule of law may lead to the view that the rule of law exists in regimes whose laws are morally objectionable (Craig, 1997: 469). As Timothy Endicott eloquently opines, '[t]he law may offer citizens the certainty that they will be dealt with arbitrarily' (Endicott, 1999: 3). The proceduralization and judicialization of the political process through the empowerment of courts has also been criticized as creating tensions with another facet of democracy, that of majoritarianism.

A substantive understanding of the rule of law raises the question of its relationship with democracy and human rights. Recently, UN member-states have declared that the ideas of '. . . protecting and promoting all human rights, the rule of law and democracy . . . are interlinked and mutually reinforcing' (UN, 2005b: para 119). Thus the rule of law has to be coupled with the protection of democracy and human rights, the latter not being a sub-category of the rule of law but standing on a par with it (Quénivet, 2006: 39) (see the chapter on democratic governance). This substantive understanding is, however, criticized on the grounds that rule of law is ultimately used as a mask for substantive inequality and that value neutrality is impossible (Craig, 1997: 474–6).

Definitions of the rule of law used by IOs

The UN uses the following definition of the rule of law:

The rule of law refers to a principle of governance in which all persons, institutions and entities, public and private, including the State itself, are accountable to laws that are publicly promulgated, equally enforced and independently adjudicated, and which are consistent with international human rights norms and standards. It requires, as well, measures to ensure adherence to the principles of supremacy of law, equality before the law, accountability to the law, fairness in the application of the law, separation of powers, participation in decision making, legal certainty, avoidance of arbitrariness and procedural and legal transparency (UN, 2004b: para 6).

The OSCE has defined rule of law in the following way:

They [declaring States] consider that the rule of law does not mean merely a formal legality which assures regularity and consistency in the achievement and enforcement of democratic order, but justice based on recognition and full acceptance of the supreme value of the human personality and guaranteed by institutions providing a framework for its fullest expression (OSCE, 1990: para 2).

Comments on the general definition given by the contributors

Our definition brings together the major procedural elements of the rule of law concept but highlights its interrelationship with ideological and substantive aspects. In this form, it is applicable at both domestic and international levels as well as in a peacebuilding context.

II. Content

Formal components

Predictability of the law and equality before the law

Predictability of the law involves a set of formal and procedural requirements concerning the promulgation and enforcement of legal acts, such as publicity of enacted rules, clarity and comprehensiveness of rules, stability and predictability in legal change (fixed procedures for reform), non-retroactivity, and reliability of enforcement. This last element is closely related to the idea of equality before the law, namely that all citizens should be subject to the same legal rules.

In the context of peacebuilding, one of the main challenges is consistency in the application of rule of law projects. The UN has been accused of inconsistent, unclear, and even contradictory policies in the field of rule of law. There are allegations of double standards when deciding where to develop rule of law projects, thus undermining their legitimacy. Moreover, the implementation of rule of law projects has been plagued by indeterminacy with regard to the applicable law. The UN has vacillated between using the pre-existing legal framework and imposing foreign models/codes or following the rules preferred by the dominant political or ethnic group. Indeterminacy creates confusion, leading to the disillusionment of the local population (UN, 2000c: para 79).

The UN has examined the possibility of developing model codes, especially for criminal justice, adaptable to regional particularities, that could be applied *ad interim* pending the re-establishment of local rule of law (UN, 2000c: para. 83). Recent studies, however, seem to have abandoned—or at least curtailed—the idea of foreign conceived solutions (UN, 2004b: para 15). UN reform proposals also focus on the need for a Rule of Law Assistance Unit within the Peacebuilding Commission that will create a pool of precedents in rule of law implementation, thus building on UN institutional memory and encouraging coherent decision-making (UN, 2005a: Addendum 2, para 6; UN, 2006b: para 52).

Reform of judicial institutions

The rule of law concept favours checks and balances between state powers as a means of circumscribing arbitrariness. In the same framework, the judiciary must be independent from external influences, competent, and representative of the various ethnic and social groups of the territory. Judicial independence has been one of the most challenging components of rule of law projects as those exercising governmental power have frequently been tempted to control the judiciary. Legislation concerning safeguards against removal of judges and prosecutors from office is often poorly drafted or altogether lacking, so that authorities may easily dispose of judges that do not 'cooperate' (see UN, 2000a). A further issue is the appointment of judges on short-term contracts subject to periodical renewal by executive authorities (Quénivet, 2006: 57), a practice which seriously undermines the rule of law ideal.

Moreover, the judicial system must function effectively and the administration of justice has to be swift and fair. Rule of law projects aim at recruiting judges and creating a pool of competent lawyers, while taking care of their training and providing the necessary infrastructure. International judges and prosecutors may be used where appropriate. Apart from adequate infrastructure and human resources, however, there is an apparent need for changing the attitudes of legal professionals and the society towards those institutions (Tolbert & Solomon, 2006: 45). It is precisely on that point that international administrations have failed to set an example. In Kosovo, for instance, the ethnic composition of the judiciary created friction between the international administration and the judges, culminating in the refusal of the Kosovo Force (KFOR) to abide by a court order to release Albanian suspects.

In the same vein, care should be taken that courts are accessible to everyone, that there is the possibility for free legal aid for the poor and that there is compliance with judicial rulings. Proceedings should be held in public. Efficient measures for protecting witnesses should also be taken. In the case of multi-ethnic societies, there must be adequate facilities for translation of documents and legal counselling in all languages. Programmes for the eradication of illiteracy and human rights education are also essential in raising the awareness of the population concerning their rights and the best way to protect them. These requirements remain, of course, dead letter if there are no remedies against the acts of the public authority.

Apart from judicial reform, rule of law projects also focus on administrative and security sector reform. In the case of peace operations the functioning of the administration may be seriously compromised and plagued by corruption, while the security sector has either collapsed or is in need of urgent reform. The rule of law should be developed hand in hand with human security projects. Civil police should be reformed in order to avoid abuses and further respect for human rights. Substantial resources should be dedicated to the reconstruction of prisons and the proper staffing of civil police forces.

The fight against impunity

The question of transitional justice overlaps with the idea of an efficient administration of justice, and focuses on accountability for past human rights abuses. This component contributes crucially to the re-establishment of faith in state institutions and has been implemented through various measures. On the one hand, ad hoc international tribunals and 'hybrid' courts or chambers have been created with a mix of international/national judges and jurisdiction over crimes under both domestic and international law. In this case, the UN insists on the prohibition of capital punishment and the application of fundamental human rights standards (UN, 2004b: para 10). The UN has also condemned peace agreements for providing blanket amnesties covering responsibility for the most egregious international crimes (*ibid*). On the other hand, setting up mechanisms of truth and reconciliation, as well as programmes of reparation, and vetting the public service to screen out individuals associated with past abuses, form part of rule of law projects (UN, 2004b: paras 50–5). Substantial resources should be devoted to those processes which should also be dependent on local participation. Programmes of reparation must help to fully integrate the victims in society and restore their dignity. Finally, the administration of transitional justice should be applied even-handedly, in order to avoid accusations of selectivity and a 'victor's justice', which will undermine its legitimacy.

Accountability of international administrations

One of the core components of the rule of law in a post-conflict peacebuilding setting is that of accountability of governmental power. The question is raised whether the UN—and more broadly all IOs—are bound to promote the rule of law and also whether they are bound by the rule of law. The first aspect raises the issue of a positive obligation for the UN to re-establish and maintain the rule of law where necessary.

The second aspect is linked to the idea of accountability of IOs when mandated to implement rule of law projects. This is all the more important in the context of peace operations including peacebuilding components where there is a strong tendency to govern through executive decrees and to concentrate power in the hands of one entity, such as the Office of the High Representative (OHR). There have been allegations of abusive use of powers in peace operations: legal regulations failing to respect international human rights standards, extensive use of legally questionable detentions, absence of remedies and effective mechanisms for reviewing executive decisions set the scene for advocating the recognition of accountability. This 'governmental' aspect of international administrations is very crucial. The Constitutional Court of Bosnia and Herzegovina, for example, asserted a right to judicial review of the acts of the OHR on the basis of the doctrine of functional duality (suggesting that the OHR acted both as a national organ of Bosnia and Herzegovina and as an international authority when adopting decisions concerning the national law of Bosnia and Herzegovina). Thus it is clear that, in a peacebuilding context, the UN and other IOs undertaking governmental responsibilities in the framework of the realization of the rule of law should be both promoters and servants of both local and international rule of law standards.

Substantive components

Human rights and the rule of law

The relationship between the rule of law and human rights constitutes one of the most controversial aspects of the rule of law idea. A wide conception of the rule of law argues in favour of the inclusion of human rights within this precept. Nevertheless, even a narrow understanding of the rule of law comprises some human rights located in a twilight zone between the formal and the substantive. For example, the tenet *nullum crimen sine lege* (non-retroactivity for crimes) embodies the idea of legislative predictability and governmental legality, while the right to access to court, the right to a remedy, the right of the defendant to be charged within an appropriate time period, the right to fair trial in general, and the prevention of unlawful detentions, form part of a well-functioning judicial system—a crucial component of rule of law projects. For those reasons, it is suggested that the rule of law incorporates the idea of human rights protection.

One of the risks of coupling rule of law with international human rights law is to transfuse to the former the ambiguities and controversies of the latter. Moreover, a view that the implementation of the rule of law requires a state to adhere to major human rights treaties and fully apply human rights standards may be considered a new form of Western colonialism. Besides, it is suggested that the purpose of reducing the arbitrariness of governmental power is not really served by a rights-focused view on the rule of law, because the community's beliefs—constituting the primary source of human rights standards—are themselves arbitrary and subject to radical modifications (Coyle, 2006: 275). Nevertheless, it is evident that rule of law projects must go hand in hand with respect for fundamental international human rights standards.

Democracy and the rule of law

The concept of democracy is also closely related to the idea of the rule of law. To the extent that separation of powers and participation in the decision-making process are seen to be part of the rule of law concept, the idea of democracy becomes embedded in the rule of law. On the other hand, the concept of the rule of law goes well beyond a narrow reading of the right to democratic governance, namely the periodic conduct of free and fair elections. In the context of peacebuilding, implementation of rule of law projects focuses more on the active participation of the local element in institutional rebuilding through consultation and collaborative governmental structures than on the immediate organization of elections (see also in this sense the chapters on capacity-building; civil society; and local ownership). The example of Bosnia and Herzegovina, where the early organization of elections risked derailing the peacebuilding process, constitutes an illustrative example of the different needs of rule of law projects in peacebuilding (Oellers-Frahm, 2005: 224). Finally, democratic governance also requires that all actors involved operate in a transparent way, that there is access to information about public affairs as well as respect for the right to due process in public administration.

Objectives

The general objectives of rule of law projects can be summarized as follows: protecting against anarchy and arbitrariness and embedding a feeling of reasonableness and legal certainty. But the real challenge of rule of law projects is changing the mentality of the people towards governmental structures and restoring confidence in state institutions. Therefore, rule of law projects should focus on educational programmes and participation of the local element in the reconstruction effort in order to reinforce a culture of lawfulness and justice.

Ideological issues

Constitutionalism and constitutionalization

While the emergence of the rule of law on the domestic plane is closely linked to the notion of constitutionalism, that is, government under law, the emergence of the rule of law concept on the international plane is linked to the trend towards constitutionalization of the international legal system. This constitutionalizing process is the result of a number of factors: the shift from an exclusively state-centric and voluntaristic order to a more individually oriented one, the increasing institutionalization of international society with concomitant calls for legal constraints on the expanding powers of IOs, the emergence of the notion of international community, the hierarchization of norms, and the strengthening of human rights law. This trend in turn feeds back into domestic processes through the promotion of rule of law projects by IOs in a peacebuilding context.

Economic liberalization

The promotion of the rule of law in war-torn societies and the pursuance of liberal economic policies are closely interlinked. Nowadays, international financial institutions are heavily involved in post-war reconstruction and more particularly in the implementation of legal reform projects through consultations and drafting of various legal codes. This process leads towards uniformity in laws around the world. The World Bank in its conceptual elaboration of the rule of law insists on the elements of equality, transparency, institutional efficacy, and clarity of legal rules/predictability of legal reforms. These elements allegedly create a safe environment favouring foreign investment and the growth of a market economy. Nevertheless, radical economic reforms in a peacebuilding context, including extensive privatizations, may go against the principle of self-determination of local populations, namely their right to 'freely pursue their economic, social and cultural development' (OHCHR, 1966: Art 1, para 1).

Actors

Rule of law projects in a peacebuilding context involve both the international community and the local population and their government.

The international community component includes the UN and several of its agencies, other international and regional organizations, international financial institutions, private donors, and international experts (Mani, 1998: 2–3). The UN has a central role in rule of law programmes. As the UN Secretary-General has observed, '[s]upporting Member States to strengthen the rule of law is central to the work of the United Nations system…' (UN, 2006b: para 10). The role of international NGOs is also crucial. They contribute to the day-to-day progress of rule of law operations and enhance a 'bottom-up' approach to rule of law. They work with both civil society and public authorities.

Local populations and governments are at the other end of the rule of law spectrum; they usually constitute the recipients of rule of law aid and the target of reform plans. Their cooperation is important and the UN has been at pains to conceptualize the manner of their participation in the implementation of rule of law projects.

Challenges and dilemmas

Rule of law projects and local participation

Rule of law projects are not deployed in a complete institutional vacuum. In many cases there is a governmental authority that simply needs to be assisted, while even in cases of anarchy there is always a *people* who must be consulted. Consequently, at the heart of the rule of law projects lies the policy dilemma of how to reconcile the far-reaching role of the international presence with the need for extensive local ownership in project drafting and implementation.

The UN is increasingly aware of the need for local participation in rule of law reforms. As the Secretary-General has noted:

To be effective, efforts to strengthen the rule of law must be led by host-country authorities and implemented by national actors. International expertise and resources should be made available to assist host-country Governments in that regard. Such efforts must be based on the culture and legal framework of the host country, including the international standards they have adopted, and not on imported models (UN, 2007a: para 57).

In this framework, UN-mandated rule of law projects should contain clear rules concerning the form of participation of the local element therein. In that way, the UN could deal with the complex duty of checking and guiding the local element while simultaneously taking into account its views and encouraging its participation.

The element of local ownership also limits the choice of the normative basis for rule of law projects. Project implementation should be consent-based and imposition through UN Security Council resolutions should be the last solution (Oellers-Frahm, 2005: 189), when the legitimacy of local authorities is challenged because they do not represent the local population (illegal occupation in East Timor, minority considerations in Kosovo), or when it is extremely difficult to identify local entities who can be consulted and to whom project implementation could be entrusted. Moreover, the use of the UN Charter Chapter VII for rule of law project implementation, in the context of post-conflict peacebuilding, may stretch to its outmost the notion of a threat to the peace, and also runs counter to the idea that Chapter VII measures should have a provisional and policing character.

Cultural and legal traditions v imported models

One of the crucial elements of a rule of law mission is the question of the applicable law. Frequently, local codes may not conform to international human rights standards and may require reform. Consequently, there is a need for legal change, while there is also a need for short-term solutions to avoid legal chaos. UN-drafted rule of law projects have initially favoured the imposition of foreign models. While offering some certainty, these models are not well adapted to local particularities and signify an unwillingness of the peacebuilders to understand

and apply local law. In addition to this, a rule of law framework within traditions and customary legal systems may well exist. It is thus important to follow an assisting rather than a substituting policy of legal reform (Quast, 2004: 46–7). Nevertheless, despite preserving legal continuity, this risks leading to a legitimization of human rights abuses, inherent in some local legal traditions. For that reason, the UN may opt for the solution of the reinstatement of local customs while incorporating human rights standards and provisions for the protection of vulnerable groups. This policy will contribute to the education of the local population and the change of traditional perceptions, thus better embedding rule of law ideals in the society (Danne, 2004: 218–28).

Accountability of international actors

Despite stressing the importance of the rule of law for the accountability of international actors in their peacebuilding activities, practice shows an abusive use of powers (eg controversial legal regulations, legally questionable detentions) and there is little prospect of holding IOs responsible for human rights violations and administrative misconduct (see also on this issue the chapter on peace operations). For example, while UN administrative authorities have proclaimed the 'applicability' of human rights standards in the exercise of transitional administration functions (UN, 1999a; 1999b), the relevant mechanisms for concretizing the notion of 'applicability' are clearly inadequate: the broad *rationae materiae* and *rationae personae* immunities sought by the UN (OHR, 1995: Annex 10, Art 3, para 4; UN, 2000b), the recommendatory nature of the decisions of reviewing authorities, and recognition of the international administration as the 'final arbiter' of its own acts, leave no clear and effective remedy for potential victims.

In spite of the recognition that when undertaking 'executive or judicial functions, UN -operated facilities must scrupulously comply with international standards for human rights in the administration of justice' (UN, 2004b: paras 10 & 33) and the submission by international administrations of reports to the Human Rights Council on the human rights situation in the administered territories, the gap of accountability has not closed. Indeed, it was accentuated when the European Court of Human Rights (ECHR) recently declared inadmissible claims against acts of the international administration in Kosovo on the basis that 'the Convention cannot be interpreted in a manner which would subject the acts and omissions of Contracting Parties which are covered by UNSC Resolutions and occur...in the course of such missions, to the scrutiny of the Court' (ECHR, 2007: para 149).

The absence of effective accountability mechanisms, while allowing the international administration to proceed unimpeded in its projects, constitutes a serious obstacle for rule of law success. Double standards and absence of control render rule of law precepts dead letter and de-legitimize the work of the UN and other IOs in this field.

Importance of rule of law projects in post-conflict peacebuilding

Rule of law projects constitute a cornerstone of peacebuilding processes. In the short term, the rule of law is perceived as a necessary prerequisite for rebuilding governmental structures, embedding law and order, and enhancing people's faith in state authority. In the long term, respect for the rule of law favours economic development and the prosperity of the population, social justice and the protection of human rights. Ultimately, the rule of law is a primary condition for the long-term viability of the state.

III. Implementation

Controversies over implementation

International v *local management*

While one would expect rule of law projects to lead to a strengthening of local governmental structures, and eventually to the full assumption of governmental responsibilities by the local element, this is not always the case. The length of time required to transfer powers to the local element can vary according to the circumstances. The need to train local staff before charging them with rule of law responsibilities may cause considerable delays (eg as in East Timor). Moreover, indeterminacy with regard to the future status of a territory, or a stalemate in the peacebuilding process because of the lack of cooperation of domestic authorities, may reverse the evolution of rule of law projects towards local ownership. It is thus argued that local ownership should be the exit strategy and not the starting point in this process (Chesterman, 2004: 152).

Rule of law v *human security*

The relation between rule of law and human security issues in the framework of rule of law project implementation has been controversial. By invoking the need for security as a necessary prerequisite for order and legal reform, international administrations and local authorities supposedly implementing rule of law projects have violated human rights and neglected due process requirements. Checks and balances have been ignored in order to accelerate the process of reform and lengthy legal reviews of new legislation have been criticized for overburdening an emerging system. It has even been asserted that 'full human rights protection was not possible in such a reconstructive context' (ECHR, 2007: para 108). On the other hand, the absence of a secure environment makes impossible the realization of rule of law projects. Thus, security considerations should be taken into account, not as a means in themselves, but as a tool for backing up and providing protection for rule of law project implementation.

Coordination between IOs

Cooperation among different actors involved in rule of law project implementation is problematic. International actors are frequently engaged in overlapping and contradictory projects because of the diversity of their aims and the multidimensional character of rule of law projects that give rise to a variety of institutional actions. The lack of coordination is also due to the lack of shared understanding concerning the concept of the rule of law.

The newly established UN Peacebuilding Commission is projected to become the forum for addressing intergovernmental coordination and for creating a common operational framework for rule of law projects. The Rule of Law Assistance Unit, the new proposal for a Rule of Law Coordination and Resource Group (UN, 2006b: para 48), and the creation of a Peacebuilding Fund may reduce the antagonism and the cacophony between international agencies, though an opposite trend towards self-containment and autonomy can be traced back in the same UN report (*ibid*: para 21).

The top-down approach

One can observe that rule of law orthodoxy features a top-down emphasis focusing on state institutions and bureaucratic administration models, which ignores the social synergies at the local level that constitute the main force of rebuilding (Golub, 2007: 48). Technocratic institutional reforms frequently neglect cultural particularities and lead to a sterile mimicry of Western models. State-driven, and thus following statal models in the context of peacebuilding, the UN unavoidably orients rule of law projects towards a top-down approach (with regard to capacity-building or security sector reform). This bias has been strongly criticized. Many times the UN has invested in corrupt and failed governments that do not give priority to embedding the rule of law, and it has tried to reform institutions and laws without taking into account the real needs of the population. The latter is ultimately the entity in need of help and should be the beneficiary of rule of law reform projects. A social development approach can be realized when channelling aid through domestic NGOs, using traditional gatherings and customary practices, and by prioritizing the education of the poor and the marginalized, the protection of their rights and their environment. Thus, war-torn societies better embrace rule of law projects and pressure institutions to change and develop, leading to better legal implementation.

Appraisal of past practices and concluding remarks

Over time, rule of law projects that include peacebuilding components within peace operations have become more sophisticated and multidimensional. The UN and other IOs have identified weak points and have taken some measures to improve efficiency (clearer mandates, better coordination, creating a pool of institutional memory). The ongoing debate on UN reform includes in its agenda the role of the UN in state-building. While initially the debate oscillated between, on the one hand, a robust intervention in rule of law project implementation (UN, 2004a: paras 177 and 264) and, on the other hand, proposals for an ancillary role for the UN, it is this latter approach that has gained pace recently. The Secretary-General has observed that increasingly the UN 'is looking to national led strategies of assessment and consultation carried out with the active and meaningful participation of national stakeholders' (UN, 2004b: para 15) and has advocated leaving process leadership and decision making to them (*ibid*). The balance between local ownership and UN leadership is also reflected in the 'light footprint' proposals of the Peacebuilding Commission. In the same vein, the new UN Office of the Rule of Law and Security Institutions aims at efficient but swift interventions based on a coherent and collaborative framework and results-oriented management (UN, 2007b). The European Union, for its part, stresses the importance of rapid rebuilding and subsequent hand-over to local ownership (Council of the European Union, 2003: 4) and concludes that an exit strategy should be projected already when the mission is launched (*ibid*: 12).

This careful approach is the result of the sore experience of IOs in peace operations (Somalia, Kosovo). In the case of Kosovo, not only was the launching of the UN international administration the outcome of serious compromise between different approaches, the administration also failed to map out a clear strategy, thus leaving Kosovo in limbo and the local population disenchanted. The lack of accountability of the international administration, the failure to reconcile the two ethnic groups, and the subsequent elaboration of Kosovo's future status behind closed doors provoked the hostility of the local element towards the international presence. As a result, rule of law reforms in Kosovo remain suspended and precarious today, even following self-proclaimed independence.

It is very difficult to refer to best practices concerning rule of law implementation in the context of peacebuilding, since projects are contextualized on the basis of the particular necessities of each situation and the relevant mandate. It is certain, however, that a balance between decisive intervention of international actors where governmental structures are lacking, and a gradual and rapid involvement of the local element in the ongoing process of rule of law rebuilding may be the best strategy. Still, such an approach begs the question as it remains very vague and subject to different understandings. But it may be that this flexibility and this generality constitute both the weakness and the strength of rule of law missions.

Selected Bibliography

Chesterman, S (2004), *You, the People: The United Nations, Transitional Administration, and State-building*, Oxford: Oxford University Press.

Council of the European Union (2003), *Comprehensive EU Concept for Missions in the Field of Rule of Law in Crisis Management*, 9792/03, 26 May.

Coyle, S (2006), 'Positivism, Idealism and the Rule of Law', *OJLS*, 26: 257–88.

Craig, P (1997), 'Formal and Substantive Conceptions of the Rule of Law: An Analytical Framework', *Public Law*, 467–87.

Danne, AP (2004), 'Customary and Indigenous Law in Transitional Post-Conflict States: A South Sudanese Case Study', *Monash U. L. Rev.*, 30: 199–228.

ECHR (European Court of Human Rights) (2007), *Behrami v France*, Application No 71412/01, Decision on Admissibility, 2 May 2007, available at: <http://www.echr.coe.int/echr>.

Endicott, T (1999), 'The Impossibility of the Rule of Law', *OJLS*, 19: 1–18.

Fallon, RH, Jr (1997), ' "The Rule of Law" as a Concept in Constitutional Discourse', *Columbia L. Rev.*, 97: 1–56.

Golub, S (2007), 'The Rule of Law and the UN Peacebuilding Commission: A Social Development Approach', *Cambridge Rev. of Int'l Aff.*, 20: 47–67.

ICJ (International Court of Justice) (1950), *Asylum Case (Colombia v Peru)*, Judgment, ICJ Reports 1950, 266.

—— (1989), *Elettronica Sicula SpA (ELSI) (United States of America v Italy)*, Judgment, ICJ Reports 1989, 15.

Lorenz, FM (2000), 'The Rule of Law in Kosovo: Problems and Prospects', *Criminal Law Forum*, 11: 127–42.

Maddex, RL (2000), 'Rule of Law', in *International Encyclopedia of Human Rights: Freedoms, Abuses, and Remedies*, Washington: CQ Press, 305–6.

Mani, R (1998), 'Conflict Resolution, Justice and the Law: Rebuilding the Rule of Law in the Aftermath of Complex Political Emergencies', *International Peacekeeping*, 5: 1–25.

Oellers-Frahm, K (2005), 'Restructuring Bosnia-Herzegovina: A Model with Pit-Falls', *Max Planck UNYB*, 9: 179–224.

OHCHR (Office of the High Commissioner for Human Rights) (1966), International Covenant on Civil and Political Rights.

OHR (Office of the High Representative) (1995), The General Framework Agreement for Peace in Bosnia and Herzegovina ('Dayton Agreement'), 14 December 1995.

OSCE (1990), Document of the Copenhagen Meeting of the Conference on the Human Dimension of the CSCE, 29 June 1990, available at: <http://www.osce.org>.

Quast, SR (2004), 'Rule of Law in Post-Conflict Societies: What Is the Role of the International Community?', *New Eng. L. Rev.*, 39: 45–51.

Quénivet, N (2006), 'Promoting and Abiding by the Rule of Law: UN Involvement in Post-conflict Justice', in Arnold, R, & Knoops, G -JA (eds), *Practice and Policies of Modern Peace Support Operations under International Law*, Ardsley, NY: Transnational, 35–66.

Raz, J (1977), 'The Rule of Law and Its Virtue', *The Law Quarterly Review*, 93: 195–211.

Salmon, J (2001), *Dictionnaire de droit international public*, Brussels: Bruylant.

Tamanaha, B Z (2002), 'The Rule of Law for Everyone', *Current Legal Problems*, 55: 97–122.

Tolbert, D, & Solomon, A (2006), 'United Nations Reform and Supporting the Rule of Law in Post-Conflict Societies', *Harvard Human Rights Journal*, 19: 29–62.

UN (1992), *An Agenda for Peace: Preventive Diplomacy, Peacemaking and Peace-keeping, Report of the Secretary-General*, A/47/277, 17 June.

—— (1999a), *On the Authority of the Interim Administration in Kosovo*, UNMIK/REG/1999/1, UN Interim Administration Mission in Kosovo (UNMIK), 25 July.

—— (1999b), *On the Authority of the Transitional Administration in East Timor*, UNTAET/REG/1991/1, UN Transitional Administration in East Timor (UNTAET), 27 November.

—— (2000a), *On the Appointment and Removal from Office of International Judges and International Prosecutors*, UNMIK/REG/2000/6, UN Interim Administration Mission in Kosovo (UNMIK), 15 February.

—— (2000b), *On the Status, Privileges and Immunities of KFOR and UNMIK and Their Personnel in Kosovo*, UNMIK/REG/2000/47, UNMIK, 18 August.

—— (2000c), *Report of the Panel on United Nations Peace Operations (Brahimi Report)*, A/55/305, 21 August.

—— (2004a), *A More Secure World: Our Shared Responsibility, Report of the Secretary-General's High-level Panel on Threats, Challenges and Change*, A/59/565, 2 December.

—— (2004b), *The Rule of Law and Transitional Justice in Conflict and Post-Conflict Societies, Report of the Secretary-General*, S/2004/616, 23 August.

—— (2005a), *In Larger Freedom: Towards Development, Security and Human Rights for All, Report of the Secretary-General*, A/59/2005, 21 March.

—— (2005b), *World Summit Outcome Document* (2005), A/RES/60/1, General Assembly, 20 September.

—— (2006a), *The Rule of Law at the National and International Levels*, A/RES/61/39, General Assembly, 18 December.

—— (2006b), *Uniting our Strengths: Enhancing United Nations Support for the Rule of Law*, Report of the Secretary General, A/61/636-S/2006/980, 14 December.

—— (2007a), *Comprehensive Report on Strengthening the Capacity of the United Nations to Manage and Sustain Peace Operations, Report of the Secretary-General*, A/61/858, 13 April.

—— (2007b), 'Top UN Rule of Law Officials Outline Goals of New Office', 2 October, available at: <http://www.un.org/apps/news/story.asp?NewsID=24140&Cr=rule&Cr1=law>.

Security Sector Reform

Heiner Hänggi

Definition

Security sector reform covers all activities aimed at the effective and efficient provision of state and human security within a framework of democratic governance. In the context of post-conflict peacebuilding, SSR is closely linked to related activities such as disarmament, demobilization, and reintegration; small arms control; and transitional justice.

I. Term

Origin and context

Security sector reform (SSR)—or 'security system reform' as it is sometimes referred to by developmental actors—is a relatively new concept essentially aimed at the effective and efficient provision of state and human security within a framework of democratic governance. It is driven by the understanding that an ineffective, inefficient, and poorly governed security sector represents a decisive obstacle to sustainable development, democratization, conflict prevention, and post-conflict peacebuilding. The need for comprehensive reform of the security sector had been identified earlier, but it was speeches by the United Kingdom (UK) Secretary of State for International Development, Clare Short, and policy statements by the newly created UK Department for International Development (DFID), in the late 1990s, that made SSR prominent as a term. Since then, the concept has received growing support among actors in such diverse fields as development assistance, democracy promotion, conflict prevention, and post-conflict peacebuilding.

Three major developments have nurtured this trend. First, during the 1990s, with some of the political constraints of the Cold War lifted, the development community had more leeway to address issues that until that point had been considered largely outside their fields of activity. These included the reduction of military expenditure for development purposes, the application of the democratic governance and public sector reform paradigms to the security sector, and the broader challenges of the security-development nexus in conflict trans-formation. Against this background, the SSR approach provided an overarch-ing concept that intellectually justified the development community's venture into security-related activities. Following the lead of the UK, other Western donor countries and multilateral development actors such as the Development Assistance Committee (DAC) of the Organisation for Economic Co-operation and Development (OECD) and the United Nations Development Programme (UNDP) soon began to embed SSR in their development assistance policies and programmes.

Second, following the end of the Cold War, Western governments began to emphasize, bilaterally as well as through multilateral security institutions such as the Organization for Security and Co-operation in Europe (OSCE) and the North Atlantic Treaty Organization (NATO), the promotion of democratic civil-military relations in Central and Eastern European transition countries. With other multilateral actors coming into the picture, notably the European Union (EU) and the Council of Europe, this approach soon began to expand to non-military elements of the security sector such as the police, border guards, and judicial institutions. While these multilateral security actors were engaged in a wide range of SSR activities throughout the 1990s, they have only recently begun to label them as such and, in the case of the EU, to draw up their own SSR policy frameworks. At the same time, SSR, albeit not necessarily under this label, has been recognized as a key element in the political transition of countries in Africa, the Asia-Pacific, and Latin America.

Third, SSR has gained the most practical relevance in the context of externally assisted reconstruction of states emerging from violent conflict. The growing number of international peace operations, along with a wider spectrum of related activities, has led to the increasing involvement of peacekeepers and civilian administrators in longer-term reconstruction and development tasks, including the reform and often even reconstruction of the security sector. SSR-related activities have included transitional justice and rule of law; disarmament, demo-bilization, and reintegration of former combatants; small arms and light weapons control; and mine action. Given its broad scope, SSR has provided a useful con-cept which addresses a host of post-conflict security and governance challenges within a coherent framework. As evidenced by the February 2007 open debate of the UN Security Council on SSR and the Secretary-General's report on UN approaches to SSR released in January 2008, within the UN system SSR is viewed increasingly as central to success in post-conflict peacebuilding efforts, particularly in terms of ensuring the transition from peacekeeping to longer-term reconstruction and development.

'Security sector reform' is the term of choice in this Lexicon because it has emerged as the term most commonly used by practitioners as well as analysts. 'Security system reform'—as referred to by the OECD DAC in line with its devel-opmental approach—reflects the multi-sectoral nature of the security and justice system. Both terms are often used interchangeably, for instance by the European Commission in its 2006 Communication on European Community support to SSR (European Commission, 2006). As early as 2002, UNDP's Bureau for Crisis Prevention and Recovery began to promote a new term, namely 'justice and security sector reform', in order to emphasize that the justice and security sectors are inextricably linked. Other UN entities such as the Department of Peacekeeping Operations (DPKO), however, normally employ the term 'security sector reform' and will use the term 'rule of law' when referring to activities related to the police, judicial, and penal systems and other law enforcement agencies. 'Security sector transformation' is a term preferred by authors who wish to underline the need for fundamental change in security sector governance rather than mere reform. 'Security sector reconstruction' is a alternative term used to highlight the peculiarities linked to the specific challenges of SSR in post-conflict environments. Finally, 'security sector governance' is an analytical term applied to security governance on the state level. It takes into account the variety of actors and mechanisms—state and non-state, hierarchical and non-hierarchical—which are involved in the provision of security and justice. From this perspective, SSR may be conceived as a means to enhance good governance of the security sector.

Understandings

Despite its growing presence in international relations discourse and practice, SSR remains a contested concept, particularly as regards understandings of the scope of the security sector. A narrow notion reflects traditional state-centric understandings of security, focusing on those public sector institutions responsible for the provision of internal and external security, as well as on the civilian bodies relevant for their management, oversight, and control. An expanded understanding that still falls within the narrow notion of the security sector would include justice institutions—or the 'justice sector' in the security system perspective—in recognition of the linkages and the complementary relationship between security and justice. This is, however, not necessarily shared by the entire SSR community: there is concern that the justice sector might become 'securitized' by its incorporation in the SSR concept, and also fear of a loss of clarity and focus if the security sector is not confined to core security actors. Although not generally accepted as falling under the SSR paradigm, it should be noted for completeness that the narrowest understanding would focus on the reform of the traditional security forces such as armed forces and police as well as the relevant 'power' ministries (defence, interior), thereby excluding the democratic governance perspective inherent to the SSR concept.

Broader understandings of SSR emphasize that security and justice services are—more often than not—delivered by non-state actors ranging from customary justice providers to armed groups and private military and security companies, and that civil society organizations have an important role to play owing to their potential for monitoring government policy and practice on security (and justice) issues. This shift from an exclusive focus on government (a narrow understanding) to governance (a broad understanding) is particularly relevant in post-conflict situations where security and justice have been both privatized and internationalized in important respects, suggesting that SSR entails far more than simply the reconstruction of the state security forces and relevant oversight institutions (for further discussion on the issue of privatized security, see the chapters on non-state actors; peace operations; and the private sector).

For these reasons, most academic and policy-oriented studies dealing with SSR adhere to a broad understanding of the concept as embodied in the OECD DAC Guidelines endorsed by the member states in 2004 (OECD, 2005) and the OECD DAC Handbook on Security System Reform adopted in April 2007 (OECD, 2007). At the same time, these policy and operational guidelines have been increasingly embraced by relevant international actors such as leading donor countries, international organizations, and non-governmental organizations (NGOs), and thus reflect a widely used definition of SSR. Accordingly, the security sector (or security system as it is referred to by the DAC) is defined as including all those institutions, groups, organizations, and individuals—both state and non-state—with a stake in security and justice provision (OECD, 2007: 22). These include the following actors:

- Core security actors: armed forces; police; gendarmeries; paramilitary forces; presidential guards; intelligence and security services (both military and civilian); coast guards; border guards; customs authorities; and reserve or local security units (civil defence forces, national guards, militias).

- Security management and oversight bodies: the executive; national security advisory bodies; legislature and legislative select committees; ministries of defence, internal affairs, foreign affairs; customary and traditional authorities; financial management bodies (finance ministries, budget officers, financial audit and planning units); and civil society organizations.

- Justice and rule of law: judiciary; justice ministries; prisons; criminal investigation and prosecution services; human rights commissions and ombudsmen; and customary and traditional justice systems.

- Non-statutory security forces: liberation armies; guerrilla armies; private security companies; and political party militias.

SSR means—again according to the DAC definition—transforming the security sector/system:

which includes all the actors, their roles, responsibilities and actions—working together to manage and operate the system in a manner that is more consistent with democratic norms and sound principles of good governance, and thus contributes to a well-functioning security framework (OECD, 2005: 20).

Although falling slightly short of the broader definition of the security sector introduced by the DAC, the UN Secretary-General's 2008 report reflects a similar understanding of SSR. Accordingly, SSR:

describes a process of assessment, review, and implementation as well as monitoring and evaluation led by national authorities that has as its goal the enhancement of effective and accountable security for the State and its peoples without discrimination and with full respect for human rights and the rule of law (UN, 2008: 6).

II. Content

Core components

Although the security sector has unique characteristics given the central role that the legitimate use of force plays in the provision of security, it shares many common characteristics with other areas of public service delivery. As UN Secretary-General Kofi Annan noted in 1999, the security sector 'should be subject to the same standards of efficiency, equity and accountability as any other [public] service' (Annan, 1999: 5). Thus, the overarching objective of SSR is to ensure that security and justice institutions perform their statutory functions—to deliver security and justice to the state and its people—efficiently and effectively, consistent with democratic norms and the principles of democratic governance, rule of law, and human rights. Although there are no universally accepted models of SSR, a number of key elements of the SSR concept are widely recognized as being the most crucial. According to Nathan (2007), these include the following:

- The security forces are, at all times, subordinate to the civilian authorities, particularly the executive government and parliament. They fulfil their mandates in accordance with international and constitutional law and with government policy. Security personnel must be trained to discharge their duty professionally and should reflect the diversity of their societies, with women and minorities adequately represented.

- The executive government determines security policy and exercises civilian control over the security forces. It is accountable to citizens, primarily through parliament and regular free and fair elections but also through media scrutiny, public debate, referenda, and other forms of public consultation.

- Parliament approves security legislation and budgets, performs oversight functions with respect to the security services and provides a forum for political parties to deliberate on security policy and activities.

- Independent courts perform judicial functions and various statutory bodies might have a watchdog function in relation to security services.

- Individuals, the media and civil society organizations are free to engage in research, debate, advocacy, and other activities that might be critical or supportive of the security services and government's security policy.

Given the scope and complexity of the concept, the range of possible SSR activities is quite extraordinary. However, two major categories of reform activities can be distinguished—each reflecting one of the two core elements of SSR:

- First, measures aimed at restructuring and improving the capacity of the security forces and justice institutions. These SSR activities include, among others, partial reforms such as defence, intelligence, police, border management, judicial and prison reform. From a broad SSR perspective, activities aimed at integrating armed non-state actors and the private sector into security governance might also be considered as a part of this category of SSR activities. In line with a holistic approach to SSR, it is imperative to link each area of engagement because efforts concentrated in one area will fail unless complementary work is carried out in other areas.
- Second, measures aimed at strengthening civilian management and democratic oversight of the security forces and justice institutions. These SSR activities include, among others, reforms of the relevant ministries and their management capacities (including financial management), of the parliament and its relevant select committees (such as defence, interior, etc) as well as of the relevant judicial oversight bodies. From a broad SSR perspective, capacity-building in favour of specialized civil society actors such as think tanks, media and NGOs would also fall into this category of SSR activities.

Beyond these broad categories of SSR activities, a number of cross-cutting reform measures have an impact on, or even link, several component parts of the security sector. Such activities include the development of norms, standards and good practices specific to the security sector, the strengthening and adaptation of the constitutional and legal framework of security sector governance, and comprehensive and inclusive national security reviews as a precondition and catalyst for successful SSR. Thus, SSR as commonly understood favours a holistic approach—first, by integrating all those partial reforms touching on defence, the police, and the judicial system which in the past were generally seen and conducted as separate efforts; second, by linking measures aimed at increasing the efficiency and effectiveness of security forces to overriding concerns of democratic governance; and third, by considering non-state actors—both non-statutory security forces and civil society actors—as relevant for security sector reform and governance.

SSR and the post-conflict environment

A high proportion of the activities currently subsumed under the heading of SSR take place in post-conflict societies. Clearly, engaging in SSR in post-conflict environments poses special challenges and also presents particular opportunities. On the one hand, there is often considerable public demand for change in these countries, including the 'right-sizing' and reform of the security sector, as well as willingness on the part of the international community to actively support reforms, including SSR. On the other hand, SSR seems to be particularly difficult given widespread insecurity, weak or absent state institutions, fragile inter-ethnic relations, tense political situations, and the precarious socio-economic conditions of post-conflict countries. This is further aggravated by the fact that the degree of privatization and internationalization of the provision of security tends to be much greater in post-conflict environments than in other SSR contexts. Such settings are more often than not characterized by the strong presence of armed non-state actors, such as rebel groups and warlords, whose political ambitions and economic stakes will have to be taken into account in post-conflict peacebuilding. Furthermore, international intervention is the rule rather than the exception in post-conflict peacebuilding, and often for a considerably longer period of time than initially expected. This tends to be contrasted with a shortage of local capacity and, thus, with a lack of local ownership in post-conflict peacebuilding in general, including SSR in particular.

Despite these distinct patterns, SSR in post-conflict settings follows the same two key principles as SSR in non-conflict environments, namely (re-)establishing security forces to provide public security in an effective and efficient manner and within a framework of democratic governance. What makes post-conflict SSR different, however, is the fact that it has to tackle a third objective, namely, that of addressing the specific legacies of violent conflict by focussing on issues that are rarely pursued in SSR programmes. Such issues include the need to disband non-statutory armed forces, or to integrate them into new statutory ones; to disarm, demobilize, and reintegrate large numbers of former combatants, including child soldiers; to overcome the challenges posed by the remnants of war including the proliferation of small arms and light weapons and landmines; to redress past crimes and atrocities; and to promote reconciliation. Thus, in addition to the standard reform activities aimed at security forces and justice institutions, as well as at their management and oversight mechanisms, SSR in post-conflict situations is also heavily dependent on more or less urgent SSR-related activities such as the engagement of armed non-state actors, disarmament, demobilization, and reintegration programmes, small arms control, mine action, transitional justice, and the establishment of the rule of law.

The large variety of SSR-related interventions and the high level of international engagement mean that taking an integrated approach to SSR is vital to success. This is of particular importance in the context of peace agreements and peace operations, which both tend to establish frameworks for SSR which may, or may not, facilitate transition from initial stabilization to longer-term reconstruction and development.

III. Implementation

The challenges of implementation

Given its broad scope and sensitive nature, SSR faces a number of challenges relating to its implementation. These include, among others, the cross-cutting nature of SSR, the role of external actors in supporting SSR, and the tension between external support for and local ownership of SSR processes.

The first challenge of implementation stems from the fact that the SSR concept bridges those previously separate international discourses of security policy, peacebuilding, democracy promotion, and development cooperation. These cross-sectoral characteristics make the SSR approach innovative and promising while simultaneously rendering it more demanding in terms of conceptualization and, especially, its implementation. The cross-cutting nature of the SSR concept thus requires close collaboration between very different epistemic communities, in particular between the development and conflict transformation community on the one hand and the traditional—often military-focused—security community on the other. However, both communities have struggled to reconcile their worldviews in a cooperative manner, thus complicating collaboration in the field. Furthermore, although it is recognized in development cooperation that security issues can no longer be excluded, the development community is still rather reluctant to cooperate with security—particularly military—actors who are more often seen as part of the problem than part of the solution. In post-conflict contexts, there is a cleavage between the peacekeeping community, which views SSR—with an emphasis on security actor capacity-building—as a short-term exit strategy, and the conflict transformation community, which considers SSR—with an emphasis on the democratic governance dimension—as a component part of longer-term reconstruction and development.

The second significant challenge of SSR implementation refers to the way that the cleavages between the different communities tend to nurture different approaches among national and international institutions, resulting in incoherent donor policy. Depending on what is considered to be in line with the national interest, development ministries may argue for a reduction in military expenditure commensurate with development needs and for an application of principles of democratic governance to the security sector; ministries of economic affairs and trade may lobby for the arms industry; ministries of defence may argue for a continuation of military-to-military cooperation; and ministries of foreign affairs may either promote democracy and human rights, or respect for traditional ties with non-democratic regimes. These diverging institutional interests in SSR often result in the mere continuation of traditional programmes of development assistance, economic relations, or political and security cooperation under the guise of SSR. Another source of incoherence in donor policy is the lack of coordination and, in some cases, even the competition between different international organizations, governments, and NGOs engaged in supporting SSR. As various actors have adopted divergent approaches to SSR, there is some risk of duplicating or contradicting the efforts of others. This is further aggravated by the fact that divergent approaches, rather than joint efforts, permit local authorities to play external actors off against each other, thereby undermining external support for domestically driven SSR.

The difficulty of balancing local ownership with external support for SSR programmes is the third important challenge to the successful implementation of SSR. In most cases, and with few exceptions in post-conflict situations, SSR programmes are initiated and funded by donor states or multilateral organizations, which generally also provide the bulk of implementation expertise and, more often than not, the political pressure to move the process forward in the face of local resistance or inertia. Given this reality, the natural tendency is for external actors to promote their own reform models. In practice, however, externally generated reform prescriptions inevitably collide with the unique framing conditions present in each context, which can include the extent to which the conflict continues in the post-war period, the nature of the pre-conflict security sector, and the relative strength of inclusive, pro-reform political forces within the domestic political sphere. In most cases, these conditions impose real limits on the scope, speed, and depth of SSR, and limit the willingness of local political actors to support such initiatives. A particularly difficult yet crucial challenge is to find a balance between external imposition and local ownership, while at the same time ensuring that SSR processes contribute to long-term peacebuilding and are not hijacked by local political actors for partisan gain. This tension is inherent in the SSR concept itself and is thus not amenable to easy solutions.

Lessons learned

Given that SSR is still a fairly new concept, it lacks conceptual and normative clarity. Also, its broad scope and its application in different contexts make it difficult to generate a clear set of lessons learned and good practices. However, a number of key principles can be drawn from policy statements and study reports developed by intergovernmental policy actors (eg OECD, 2007; UN, 2007b, 2008) as well as non-governmental ones (eg Nathan, 2007; Hänggi & Scherrer, 2007). These include the following eight points:

- SSR should be based on the same principles of accountability and transparency that apply across the public sector, in particular improved governance through greater civilian and parliamentary oversight of security processes. It is crucial but not sufficient that the security forces perform their statutory functions efficiently and effectively; they must perform them in accordance with democratic norms and the principles of democratic governance, the rule of law, and the protection of human rights. Consequently, reforms aimed solely at modernizing and professionalizing the security forces and thereby increasing their capacity without ensuring their democratic accountability are not consistent with the SSR concept. As difficult or seemingly counter-productive as it may seem in the short term, particularly in post-conflict environments, investing in participative, locally owned reform processes and oversight mechanisms is seen as critical for the long-term success of SSR.

• SSR must be addressed holistically, taking into account all institutions and actors that play a role in security sector governance. A particular challenge of post-conflict SSR is to simultaneously engage armed non-state actors and build government capacity to provide security to the people in an accountable way (human security); to build capacity of security forces and justice institutions, and establish appropriate management and oversight mechanisms; to construct or reconstruct (rather than reform) the security sector and to tackle SSR-related issues such as disarmament, demobilization, and reintegration as well as transitional justice; thus, there is a need to steer away from a piecemeal approach to SSR. At the same time, SSR programmes do not have to encompass all actors and dimensions of the security sector. They do, however, need to be designed and implemented in full awareness of the complex interdependencies that characterize the security sector. The development of a nationally owned and inclusive concept of security, based on a thorough needs assessment, is an important first step in developing a holistic approach.

• In many countries and in post-conflict countries in particular, the security of women and children warrants special attention because they are exposed to a high level of general and also gender-based violence and insecurity. Women and children are marginalized in political decision-making and in the determination of security priorities and resource allocation. The security services, headed and predominantly staffed by men, neglect gender-based violence, and are themselves guilty of this form of violence, as well as discrimination against their female members. A key SSR challenge is therefore to integrate a gender-sensitive approach that promotes the different security needs of women, men, boys, and girls. Of particular importance is the full involvement and equal participation of women in SSR programmes.

• SSR must be context-specific because each country engaged in SSR constitutes a special case and hence a different reform context. Consequently, the way SSR is approached and implemented very much depends on whether a country finds itself in a long-term democratization process, in transition from war to peace or in a post-conflict setting. Another important contextual factor is the regional security environment, which may be more or less amenable to SSR at a national level. A comprehensive SSR process is most easily achieved where a country has embarked on a process of long-term democratization and development, as well as in those post-conflict states in which local stakeholders interested in engaging in SSR and international peace operations offer a basis for reconstruction and sustainable development. In many other cases, however, it can be considerably more difficult to carry out SSR activities.

- SSR depends on local ownership because the reform of the most sensitive sector of the state must be shaped and driven by local actors and supported, if necessary, by external actors. Local ownership entails the need to ensure that local actors are involved in the SSR process from the outset and that they acquire enough capacity to enable the smooth handover of tasks from external actors when the time is right. As local ownership is an essential condition for the development of effective and accountable security and justice institutions, it is important that international actors consider national frameworks and local knowledge already in place before embarking on SSR processes. This may be extremely difficult in some countries, particularly in post-conflict environments, but it is a pragmatic imperative as well as a matter of respect. SSR that is not locally shaped and driven is not sustainable.

- Since local ownership is fundamental, the general strategy of external actors should be to support domestic actors engaged in SSR, including local women's organizations and human rights actors. Areas for external actors' support to SSR include: the provision of funds; the stimulation and facilitation of policy dialogue and transformation; technical advice on security issues; training and education activities; generating lessons learned and best practices; and norm setting (in the case of regional and international organizations). As SSR constitutes a fundamentally political activity necessitating a careful appreciation of who the 'reformers' are as opposed to the 'spoilers', the international community needs to remain cognisant of the fact that it is supporting the redistribution of the means of power within a state, and should therefore avoid purely technical solutions. External actors must proceed with sensitivity, care, and caution in dealing with SSR, and act in a coherent and coordinated way.

- In order to be effective, external assistance to nationally led and owned SSR programmes needs to be well coordinated. Coordination between local and external actors involved in SSR programmes is clearly vital but it presupposes coordination within and among all relevant international actors. Such coordination often remains poor in practice, whether because different mandates cover SSR only partially or because actors are reluctant to coordinate. Leading donor countries try to meet the challenge of internal coordination by following a 'whole-of-government' approach, integrating security (defence), political (diplomacy), and socio-economic (development) perspectives. International and regional organizations such as the UN and the EU face a similar challenge in developing overarching, 'whole-of-system' approaches to SSR. Coordination between international actors remains extremely difficult but some points of reference for improved coordination among donor countries and organizations are provided by the OECD DAC Guidelines on SSR (OECD, 2005), an over-arching EU policy framework on SSR—based on the 'EU Concept for ESDP Support to SSR' (Council of the European Union, 2006) and on the European Commission Communication on European Community support for SSR (European Commission, 2006) adopted in 2005 and 2006, respectively—as well as the UN Secretary-General's report on United Nations approaches to SSR (UN, 2008).

• SSR must be conceived as a long-term endeavour that takes place over several years (if not decades) and which requires substantial resources and commit-ment, particularly in post-conflict countries. A host of security needs might be urgent but there is never a quick-fix solution. Short-term targets lead to dys-functional and unsustainable outcomes. Institutional capacity, affordability and sustainability of programmes, sequencing, timing, and flexibility are all aspects of SSR that need to be balanced against each other. In particular, there is a need to address in this context the deficits of external actors' capacity to support long-term SSR programmes, and the lack of domestic actors' capacity to absorb substantive external assistance.

Selected Bibliography

Annan, K (1999), 'Peace and Development—One Struggle, Two Fronts', Address of the UN Secretary-General to World Bank Staff, 19 October.

Bryden, A, & Hänggi, H (eds) (2004), *Reform and Reconstruction of the Security Sector*, Münster: Lit Verlag.

—— & Hänggi, H (eds.) (2005), *Security Governance in Post-Conflict Peacebuilding*, Münster: Lit Verlag.

Brzoska, M, & Law, DM (eds) (2006), *Security Sector Reconstruction and Reform in Peace Support Operations*, Special Issue of *International Peacekeeping*, 13/1, March.

Council of the European Union (2006), *EU Concept for ESDP Support to Security Sector Reform (SSR)*, doc 12566/4/05.

European Commission (2006), *A Concept for European Community Support for Security Sector Reform*, Communication from the Commission to the Council and the European Parliament, SEC(2006) 658.

Hänggi, H, & Scherrer, V (2007), *Towards a Common UN Approach to Security Sector Reform: Lessons Learned from Integrated Missions*, Geneva: Geneva Centre for the Democratic Control of Armed Forces.

Law, D (ed) (2007), *Intergovernmental Organisations and Security Sector Reform*, Münster: Lit Verlag.

Nathan, L (2007), *No Ownership, No Commitment: A Guide to Local Ownership of Security Sector Reform*, Birmingham: University of Birmingham.

OECD (2005), *Security System Reform and Governance: Policy and Good Practice*, DAC Guidelines and Reference Series, Paris: Organisation for Economic Co-operation and Development.

—— (2007), *The OECD DAC Handbook on Security System Reform: Supporting Security and Justice*, Paris: OECD.

Schnabel, A, & Erhart, HG (eds) (2006), *Security Sector Reform and Post-Conflict Peacebuilding*, Tokyo: UN University.

UN (2007a), *Maintenance of International Peace and Security: Role of the Security Council in Supporting Security Sector Reform*, Concept Paper prepared by the Slovak Republic for the Security Council open debate, S/2007/72, 9 February.

—— (2007b), *Statement by the President of the Security Council*, S/PRST/2007/3, 21 February.

—— (2008), *Securing peace and development: the role of the United Nations in supporting security sector reform*, Report of the United Nations Secretary-General to the General Assembly and the Security Council, A/62/659-S/2008/39, 23 January.

State-building

Marwa Daoudy

Definition

State-building falls within the scope of international programmes through which bilateral or multilateral agencies mobilize resources in order to set up or reinforce weakened or non-existent institutions in those states that are considered to be fragile, weak, moving towards failure, or which have already collapsed. The objective is to build peace and promote security through the political, economic, and social development of states either threatened or affected by violent conflicts.

I. Term

Origin and context

The emergence of the modern state goes back *inter alia* to the peace treaties of Westphalia in 1648. The treaties introduced the notion of a sovereign entity set up within a defined territory and in which both the population and the territory are under the control of non-religious political authorities. Mutual recognition validates the sovereignty of such entities. However, scholars continue to disagree about the factors that caused the emergence of the modern state between the 16th and 17th centuries. Milliken and Krause articulate five centuries of history around the three main functions of the modern state, according to their ideological standpoint: *security*, thanks to a social contract appropriating the means of violence; *legitimacy*, resulting from the representation of a state's identity; and *growing wealth*, fostered by modern capitalism and imperialism (2002: 755–62). These authors point to the various paradoxes underpinning research into the crisis of the modern state. To use the expression coined by Tilly: 'States make war and war makes states' (1985: 170).

Ever since the 16th century, state-building has had the advantage of building on the institutional monopoly over violence, in order to ensure the security of its population and confine it within a consolidated territory. Contrary to empires, which are made up of different components, the state is supposed to be the central and cohesive entity. It may, nonetheless, acquire a *de jure* or *de facto* stature depending on whether it is recognized by the international community as a sovereign entity, regardless of the actual ability of the government to exercise control over its territory (Jackson quoted in Ottaway, 2002: 1003).

This raises the issue of state collapse as an indispensable stage in the ongoing state-building process, particularly in the context of the painful emergence of a new post-colonial order (Doornbos, 2002: 798). The analysis of state-building, which began as a regional and sometimes even a specifically African phenomenon, gradually started to take on a global dimension (Yannis, 2002: 819). The most vulnerable post-colonial entities then had to meet the challenges posed by the relaxing of the international structure inherited from World War II. State failure was the result of a lack of legitimacy, be it vertically, in the state's relation to its society, or horizontally, in the relations between the different political groups involved in an ethnic or social conflict (Bächler, 2004: 2). In the 1960s, the term used most frequently by scholars in the context of peacebuilding efforts was 'nation-building' (Deutsch, 1963). This term actually validated the efforts deployed by some international actors, including the United States, in their peacebuilding programmes. However, because it implies the idea of a national identity that is built throughout a long historical process, this notion did not receive endorsement by the UN. Instead, the UN progressively adopted an operational and tangible definition of state-building which reflected the administrative practices of multilateral agencies. From then on, state-building appeared to be a crucial factor for the sustainability of peacebuilding efforts.

Progressively, the various actors involved started to develop different approaches to the issue. The UN was reluctant to adopt practices which could have been perceived as neo-colonialist and, at the end of the 1980s, adopted a functionalist approach to peacebuilding: states started to be considered as institutions fulfilling specific functions which needed to be coordinated. On the other hand, the World Bank used the sovereign state as the central unit of its development policies.

The end of the Cold War constituted a real turning point which, subsequently, implied a change in the nature of conflicts and the appearance of new stakes in the field of peacebuilding. With superpowers cutting off their economic assistance, internal conflicts were triggered within weak states. These conflicts, which further complicated humanitarian and security issues, occurred in Africa, Central America, South-Eastern Asia, and South-Eastern Europe. From then on, such conflicts raised new issues, such as the intervention of international actors (states or non-state actors) and the implementation of stabilization and peace restoration strategies (peace operations). However, the linkage between state failure (or collapse) and international security was only first highlighted with the 11 September 2001 attacks, which had been prepared under the ægis of an already failed state: Afghanistan (Klotzle, 2006: 5–6).

Semantic and linguistic difficulties

The terminology itself raises various semantic and linguistic problems. The terms associated with state-building describe a whole range of situations, from 'fragile states' to 'failing states', to 'failed state', and to 'collapsed state', though some believe they all describe exactly the same thing. Similar categories have been introduced by some international players, eg 'rogue states', 'states with an instability risk', 'weak performers', or 'low-income countries under stress'. The present chapter does not deal with all of these notions. Milliken and Krause highlight the fact that literature and practice do not draw any distinction between failed states and collapsed states—an extreme phenomenon which remains the exception. Such authors consider it necessary to understand the phenomenon better before finding a solution. One possibility might be to develop a definition of 'state collapse' which would go beyond sheer institutional collapse to account for functional failure *per se* (Milliken & Krause, 2002: 764–5). Thus, the authors challenge Tilly's formula by linking provision of security to state-building. Such an approach would entail a better understanding of the role of the state as seen through the prism of militarization and the circulation of the means of violence within the relevant societies (Milliken & Krause, 2002: 756–7). Others oppose the process (failing) to the result (failed) or observe that collapse and failure may occur independently. Iraq is an example of a collapsed state that has never been a failing state (Schwarz, 2005).

The terminology used is another factor which influences the way an ongoing process is perceived. The notion of 'state failure' may entail a value judgment related to the moral, political, and economic failure of a society that has not managed to reach or maintain minimum standards of accountability in its governance. Such failure serves to justify externally-led intervention (Yannis, 2002: 818). Thus, this notion has been replaced by 'state collapse', which has fewer connotations.

II. Content

Premises and dilemmas of state-building

State reform policies aim at eradicating conflicts and restoring sustainable peace by implementing predefined state-building programmes. However, depending on the strategies and the premises underpinning the approach adopted, reform may actually be a source of conflict. To find the best solutions, it is therefore necessary to define and differentiate processes which lead to a state's failure or to its collapse. What are the influencing variables? Would identifying them make it possible to better prevent a state's progressive or final disintegration? What are the internal and external implications? What are the issues at stake for internal actors *vis-à-vis* international actors?

The underlying theory is that of the state. It is obvious that rebuilding efforts take place within the same borders and framework as the former state. The previous order maintains its legitimacy and must be restored, without there necessarily being any prior reflection about the mechanisms that brought about the collapse of its institutions. While past state-building efforts were characterized by states simply disappearing, being divided up into smaller units or being conquered by a more powerful neighbour, recent state-building efforts have focused on state restoration (Ottaway, 2002: 1001). Ever since the 1980s, the discourse in political science has hinged on the notion of the modern state, its birth and status as the central unit in the analysis of international relations. Today, the debate is structured around the crisis of the post-colonial state and its institutions (Milliken & Krause, 2002: 753) and dovetails with research that calls into question notions such as identity, power, and accountability of international actors within a broader reflection on national sovereignty and the challenging of its limits.

Thus, the interlocking of internal and external influencing variables, which are at the root of the crisis affecting post-colonial states, opens the door to a reflection on the dynamics that mobilize, divide, or confront local and international actors. Some consider the state's collapse as a considerable threat to international security—a perspective which puts this issue at the top of the global security agenda (Fukuyama, 2004; Krasner, 2004; Rotberg, 2004). The aim is no less than to preserve peace, stability, and the rule of law of the international community whose responsibility it is to protect failed states. Others define the international community as a 'conglomerate of industrialised democracies and the multilateral agencies over which they have preponderant influence' (Ottaway, 2002: 1001). This aim echoes the strengthening of systems and resources inherent to local capacity-building efforts and the peaceful settlement of disputes.

A new interventionist consensus emerges from this process whereby statehood is granted to a country combining all necessary qualification criteria. Thus, conflict prevention, resolution or transformation may be achieved through institutional reforms in so-called fragile states, through sustainable human development policies or through the implementation of democratic governance principles (Chesterman, 2005; International Alert & Saferworld, 2005).

Situations in which a state's essential functions fail, while its institutions continue to operate, are problematic. Ever since the nineteenth century, the model of the Western welfare state has been based on the state's core functions, of ensuring the economic, social, and general well-being of its population. In the case of post-colonial societies, these core functions may take on a neo-patrimonial character and give rise to social conflicts which, in turn, may lead the collapse of the state.

Even if they collapse, most post-colonial states are recognized as enjoying, *de jure*, sovereign rights. However, Ottaway draws a distinction between different types of *de facto* states. On one side of the continuum, there are 'raw power states': that is, states with weak institutions not recognized by their peers, but which manage to exercise actual power over their territories and their population. In such states, internally-led efforts are made toward rebuilding the state's institutions, even if they remain undemocratic. This type of situation is exemplified by Somaliland or the Democratic Republic of Congo. On the other side of the continuum are states in the Weberian sense, that is, states both *de jure* and *de facto*. Such states manage to control effectively their territories thanks to strong institutions governed by the rule of law and a sound administration. Externally-led rebuilding efforts try to fast-track states to attain this ideal model. In such situations, states are required to take short cuts and end up missing out on historical and conflictual stages that are absolutely necessary to the political and social maturation of such a project (Ottaway, 2002: 1003–4).

The elusive concept of sovereignty

State-building and its political agenda thus seem to be heading toward a fundamental redefinition of the notion of sovereignty. Some authors have advocated doing away with the classic ideal of Westphalian sovereignty (Keohane, 2003: 276). However, the risk is that the issue of sovereignty will be abandoned in favour of tutelage by the UN or some vague 'mandate' (Doornbos, 2002: 811) (see the chapters on responsibility to protect and transitional administration). New, ideologically significant concepts have therefore been put forward. This is the case for the new concepts of 'shared' or 'conditional' sovereignty which are applied to internationally sovereign states unable, as of yet, to fulfil their core functions (Krasner, 2004).

At the heart of the matter is the lack of internal legitimacy of such approaches and the subsequent tension between national identity and a representative state based on a social contract. Some go so far as to say that some state-building efforts are nothing but a resurgence of the imperial powers' past glory (Paris, 2002; Knaus & Martin, 2003). The causes of, and the appropriate answers to, the collapse of a state are to be grasped in the relation of the state to society. Given the fact that local governance structures may take over, state collapse does not necessarily imply failure of state functions, chaos, and disorder. In addition, a stable and reliable (re-)building process has to be internally led. Any intervention from outside tends to have negative consequences. This is why rebuilding policies drawn up by multilateral agencies and donating parties have now come to include a new discourse and new commitments in terms of conflict management by referring to development policies, participatory democracy, and respect for human rights, with a view to democratic governance.

According to the criteria developed by the Organisation for Economic Co-operation and Development (OECD), standards of 'good governance' or 'democratic governance' are based on four core elements: the rule of law; management of the public sector; the fight against corruption; and the reduction of military expenditure (Bächler, 2004: 3). A first caveat lies in externally-led efforts towards institutional reform. More often than not, they actually lead to setting up organizations rather than 'established' and 'significant' institutions to over-haul the electoral system and organize free and fair elections, public institutions, a parliament, as well as judicial, military, or political institutions (Ottaway, 2002: 1004). By identifying the factors behind a state's collapse, bilateral or multilat-eral agencies devise their action according to a pre-defined state-building model which hinges on simultaneous security sector reform, support for the political system, and the economy (*ibid*: 1006; Bächler, 2004: 15–6) or on a high-priority human security strategy aimed at restoring the state's capacity to control its terri-tory and population (Klotzle, 2006: 14–5).

Though such efforts seem coordinated, they suffer from the multiplicity of prescriptions that have been prepared in advance without any consideration for either the specificities of each situation or the competition between different international donors, each driven by their own development agenda rather than by the country's needs or interests. A new pattern of domination is thus estab-lished *vis-à-vis* local entities without there necessarily being any involvement on the part of the political elite. At the end of the day, experimenting with reform is problematic in that it may lead to bloodshed in extreme cases, such as in Iraq. An additional flaw appears when outside assistance pours in without any thought being given to the absorption capacity of the country's weakened institutions or the fact that corrupt elites may embezzle the money. Such a situation ends up cre-ating new problems instead of solving those that already exist (Klotzle, 2006: 10). Finally, there is the issue of the rebuilding process most likely to ensure stability and viability to the state in the making.

III. Implementation

Past experiences

Since the 1990s, different projects to rebuild collapsed states have been under-taken by the international donor community. In order to generalize the positive achievements of such projects, a list of best practices in the field of institu-tional reform was drawn up with the aim of optimizing present and future state rebuilding efforts (Ottaway, 2002: 1020). Such institutional practices target the following sectors: constitutional reform, devolution of power and decentraliza-tion, protection of minorities, rule of law, and human rights (Bächler, 2004: 7). Bosnia and Herzegovina, Cambodia, Mozambique, and Sierra Leone can be cited among the few significant examples (Klotzle, 2006: 6; Ottaway, 2002: 1009–12).

In Mozambique, after the end of the civil war in 1992, considerable resources were poured into the country. As regards economic development, the experience has proved more or less successful, despite the inability of Mozambique's still weak public institutions to render these measures operational. Ever since 2002 when the civil war was officially declared to be over, Sierra Leone's success has been only partial: the former state institutions have been restored, and yet the judiciary still needs to be strengthened. The new institutions are working to resolve three main issues: reconciliation, corruption, and war crimes; however, security sector reform remains incomplete and control has not been regained over the whole of the territory. In Cambodia, the state is surviving without having become fully democratic. In Bosnia and Herzegovina, the international community is still massively and fully involved from a military, civil, and financial point of view, but the state is not yet functioning autonomously because of internal resistance and the effective separation of power between the country's three components.

More recently, externally-led rebuilding efforts have led to transitional administrations in Kosovo (1999–present) and East Timor (1999–2002). Thanks to this system, the UN, whose presence was necessary to put an end to the conflicts, assumed only temporarily all or part of the state's sovereign functions (Chesterman, 2005). In the cases of Rwanda and Sudan, the involvement of the international community came at a late stage, if at all (Klotzle, 2006: 6). Following the 1994 genocide in Rwanda, two of the best practices were implemented when the International Criminal Tribunal was set up in Arusha and policies were designed to rebuild independent judicial institutions. And yet, these actions did not manage to secure a sustainable settlement. Rwanda actually found an internal solution outside the framework of the best practices developed by Western states by setting up local popular courts (Ottaway, 2002: 1020). In Iraq (2003–present), the state's collapse is the result of an external intervention. In Africa, other internally-led projects were devised to rebuild the state *de facto*. These experiments turned out to be successful, for example, in Eritrea, Ethiopia, and Uganda, where they came after a military victory. In such cases, power is exerted without the features of a democratic state having been acquired either by recognition or through the participation of the population. On the other hand, in Somalia, the *de jure* state has survived despite two externally and internally led attempts to rebuild the state (1992–1993). The central government has no effective control over its territory and population except in Somaliland, which has *de facto* acquired the status of state.

Assessment of institutional practices

It is possible to establish a cross-cutting assessment of institutional practices by analyzing these few experiences. Generalizing best practices in terms of state rebuilding appears artificial and insufficiently rigorous, since it leaves little room to consider the specificities of each individual situation. Optimal governance strategies and international regulation mechanisms aimed at preventing or repairing state failure and/or collapse must operate according to the specific historical and social contexts in which they are embedded. This implies prior identification of the factors which contributed to such a collapse, as well as the subsequent implementation of solutions. In the cases of Afghanistan, Bosnia and Herzegovina, and Kosovo, lack of state autonomy and the setting up of artificial institutions has led to a loyalty deficit on the part of the population. It has also contributed to bogging down the rebuilding effort. In addition, the thorny issue of international recognition complicates matters even further when it comes to the nature of the states in question. Despite legal and political controversies over the legality of its self-proclaimed independence, Kosovo seems to have achieved the highest degree of state-building. Nevertheless, whatever the circumstances of the conflict, there is no absolute state-rebuilding scheme which may be modelled on Western democratic countries with market economies.

Before any action is taken to prevent or to deal with the consequences of a state's collapse, a careful analysis must be undertaken to identify background variables, conditional factors, and the dynamics which have caused the state to collapse. The international donor community must step aside in favour of internal actors and only play an advisory or facilitator role in the identification of internal and external signs of vulnerability, regardless of whether they are the result of poverty, the monopoly on power by given social or ethnic groups, or of attempts at destabilizing the country from the outside. Post-conflict stabilization and rebuilding efforts must take into account the needs, interests and traditions of internal actors. The time factor is of paramount importance since international actors, provided they are patient, may achieve much more realistic objectives by taking local contexts and their evolution into consideration.

Despite the fact that externally-led efforts are sometimes absolutely necessary to restore peace, the need for internal actors to claim and take on a central part in the political rebuilding process is crucial for the success of externally-led reform policies. Finally, if international actors are made accountable—and this is still not part of the state rebuilding paradigm—it is possible to demystify discourse by making internal actors take on their political, social, and economic responsibilities. State-rebuilding efforts should go hand in hand with a strong political will together with the resources necessary to achieve the goals that have been set. Institutional reform cannot be the starting point as it must mature and can only take place in the context of a relationship that is progressively built up between state and society.

Selected Bibliography

Bächler, G (2004), *Conflict Transformation through State Reform*, The Berghof Handbook, Berlin: Berghof Research Centre for Constructive Conflict Management.

Chesterman, S (2005), 'State-Building and Human Development', *Human Development Report Office*, Occasional Paper.

Deutsch, KW (1963), 'Nation-Building and National Development', in Deutsch, KW, & Foltz, WJ (eds), *Nation-Building*, New York: Atherton, 1–16.

Doornbos, M (2002), 'State Collapse and Fresh Starts: Some Critical Reflections', *Development and Change*, 33/5, 797–815.

Fukuyama, F (2004), *State-Building: Governance and World Order in the Twenty-First Century*, London: Profile Books.

International Alert & Saferworld (2005), *Developing an EU Strategy to Address Fragile States: Priorities for the British EU Presidency in 2005*, London: Saferworld and International Alert, Executive Summary and chapter 1.

Jackson, R (1990), *Quasi-States: Sovereignty, International Relations and the Third World*, Cambridge: Cambridge University Press.

Keohane, R (2003), 'Political Authority after Intervention: Gradations in Sovereignty', in Holzgrefe, JL, & Keohane, R (eds), *Humanitarian Intervention: Ethical, Legal and Political Dilemmas*, Cambridge: Cambridge University Press.

Klotzle, K (2006), *International Strategies in Fragile States: Expanding the Toolbox?*, CAP Policy Analysis, No 1, Bertelsmann Group for Policy Research.

Knaus, G, & Martin, F (2003), 'Lessons from Bosnia and Herzegovina: Travails of the European Raj', *Journal of Democracy*, 14/3: 60–74.

Krasner, S (2004), 'Sharing Sovereignty: New Institutions for Collapsing and Failing States', Working Papers, No 1, Centre on Democracy, Development and the Rule of Law, Standford University on International Studies.

Milliken, J, & Krause, K (2002), 'State Failure, State Collapse and State Reconstruction: Concepts, Lessons and Strategies', *Development and Change*, 33/5: 753–74.

Ottaway, M (2002), 'Rebuilding State Institutions in Collapsed States', *Development and Change*, 33/5: 1001–23.

Paris, R (2002), 'International Peacebuilding and the "Mission Civilisatrice"', *Review of International Studies*, 28/4: 637–56.

Rotberg, I (ed) (2004), *When States Fail: Causes and Consequences*, Princeton: Princeton University Press.

Schwarz, R (2005), 'Post-Conflict Peacebuilding: The Challenges of Security, Welfare and Representation', *Security Dialogue*, 36: 429–46.

Tilly, C (1985), 'War-Making and State-Making as Organised Crime', in Evans, P, Rueschmeyer, D, & Skocpol, T (eds), *Bringing the State Back In*, Cambridge: Cambridge University Press, 169–91.

Yannis, A (2002), 'State Collapse and its Implications for Peacebuilding and Reconstruction', *Development and Change*, 33/5: 817–35.

Transitional Administration

Richard Caplan

Definition

A transitional administration is a formally constituted international body that has been entrusted temporarily with responsibility for the principal governance functions of a state or territory. In the context of post-conflict peacebuilding, transitional administration represents an international response to an internal conflict whose belligerents are unable to arrive at or to implement a peace settlement or to govern themselves peacefully.

I. Term

Transitional administration refers to the temporary assumption of responsibility of the principal governance functions of a state or territory by an international organization or organizations, often but not always led by the UN. The terms 'international administration', 'international trusteeship' (or 'neo-trusteeship'), and 'international protectorate' are sometimes used interchangeably with that of 'transitional administration'; however, only 'international administration' (or 'international territorial administration') is considered to be an acceptable substitute.

'Trusteeship' has a very precise meaning, as defined by Chapter XII of the UN Charter, which limits the use of that institution to certain non-self-governing territories administered in conformity with the stated purposes of the UN-established international trusteeship system and under the supervision of the UN Trusteeship Council.

A 'protectorate' is a state or territory whose government has agreed to surrender the conduct of its foreign relations, and possibly other sovereign competences, to a state without formal incorporation into or annexation by that state (Crawford, 2006: Chapter 7). While some scholars maintain that transitional administration represents protection 'in a new guise' (Wilde, 2001: 602), the circumstances that have given rise to the establishment of transitional administrations and some of the normative constraints that govern their operation—reflected, for instance, in the international organizational nature of all transitional administrations—can be said to distinguish them from protectorates.

Another synonymous term used, albeit very rarely, is 'substitution mission', referring to situations in which an international body substitutes itself for the national institutions (Council of the European Union, 2003: 9). 'Transitional administration' is the term that the UN Department of Peacekeeping Operations employs to describe its own operations of this kind (UN, 2006: para 3.3), although 'transitional civil administration' has also been used, arguably to emphasize the civil aspects of transitional administration over which the UN has exercised responsibility on numerous occasions (UN, 2000: paras 76–83).

Transitional administration derives its origins from a large body of cognate historical experiences in the first half of the twentieth century (Chesterman, 2004: Chapter 1). International organizations first exercised territorial administration with the League of Nations administrations of the Saar Basin, the Free City of Danzig, the Colombian town and district of Leticia, and, to a lesser extent, Upper Silesia after World War I. Other transitional administrations were envisioned for the Fiume in Dalmatia in 1919, Memel in what is now Lithuania between 1921 and 1923, Alexandretta in Syria in 1937, and Jerusalem and Trieste in 1947 (Wilde, 2001). The UN first exercised territorial administration as part of the UN Operation in Congo (UNOC) between 1960 and 1964 and with the UN's administration of West Irian from 1962 to 1963 (UNTEA). These experiences and blueprints have been the source of inspiration for the wave of contemporary initiatives, whose intellectual origins lie with the end of the Cold War. In the early post-Cold War period, the ideas of 'United Nations conservatorship' (Helman & Ratner, 1992–93), 'international trusteeship' (Lyon, 1993), and similar notions gained currency among scholars and analysts as a possible means of coping with the problem of so-called state failure (see, further, the chapter on state-building). These ideas were then adopted and adapted for use by policymakers for the purpose of post-conflict peacebuilding.

A transitional administration can be distinguished from an interim or provisional government, which refers to temporary domestic governance arrangements established during the period between the collapse of one regime and the creation of a new one. However, Guttieri and Piombo's use of the term 'international interim governments' includes transitional administrations (Guttieri & Piombo, 2007: Chapter 1). Such arrangements have been used commonly in transitions from autocratic or communist rule to democratic rule (Shain & Linz, 1995).

Transitional administration is also distinguished from military occupation, although many of the challenges that a transitional administrator and an occupying power face may be similar. A transitional administration is usually established with the authorization or at least the endorsement of the UN Security Council whereas a military occupation is likely to attract no more than Security Council recognition (see also the chapter on peace operations). For instance, while the Security Council acknowledged a central role for the Coalition Provisional Authority (CPA) in post-Saddam Iraq, UN Security Council Resolution 1483 affirmed that the United States (US) and the United Kingdom (UK) were occupying powers and that the occupation was a US–UK undertaking, not a UN-sanctioned one. In contrast with military occupations, moreover, transitional administrations are normally established with the consent of the parties, even if that consent may in some cases be only grudging. The distinction between transitional administration and military occupation is reflected in the differential legal norms that apply to the two institutions, although the usefulness and validity of this distinction have been called into question (Ratner, 2005).

II. Content

Objectives and functions

In the context of post-conflict peacebuilding, transitional administration represents an international response to an internal conflict whose severity is thought to have rendered it difficult if not impossible for the local parties to govern themselves. In such cases, either violent conflict has generated an acute administrative, political, and strategic vacuum, or local structures have remained intact but the internal situation has been a highly unstable one. The purpose of the transitional administration under such circumstances is twofold: to administer the territory while at the same time fostering the development of local autonomous capacity for self-government. In some cases an unresolved dispute between the parties may be an obstacle to achieving full self-government and the transitional administration will thus also have responsibility for promoting a resolution of the dispute or for helping to implement a decision or a settlement when one has been reached. Not all transitional administrations serve a post-conflict peacebuilding purpose; they may also be used, for instance, to facilitate the transfer of sovereignty or territorial control from one entity to another.

Transitional administrations differ from one another with respect to the degree of authority or control that the transitional administrator and associated international bodies may possess. At one end of the spectrum are supervisory administrations, which have responsibility for monitoring the governance of a state or a territory by the local parties. An example of a supervisory administration was the UN Transitional Authority in Cambodia (UNTAC) from 1992 to 1993. At the other end of the spectrum transitional administration takes the form of direct governance, as exemplified by the UN Interim Administration Mission in Kosovo (UNMIK), from 1999 to 2008, and the UN Transitional Administration in East Timor (UNTAET), from 1999 to 2002. Operations between these two poles exhibit varying magnitudes of authority, such as the UN Transitional Administration for Eastern Slavonia, Baranja and Western Sirmium

(UNTAES) in Croatia, from 1996 to 1998, and the international administration of Bosnia and Herzegovina, from 1996, which has no formal name.

Different scholars employ different terms in their categorizations of transitional authority. For instance, Doyle and Sambanis distinguish between 'supervisory', 'executive', and 'administrative' authorities (Doyle & Sambanis, 2006: 332), whereas Chopra distinguishes between 'governorship', 'control', 'partnership', and 'assistance' (Chopra, 1999: 16). In all cases, the scope of a transitional administration's interest in—if not actual responsibility for—the functioning of a state or territory is quite extensive. Indeed, never before in recent history have multilateral organizations had such broad authority for the governance of a state or territory. The chief functions of a transitional administration can be grouped into six broad categories of activity:

- the establishment and maintenance of public order and internal security through the temporary assumption of responsibility for law enforcement and/or the monitoring and training of local police; the administration of justice and/or the development of domestic judicial institutions, including the training of local judges; and the establishment and maintenance of penal institutions;
- the provision of humanitarian assistance;
- the return and reintegration of refugees and internally displaced persons;
- the performance of basic civil administrative functions, including the reconstruction and operation of public utilities, the regulation of local businesses, the establishment and maintenance of a tax regime, the running of schools and hospitals, the regulation of the media, etc.;
- the exercise or oversight of the exercise of political authority, including the appointment and removal of local public officials; the development of local political institutions, including the holding of elections to these institutions;
- economic reconstruction and the promotion of economic development.

The normative basis

The sources of authority for the establishment of transitional administrations are both legal and normative. There is no explicit UN Charter basis for transitional administrations, UN or otherwise, but nor is there for other well-established UN practices such as peacekeeping (see the chapter on peace operations). Like many other actions authorized by the Security Council and undertaken for 'the maintenance of international peace and security', these instruments may not be specified by the Charter but they are sanctioned by a broad interpretation of the functions and powers of the Security Council in Chapter V (Article 24), the nature of 'threats to the peace' and 'breaches of the peace' (Article 39), and the actions that the Security Council may take in response to them in Chapter VII (Articles 41 and 42). As the UN Secretary-General's High Level Panel on Threats, Challenges and Change observed in 2004:

The language of chapter VII is inherently broad enough . . . to allow the Security Council to approve any coercive action at all, including military action, against a state when it deems this 'necessary to maintain or restore international peace and security' (UN, 2004: para 193).

The normative basis of authority for the establishment of transitional administrations derives in part from widespread recognition of the need for, and even the responsibility of, the international community to rebuild states and territories ravaged by war. Such recognition reflects awareness of the importance of taking measures to consolidate a fragile peace in the aftermath of violent conflict so as to prevent the resumption of hostilities—an approach encapsulated by the concept of post-conflict peacebuilding (Galtung, 1975: 282–304; UN, 1992: para 21) and embodied in the UN Peacebuilding Commission, which was established in December 2005 (for further development on the Peacebuilding Commission, see the introduction to this Lexicon).

Many states also accept that there is a responsibility to rebuild, especially if their own efforts to protect a population from a humanitarian crisis have led to military intervention (see the chapter on the responsibility to protect). As the International Commission on Intervention and State Sovereignty (ICISS) concluded in its 2001 report:

The responsibility to protect implies the responsibility not just to prevent and react, but to follow through and rebuild. This means that if military intervention action is taken—because of a breakdown or abdication of a state's own capacity and authority in discharging its 'responsibility to protect'—there should be a genuine commitment to helping to build a durable peace, and promoting good governance and sustainable development (ICISS, 2001: para 5.1).

Transitional administration thus represents one of the most ambitious forms of post-conflict peacebuilding.

The multilateral nature

A characteristic feature of all transitional administrations is their international organizational nature. In contrast with the League mandates and UN trusteeship systems historically, no single state today would likely be entrusted with responsibility for the transitional administration of a state or territory. Instead, this function is performed most commonly by the UN or, in some instances, by an ad hoc international organization such as the Office of the High Representative (OHR) in the case of Bosnia and Herzegovina. Not only would it be politically unacceptable in a post-colonial era to entrust responsibility for the administration of a war-torn or contested state or territory to a single state, but the costs would also likely be too great for one state alone to bear. In contrast with cases in the past where the League or the UN itself has administered territories, the number of other international actors—both governmental and non-governmental—likely to be involved in a transitional administration today is very great. The multilateral character of transitional administrations arguably lends legitimacy to these operations. The multiplicity of actors, however, can create problems of coordination similar to those that sometimes bedevil complex peace operations, as different organizations may have different strategic objectives and may vary in their appreciation of available tactical approaches (see for instance the chapter on civil-military interface).

III. Implementation

The challenges of implementation

Notwithstanding the legitimacy that multilateralism helps to confer on transitional administrations, the institution tends to suffer from difficulties in practice that call into question its legitimacy. Transitional administrations, by their very nature, represent alien rule and thus a violation of the principle of self-determination. Even if these arrangements are designed ultimately to enhance local capacity for self-governance, and even if they enjoy broad support among the local population, the fundamental political illegitimacy associated with the suspension of sovereignty, albeit only temporarily, is inescapable.

A related problem is that transitional administration invariably operates on the basis of an accountability deficit (Caplan, 2005: Chapter 9). Transitional administrators are accountable to the agencies that appoint them but not to the local population on whose behalf they administer the territory. The local population thus cannot challenge the actions of the transitional administration, although the adoption of appeal procedures has been recommended by the Council of the European Union, among others (Council of the European Union, 2002: 15–6). In cases where executive, legislative, and judicial authority is concentrated in one individual—the transitional administrator—the accountability deficit can be especially acute. For this reason, Sergio Vieira de Mello, the first transitional administrator of Kosovo and then East Timor, likened the institution to 'benevolent despotism' (Vieira de Mello, 2001). The accountability deficit can be mitigated, but not eliminated, through the establishment of consultative mechanisms that allow for input from local authorities (see, further, the chapters devoted to peace operations and rule of law).

Another related problem is that transitional administrations can often inhibit the realization of the very outcome that they are meant to facilitate, notably local capacity-building. While the importance of building local capacity is widely recognized, in practice it is often given too little emphasis because international authorities are inclined to rely on international agencies and personnel to ensure that territorial administration is conducted competently and in conformity with the requirements of an administration's mandate. However, such practices may come at the expense of training local cadres adequately and preparing the population for the assumption of responsibility for governance (for a similar assessment see the chapter on local ownership).

Because their mandates are so extensive, transitional administrations are costly operations. Bosnia and Herzegovina received nearly seven times the external assistance per capita than Germany did in the first two post-conflict years, while Kosovo has been the recipient of twenty-five times more money on a per capita basis than post-Taliban Afghanistan (Dobbins, 2003: 96). The costs of transitional administration, combined with the unease of exercising sovereignty on behalf of a people, explain in part the appeal of the 'light footprint' approach that has characterized international assistance efforts in Afghanistan (UN, 2002: para. 98). Such an approach, rather than supplanting local authority, seeks instead to reinforce local ownership.

In contrast with other assistance missions, the light footprint approach not only provides extensive external support but also means that third parties are closely involved in governance and the transition to a new political regime (Chesterman, 2004: 88–92). The light footprint approach carries its own risks, however, most notably a lack of control over local actors whose policies may not necessarily be conducive to peacebuilding. In Bosnia and Herzegovina, for instance, international authorities drafted a constitution which contained provisions that barred from public office (elective or appointive) any person under indictment by the International Criminal Tribunal for the former Yugoslavia. In Afghanistan, no such restrictions on the participation of alleged war criminals in public life have been in effect (see on this controversial issue the chapters on international crimes and reconciliation).

Lessons learned

The apparent inappropriateness of the transitional administration model for post-Taliban Afghanistan points to some of the necessary conditions for the success of a transitional administration. There are at least three such conditions: (1) the territory in question needs to be small enough to ensure that the transitional authority is able to exercise adequate control; (2) external parties must be willing to expend considerable resources—military and civilian—in support of the administration over an extended period of time; and (3) ideally, the local population will be willing to work with the transitional authorities to achieve agreed upon aims. Where there is significant local resistance, it may not be possible for international authorities to impose results by fiat.

Another alternative to transitional administration, albeit one that is very much in the same spirit, is what Krasner calls 'shared sovereignty' arrangements (Krasner, 2004). This involves oversight or control by external actors of some of the domestic authority structures of the target state on a consensual basis. It is similar to a 'supervisory' transitional administration although the scope of shared sovereignty arrangements is normally narrower. Arrangements of this kind were established historically for the multilateral management of the Ottoman Empire's public debt and, more recently, for the exploitation of Chad's oil resources, the revenue from which the Chadian government committed to poverty reduction programmes in exchange for technical assistance. Under this scheme, direct oil revenues could be neither allocated nor disbursed without the approval of an oversight committee, thus helping to ensure that the oil proceeds would not be lost to corruption (in actual practice, oversight has proved to be more nominal than real). Similar, though more robust, arrangements could conceivably be applied to war-torn states where, for instance, external actors might have sole or co-responsibility for the judiciary or the police to ensure that the rule of law is respected and minority rights are protected.

There are no standard formulae for a successful transitional administration. The uniqueness of each situation will generate its own particular set of challenges. However, a list of best practices would include the following:

- *Clarity of aims:* a transitional administration can only succeed if it has clear ends and if the benchmarks of success in relation to those ends are also well defined.

- *Coordination:* coordination of effort is vital for the success of any complex peace operation. A transitional administration needs to achieve reasonable coordination among the many disparate international actors, governmental and non-governmental, engaged in the peacebuilding efforts.

- *Transparency and accountability:* a transitional administration needs to act in an open and accountable manner with respect to both the local and international communities.

- *Consultation:* a transitional administration must establish formal channels of communication that allow it to be sensitive and responsive to the interests and concerns of the principal local constituencies.

- *Capacity-building:* a transitional administration must give priority from the start to strengthening local ownership, without which it will be impossible to establish self-reliance.

Selected Bibliography

Caplan, R (2005), *International Governance of War-torn Territories: Rule and Reconstruction*, Oxford: Oxford University Press.
Chesterman, S (2004), *You the People: The United Nations, Transitional Administration and State-Building*, Oxford: Oxford University Press.
Chopra, J (1999), *Peace Maintenance: The Evolution of International Political Authority*, London: Routledge.

Council of the European Union (2002), Committee for Civilian Aspects of Crisis Management, *Basic Guidelines for Crisis Management Missions in the Field of Civilian Administration*, 9369/1/02 REV1, 30 May.

—— (2003), *EU Concept for Crisis Management Missions in the Field of Civilian Administration*, 15311/03, 25 November.

Crawford, J (1979), *The Creation of States in International Law*, 2nd edn, Oxford: Clarendon Press.

Dobbins, JF (2003), 'America's Role in Nation-Building: From Germany to Iraq', *Survival*, 45/4: 87–110.

Doyle, MW, & Sambanis, N (2006), *Making War and Building Peace*, Princeton: Princeton University Press.

Galtung, J (1975), 'Three Approaches to Peace: Peacekeeping, Peacemaking and Peacebuilding', in Galtung, J., *Peace, War and Defence: Essays in Peace Research*, Copenhagen: Christian Ejers, 282–304.

Guttieri, K, & Piombo, J (eds) (2007), *Interim Governments: Institutional Bridges to Peace and Democracy?*, Washington, DC: United States Institute of Peace Press.

Helman, GB, & Ratner, SR (1992–93), 'Saving Failed States', *Foreign Policy*, 89: 3–20.

ICISS (International Commission on Intervention and State Sovereignty) (2001), *The Responsibility to Protect*, Ottawa: International Development Research Centre.

Krasner, SD (2004), 'Sharing Sovereignty: New Institutions for Collapsed and Failing States', *International Security*, 29/2: 85–102.

Lyon, P (1993), 'The Rise and Fall and Possible Revival of International Trusteeship', *Journal of Commonwealth and Comparative Politics*, 31/1: 96–110.

Ratner, SR (2005), 'Foreign Occupation and International Territorial Administration: The Challenges of Convergence', *European Journal of International Law*, 16/4: 695–719.

Shain, Y, & Linz, J (1995), *Between States: Interim Governments and Democratic Institutions*, Cambridge: Cambridge University Press.

UN (1992), *An Agenda for Peace, Preventive Diplomacy, Peacemaking and Peacekeeping*, Report of the Secretary-General Pursuant to the Statement Adopted by the Summit Meeting of the Security Council on 31 January 1992, A/47/277–S/24111, 17 June.

—— (2000), *Report of the Panel on United Nations Peace Operations* (Brahimi Report), A/55/305-S/2000/809, General Assembly and Security Council, 21 August.

—— (2002), *The Situation in Afghanistan and its Implications for International Peace and Security*, Report of the Secretary-General, A/5/875-S/2002/278, General Assembly and Security Council, 18 March.

—— (2004), *A More Secure World: Our Shared Responsibility*, A/59/565, General Assembly, 2 December.

UN (Department of Peacekeeping Operations) (2008), *United Nations Peacekeeping Operations: Principles and Guidelines*.

Vieira de Mello, S (2001), 'UNTAET: Lessons to Learn for Future United Nations Peace Operations', presentation to the Oxford University European Affairs Society, Oxford, 26 October.

Wilde, R (2001), 'From Danzig to East Timor and Beyond: The Role of International Territorial Administration', *American Journal of International Law*, 95/3 583–606.

Transitional Justice

Anne-Marie La Rosa and Xavier Philippe

Definition

Transitional justice sets out to address the legacy of a violent past, linked to an armed conflict or other situations of violence or oppression, by bringing about major political changes. It is based on adherence to applicable law (both at the international and domestic level) and an integrated approach to justice where the victim is at the heart of the process. It comprises both judicial and non-judicial aspects in order to ensure that its main goals—of truth-seeking, reparation, enforcement, and sanctions—are attained.

I. Term

Origin and context

The modern concept of transitional justice was first employed at the end of World War II, albeit without official endorsement, when there were concerted efforts to rebuild Europe and to achieve sustainable peace. In fact, one of the first times the international community coordinated its work to bring to trial persons who had committed international crimes was in its establishment of 'denazification' programmes in Germany. Historically, then, transitional justice was first associated with periods following interstate conflicts but, at the end of the 1980s it was broadened to encompass the setting up of new 'democratic' regimes after periods of unrest, whether the unrest was due to non-international armed conflicts, internal strife, or the transition from an authoritarian/totalitarian regime to democracy.

Previously, the notion of post-conflict justice had been a purely theoretical one. At the end of World War I, the international criminal justice system, which had been provided for in the Versailles Treaty, remained unimplemented. First, because the Kaiser had sought refuge in the Netherlands, and the competent international tribunal to try him was not constituted. Second, the Allies waived their prerogative to try war criminals and left this task to a court in Leipzig. The Allies' list first contained 890 names. It was later reduced to forty-six names, and finally only eleven were brought to justice, of whom six were convicted, receiving token sentences.

There is no consensus on the origins of the concept, yet the etymology of both words has much to tell us. The adjective 'transitional' comes from the Latin *transitio*, which implies a change from one state to another. Some scholars interpret this change as the move from a situation of open violence to a situation of sustainable peace, which is usually built on democratic values. In political terms, such a change implies that the former regime is moribund and that the budding regime has not yet managed to assert itself. A transitional country is thus characterized by the emergence of a new political order which has not—as yet—established its foundations and structures.

The question of the kind of 'justice' involved is even more controversial. There is generally agreement that the term 'justice' has to be understood in a broad sense: thus it should not be limited to mere prosecution of violations. Arguably, it aims to include all of the following: to determine legal responsibility, to punish the perpetrators (retribution), to identify victims' needs and demands (reparation), and to rebuild society in such a way that it is recognized by the entire population (rebuilding). A global approach to both judicial and non-judicial justice is therefore recommended in complex political contexts where it is necessary to take into account a number of different and sometimes opposing objectives, such as: peacebuilding and consolidation of democracy; public security; reconstruction of society; economic development; and restoring the capacity of national institutions based on the rule of law (see notably on these objectives the chapters on capacity-building; democratic governance; recovery; and conflict economies).

Linguistic and semantic issues

Although, nowadays, the English expression 'transitional justice' no longer raises any major problem from a purely linguistic perspective, one of the main semantic challenges posed by transitional justice arises from its still experimental nature and the context in which each experience of transitional justice has taken place. The initial lack of cohesion and harmony of work undertaken in its name goes a long way towards explaining the different terms used. Some institutions, such as the International Centre for Transitional Justice (ICTJ), the bulk of whose work is devoted to transitional justice as its name suggests, have sought to correct this situation (see <http://www.ictj.org/en/index.html>).

Meanings

Literature on the topic offers many different definitions of transitional justice. The main actors and international organizations base their work on definitions that are more or less expansive, depending on their mandate and aims. These definitions do, however, have common features.

First, transitional justice is characterized by the clash between a violent past and the major political changes that affect post-conflict societies. As such, transitional justice is both retrospective and prospective. Its goal is to make it possible for war-torn societies and communities to start anew, impose or restore sustainable peace, and set up more democratic and fair societies (Bell *et al*, 2004: 305–28).

Second, transitional justice puts the victim at the heart of the process, regardless of the means used to achieve this. Put differently, the victims of past violence and their beneficiaries have the 'right to know' and to receive reparation for the abuses they have had to endure.

Third, the definitions of transitional justice share a certain number of objectives. They assume that prosecution of serious violations of international humanitarian law and human rights is a state obligation, as well as putting an end to the abuses. Moreover, the definitions include different aims, such as 'truth-seeking' and 'reparations to the victims and their beneficiaries'. Such obligations are at the heart of the process. Other definitions highlight the importance of institutional reform and sometimes include issues specific to the administration of justice. Finally, some definitions consider reconciliation as a separate ultimate goal for transitional justice, which calls for specific measures. Some scholars are ill at ease with this last definition, considering its contours difficult to define from both an individual and a collective point of view. They believe that, like peaceful coexistence, reconciliation is an intended consequence which follows naturally from the achievement of the other objectives cited previously.

Fourth, the objectives of transitional justice may be achieved by setting up both judicial and non-judicial framework processes, either alternatively or simultaneously. A typology of such processes is described below. Increasingly, views expressed in the literature go beyond a single, linear approach, preferring an integrated approach to transitional justice and its necessary processes and mechanisms, although disagreement still exists with regard to their sequence and timeframe.

Official definitions used by international organizations and the different stakeholders

Several definitions are relevant here, characterized by their wide fields of application. Notably, in a 2004 report, the UN Secretary-General supported a broad approach to 'transitional justice', which he defined as:

the full range of processes and mechanisms associated with a society's attempt to come to terms with a legacy of large-scale past abuses, in order to ensure accountability, serve justice and achieve reconciliation. These may include both judicial and non-judicial mechanisms, with differing levels of international involvement (or none at all) and individual prosecutions, reparations, truth-seeking, institutional reform, vetting and dismissals, or a combination thereof (UNSG, 2004: para 8).

While the UN High Commissioner for Human Rights uses the same definition, the one employed by the UN Office for the Coordination of Humanitarian
Affairs (OCHA), though similar, focuses on the unique character of each situation (OCHA, 2003: 32). The generic definition given by the ICTJ sums up the
overarching philosophy:

Transitional justice refers to a range of approaches that societies undertake to reckon with
legacies of widespread or systematic human rights abuse as they move from a period of
violent conflict or oppression towards peace, democracy, the rule of law, and respect for
individual and collective rights (ICTJ, 2001).

II. Content

Transitional justice mechanisms should not be envisaged as separate mechanisms
but regarded as complementary. They can be broken down according to the main
goals of transitional justice, which are: truth-seeking, reparations, enforcement,
and sanctions. Institutional reform is often a precondition to the effective and
efficient implementation of transitional justice mechanisms.

Truth-seeking

Truth-seeking processes are part of 'restorative justice' initiatives, whereby crimes
are considered as wounds that need to be healed. They are mechanisms and processes which, like criminal justice, aim at establishing the facts by paying close
attention to the historical, political, economic, and social context in which abuses
were perpetrated. While criminal action focuses on the charges made against the
defendant, truth-seeking aims at depicting a broader picture of the past and the
abuses committed. Such processes delve not only into individual violations, but
also into the institutional structures which allowed, facilitated, ordered, or sponsored them. They make it possible to identify responsibilities and also provide an
opportunity to garner useful evidence for future criminal action.

  Truth-seeking mechanisms are different from criminal prosecution because
they make it possible for victims to tell their stories and enable direct confrontation between victims and perpetrators. Such a process is often the victims' first
forum to make public facts that they have had to keep to themselves, but it also
gives them the opportunity to have their status recognized. In addition, it gives
the perpetrators a chance to acknowledge their participation in the abuse, to take
responsibility for them, and to repent or apologize to the victims. In this context,
the confrontation is intended to create a shock and make the perpetrators aware
of the precise consequences of their actions. Truth-seeking also aims to lead to
catharsis on the basis that if the truth becomes widely known, as time goes by, it
can no longer be challenged or deformed (see also the chapter on reconciliation).

Truth-seeking mechanisms lead to the production of official reports. Such reports have two goals. First, they serve as a basis to prepare recommendations and corrective measures. Second, the testimony of all the actors and observers crystallizes the history of this otherwise 'murky' period and makes it possible to determine the responsibilities of the different protagonists. Such mechanisms, however, place the burden for implementing recommendations onto the political authorities. In principle, there is no reason why the bodies in charge of uncovering the truth should not also exercise real decision-making power, yet governments have always shied away from granting them such authority.

Truth and Reconciliation Commissions are typical example of mechanisms that try to shed light on past events. They are official, temporary, and non-judicial commissions in charge of establishing the facts. They investigate a wide range of violations of international humanitarian and human rights law committed during a given period of time. Once again, victims are placed at the heart of the process and the report drafted by the relevant commission seeks to disclose the facts it has observed and draw up both recommendations and measures likely to prevent such a situation from re-occurring (UN Secretary-General, 2004: para 64). The first such experiences, which took place in Latin America at the beginning of the 1980s, have greatly influenced the way in which subsequent commissions in Africa, Asia, Central America, and Eastern Europe have been organized and have functioned (for an assessment of these experiences see the chapter on reconciliation).

However, truth and reconciliation commissions are not the only bodies able to reveal the truth. Other bodies may fulfil the same purpose. For instance, national or international fact-finding commissions may pursue similar goals. Yet, for lack of a comprehensive and integrated system, fact-finding commissions can meet resistance if they have not been granted enough powers, if they are not integrated enough, or if they are insufficiently accepted by the population.

Reparations

Prior to the programme established by the German government in the 1950s to compensate the victims of the Shoah, the issue of reparation was dealt with exclusively at interstate level. The Versailles Treaty, for example, which was signed six months after the Armistice, made it an obligation for Germany to compensate the Allies for the damage it had caused during World War I (Arts 231, 232). Nowadays, it is widely accepted that when serious violations of fundamental human rights and international humanitarian law occur, states must not only prosecute the perpetrators, they must also ensure that victims obtain reparation, if necessary by substituting for the defaulting perpetrators (UN General Assembly, 2005: Principle II). By setting up reparation programmes, public authorities show that such violations call for a reaffirmation of victims' rights. Such reparation mechanisms should also help to restore the population's trust in public authorities, the credibility of which has often been seriously undermined.

In the context of transitional justice, reparation integrates the usual aspects of responsibility, but also goes much further by including reparation which falls outside the ambit of traditional legal obligations. Reparation may take on different forms: it may be monetary or not, collective or individual. More specifically, emphasis may be put on restitution and a return to the status quo ante, if possible, by ordering restoration of liberty, return to the place of residence, or restitution of employment or assets (UN General Assembly, 2005: Principle IX). When this is not possible, appropriate compensation should be paid. Reparation can include public policies in favour of the victims or their beneficiaries with regard to access to public services and equal opportunity. It can also cover rehabilitation and reintegration measures, as well as more symbolic measures (such as official apologies, guarantees of non-repetition, the building of memorials, commemoration ceremonies), which are often important to the victims. In order to guarantee effective payment of reparation to the victims, such initiatives may—or should—go hand in hand with national or international funds.

Law enforcement

In cases of particularly serious violations of international human rights and humanitarian law, criminal prosecutions should remain the cornerstone of justice. This is part and parcel of transitional justice. When criminal prosecutions are 'appropriately' pursued, they may contribute to ending abuses and preventing repetition, by making conviction for crimes appear inevitable. Criminal law enforcement makes it possible, to a certain extent, to establish a chronological account of past events and to give a sense of justice to the victims, despite this not being the main objective of such prosecutions. In transitional societies, when criminal law enforcement is pursued at the national level, it also contributes to building trust in the state's ability and willingness to ensure that laws are respected.

Nowadays, in the context of transitional justice, criminal justice may take on different shapes and be exercised in different ways in different places. It may be applied at national or international level or at both levels simultaneously. International criminal justice is best exemplified by international criminal courts and tribunals. Such courts are usually created by states collectively and have the authority to try alleged perpetrators for crimes falling under their jurisdiction. These courts are deemed international because they have been established by an agreement between states. International courts may be permanent criminal courts, such as the International Criminal Court (ICC), or temporary ad hoc tribunals, such as the International Criminal Tribunals for Rwanda and the former

Yugoslavia, respectively (ICTR, ICTY). They may be headquartered on the territory where the crimes were committed, or elsewhere.

In any event, the efforts made by such international criminal tribunals in punishing serious violations of international humanitarian and human rights law must be coordinated at the national level, on the basis of complementarity, with jurisdiction given either in favour of the states (as in the case of the ICC) or in favour of the international criminal tribunals (as with the ad hoc courts such as the ICTR or ICTY). In other words, transitional justice may benefit from such complementary criminal mechanisms which promote cooperation between national and international tribunals. Such an articulation, which implements the principle of 'universal jurisdiction', reinforces the states' prosecutorial action and helps them to fulfil their international obligations (see international crimes).

The end of the twentieth century was marked by an interesting turn of events which was intended to combine the advantages of both levels of jurisdiction within one single body, the so-called mixed, hybrid, or internationalized tribunals. This category covers a certain number of models developed in contexts as different as Bosnia and Herzegovina, Cambodia, Kosovo, Timor Leste, and Sierra Leone. Such courts offer a blend of internal and international characteristics: in their foundation, membership, the law they apply—both in substance and form—as well as in their position in the global legal order. The Special Court for Sierra Leone is the most internationalized of these tribunals. It was set up by a treaty between the UN and the Sierra Leone government. Its competence and membership is mixed. Because of its features, this is a *sui generis* court that was not based on an existing model. Yet, in the case of Cambodia, the crimes committed during the period of 'Democratic Kampuchea' are addressed in accordance with an agreement between the government and the UN, by the setting up of Extraordinary Chambers in the Courts of Cambodia and thus remains a national matter. This has also been the case in Bosnia and Herzegovina, Kosovo, and Timor Leste (for a typology on the different forms of transitional justice, see the introduction to this Lexicon).

Sanctions

Transitional justice has often been unfairly considered as a process which guarantees amnesty to the perpetrators of violations. And yet, even in its non-judicial aspects, transitional justice is far from dismissive of sanctions as an element of justice. The range of sanctions available is wide and context-dependent. But an element common to all experiences of transitional justice is their break with the principle of proportionality between the degree of gravity of the infraction committed and the sentence. In such contexts the penalty is often not as severe as the sentence which would usually apply in times of peace. However, such a break is not specific to non-judicial processes. Determining sanctions in criminal matters is also based on the attitude of the person being prosecuted. Depending on that person's cooperation and behaviour during the trial, the sentence may be substantially reduced (ICTY, 2003). Thus, it is one approach that is expressed differently in different contexts.

The connections between transitional justice and sanctions are manifold, since the range of sanctions available is significantly wider than in ordinary criminal matters and includes administrative, financial, psychological, and other sanctions. The scope of the sanctions depends on the cultural context. Some forms of non-judicial transitional justice have even included custodial sentences. This may be problematic if the members of the commission have no in-depth experience in criminal sentencing. If such an option is to be chosen, it is preferable to plan a specific structure in the process to deal with the issue of sentencing, ensuring that sufficient expertise is guaranteed and that procedures are respected.

Ideological and institutional stakes

Transitional justice is a dynamic process and, paradoxically, its strengths are also its weaknesses. The Gordian knot of transitional justice is hard to cut: the obligation of justice and peace is closely connected to considerations about the past and the future, collective and individual perceptions, as well as the judicial and political context. Indeed, the political nature of the process must be instantly acknowledged, not denied. Nevertheless, these political considerations—the drivers of the entire process—should be circumscribed to prevent them from taking over. To do so, there are certain prerequisites.

First, the mechanisms and frameworks of transitional justice must be based on respect for human rights and be understood in the context of the obligations imposed on states by international law. These obligations include ending the abuse, prosecuting and punishing its perpetrators, providing for necessary reparation, and preventing repetition. The rhetoric of transitional justice should not serve as an excuse to undermine the normative legal framework, which should continue to apply.

Second, even before setting up transitional justice mechanisms, there should be efforts made to reinforce the state's capacities and those of its institutions (see the chapters on state building and capacity-building). This may seem paradoxical, but experience has shown that, for such a process to be successful, institutional and procedural work has to be accomplished beforehand. If such preparatory work is not done, transitional justice may prove more detrimental than beneficial for the state. In the absence of adapted mechanisms that are accepted by everyone, transitional justice mechanisms lose their effectiveness. In this context, one suggestion is often to vet or weed out the civil service. As long as the rights of the persons concerned are respected, such a process should help the state to establish true rule of law. However, mechanisms which may incur administrative sanctions should be controlled and monitored because there is a real risk of abuse and settling of scores, which may jeopardize the entire system.

Third, to reach the goals pursued by transitional justice, an integrated approach is necessary. This requires a timely and wise combination of the mechanisms and procedures necessary for criminal prosecutions, including truth-seeking with regard to past events, particularly by helping the victims' families in finding their loved ones and learning about their fate. Implementation of such an approach presupposes prior analysis of context-specific characteristics. It also excludes implementation of a predefined model without making sure that it meets all requirements of a given situation and that it corresponds to the wishes of all parties concerned.

III. Implementation

The challenges of implementation

According to the definition given previously, transitional justice aims to promote the reconstruction of post-conflict societies by using all the operational means and skills available. It is thus meant to contribute to restoring and maintaining sustainable peace as well as to put in motion a transition towards democracy. However, there are enormous challenges and obstacles to be overcome.

First, the ideal combination of criminal action and truth-seeking mechanisms is often a mirage. Frequently, nothing changes. Inertia is one of the big challenges facing justice in post-conflict situations. Without going as far as blanket amnesties, very often there is no justice simply because there is no prosecution. The international community has undertaken too few and too limited actions for any definitive, general conclusions to be drawn, and in any event it is important always to remember the specificity of transitional justice. It is an extraordinary kind of justice meant to find pragmatic solutions to very tangible problems, and theorization and repetition of positive experiences from one context is no guarantee of their success in other contexts.

Second, transitional justice is part of a global peacebuilding process. Once again, transitional justice cannot function in a vacuum without considering other aspects of post-conflict peacebuilding. However, this is more easily said than done: many obstacles make integration of the process and its result unpredictable. Words such as 'cooperation' and 'consultation' often remain wishful thinking. While there is no magic formula, it is nonetheless indispensable to integrate transitional justice into the reconstruction process immediately. The chances of success for transitional justice will be greatly enhanced if it has been designed as part of a more global process. It should not be an alternative solution pieced together *a posteriori* because the process had not been thought through earlier. Reflection about transitional justice must start even before the end of the conflict so as to be better integrated into the peace process from the outset.

Third, transitional justice requires political will to implement the results of the process if it is to have its full impact. It must be thought of as a 'social contract' between the political leadership and the population as a whole, aimed at coming to terms with the past while also paving the way for the future. This implies two unavoidable consequences. One is that governmental authorities must fulfil their responsibilities and implement all findings drafted by the entities in charge of managing the process, especially in terms of reparation. The other is that they cannot later challenge the results of the process, through leniency or the granting of amnesties, even years afterwards.

Operational aspects and lessons learned

Operational aspects rest on the principles mentioned previously—realism, pragmatism, and efficiency. And yet, one of the fundamental aspects of transitional justice is the availability of resources necessary for implementation. This is not specific to transitional justice, but these needs are particularly acute when it comes to human resources. While financial resources may be indispensable, they are easier to come by than the necessary skills for transitional justice to function correctly. Training judges and finding interpreters, investigators, or judicial administrators, is often a real challenge. The international community's good will may compensate for some of these shortcomings, but the transitional justice process must remain in the hands of the people concerned (see the chapters on local ownership and capacity-building). Applying ready-made solutions, or externally imposed models, is a recipe for failure. Although it is hard to strike a balance between internal and external resources, it is essential to favour the former (and thus, give the necessary training as early as possible).

In addition, there is an obligation to implement a clear and transparent process to which the population will be committed. In some instances, transitional justice may be a successful experience from a technical point of view (reports, proposals), but a failure from a political standpoint because of the lack of endorsement from the population, or disregard for the 'contract' on the part of the political leadership. As soon as problems arise, there are a number of pitfalls that must be overcome. In the context of transitional justice, the way communication is managed on a daily basis can have a real impact on the outcome of the process. In addition, though imitating other experiences of transitional justice may be dangerous, mistakes made in different contexts may be very informative. In this sense, a comparative approach to transitional justice is necessary.

Acceptance by the population also depends on the consultation processes with, and participation of, the social groups in question. Such processes should make it possible to gain greater insight into the contextual characteristics which need to be taken into consideration when assessing the situation and drawing up the relevant mechanisms. Furthermore, past experiences have often highlighted the importance for the transitional justice process of arriving at a schedule that specifies the intended timing and delivery of each of its objectives.

Finally, in considering long-term objectives, transitional justice is clearly only a starting point for a much broader project aimed at establishing social justice. With such an understanding of transitional justice it is possible to go beyond a limited notion of justice, by not restricting it to criminal functions, but acknowledging that it has a much broader meaning and scope and is an essential exercise to heal a severely wounded society.

Normative and institutional choices depend on such contextual analysis: it is the guarantee of a successful peacebuilding process. However, there are a few general rules that should be born in mind. First, the transitional justice process should be placed as high as possible in the hierarchy of standards, if possible, even in the constitution. This will prevent transitional justice from being challenged too easily at a later stage. Second, the chosen structures have to be operational. This implies that it is possible—and even preferable—to use the structures in place if they present the necessary guarantees of impartiality and efficiency. Nonetheless, should there be the slightest doubt about such structures, they must be disregarded and replaced by new ad hoc institutions. Transitional justice should not embark on unrealistic institutional solutions. Third, there should be explicit procedures as well as a clear distribution of authority between the different bodies. This should be provided for in a law (or an equivalent normative act) that defines clearly the obligations and guarantees of all parties.

Selected Bibliography

Battle, GG (1921), 'The Trials before the Leipzig Supreme Court of German Accused of War Crimes', *Virginia Law Review*, 8: 5–17.
Bell, C, Campbell, C, Ni Aolain, F (2004), 'Justice Discourses in Transition', *Social and Legal Studies*, 13/3: 305–28.
Bickford, L (2004), *Encyclopedia of Genocide and Crimes against Humanity*, Macmillan Reference USA, 3: 1045–7.
Elster, J (2004), *Closing the Books: Transitional Justice in Historical Perspective*, New York: Cambridge University Press, 1–23.
De Greiff, P (ed) (2006), *The Handbook of Reparations*, Oxford: Oxford University Press.
ICTY (International Criminal Tribunal for the Former Yugoslavia), *Plavsic case*, IT-00–39&40/1.
OCHA (UN Office for the Coordination of Humanitarian Affairs), (2003), *Glossary of Humanitarian Terms in Relation to the Protection of Civilians in Armed Conflict*.
OHCHR (Office of the UN High Commissioner for Human Rights) (2006), 'Study by the Office of the United Nations High Commissioner for Human Rights on Human Rights

and Transitional Justice Activities Undertaken by the Human Rights Components of the United Nations System', UN E/CN.4/2006/93, 7 February.

Teitel, RG (2000), *Transitional Justice*, Oxford: Oxford University Press.

UN General Assembly (2005) A/RES/60/147 adopted on December 16th 2005 to which are attached 'the Basic Principles and Guidelines on the Right to a Remedy and Reparation for Victims of Gross Violations of International Human Rights Law and International Humanitarian Law'.

UN Secretary-General (2004), Report on the 'Rule of Law and Transitional Justice in Conflict and Post-Conflict Societies', UN Security Council, S/2004/616, 23 August.

- **Online resources**

ICTJ (International Center for Transitional Justice), available at: <http://www.ictj.org>.

Index